MANAGEMENT LAUREATES:

A Collection of Autobiographical Essays

VOLUME 2

Editor: ARTHUR G. BEDEIAN
Ralph and Kacoo Olinde Distinguished Professor,
College of Business Administration, Louisiana State University

MANAGEMENT LAUREATES:

A Collection of Autobiographical Essays

by

FREDERICK I. HERZBERG

ROBERT J. HOUSE

EDWARD E. LAWLER, III

PAUL R. LAWRENCE

EDMUND PHILIP LEARNED

HARRY LEVINSON

EDWIN A. LOCKE

DALTON E. McFARLAND

JOHN B. MINER

HENRY MINTZBERG

WILLIAM H. NEWMAN

CHARLES PERROW

JAI PRESS INC.

Greenwich, Connecticut   *London, England*

Library of Congress Cataloging-in-Publication Data
(Rev. for vol. 2)

Management laureates.

Vol. 2: by Frederick I. Herzberg ... [et al.].
Includes bibliographical references.
1. Executives--United States--Biography.
2. Executives--Canada--Biography.   3. Industrial
management--United States.   4. Industrial manage-
ment--Canada.   5. Master of business administration
degree--Canada.   6. Master of business administration degree--Canada.   I. Ansoff, H. Igor.
II. Bedian, Arthur G.   III. Herzberg, Frederick.
HC102.5.A2M32   1992   658.4′092′273 [B]
ISBN 1-55938-469-7 (v. 1)
ISBN 1-55938-470-0 (v. 2)

CONTENTS

PREFACE

For many years, I have contemplated compiling a volume such as this, containing the autobiographies of the management discipline's most distinguished laureates. The impetus to do so was reinforced when, in preparing my Academy of Management presidential address, I re-read Theophile S. Krawiec's *The Psychologists* (1972-1978). Phil argues, and I agree, that "one way to learn about and understand psychology is to study psychologists as they reveal themselves in writing about their lives" (1972, p. vi). Moreover, I would make the same argument for management and its leading thinkers, since I share the belief that you cannot fully understand an individual's work without knowing a great deal about the person behind that work.

Unfortunately, the available management literature provides little insight into the personal and intellectual lives—the frustrations as well as the triumphs—of the individuals in the management discipline. Although such understanding could be conveyed in many forms, perhaps the most intimate and fascinating of these for gaining behind-the-scenes insights is the autobiography. Thus, as self-exemplifying exercises, the autobiographies in this volume, as in the two companion volumes, offer the reader not only a glimpse of the subjective determinants and personal experiences of the management discipline's most distinguished laureates, but also a deeper understanding of what management is and what it is becoming. Those who have contributed to this undertaking are all distinguished by their successes, comprising a sample of the highest achievers in the management discipline. They are widely diversified in background and involvement in various areas of management, and their experiences are indelibly marked by societal and intellectual trends that span the entire twentieth century. To borrow a term from Robert K. Merton (cited in Riley, 1988, p. 25), the management laureates included in this undertaking are "influentials." Their lives have had and continue to have significant consequences for both management and society.

The difficulty and trepidations of preparing a verbal portrait of one's life should not be underestimated. Any sincere attempt to portray an unencapsulated personal and intellectual history is risky. It requires that one stand naked in front of oneself in a state of self-communion. Such immersion in the self, with its inevitable introspection, retrospection, and interpretation, may well lead to conflict with others, as well as result in internal dissensions. Moreover, the honest reconsideration of one's own motivations and thoughts may not only influence the rest of one's career, but also impart a sense of premature semi-closure. In this sense, preparing an autobiography is an adventure.

Editorial intervention has been purposefully kept at a minimum. Although all contributions open with a photograph and conclude with a complete bibliography of the author's published works, no rigid model was specified. Thus, the various accounts reflect a diversity of approaches, interests, and experiences. Contributors were free to choose not only their manner of presentation, but also the aspects of their lives they wished to emphasize. Some have offered rounded autobiographies, while other have emphasized intellectual and scholarly achievements. Many are laced with "confessions" of one sort or another, and virtually all reflect on the many people who have influenced their lives and their work.

It is an accepted psychological fact that such personalized accounts do not proceed as mechanical reproduction, but tend toward creation (Misch, 1951, p. 11), suffering from what Lindzey (1974) has labeled an "astigmatism imposed by personal needs and too little perspective" (p. ix). For this reason, autobiographies should not be regarded as objective narratives. The lack of objectivity is offset, however, by certain advantages. In methodological terms, autobiographers are the "ultimate participants in a dual participant-observer role," having privileged (if not monopolistic) access to their own inner thoughts (Merton, 1988, p. 18). By providing insights that are direct and not secondhand, the autobiographer is better qualified than anyone else to describe his or her private feelings. Autobiographies, therefore, should be regarded not as objective narratives, but as a means for evaluating an individual's self-definition (Sjoberg & Kuhn, 1989, p. 312), documenting inner thoughts that are unobtainable from other sources.

Autobiographers, however, are not without some measure of control over errors in recollection and observation. By using historical documents and other external facts, one can transform the remebered past into what Merton (1988) has termed a "series of hypotheses to be checked" (pp. 18-19). Empirical contemplation of reality, therefore, can afford at least some protection from excessive tendentiousness. The incentive to minimize such bias is high, of course, since narrators who exaggerate their positions or engage in shallow attempts at self-justification risk damaging their professional credibility.

It is an historical truism that the past is invariably interpreted in terms of the present (Sjoberg & Kuhn, 1989). A review of the narratives in this volume, supplemented by correspondence and conversations with the authors, indicates that the narrators are no exception to this historical axiom. Each invariably interprets his reminiscences in light of what has occurred since. For virtually all, writing an autobiography has been an emotionally moving experience, leading to self-revelation as each author recalled facts and feelings, actions and reactions, the incidents that prompted him, the persons he met, and the transactions in which he was involved. Several contributors have divulged that this self-revelation has enabled, if not forced, them to perceived their lives as a single whole. As a consequence, each of this latter group has benefitted by growing in ways that others could not do for them (Misch, 1951).

Further review of the following narratives highlights a second historical truism (Riley, 1988). Though the management laureates included in these volumes are indeed "influentials," they were likewise *influenced by* the social, cultural, and environmental changes to which they were exposed. Collectively, the narratives clearly show how management thinkers living at a particular point in history have been influenced by existing social policies, practices, and structures; and how these influences have, in turn, affected their thinking. The narratives, as a group, also show that the experiences, interests, accomplishments, and failures of the various contributors were in no small way a function of the historical moment at which they entered the management discipline (Merton, 1988). For instance, those entering the discipline shortly after World War II were in an appreciably different historical context than their predecessors. As several of the contributors suggest, their common wartime experiences greatly influenced the intellectual evolution of management thinking by introducing new theoretical concepts and redirecting scientific attention to new research domains.

The relevance of historical context underscores a final point. As Phil Krawiec, for one, is found of observing, "autobiographies are an introduction to the past of our discipline" (personal interview, January 28, 1990). Contemporary as they now seem, the autobiographies in this volume are also a contribution to the history of management. Even today, readers can sense in these accounts the attitudes of earlier generations and their interpretations of changing social policies, practices, and structures. Tacitly and explicitly, the narratives also tell of dominant research philosophies and the importance of reference groups and reference individuals, the significant others who helped shape the character of contemporary management thought and inquiry.

In perusing these narratives, one might ask why only North Americans, and exclusively males at that, are included as contributors to the present volumes? Historically, the professional study of management has been predominantly American. With the spread of management training on six continents, this condition is quickly changing. Likewise, the entry over the last two decades of numerous female scholars who are now notably influencing management thought is a welcomed phenomenon. Consequently, it is hoped that any future volumes will not only be truly international, but also include distinguished female contributors. Thus, the absence of international and female contributors should not be interpreted to suggest that the editor is xenophobic or sexist, but rather to reflect an absence of appropriate candidates either belonging to the cohorts from which autobiographers were selected or who had not already prepared autobiographical memoirs.

Special thanks goes to the contributors. It is hoped that each will find some satisfaction in the immortality that the present undertaking provides. All have hereby gained a medium of access that will allow them, decades after they are gone, to speak to those management scholars who will be heirs to their intellectual legacy.

Arthur G. Bedeian
July 1991

REFERENCES

Krawiec, T.S. (1972-1978). *The psychologists* (Vols. 1-2). New York: Oxford University Press. (Vol. 2): Brandon, VT: Clinical Psychology Press.

Lindzey, G. (Ed.). (1974). *A history of psychology in autobiography* (Vol. 6). Englewood Cliffs, NJ: Prentice-Hall.

Merton, R.K. (1988). Some thoughts on the concept of sociological autobiography. In M.W. Riley (Ed.), *Sociological lives* (pp. 17-21). Newbury Park, CA: Sage.

Misch, G. (1951). *A history of autobiography in antiquity* (Vol. 1). Cambridge, MA: Harvard University Press.

Riley, M.W. (Ed.). (1988). Notes on the influence of sociological lives. *Sociological lives* (pp. 23-40). Newbury Park, CA: Sage.

Sjoberg, G., & Kuhn, K. (1989). Autobiography and organizations: Theoretical and methodological issues. *Journal of Applied Behavioral Science, 24*, 309-326.

If I have seen farther, it is by standing on the shoulders of giants.

—Sir Issac Newton

Happiness and Unhappiness:
A Brief Autobiography

FREDERICK I. HERZBERG

I was born April 18, 1923, 8 George Street in the old shoe manufacturing town of Lynn, Massachusetts. Our neighborhood of working-class row houses was ripped down in recent years as part of a renovation project. I remember only the kitchen of the house and the man on the corner with a broom on his face (a beard), who I recall being used as the bogeyman. My father, Lewis, was a foreman of shoe lasters in one of the many factories. He had been born in Lithuania, and was proud of having attended a yeshiva there before immigrating to England with his parents as a boy. As a young man he came to America to work in the factories of Lynn and then brought over his brother, Phillip. The rest of the family remained in England, where I still have cousins. My mother, Gertrude, had been given the surname of Koppelman when she came through Ellis Island as a young child, virtually alone at age 12 or 13, to live with her older brother, Jacob. She had immigrated from a small *stetl* on the Polish-Russian border, no longer feeling welcome in the home of her newly remarried father. She was employed like so many immigrant children in the factories of Lynn, where she grew up, met, and married my father. She never learned to read English. I was one of five children—very much a loner since I was five years younger than the next youngest.

When I was six, we moved to New York City where my father began work as a painter, and where I was enrolled at PS 169. My sister, Pearl, who had the job of looking out for me when I was small, says that I was a "cute" kid with curly red hair, but hyperactive in the more restricted space of our New York apartment in the largely Irish Catholic neighborhood of

Washington Heights and afraid of the dark stairs in the halls outside the apartment. (I still remember her patient reassurance on those dark stairs.) At PS 169 I had kind teachers, Miss Hohenstein and Miss Oaks, and one terribly anti-semitic one, Miss O'Connell. But the teacher that influenced me most was my history teacher, a stern lady, always dressed in black, who was pleased and amazed at my knowledge of the ancient Greek heroes such as Achilles and Hercules. I had fallen in love with history as soon as I learned to read, which was some time before I attended school. I read whatever was available, chiefly dime novels during elementary school, then historical novels from the library, and finally the writings of historians. I particularly remember reading and re-reading Lytton Strachey's *Emminent Victorians*, which I discovered sometime during junior high school.

I was 13 years old when my father lost his painting business during the Great Depression. Part of the family moved to Norfolk, Virginia, where they got work in the shipyards. I convinced my father to let me stay in New York, where I could help support myself with a variety of odd jobs and work toward a scholarship to City College, one of the first to give educational opportunities to the immigrants of New York and their children.

CITY COLLEGE OF NEW YORK (CCNY)

In 1940 I placed high enough on the Regents' exam to enter City College of New York as a history major. In those days, to study history was to memorize dates, and the textbook indentations aided memorization. I would argue with Professor Shapiro and he would answer, "Well, let's look at the book," and the book, of course, was the *Old Testament* according to J. S. Shapiro. He would open the book and say, "Herzberg, you're wrong, it says right here." And I would say, "But, Professor, you wrote the book." And he would look at me with incomprehension as if to say, "What the hell did that have to do with it?"

That experience led to two great effects on my thinking. First, it led me to distrust textbook writers. Second, it got me out of the history department and into the psychology department. The psychology department at that time was led by a great professor, not a contributing scholar, but a great synthesizer, the psychologist, Gardner Murphy. He is best known for a book called *The Bio-Social Approach*. He ended up his years as the research director of the Menninger Institute. Two other important influences at City College were Karen Horney and Jacob Moreno. The psychoanalyst, Dr. Horney used to give lectures in her apartment with students sitting around on the floor. I overcame some of my shyness in Moreno's famous psychodrama sessions where I acted as an alter ego on his Psychodrama Stage.

I played football for CCNY until my senior year (1943), when I suffered a broken sternum during a game. Not only could I no longer play on the team, but more serious to making ends meet financially and to finishing my degree, I could no longer eat at the training table. I enlisted in the army, and after finishing infantry training at Fort McClelland in Alabama, was assigned to an Army Specialized Training Program in Italian language and culture at Amherst College in Massachusetts. There I met and later married my commanding officer's niece, Shirley Bedell.

WORLD WAR II

I was not destined to be part of the invasion of Italy. The army shortened the ASTP course as D-Day neared. They needed more foot soldiers for the invasion. A description of what happened to the specialized training units and casualties sustained can be found in a book by Louis E. Keefer, *Scholars in Foxholes* (MacFarland Publishers, 1988). I participated in the invasion of southern France, as a sergeant in charge of mortars for the 63rd Infantry Division, then volunteered to become a battle patrol leader assigned to go behind enemy lines, take prisoners, knock out observation posts and bunkers, and gather intelligence of German positions. I got several recognitions, one being, a Bronze star for leading patrols across the frozen Saar River.

At the tail end of the fighting I was reassigned (probably because of knowledge of Yiddish and other languages), taken to a nearby castle for instructions, and told to drive some half-tracks down the autobahn as quickly as possible and help at the liberation of Dachau Concentration Camp near Munich, Germany. The first thing we saw as we entered were the rows of railroad cars filled with lime-covered corpses; the next, as we broke into the guards' houses, were the housefraus packing up china and other loot.

I was made operations sergeant for military administration of the camp for several months until the UN Relief Organization came in to assume the task. I went around the whole time powdered with DDT because typhus was rampant. But that was the least of my problems. I had just turned 22. Nothing in my education in history or psychology had prepared me for this experience. The shock has influenced all my thinking. There are always around 15 percent nuts in any society. But a whole society had gone insane. During my months at Dachau, I was able to go to other camps and help find relatives for some of the displaced persons. I also interviewed many Germans who worked in the camps and also many who lived in Munich and claimed to know nothing about what went on! How could apparently normal people do such terrible things? I concluded that the most important role of a psychologist was to help keep the sane from going insane.

When the UN took over, I was sent to Queens University, Belfast, Northern Ireland for rest and recreation. I signed up for tutorials in anthropology but actually spent most of my time in the pubs in Dublin, Ireland, which remained neutral during the war. There were lots of fights at the time between black and white soldiers. My last recognition of war came from the Red Cross, for coming to the aid of some black soldiers outnumbered by a bunch of whites from a tank unit. A case of measles delayed my return home until March 1946.

GRADUATE SCHOOL

Shirley and I stayed in New York where I completed the few credits needed for my bachelors degree at CCNY, and proceeded to the University of Pittsburgh for graduate studies under the direction of Dr. Wayne Dennis of Hopi Indian fame, and John Flanagan, who was in charge of the Army Aviation Personnel Program, Selection, Training, and Evaluation.

I was a good student in terms of passing any test you gave me but I had broader experiences in the war and in work than most. I knew the academic subject matter but didn't believe in it as much as those with narrower experience. I was like a scanning mechanism looking to see which of the academic materials made any sense or was useful. Of course, you can rationalize any program of study and say "all of this is appropriate and necessary and an integral part of the well-trained person." You can always find glue. I had experienced some startling realities, but much of what they were teaching me about reality seemed unimportant—the minutiae of life, not the essentials. The learning theory of Tolman and Hull looked like a good parlor game but no more. When I realized that people were taking these games seriously, I began to wonder whether there was something that I was missing. What was wrong with me that I couldn't take them seriously? I hadn't learned at that time that pedantry is psychological seriousness, not necessarily reality. I came to realize that the language of pedantry simply explained in pedantic language what my mother had explained to me more directly. Second, I was looking for ideas to tie what was significant together—I didn't need to tie all the junk together.

In 1948 our son Mark was born and I accepted a position as Principal Personnel Administrator for the City of Richmond, Virginia, to set up a Merit System program required under a new City Charter. I installed Employment Procedures and Regulations, Testing and Examinations for all City employees as well as job classification and evaluation systems for all the jobs in the City government. I soon became involved in the problem of Selective Certification for Blacks. This was a highly political issue but we did succeed in hiring the first black policeman and public health nurses in Virginia. Upon completion of the successful installation of the new Mandated Merit System program, I returned in 1949 to the University of Pittsburgh to complete my doctoral degree in psychology.

I combined what would be termed an internship today with studies in electroshock therapy for doctoral thesis at the Mayview State Hospital, under the clinical direction of Dr. Carroll Whitmer, who was at that time, the director of the clinical training program at the University of Pittsburgh.

The realization of what was happening to all the data that I was collecting in the mental hospital had a great influence on me. All that test data were just filling up files—they were not useful to the people they were supposed to help. It finally dawned on me that I was using all that training and all those exams to perpetuate a lot of pretense. Put that in juxtaposition with doing a Ph.D. dissertation on electroshock therapy and looking after a corridor of patients like those in "One Flew Over the Cuckoo's Nest."

Here were these people convulsing, attended by foreign doctors—the only ones willing to work in mental hospitals—and I found myself filling up protocols by asking them, "What do you see on this card?" After all the tests, the only way I could tell that someone was mentally ill was that he was in the hospital; otherwise why was he in the hospital? That remained the best diagnostic technique I had. Obviously we were missing the boat. What had happened was that psychology had gotten procedurized. We had mythicized our procedures because procedures always sell.

What had happened in Europe during World War II had happened outside a mental hospital. People who had done hideous things could talk very rationally about them. Human beings had done these things in society. What hits the front pages is people who act out the bizarre and incomprehensible behaviors when the play is not on, such as throwing kids off a roof. But as soon as the play goes on, they call it War, and call it Normal.

PUBLIC HEALTH SCHOOL

There was no rational explanation for what occurred in World War II. It was a sickness beyond comprehension, the sickness of the soul. So I went to Public Health School and began to ask, "What is a healthy population like?" In clinical training a psychologist is taught nothing but illness, illness, illness. You begin to think you are well because you are not as sick as those you are seeing around you. I personally knew that many of those doing therapy on the mentally ill and acting like paradigms of mental health were nuts themselves. But I found that at that time no one had a concept of what health is.

In Public Health School we knew only when things went wrong, not when they went right. We had biological clues when things went wrong—pain. But we had no clues when things went right. We had completely lost the other dimension. Progress was always getting away from the pains of the present.

In other words, I found that every so-called positive was just described as an antonym of the negative, so the positive was assumed to emanate from the negative. This illusion led to the idea that all positives were the result of sublimation of pain. And "positive thinking" was always wishy-washy homilies. *There was no substance to positives.* This was not true in the areas where breakthroughs were being made—that is in the hard physical sciences. They were pure sciences because they were going in positive directions. That is perhaps the basic distinction between the pure sciences and the social sciences. In psychology we were going around in circles, hung up on the procedure of illness, because we had no concept of what wellness was.

Amelioration in Public Health School still meant removal of disease. But when polio was wiped out, it didn't open up a whole new life for parents who no longer had to suffer through dread of the polio season; now they had to suffer through the drug epidemic, which still continues.

I wrote a thesis paper out of sheer frustration called "Mental Health is Not the Opposite of Mental Illness." It was a protest.

I studied with an industrial psychiatrist named Graham Taylor. He is at William Allan Memorial Institute in Montreal now. He and another industrial psychiatrist, Allan McLain of IBM, came out of Cornell. They, like the Menningers and the Tavistock group, were intent on bringing the knowledge gained from war experiences into industry.

Thomas Parran, former Surgeon General of the United States, who wrote *Shadow on the Land*, the first expose of the problem of venereal disease, was the dean at Public Health School. He had a concept of public health as something that went beyond fear of illness. He had a great influence on me.

JOHN FLANAGAN

After getting my Ph.D. in clinical psychology with an emphasis in physiology, I worked in the aftermath of the Air Force Psychology program under John Flanagan, who developed the critical incidents classification test for flight crews—selecting those able to function as pilots, bombardiers, and gunners for the Army Air Corps during World War II. Measurement techniques usually select items and test them out, that is, a pilot can read, has good eyesight, dresses neatly, and so on. Flanagan asked what are the *critical* requirements for what a pilot has to do? Flanagan would ask trainers, "When was the last time you had to take the controls away from a student pilot? What did the student do?" He collected thousands of incidents from such questions and translated these into critical behaviors that differentiated promising pilots from, for example, promising navigators. His results were much better than previous selection and classification procedures—of course, he had thousands to test with.

I had been specializing in tests and measurements and came to my study with Flanagan numbed with numbers—numbers that were being manipulated usually by academics who had no experience in the war or in the workplace. I had done many surveys using questionnaires and knew their limitations only too well. I saw at once that Flanagan's focus on real happenings in individual lives had external validity built-in.

The late forties and early fifties were a period of high hopes for students of psychology. Primarily because study was free, through the GI Bill of Rights, the Affirmative Action program for GIs and second, because psychology was a field where you could get a doctorate degree without having to study medicine. There was a demand—lots of jobs, particularly teaching jobs and jobs in the Veterans Administration. The universities exploded. Often you could make more money going to graduate school than you could going to work. I remember that I had to take a 50 percent cut in salary when I went to work. I was an instructor in the Psychology Department, had a fellowship in the Graduate School of Public Health, had a research grant from the National Research Council, and worked as a consultant for John Flanagan. I was making so much money I couldn't afford to get my degree.

JOB ATTITUDES: RESEARCH AND OPINION (1957)

After graduating from Public Health School I took a job as research director of Psychological Services of Pittsburgh. A great influence on me during this period was my experience being a consultant to Harold Geneen of ITT fame. I was greatly impressed by his confidence and success but increasingly turned off by his coldness when it came to what he considered a choice between people and profits.

We did lots of morale surveys, and I discovered that the "for instance" examples that respondents gave contradicted the answers they had given to the rating scales. I was asked by a Chairman of the Board "What do people want from their jobs?" Like a good psychologist, I said, "I don't know, but if you'll give me enough money I'll find out." My staff and I reviewed the literature on job attitudes including over 2,000 sources. At the end, we found that the research results were contradictory. We could find support for any bias you had, although there did appear to be a pattern in the research results suggesting that different factors caused job satisfaction and dissatisfaction.

MOTIVATION TO WORK (1959)

After these disillusioning experiences with psychological research in industry, I decided to adapt Flanagan's critical-incident method to a research study on job satisfaction and attitudes to a study of 200 accountants and engineers.

To elicit critical events, we asked, "Describe a time, an incident, when you felt good on the job and a time, incident, when you felt bad on the job." We analyzed the data according to factors. And of course we had to use words for factors that could be interpreted in a variety of ways. But we found that job satisfaction tended to result from intrinsic factors: achievement, recognition for achievement, work itself, responsibility, advancement, and growth. In contrast, job dissatisfaction tended to result from extrinsic factors: company policy and administration, supervision, interpersonal relations with co-workers, salary, working conditions, and security.

CASE WESTERN RESERVE UNIVERSITY

Just as this study was ending, I accepted an appointment to Case Western Reserve University in Cleveland, Ohio, where my job was divided evenly between the medical school and the psychology department. While Shirley was tying up loose ends in Cleveland, I slept on a bed in my office at the University and wrote the results of the study which I co-authored with Bernard Mausner and Barbara Block Snyderman, *Motivation to Work* (1959).

The results of this study caused great controversy and consternation in industrial psychology, chiefly because it called into question the attitude measurement instruments on which psychologists make their livings. Freud had the same problem, when he published his work on psychoanalysis. It called into question the electrical current instruments being used on the mentally ill at the time—instruments belonging to vested interests in the medical profession. Instruments and procedures always become the security blankets of practitioners. The glaring error in psychological measurement instruments is that they assume that healthy is the opposite of *un*healthy and that satisfaction is the opposite of *dis*satisfaction. The ubiquitous prefix creates the assumption that dynamically different states can be polar opposites. The major criticisms of Motivation-Hygiene theory rest on the argument, "My instruments don't show two continua." But these instruments are based on a single continuum (1,2,3,4,5,etc.) with polar opposites.

The Western tendency to try to solve paradoxes can be illustrated in the use of antonyms in our languages. These antonyms make paradoxical feeling states, such as *happiness* and *unhappiness*, appear to be opposite ends of the same continuum. If these feelings are highs and lows of the same feeling continuum, the logical mind assumes that they are caused by presence or absence of the same factors. My research in job attitudes has illustrated the fallacy of this assumption.

Motivation to Work (1959) and subsequent replications revealed that what made people satisfied and happy on the job was what they were doing; whereas what made them dissatisfied and unhappy on the job was the situation or environment in which they were doing it. Achievement was the most frequent satisfier. In other words, performance (behavior) led to satisfaction and positive attitudes. I called the environmental factors *hygienes* because of my public health background and the doing of performance factors, *motivators*. I cited the distinction Hannah Arendt had made between the terms *work* and *labor* in her book *The Human Condition* (University of Chicago Press, 1958) which I thought helped clarify the distinction between motivation (growth-creativity) and hygiene (pain-avoidance.) Although my theory is usually compared to Abraham Maslow's, it was not an influence on me because I was not familiar with Maslow's 1956 book but only with his earlier animal research.

My research certainly supports Maslow's theory of the existence of human self-actualization needs, which I call *motivator* needs. However, it does not support his theory that self-actualization needs are dependent on satisfaction of lower order needs. On the contrary, Motivator and Hygiene needs appear to operate independently, except at the extremes.

THEORY APPLICATIONS TO MENTAL HEALTH-MENTAL ILLNESS

I became interested in applying my theories to problems of abnormal psychology because one of my old professors, Dr. Roy Hamlin, was psychologist for the VA hospital. His interest was in treatment of schizophrenics, so the first clinical study was done on that population. Motivation treatment consisted of teaching the schizophrenics to play golf during their therapy sessions. They played a wild game of golf, but the study controls showed that their behavior improved as a result of this treatment, which came to be called Activation Therapy, and which is not generally identified with Motivation-Hygiene theory. (Innovation in the field of psychology generally consists of changing the name of the treatment. Every treatment known to modern psychology was invented by primitive cultures— from dream analysis, to shock therapy, to behavior modification.) If you will recall the movie "One Flew Over the Cuckoo's Nest" when the inmates escaped and went on a fishing trip—they behaved much more "normally" than they were able to behave inside the mental hospital.

The articles I did with Roy Hamlin (1961, 1963) were partly based on Motivation-Hygiene studies conducted by his students on schizophrenics at Danville, Illinois VA hospital. The studies I conducted with my student, Fantz (1962), at a rehabilitation hospital showed markedly different Motivation-Hygiene profiles between patients who improved and those who didn't.

Motivation-Hygiene concepts of mental health and illness had been developed through the study of functioning populations in the pursuit of what is universally accepted as "normal" and "human" activity—work. Most definitions of mental health and illness have had their origins in the study of acknowledged abnormal populations. After comparing profiles of functioning and nonfunctioning populations, I concluded that behavioral scientists normalize the average unhappiness leading to normalized pathology. Each society then normalizes its own pathology. Why? One of the difficulties we have in psychology and have always had in psychological measurement, is no zero point. What is the zero point of intelligence, for example, or what is the zero point of aptitude to go to business school? (Is it the zero point of greed?) So what do we use? Averages. In physics we at least have a concrete idea of absolute zero. We can take some reference point on the Fahrenheit scale and say that zero is the freezing point of water. In psychology we say that the freezing point is the average temperature.

I thought a more valid approach would be to judge degrees of mental health on the motivator continuum, where most good events → feelings occurred and to judge mental illness on the hygiene continuum where most bad events → feelings occurred. I therefore extended my micro theory of motivator-satisfaction/hygiene-dissatisfaction to a macro theory of mental health-mental illness (see Figure 1):

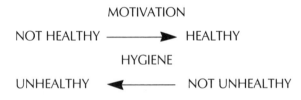

Figure 1. Mental Health/Mental Illness Continua

To help managers understand the major individual differences which could be classified as Normal within this theory, I began using the following terms:

1. "The Best of All Possible Worlds" (from Voltaire's *Candide*) for a healthy and not unhealthy individual.
2. "I'm All Right, Jack" (from the 1960 Peter Sellers film of the same name) for the not healthy (bored) but not unhealthy (suffering little pain).
3. The "Starving Artist" for the healthy (very motivated-satisfied) individual who is yet very dissatisfied-unhealthy (suffering a great deal of pain from poor hygiene).
4. The "Down and Out" for the individuals who find themselves in poor environments with few motivators and are unhealthy and not healthy either.

I insisted then and still insist that starving artist and down and out individuals are normal though unhealthy because they want to avoid pain from their environment and are trying, although not succeeding. Their pain and distress is a normal symptom of environmental factors that need to be remedied, just as fever is a normal reaction to infection. The "I'm All Right, Jack" Motivation-Hygiene profile shows unusual amounts of motivator slippage (no satisfaction). The "Starving Artist" shows little motivator slippage but concentration of hygiene dissatisfaction in their lives to one or two very painful factors.

In contrast to these degrees of healthiness and unhealthiness that I classified as normal, the nonfunctioning populations, schizophrenics, and so forth demonstrate much rarer Motivation-Hygiene profiles—virtual absence of motivator factors, especially in events that they report make them feel good. Almost all their good and bad feelings are hygiene-related. I soon saw the similarity with insane societies, like Germany (1932-1945), in which it became the mode for individuals to relinquish their motivator-satisfaction-health for hygiene-relief from the leader and group. I decided to call this inversion *abnormal* and to try to draw a sharp distinction between normal mental illness-dissatisfaction of poor hygiene and the abnormal patterns of seeking long-term happiness through hygiene relief that characterizes the psychologically abnormal—particularly the psychopath. I set up the Industrial Mental Health Program at Case Western Reserve University to explore and apply these ideas.

LEVELS OF GROWTH

As I tried to explain the underlying growth dynamic of the motivators to managers and to my students as Case Western, I noted that the levels of growth were related to the less frequent and most long-term motivators: (1) *Knowing more* from successes and failures (achievements); (2) *understanding more* from relationships of various achievements and feedback (recognition for achievement); (3) *thinking and creating more* from interesting job content (work itself); (4) *effectiveness in ambiguity* from adult behavior (responsibility-advancement); (5) *individuation* from development of unique expertise and identity that doesn't rely on approval of others for satisfaction (growth-self-actualization); (6) *real growth* from growth in ethical behavior—no need to make others look smaller in order to feel taller. I suggested that these levels of growth be incorporated into appraisal systems and published an article on the subject just before leaving on a Fulbright fellowship to Finland (*Manage*, 1965).

Shirley was in her last year of medical school at Case Western and so our son Mark went with me. We enjoyed the country and people tremendously. In addition to teaching, I conducted a study of job satisfaction-dissatisfaction among Finnish supervisors, using a written critical events form for the first time. This overcame the problem of possible interviewer bias and yet the profile results still supported Motivation-Hygiene theory of two dynamically independent need systems. Strangely, to me, the major psychological journals refused to publish the results, which had to appear in a more "popular" journal (*Personnel Psychology*, 1965). I was shocked. I had left the consulting firm of Psychological Services of Pittsburgh for what I thought would be the "purer" environment of academia. By now what came to be known as the "Herzberg Controversy" was in full swing. But in the words of the old Chinese proverb, "Happiness is the best revenge." I enjoyed my work with Finnish companies and the adventure of exploring the country, traveling by reindeer sled in Lapland. I was cheered by an invitation from the Sociological Research Laboratory at the University of Leningrad to present my work to them in lectures at the Institute of Philosophy. Khrushchev was in power and the first brief thaw in Soviet-American relations was taking place.

One of the biggest thrills in my life was running across the Neva River bridge in Leningrad to give my first lecture there. I was able to assist Professor V.A. Yadov and A.G. Zdravomslov in their landmark study of Soviet worker attitudes first published in the Soviet journal *Questions of Philosophy*. Their study of 2,665 workers under the age of 30 found that the highest relationship between satisfaction and performance was with the nature of the work that the employee was doing. And contrary to what the Soviet researchers hoped to prove, the lowest relationship was with the social value of the work.

Also, while I was in Finland, I put together my lecture notes and data from the Motivation-Hygiene research studies to date into a book titled *Work and the Nature of Man* published in 1966. The book asked what these research findings meant and summed up my theory in two archetypes from the *Bible* which I had been using for some years in lectures to students and managers: Adam, the hygiene-pain avoidance nature of man, that we share with other animals, and Abraham, the growth seeking nature of man that is distinctly human and transcends the biological dying process. I tried to make the point that industry's models of man have historically focused only on our Adam nature. Also in this book were my theory of mental health-illness, levels of growth, and reports of the first job enrichment applications of my theory on stockholder correspondents at AT&T. At the end of my sabbatical I flew back to Israel in time to observe the 1967 Six-Day War.

JOB ENRICHMENT FOR MINORITIES

The idea of pushing down responsibility, of course, had been around for a long time, but before job enrichment based on Motivation-Hygiene theory, it did not have a behavioral science base.

The first job enrichment project based on my theory was carried out in a large Canadian chemical company. I had been lecturing to executive officers in the Laurentian mountains, and a French Canadian, who was an executive in personnel, where front-office minorities are always placed, implemented a job enrichment project among lower-level jobs, which of course were held by French Canadians. The workers performed well taking responsibilities on the enriched jobs, removing the justification for denying them advancement into higher level jobs. As a result, many French Canadians were promoted in this company.

The same thing happened with women's jobs at AT&T. The first job enrichment projects there were on jobs that had been limited to women: stockholder correspondents, service representatives, operators, telephone directory clerks. We called it "collapsing the job," giving workers responsibility for all the jobs in a territory (client area). The women (called "girls at the time), proved they could do it all. Many of them were promoted, as a result. Women were granted extra pay for past discrimination, AT&T was admonished twice for discrimination—once by women and once by the American Jewish Congress because they had no Jewish executives. In the latter case, they had the nerve to try to use me as a cover-up—"See our consultant Frederick Herzberg."

The earliest job enrichment project for chiefly black workers in this country was on jobs of cleaning women in a VA hospital. The hospital administrator had called for help with these "illiterate, itinerant, absentee" women. I looked at the rooms and saw that there was dust under the bed but the door knobs were polished. I got to know several of these women and one of them invited me to her home and showed me around—it was very clean—no dust under the bed there. She explained to me that the inspectors never looked under the beds, but always inspected the brass door knobs. If someone threw up in the hall right after inspection, it didn't get cleaned up until the next inspection. So we enriched these jobs: (1) Gave each worker responsibility for a certain area (client relationship); (2) put up a sign saying "Any complaints about cleanliness of this area should be referred to Mrs. _____ telephone #_____ (accountability); (3) they were allowed to schedule their own work within certain limits—they scheduled to the patients' and nurses' needs rather than to the inspector's—and covered for each other when there were problems at home; (4) control of resources—they were given a budget for supplies and allowed to order what they wanted. This, of course, angered the purchasing agent. He tried to tell one of the women that the Murphy's soap she had ordered was toxic. She complained to me and I had the university pharmacologist examine it for her. She posted his analysis on the bulletin board: "Murphy's soap is completely safe." The maids were also allowed to design the storage in their broom closets. A carpenter was assigned to follow their instructions.

The incident that stands out in my mind from this project occurred when I came out of the movie late at night with my wife and met Nellie, one of the maids and her husband. We asked them to have a cup of coffee with us but Nellie replied, "No, I have to check my ward."

Absenteeism went down on this project, costs of cleaning materials went down, and the wards were kept much cleaner (in fact, one of the doctors who habitually spilled pipe ashes on the floor was told by the maid on duty to clean them up. Of course, this doctor got angry, but he cleaned up his ashes on the sly. And the purchasing agent got angry. He said, "These people can't handle money." I told him "You try bringing up six kids on $3,000 a year, and you'll learn how to handle money."

So early job enrichment was done in low level jobs and among minorities and women, where management thought "it couldn't work" but it did, and it has worked to remove justifications for institutional denial of human needs of minorities and women.

JOB ENRICHMENT AT THE EXECUTIVE LEVEL

Managers had tended to say that their own jobs were already enriched, but this analysis tends to confuse managerial pressures (hygiene hassles) with enrichment. Work on jobs at higher levels have tended to work only at placating hygiene egos and further screwing up the works. Job enrichment is actually needed even more at the executive level, where transferring people to the right job is hindered by status problems of "appearance of demotion."

In one company, which had hired a consulting firm to find capable vice presidents, the president complained that they weren't doing anything. I found that he was quite right because he wouldn't let them. I assigned each of these vice presidents to write job descriptions for the others and let the one described make corrections on the description. The president complained that these descriptions "left him nothing to do" but they were adopted within about three months. If a "one-man show" works, OK, but in this case, the one-man show hadn't been working. The president hadn't been capable of doing all those jobs.

I began learning about the problems of job enrichment at the supervisory level while I was still working at Psychological Services of Pittsburgh. I went to the Alcoa plant in Tyler, Texas to help develop an instrument for evaluating jobs—especially those of the pot-line supervisors. Alcoa used the Hall process which involved lines of huge pots presided over by pot-line supervisors, shift foremen, and general foremen. I used the "forced choice" technique. This technique prevents the evaluator from knowing whether he is saying something good or bad about the person being evaluated. It is based on descriptions of characteristics of "best foremen" and "worst foremen." On each characteristic you take two good statements about a good foreman, two bad statements about a good foreman, two good statements about a bad foreman and two bad statements about a bad foreman and you ask the evaluator, "How willing are you to say this about _____?" They have to choose a number, even if the statement doesn't fit at all. The instrument I finally developed had 31 choices.

The scale generally broke into technical and interpersonal competence. Before administering it, I asked supervisors and managers to give me their impressions of the instrument. The pot-line supervisors said, "You have captured our job perfectly except we don't handle interpersonal relations problems—the managers do that." The managers said,"You have captured the job of pot-line supervisor perfectly except they don't handle technical problems—we do that."

So I took my clipboard and followed the pot-line supervisors around, recording what they did. I found that they were very busy looking into everything and doing nothing. I told the plant manager, and he explained that these supervisors had been work leaders, who they had made supervisors to get them out of the labor bargaining unit. Management knew very well that this expensive scale I have been hired to develop was to be used to evaluate people who really had nothing to do. This has usually been the role of elaborate job evaluation scales in industry.

In summary, job enrichment has contributed to equal opportunity for minorities and women. This contribution has occurred serendipitously. It was not planned. In general, we were allowed to enrich jobs where productivity problems were most acute. Some job enrichments at supervisory and management levels haven't succeeded because there was no job there. You cannot enrich a featherbedding job. Many survey instruments have been designed and used to maintain the fiction that there are jobs where there are none. More ingenuity has gone into maintaining this fiction in industry than into designing content jobs. I published my definition of job enrichment and examples from AT&T in "One More Time: How Do You Motivate Employees?" (*Harvard Business Review*, January 1968). (This article has proved to be the most popular in *Harvard Business Review* history with over 1.3 million copies sold to date.)

TEXAS INSTRUMENTS

Texas Instruments saw my work and sent Scott Myers to study with me. He replicated the critical events study and published it as "Overcoming Union Opposition to Job Enrichment" (*Harvard Business Review*, May-June 1971).

In the meantime I was working at AT&T, where Bob Ford and Roy Walters changed the word *hygiene*, which they felt had a connotation of clean toilets, to the word *maintenance*. So it became MM theory—Scott picked that up and all over Texas Instruments every desk had "We believe in MM theory."

In the White Rooms they had hundreds of women assembling the integrated circuit boards. They started participative management of the protocol type— used a few ingredients of job enrichment and got a lot of mileage out of it. I cut out after awhile as a consultant—discouraged that job enrichment could become the new umbrella for old human relations techniques. I must admit that the improvements made by Scott Myers and others at Texas Instruments included some of the job enrichment ingredients. But chiefly, it was used for political goals and to keep out unions, which was an anathema to me.

IMPERIAL CHEMICAL INDUSTRIES (ICI)

My 1969 Bureau of National Affairs (BNA) film "Job Enrichment in Action" was shot in New York but it was the exact study that was done in the Imperial Chemical Industries in Great Britain. In shooting the film we couldn't get permission to use ICI's name at that time, but the film is an accurate description of enrichment of sales jobs there. The Imperial Chemical projects were contemporaneous with the AT&T studies. At that stage, to introduce job enrichment I had to play two roles—the professor and the consultant. The study presented a couple of very unique problems. We started at Teeside, which is up in northern England, where they have the heavy chemical agricultural plants. It is a grotesque place, with factory after factory producing all kinds of fertilizers. Because of the tremendous growth that was taking place, they were having difficulties in managing the plants, particularly with the influx of labor coming in and the Trade Union Congress—the unions saw what was happening was a huge development. I was asked to go up there and see it and just make some presentations. They have a castle like the Guggenheim estate for IBM. And I would fly to Teeside in a company plane and just spend time with all the executives. The first break came when they assigned a new managing director for R&D who was a young chemist. In reviewing his operation at R&D he found that the number of patents in the company had gone way down. The lifeblood in a chemical company is its patents. The second problem was that the laboratory work that they were doing for all the installations was sloppy. The new director threw these two problems on the table. Together with my students Bill Paul and Keith Robertson, we did job enrichment in the R&D department on "technical officers" and "experimental officers." We found that Technical officers (Ph.D.s, researchers) had a lot of paper work to do, while Experimental officers (lab technicians promoted to this position) had virtually nothing to do. We pushed responsibility for lab tests down to experimental officers so that technical officers were more free to work on patents ("Job Enrichment Pays Off," 1969). Next we enriched sales jobs as the film shows. At the same time I worked at the Imperial Metals Subsidiary, where they were having terrible quality problems making zippers. I suggested that production and inspection come under the maintenance director who was also put in charge of training. His responsibility was not only to maintain machines but to produce quality. Result: the quality was improved.

CUMMINS ENGINES

Most plants are built on industrial engineering principles with the behavioral sciences as a secondary concern. Two plants are a reversal of this trend. Volvo's operations in Kalmar, Sweden and the Cummins Engine plant in Charleston, South Carolina were both built with the behavioral sciences in mind.

Cummins Engines is a family-owned company which builds diesel engines. By 1971 Cummins was preparing to open the plant in Charleston. To avoid repeating some problems found at the Columbus, Ohio plant, Irwin Miller, Chairman, Jim Henderson, CEO and Ted Marston, Head of Personnel and Labor Relations, decided to use my "cockeyed ideas" in the design of the new plant.

However, we had to work within four constraints: (1) an existing building. Cummins had acquired an old helicopter plant as the new site; (2) a production deadline; (3) a previously selected plant manager; and (4) a goal for hiring minorities. Working within these guidelines we established three major principles for the plant. The primary purpose of the plant is to manufacture diesel engines. This was to be understood by everyone in the plant whether they were in accounting or the secretarial pool. One problem was to make concrete the abstract statement of "everybody here makes engines." To do this most personnel hired for the new plant were required to assemble an engine. Even though this led to high training costs, I felt it necessary to prevent having typists, accountants, executives, and so forth, know nothing about engine assembly.

The second major principle of the plant was that of cross-training. Cross-training is the expansion of knowledge beyond building and testing engines. From the core job of engine assembly workers would learn about related areas such as shop maintenance and tool room operation.

Cross-training led to the next principle of the plant: the criteria for job evaluations. At this Cummins plant doing a good job involved performing one's tasks well and continuing to learn (*The Managerial Choice*, 1976). This also simplified the problem of job classifications. There was only one (besides the probationary training classification).

Having only one job classification led to the idea of one wage scale, although there continued to be argument on this point. The workers were given a set increase in salary each year because all workers are expected to keep learning and so to be worth more. The set annual increase prevents the pairing of money with learning, which inhibits learning.

With this emphasis on learning, Cummins Engines approached the governor of South Carolina with a proposal to change the curriculum of the state's technical schools. Rather than providing training of the traditional style, they suggested correlated teaching "to give the Cummins Engines philosophy to school training." I was familiar with correlated teaching from my work with the Division of Research of Medical Education at Case Western Reserve. The Western Reserve curriculum has largely replaced the Johns Hopkins curriculum.

It would be unrealistic to think the Charleston plant could operate without any problems. One common area of complaint is that of "I work harder so I deserve more money." Cummins had this problem primarily in the machining area because of a badly designed head line machine. The people *not* assigned to these Mickey Mouse jobs felt they deserved more money. Other problems included a "cadre" of old style managers, plant managers with nothing to do (the plant was "run" by the head of assembly and testing), and the Organization Development people who were bored and wanted more meetings to justify their existence.

UNIVERSITY OF UTAH

From 1960 to 1972 I had been promoted to the rank of Distinguished Professor, head of the Industrial Mental Health Program, chairman of the Psychology Department and professor of research in medical education at Case Western Reserve University. In addition, I was president of three consulting firms (in New York, Chicago, and Copenhagen) and on the Board of Directors of several others, most actively with a consultancy in London.

In 1972, Shirley and I decided to move West to the University of Utah in Salt Lake City where she could get an appointment to the medical school and where I was offered a post as Distinguished University Professor with considerable freedom to teach and pursue studies that interested me.

SOUTH AFRICA

In 1973 I was invited by the government of South Africa to be the keynote speaker for their first labor conference which would include blacks(labor unions were prohibited for the blacks in South Africa) and what they call coloreds. (Chinese were considered to be black, Japanese were considered to be white. And so it was just like Hitler's ideology of race—by political decision.) I met with the largest builder among the coloreds at my hotel in Johannesburg and he was denied admission. I had to get special permission to get him to come up to my room to talk. I gave lectures in many cities with the proviso that there would be no discrimination as to who could come in and hear me speak. I remember sitting with the mayor of Port Elizabeth. The blacks were all standing outside. They were allowed to come in, and one of the most beautiful things I have ever seen was that the whites got up and made room.

I went down into the gold mines where miners were black and supervisors were taxicab drivers off the Greek Islands. (The law stated that no black could be above a white.) I went down with the plant manager and with the company psychologist, who was making a survey of black morale. We had to put on very heavy clothes and start crawling through tunnels, where safety wouldn't meet our standards. (My wife, who is a physician, looked into the physical examination they gave these blacks and it was the Snyder Test, an old Air Force exam that merely requires stepping up and down and then taking the heart rate.) The psychologist was saying that he had to get 15 interviews on a checklist asking: "How do you like your supervision?"; "How do you like the canteen?"; and so forth. After he got his 15 checklist items we stopped in a cul-de-sac where there was a black with his jackhammer. The psychologist turned to me and said, "Professor, would you like to ask a question?" I said I would love to. He got his pad ready to write my question and translate for me. I said, "Ask him how he pisses down here?" The psychologist was shaken. But the black miner put down his jackhammer and answered me in perfect English, "The white bastards up there don't think us blacks have to piss."

We came back up the incline, took off our heavy clothing, took showers, went into the boardroom and had tea with the company president. He asked "What do you think morale is like down there?" I replied, "You will have a strike in six weeks." I missed it by two months and hit the *Times Herald* headlines. It was a lucky shot.

During the Plenary Session of the Labor Conference one of the industrialists who had a supermarket chain in Capetown said he wanted to try some of my ideas. I outlined the program with him and then assigned one of my students, Luther Backer, to carry out the project. It went very well because they taught the shelf packers how to use inventory control, how to run the check-out counter, and so on. It worked beautifully. In 1982 Luther Backer also did a very significant critical events study on black and white workers in South Africa ("An Intercultural Study of Work Motivation—A Useful Instrument in Industrial Relations," *Journal of Labor Relations, 6*(1), 49-65). Naturally, this made the "establishment" psychologist at the University, a guy named Bechevel, very angry. He had all kinds of "data" showing that blacks had lower IQs and that they "didn't want" responsibility. In South Africa job enrichment provided a medium for social change again.

AIR FORCE LOGISTICS COMMAND (AFLC)

The Orthodox Job Enrichment program in the AFLC began prosaically enough in 1974. The Ogden Logistics Center needed a productivity program so that they could fill in the blanks for the productivity program form sent from Washington. And I had a student who needed a field experiment for his doctoral dissertation. But the program that we started in 1974 at Ogden AFLC grew into the largest job enrichment program ever carried out. I had developed some workbooks on Motivation-Hygiene theory, *Motivation: The Management of Success* (1973), that proved useful in training and had translated the motivator factors into more specific "ingredients of a good job" published in "The Wise Old Turk" *Harvard Business Review* (1974): *Recognition* translated into *Direct Feedback, Work Itself* into the *Client Relationship, Responsibility* into (1) *Self-Scheduling,* (2) *Control of Resources,* (3) *Authority to Communicate,* and (4) *Accountability.* Advancement and Growth translated into New Learning leading to *Unique Expertise.*

Two of the hardware projects were very significant ("Efficiency in the Military," 1975). The redesign of the wing slat modification of the F-4 Phantom was a classic. They showed me workers doing nothing but drilling holes and asked, why aren't they motivated? The line from my 1969 Bureau of National Affairs (BNA) film *Modern Meaning of Efficiency*—"We don't know why there are so many errors, the work is so simple even a child can do it"—applied here. The trick is to make that connection between errors, lack of motivation, and boring work. I told them that the wing slat modification appeared to be all one job and that the workers should learn to do the whole thing. This was done and productivity and quality improved greatly. The holes I was speaking of had to be drilled with very little tolerance for error. The workers knew that this was important, but no reasonably intelligent person can concentrate on drilling holes, or watching for a light to flash on, for very long. (The second example was part of my job enrichment studies at oil refineries in Venezuela, South America.) You either enrich the jobs or expect more and more disastrous errors of the Three-Mile-Island type. As I was saying, the wing slat modification was a classic redesign case and we improved productivity, quality and worker satisfaction there. However, we observed over time that the job enrichments did not spread to other jobs in this area.

In contrast, job enrichment of the jobs of the avionics mechanics did spread through the system ("Monitoring Orthodox Job Enrichment," 1980; see also 1979 publications). A central difference between the two projects was that the avionics mechanics were serving a client external to the organization—the test pilot. The client relationship has always been an important consideration in job enrichment. But in the AFLC program we came to see that it is the central ingredient and that the other ingredients take on a new meaning in relationship to this central ingredient (see Figure 2).

The ingredient *New Learning* is more meaningful when we realize that training should be focused on what we need to know to serve the client (not just entertainment at various workshops). The ingredient *Unique Expertise* came into job enrichment from a different direction—the need for psychological privacy, which is still valid. However, no client can be well-served through rigid adherence to prescribed procedures. Workers develop unique expertise by learning from clients how to serve them better. They feed this

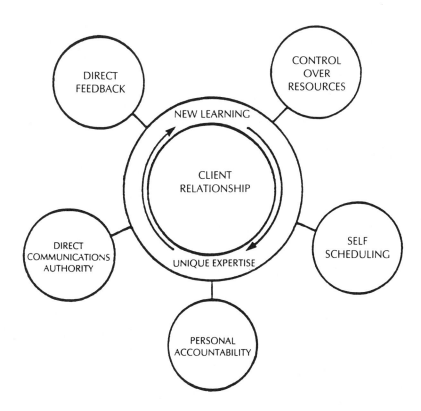

Figure 2. Client-Serving Ingredients of a Good Job

information into a more updated system, and in turn, they have the psychological privacy to continue to develop more unique expertise.

All of these ingredients—direct feedback, control of resources, communication authority, self-scheduling, and accountability make better sense when tied to the client relationship.

We used the client relationship for the first time in Imperial Chemical Industries when we looked at the sales jobs. They said that the salesman's job could not rely on job intrinsics because incentive systems were synonymous with sales. Yet the client relationship, a job intrinsic, was also synonymous with sales. The paradox was that a good client relationship was not usually thought of as an incentive. Now that I look back at AT&T job enrichments,

I can see that improving the client relationship was also the central ingredient in enrichment of the jobs of stockholder correspondents. One of the things that interfered with this insight was the "greenlight index" of the implementers of job enrichment. Their central goal came to be to cover the walls with endless disconnected "ideas" under *feedback, communication authority,* and so on. The reason for this was that few of them knew much about the jobs they were redesigning and they were unwilling to go down and look at them. The answer came after midnight in a hotel bar in New York City—not in the formal brainstorming session—an example of insight surpassing procedurized thinking. Another thing that interfered with seeing the client relationship as central was the organization charts which lent legitimacy to seeing the boss as the client of line jobs—an inversion which contributed to internal competition—the adversary system between divisions and plants of the same company. Everyone in these charts claims to be serving an external client "What's good for GM is good for the USA"; whereas most jobs should serve internal clients as well who are not the boss.

There was a period of time during the growth of the '50s or '60s when a lot of companies were manager-proof. What management did was to do nothing. Labor-management negotiations became shaking hands and just passing through costs. There was no collective bargaining, just harmony. I remember sitting with the board of directors of one of the largest corporations and the chairman of the board was telling one of the subsidiaries that the message of the conference meeting was to raise prices. Just raise prices. That was it. No efficiency, no concern. And when I said "My God, you don't believe in motivation?" I got that Mona Lisa smile. What they were saying is "Look, it sounds rational, it sounds scientific so nobody can accuse us with not being concerned with rationality and reason and science when we are dealing with people."

JAPAN

Until the mid 1970s, it was difficult to get American management interested in quality improvements, which are always the first measures of job enrichment. Then this interest came in the guise of "something new"—Quality Circles— from Japan. Dr. Ishikawa of the Japanese engineering organization that developed quality circles in Japan in the early sixties cited our *Motivation to Work* (1959) study of engineers' satisfaction with their quality achievements. Also, both *Work and the Nature of Man* (1966) and "One More Time: How Do You Motivate Employees?" (*Harvard Business Review* 1968), with its reports of job enrichment were translated and widely read by Japanese management. In 1974 I was invited to Japan to give lectures to management. Later, the critical events studies of Japanese workers published in 1981 by

Kobayashi and Igarashi showed that contrary to everyone's expectations, Japanese workers did not get satisfaction from company policy, supervision or interpersonal relationships, but like workers in the United States and other countries, their major satisfaction came from their own achievements and learning ("An Empirical Test of the Herzberg Theory of Job Satisfaction," *Tohoku Psychologica Folia, 40,* 74-83). In 1982 I was honored by the Japanese pharmaceutical industry, along with Dr. Edward Deming, by having a training center named for me.

During the 1980s, I focused on existential levels of motivation, problems of abstract work, depression in the work force and cross-cultural studies of Motivation-Hygiene theory. Some significant articles published in *Industry Week* have been "Leadership in a Period of Psychological Depression" (1980), "Humanities: Practical Management Education" (1980), "The Abstraction Revolution" (1983), "Managing Egos/East vs. West" (1984), and "Workers' Needs: The Same Around the World" (1987).

In 1988, after reading Gorbachev's *Perestroika,* I wrote to congratulate him and to ask that I be allowed to renew my work in the Soviet Union with Professor Yadov. I soon heard from Professor Yadov that he had recently been appointed head of Sociological Studies in the Soviet Academy of Sciences. He said that Secretary Gorbachev had forwarded my letter to him and that my answer was a request to meet with Yadov in New York and to prepare a paper for publication in the Soviet Union. The result was "Motivation to Work vs. Incentive to Labor" (1990).

I have continued to travel widely, working in over 30 different countries, but discussing problems with a more philosophical and global approach than previously. I no longer read the "publish or perish" journals. However, now that copyright laws have become more strict, I do get requests from some textbook writers to review and correct inaccuracies in their descriptions of Motivation-Hygiene theory and its job enrichment applications. This I am happy to do.

Enough already. Don't "Play It Again, Sam." I have had a good life with more than Andy Warhol's "fifteen minutes of fame" that should be allotted to each of us. I have been able to combine the pleasures of work with the pleasures of adventure. The sadness that is inherent in life cannot take away this human dimension. My advice to students still is to pursue the happiness of growth through the motivators at least as much as they struggle to avoid the unhappiness of pain from hygiene.

PUBLICATIONS

1952

A study pf the psychological factors in primary dysmenorrhea. *Journal of Clinical Psychology, 8.*

With G. Pascal. The detection of deviant sexual practice from perfomance on the Rorshach Test. *Journal of Projective Techniques, 16.*

1953

With D. Russel. The effects of experience and change of job interest on the Kuder Preference Record. *Journal of Applied Psychology, 37.*

1954

An analysis of morale survey comments. *Personnel Psychology, 7.*

Prognostic variables for electro-shock therapy. *Journal of General Psychology, 50.*

Psychological Service Moral Surveys. Pittsburgh, PA: Psychological Service of Pittsburgh.

Temperament measures in industrial selection. *Journal of Applied Psychology, 50.*

With A. Bouton. Further studies of the stability of the Kuder Performance Record. *Educational and Psychological Measurement, 14.*

With A. Bouton & B. Steiner. Srudies of the Stability Preference Record. *Educational and Psychological Measurement, 14.*

1955

Mental health in industry. Pittsburgh, PA: Psychological Service of Pittsburgh.

The prevalence of job dissatisfaction. Pittsburgh, PA: Psychological Service of Pittsburgh.

With D. Capwell. *Vocational selection and job attitudes.* Pittsburgh, PA: Psychological Service of Pittsburgh.

With B. Mausner. *Effect of job attitudes.* Pittsburgh, PA: Pyschological Service of Pittsburgh.

With R. Peterson. *Factors related to job attitudes.* Pittsburgh, PA: Psychological Service of Pittsburgh.

1957

With B. Mausner, R. Peterson, & D. Capwell. *Job attitudes: Research and opinion.* Pittsburgh, PA: Psychological Service of Pittsburgh.

1959

With B. Mausner & B. Snyderman. *The motivation to work.* New York: Wiley.

[Review of *Mental health in industry*]. *Personnel Psychology, 12.*

With M. Horowitz. Faculty attitudes toward experiences with a revised program of medical education. *Journal of Medical Education, 35.*

WWith S. Inkley & W. Adams. Some effects on the clinical faculty of a Critical Incident Study of the Performance of Students. *Journal of Medical Education, 35.*

1961

With R. Hamlin. A motivation-hygiene concept of mental health. *Mental Hygiene, 45.*

1962

Basic needs and satisfaction of individuals (Industrial Relations Monograph No. 2). New York: Industrial Relations Counselors.

[Comment on *The meaning of work*]. In *The worker in the new industrial environment.* Ann Arbor, MI: Foundation for Research on Human Behavior, University of Michigan.

The meaning of work to the individual. In *Basic physiology and psychology of work.* Cleveland, OH: Case Western Reserve University.

The mental health effects of the work environment. Ann Arbor, MI: Foundation for Research on Human Behavior, University of Michigan.

New approaches in management organization and job design. *Industrial Medicine and Surgery, 31.*

1963

With R. Hamlin. Motivation-hygiene concept and psychotherapy. *Mental Hygiene, 47.*

1964

Motivation-hygiene concetpt and problems of manpower. *Personnel Administration* (January-February).

1965

Are you confined by outmoded motivational theories? *Occupational Hazards* (October).

Comparison of work motivation, U.S.S.R.-U.S.A. *Soviet Life.*

Job attitudes in the Soviet Union. *Personnel Psychology* (Fall).

Motivation-hygiene theory of job attitudes. In *Proceedings of the International Congress of Social Pyschiatry.* London.

Money isn't everthing [Interview]. *The Dallas Evening News* (April 3).
Motivation to work. *Manage* (January).
Motivation to work among Finnish supervisors. *Personnel Psychology* (Winter).
The new industrial psychology. *Industrial and Labor Relations Review, 18.*
Problems of providing motivation in technical areas. In *Proceedings of the Executive Study Conference.* Princeton, NJ: Educational Testing Service.
Salary—A dissatisfier. In *Proceedings of the American Compensation Society.*
This matter of motivation [Film]. Dartnell Company.

1966

Work and the nature of man. New York: Thomas Y Crowell.
Ivan vs. Joe. *Newsweek* (January 24).
Motivation-hygiene theory. In *Proceedings of International Congress of Psychology.*
More than a living: The theories of Frederick Herzberg [Film]. New York: American Telephone and Telegraph Company.
Test case–Treasury (consultant) [Film]. New York: American Telephone and Telegraph Company.

1967

The motivation to work. In E. Fleishman (Ed.), *Studies in personnel and industrial psychology.* Homewood, IL: Dorsey Press.
Motivation through job enrichment [Film]. Rockville, MD: BNA Communications.

1968

Job motivation: Money isn't everything. *Reader's Digest* (July).
Motivating people: Money isn't everything. *Newsweek* (April 22).
Motivation, morale, and money. *Psychology Today* (March).
One more time: How do you motivate employees? *Harvard Business Review* (January-February).
To motivate: Challenge the man. *National Safety News* (May).
Une fois de plus: Comment motiver vos employes? *Harvard Business Review* (Janvier-Fevrier).

1969

Herzberg's 10 steps to becoming a sucessful businessman. *Newsletter* (BNA Communications, Inc.).

Making a job more than a job. *Business Week* (April 19).
The new kid in the company. *Innovation, 8* (December).
To be efficient and to be human. In *Plant engineering and maintenance yearbook* (Vol. 20).
With W.A. Paul & K.B. Robertson. Job enrichment pays off. *Harvard Business Review* (March-April).
With E.K. Winslow & Lt. Col. M.S. Majesty. Motivational engineering for pilot training. *Technical Report AFHRL* (October). Ohio: Wright Patterson Air Force Base.
The ABC man: The manager in mid-career [Film]. Rockville, MD: BNA Communications, Inc.
Building a climate for individual growth [Film]. Rockville, MD: BNA Communications, Inc.
Job enrichment in action [Film]. Rockville, MD: BNA Communications, Inc.
The modern meaning of efficiency [Film]. Rockville, MD: BNA Communications, Inc.
What have you done for me lately? [Film]. Rockville, MD: BNA Communications, Inc.

1970

Be efficient and be human. *Industry Week* (June 8).
Black and white of hostility. *Industry Week* (September 21).
Does money really motivate? *Purchasing* (August 6).
Does your job bore you, or does Professor Herzberg? [Interview]. *The Economist* (July, London).
Innovations in motivating salesmen. In *The marketing road to greater member firm profitability.* New York: New York Stock Exchange.
La Detaylorisation est en Marche [Interview]. *France et Monde* (May).
Management of hostility. *Industry Week* (August 24).
Man of the moment: Switched on to the behavioral scene [Interview]. *Personnel Management* (July, London).
No people shortage, just . . . turn your people on. *Industry Week* (January 19).
People are polarizing. *Industry Week* (July 27).
What people want from their jobs. *Industry Week* (October 19).
Work and the two faces of man. *Industry Week* (November 9).
Motivational engineering for undergraduate pilot training [Film]. Air Force Documentary, SPR-6-70.

1971

Are have-nots entitled to automatic equality? *Industry Week* (March 15).

Humanity and efficiency. *Ulster Businessman* (April).

Management and motivators. *Industry Week* (February 15).

Managers or animal trainers [Interview with W.F. Dowling]. *Management Review, 60* (July).

More on avoiding pain in organizations. *Industry Week* (January 18).

Motivation in an advanced technological society . . . To be efficient and to be human. In *Agent of change: Technology's impact on management.*

The negro and his bootstraps. Cleveland, OH: Case Western Reserve University.

Job enrichment: Sometimes it works. *Wall Street Journal* (December).

The games managers play. The sweet, enriched life of Professor Herzberg. *The Sunday Times* (January 19, London).

With B. Grigaliunas. Relevancy in the test of motivation-hygiene theory. *Journal of Applied Psychology, 55.*

Advantages and obstacles to job enrichment [Videotape series]. Chicago: Video Learning Centers.

Clinical case: Directory [Videotape series]. Chicago: Video Learning Centers.

Clinical case: Keypunch [Videotape series]. Chicago: Video Learning Centers.

Defining the model job [Videotape series]. Chicago: Video Learning Centers.

Implementing job enrichment [Videotape series]. Chicago: Video Learning Centers.

Initiating the job enrichment effort [Videotape series]. Chicago: Video Learning Centers.

Management by hygiene [Videotape series]. Chicago: Video Learning Centers.

Management by motivation [Videotape series]. Chicago: Video Learning Centers.

Motivation to work studies [Videotape series]. Chicago: Video Learning Centers.

Pre-implementation [Videotape series]. Chicago: Video Learning Centers.

Refining the greenlight items [Videotape series]. Chicago: Video Learning Centers.

Undertaking job enrichment [Videotape series]. Chicago: Video Learning Centers.

Why jobs die [Videotape series]. Chicago: Video Learning Centers.

1972

With B. Boyle. *Women: The emerging resource* (Coordinator guide, Vols. 1 & 2). Elk Grove Village, IL: Advanced Systems, Inc.

The end of obligation. *Industry Week* (October 16).

The equality of ignorance. *Industry Week* (October 9).

Swapping managerial garbage. *Industry Week* (October 2).

How to restore the will to work. *Industry Week* (November 20).

Documentary on job enrichment [Film].RAI Corporation.
How to restore the will to work [Film]. Cleveland, OH: Penton, Inc.

1973

With B. Grigaliunas. *Motivation; The management of success* (Coordinator guide, Vols. 1, 2, &3). Elk Grove Village, IL: Advanced Systems, Inc.
Frederick Herzberg's recipe for motivation [Interview]. *International Management* (September).
The inimitable Herzberg [Interview]. *People and Profits, 1* (3).
Why bother to work? *Industry Week* (July 16).
How do you react to hostility? *Management Magazine, Bank of America, 3* (5).
Jumping for the jellybeans [Film]. British Broadcasting Corporation.
Management by movement [Film]. Elk Grove Village, IL: Advanced Systems, Inc.
Management of hostility [Film]. Elk Grove Village, IL: Advanced Systems, Inc.
Management of hygiene [Film]. Elk Grove Village, IL: Advanced Systems, Inc.
Management of the motivators [Film]. Elk Grove Village, IL: Advanced Systems, Inc.
Motivational types [Film]. Elk Grove Village, IL: Advanced Systems, Inc.
Motivation-hygiene theory [Film]. Elk Grove Village, IL: Advanced Systems, Inc.
Myth about your employees [Film]. Elk Grove Village, IL: Advanced Systems, Inc.
The nature of man [Film]. Elk Grove Village, IL: Advanced Systems, Inc.
To be efficient and to be human [Film]. Elk Grove Village, IL: Advanced Systems, Inc.
What happened to the work ethic? [Film]. Elk Grove Village, IL: Advanced Systems, Inc.
With B. Boyle. *Women: The emerging resource: Counseling Women* [Film]. Elk Grove Village, IL: Advanced Systems, Inc.
With B. Boyle. *Women: The emerging resource: Why be concerned?* [Film]. Elk Grove Village, IL: Advanced Systems, Inc.
With B. Boyle. *Women: The emerging resource: Why women work* [Film]. Elk Grove Village, IL: Advanced Systems, Inc.

1974

With R. Walters & B. Grigaliunas. *Job enrichment* (Coordinator guide, Vols 1 & 2). Elk Grove Village, IL: Advanced Systems, Inc.
Commentaries. In *R&D Productivity*. Hughes Aircraft Co.

Coping with change: Some blind alleys for the perplexed and some pessimisms for the dismayed. *Hospital Forum* (December).

The economic crisis and work motivation. *Industry Week* (February 25).

Managing people in an era of hopelessness. *Industry Week* (November 11).

Motivation-hygiene profiles: Pinpointing what ails the organization. *Organizational Dynamics* (Autumn).

New perspectives on the will to work. *Personnel Administrator* (July-August).

The wise old Turk. *Harvard Business Revview* (September-October).

Una ves mas Comomotivar a sus empleados? *Biblioteca Harvard de Admistracion de Empresas.*

Work, satisfaction and motivation-hygiene theory [Special issue]. *Book Forum, 1* (2).

With Y. Wiener, J. Mathao, & L. Wiesen. Motivation-hygiene correlates of mental health: An examination of motivatin inversion in a clinical population. *Journal of Consulting and Clinical Psychology, 42* (3).

With R. Walters. *Implementing job enrichment* [Film]. Elk Grove Village, IL: Advanced Systems, Inc.

With R. Walters. *Ingredients of a good job* [Film]. Elk Grove Village, IL: Advanced Systems, Inc.

With R. Walters. *Job enrichment: A pragmatic view* [Film]. Elk Grove Village, IL: Advanced Systems, Inc.

With R. Walters. *Starting a job enrichment program* [Film]. Elk Grove Village, IL: Advanced Systems, Inc.

With R. Walters. *What is job enrichment?* [Film]. Elk Grove Village, IL: Advanced Systems, Inc.

1975

With W.J. Paul, Jr. & K.B. Robertson. One more time: How do you motivate employees and job enrichment pays off. *Harvard Business Review–Business Classics.*

Job enrichment—Ogden style. In *Productivity enhancement in logistical systems.* Washington, DC: U.S. Department of Commerce.

Job enrichment's "father" admits: Disparity between promise and reality. *Industry Week* (November 25).

Para quem quer motivar seu pessoal e nao sabe como [Interview]. *Supermercado Moderno* (March, Sao Paulo).

With Maj. Gen. E. Rafalko. Efficiency in the military: Cutting costs with orthodox job enrichment. *Personnel* (November-December)).

With Y. Wiener & R. Vaitenaso. *Social desirability, repression and sensitization as factors in the critical incidents method of motivation-hygiene* (Human Resources Management Publication No. 75-101). Salt Lake City, UT: University of Utah Press.

With Y. Wiener, R. Vaitenas, & K. Klein. *A new classification system for critical incidents: Implications for the defensiveness hypothesis and white collar-blue collar job feelings* (Human Resources Management Publication No. 75-101). Salt Lake City, UT: University of Utah Press.

[Discussion between Professor Herzberg and Professor Kalevsky (U.S.S.R) on *Encuentro*] [Film]. Mexico City: Instituto Mexicano del Seguro Social and Televisa.

[Documentary on Job Enrichment Research Program, *OJE-Ogden Style*] [Film, VRDO869/539CCH]. Utah: Ogden Air Force Logistics Command, Hill Air Force Base.

1976

The managerial choice: To be efficient and to be human (1st ed.). Homewood, IL: Dow Jones-Irwin.

Commentary of Maslow. In *Great writings of marketing.* Plymouth, MI: Commerce Press.

Making work work better symposium. *The Rotarian* (May).

Types of job enrichment. In *Proceedings of First International Congress of Labor and Psychology.* Mexico City: Asociacion de Psicologos Industriales.

With A. Zautra. Orthodox job enrichment: Measuring true quality in job satisfaction. *Personnel* (September-October).

OJE: What do employees think? [Film, VR/667]. Utah: Ogden Air Force Logistics Command, Hill Air Force Base.

1977

Orthodox job enrichment: A common sense approach to people at work. *Defense Management Journal* (April).

Frederick Herzberg on motivation, job enrichment and productivity [Interview]. *Bulletin on Training, BNA Communications, Inc.* (May-June).

New Approaches im management organization and job design—1. In M.T. Matteson & J.M. Ivancevich (Eds.), *Management classics.* Santa Monica, CA: Goodyear.

Motivation—Where theory conflicts with reality. *Industry Week* (July 4).

An old-new perspective of work motivation. Address to Rotary Club of Salt Lake City, Utah, July.

A la rechercle des motivations perdues. Harvard-L'expansion (Autumn).

Comparison of U.S.A. and European approaches to work motivation. Paper presented at Annual Conference Utbildningsbolget, Stockholm, October.

Motivation og jobberegelse. In F. Balvig (Ed.), *Organisations udvikling.* Copenhagen:Nyt Nordisk Forlag Arnold Busck.

1978

Getting a kick out of work [Interview with C. Kelly]. *Mgr* [*AT&T Long Lines*] (January).
Putting people back together:The human need for work. *Industry Week* (July 24).
The human need for work: The dynamics of caring. *Industry Week* (August 7).
Careerists, accomplihers and the obsolete. *Industry Week* (August 21).
Participation is not a motivator. *Industry Week* (September 4).
Humanistic management to motivating people [Interview with J. Ichikawa & K. Kitano]. *Kassei* [Japanese steeel industry magazine] (October).
Humanistic management to motivating people [Interview with J. Ichikawa & K. Kitano]. *Live* [Popular Japanese management magazine] (October).

1979

Peoples' needs haven't changed. *Communications West* (Spring).
Piecing together generations of values. *Industry Week* (October 1).
Motivation and innovation: Who are workers serving? *California Management Review, 22* (2).

1980

Commentary in retrospect on "One more time: How do you motivate employees." In L.E. Boone (Ed.), *Great writings in management and organizational behavior.* Tulsa, OK: Petroleum Publishing Company.
With M. Miner. Monitoring orthodox job enrichment. *Defense Management Journal.*
Leadership in the 80's and all the years before. In *Proceedings if the Home Office Life Underwriters Association 50th Anniversary.*
Herzberg the humanist [Interview with P. Pascarella]. *Industry Week* (September 15).
Leadership in a period of psychological depression. *Industry Week* (September 15).
Humanities: Practical management education. *Industry Week* (September 29).
Maximizing work and minimizing labor. *Industry Week* (October 13).

1981

Motivating people. In P. Mali (Ed.), *Management handbook*. New York: Wiley.

Geld verdirbt den Charkter. *Warum* (March).

Producivity and motivation [Interview].Public Pulse—Radio KSL, Salt Lake City, Utah, February 24.

Humanisierung der Argeit und Produkivitaetssteigerung [Interview]. *10 Management Zeitschrift* (July-August).

Group dynamics at the roundtable. *Industry Week* (November 16).

Productivity begins with the individual. *Industry Week* (November 30).

1982

The managerial choice: To be efficient to be human (2nd rev. ed.). Salt Lake City, UT: Olympus Publishing Company.

Where have all the management gurus gone? [Interview]. *International Management* (January).

Are today's managers risk-shy? [Interview]. *International Management* (May).

Thoughts on management. *Communicator* (May).

The lonely struggle to develop character. *Industry Week* (August 23).

1983

Herzberg on motivation (2nd ed.). Cleveland, OH: Penton/PC.

Up the staircase to productivity burnout. *Industry Week* (January 10).

Down the staircase to depression. *Industry Week* (January 24).

Remedies for depression and burnout. *Industry Week* (February 7).

Psychogical implications in the office of the future. *Human Factors* (Spring).

Herzberg on motivation for the '80s. In *How to be a better leader*. Cleveland, OH: Penton/PC.

The human need for work. In *How to be a better leader*. Cleveland, OH: Penton/PC.

Distinguished psychologistsabout psychology [Interview]. *Veliki Psiholozi O Psihologiji.*

Love and work. *World Executive's Digest* (December).

1984

[Commentary on *Origin of motivation to work*]. *Current Contents, 16* (19).

Managing egos of east and west: Existential questions and annswers [Interview with M. Miner]. *The Journal* (Summer).

Mystery systems shape loyalties. *Industry Week* (November 12).

Participation: Harmony or conflict? *Industry Week* (November 26).
Seeking answers that motivate. *Industry Week* (December 10).

1985

Chapter. In M. Stevens & R. Zimbardo (Eds.), *Critical thinking and critical writing across the curriculum*. New York: Longman.
Innovation: Where is the relish? In *Proceedings from the Second Creativity, Innovation & Entrepreneurship Symposium.*
Where is the passion? *Industry Week* (November 11).

1986

Beyond beliefs and betrayals. *Personnel* (September).
The passionless society [Interview with H. Levine]. *Personnel* (September).

1987

Herzberg on motivation (2nd ed.). Cleveland, OH: Penton/PC.
A new game in management of human resources. In *International management develpment review* (Vol. 3). Management Centre Europe, European Headquarters of the American Management Association.
Overcoming betrayals of the '80s. *Industry Week* (July 13).
Workers' needs: The same around the world. *Industry Week* (September 21).
Commentary on industrial psychology. *Veliki Psiholozi on Psihologiji.*
Commentary of *Origin of motivation to work*. In *Contemporary classics in the social and behavioral sciences.* ICI Press.
Retrospective commentary on "One more time: How do you motivate employees." *Harvard Business Review Classic* (September-October).
Innovation: Where is the relish? *The Journal of Creative Behavior, 21* (3).

1988

The corporate sages (D. Clutterbuck & S. Crainer, eds.). *Business* (September).
Darlige ledere skylker pa andre [Interview with N. Brett]. *Aftenposten* (December 17).

1989

Hvordan motiverer man medarbejdere. *FIU-Centret.*
Chapter. In N. Mather (Ed.), *Management thought–Contributions of American and European thinkers.* Jaipur, India: National Publishing House.

Chapter. In D.S. Pugh & D.J. Hickson (Eds.), *Writers on organization* (4th ed.). Newbury Park, CA: Sage.

Effectiveness in organizations. *Issues, 9.*

Appropriate motivation [Interview with S. Komago]. *The Nihon Keizai Shimbun* (December 9).

1990

With M. Miner. Motivation to work versus incentive to labor. *Journal of Sociological Studies.*

Biography of Frederick Herzberg. In D. Clutterbuck & S. Crainer (Eds.), *Makers of management: Men and women who changed the business world.* London: Macmillan.

With M. Miner. Why work? Summary of "Motivation to work vs. incentive to labor." *Business Review.*

Biography of Frederick Herzberg. In N. Mathur (Ed.), *Life and works of management thinkers.* India: Sahitya Bhawan Agra.

Managing health services using motivation-hygiene theory [Taped lecture]. The Open University of London, British Broadcasting Corporation, London, December.

Robert J. House

Slow Learner and Late Bloomer

ROBERT J. HOUSE

I am honored to present my autobiography amidst such a group of competent scholars. I will begin by describing my parents and my childhood experiences. I will then describe some of the more salient points of my career and will end with some observations concerning my beliefs about the future direction of the field of organizational behavior.

MY PARENTS

My father, of whom I am very proud, was required to quit school at the end of the fourth grade to go to work on his father's farm. In 1902, at age 15, he left the farm because he could no longer suffer his autocratic and authoritarian father.

Upon leaving the farm in central Ohio, my father went to the big city of Toledo, Ohio, where he obtained a job as a railroad worker. He began working on the railroad in about 1902 or 1903 and continued until he had saved enough money, probably $100 or so, to buy a poolroom. In 1902, unskilled railroad workers earned $9 per week, so saving $100 most likely required him to work overtime and make many personal sacrifices. He used the earnings from the poolroom to buy three slot machines. Thus, his career as an entrepreneur was launched.

Because of the competition from the "syndicate," it was necessary for him to place the slot machines in restaurants, poolrooms, after-hours joints, speakeasys, and cafes on the outskirts of Toledo. When he placed the slots closer to the center of town, the syndicate would physically destroy them to protect its turf. Thus, he spent his early years as an entrepreneur, driving

41

a Model A Ford on mud roads, back and forth across the northern part of Ohio to service the slots and collect revenues. His "locations" could be as far as forty miles apart. A forty mile trip on a mud road might take as long as an hour and a half. My mother, Mary, would often ride with him to keep him company. To prevent him from falling asleep, she would frequently sing the popular songs of the day to him.

My father's business thrived, and he expanded into pinball machines, which were different from today's pinball machines. It cost a nickel to play a pinball machine, and one could possibly win as much as $2 or $3 in a given play. My father was moderately successful, and thus we enjoyed middle-class economic status. However, I was raised in a blue-collar neighborhood as my parents found themselves uncomfortable around more affluent and more educated people. Prior to my birth, and after my father had become somewhat successful, he and my mother moved to an affluent section of Toledo, Westmoreland. The neighbors snubbed my mother and gossiped about my father's business and the kind of people who came to our house. My father saw them as "blue bloods," and thought they didn't appreciate what it took for a poor boy to make good. To him, these people really didn't believe in the "American way." Consequently, my parents moved back to a working-class neighborhood on the east side of Toledo where my sisters and I were raised. My father's success was sufficient to put my two sisters and me through university and to leave my mother a sufficient amount of funds for her remaining years after his accidental death at the age of seventy.

My mother, whose maiden name was Mary Kinn, and of whom I am equally proud, was born in 1902 on a farm near Fostoria, Ohio. She was the youngest of eleven children. Her mother died when she was ten, and her father when she was fifteen. She and her brothers and sisters sold the farm and divided the proceeds equally. At the age of fifteen, she moved to Tiffin, Ohio, where she took a room with a family and spent her inheritance obtaining a diploma for secretarial and bookkeeping skills. At the age of about seventeen, she moved to Toledo, where she took an apartment with a number of other young women. They were carefree, fun-loving young women who were referred to in those days as "flappers," although my mother would never admit to it. Nevertheless, her stories, and the stories about her in the "roaring twenties" belied her denial.

From this brief description of my parents' background, you can see that I was endowed with two role models of industriousness, risk taking, and courage. It took a lot of courage for these young people to leave the farm and come to the big city, then known as "Unholy Toledo," while still in their teens. My mother was very nurturing. My father was strongly achievement-oriented, hard-driving, and very intolerant of laziness and dishonesty. From him I learned three things: achievement motivation, the importance of controlling one's own destiny, and honesty. While my father was small, five-foot-four, and quite a gentle man, he didn't take any guff from anyone. He said it was necessary to stand on your own two feet or you'd get knocked over. From my mother I learned nurturance, hard work, respect for honesty and for the less fortunate, and humor. She loved to tell and listen to jokes, play cards (bridge and gin rummy), entertain, and party.

GROWING UP IN UNHOLY TOLEDO

If you've read any of Damon Runyon, or if you've seen the play or the movie *Guys and Dolls*, you'll have a good idea of what life was like for me as a child growing up in Toledo. It was a Runyonesque environment. Toledo was a wide-open city. People would come to Toledo from Chicago, Cleveland, Detroit, Columbus, and all the small farm towns to have a good time. Gambling houses, poolhalls, and bars were open around the clock. Anybody who wanted "action" could find it in Toledo. By virtue of my father's occupation, the people whom the family knew were either small-time gamblers or people who, like my father, ran gambling businesses: numbers, racetracks, gambling houses, pinballs, "floating" card games, and slots. These were exciting times with exciting people. Many lived a roller coaster life of up and down; win at the track or the tables one day, lose the next. Borrow a hundred and make good your marker (IOU) as promised. Welchers could never borrow a second time—the word got around. Consequently, for the most part, these were honest people who lived and worked at night and slept most of the day. While my father was not a show-off, he had a dry sense of humor and enjoyed having a good time. My mother also liked to "kick up her heels," as she would say. She was a bit of an "Auntie Mame" type.

To give you an idea of the kind of environment in which I was raised, I'll recount a few incidents that occurred in my childhood and early adolescence.

There were a number of guys who hung out at my father's shop, where he repaired the slots; at a local bar and restaurant titled "The Main Street Grill"; at the pool hall next door to my dad's shop, which he sold after he got into the slot machine business; at Charlie Bones' cigar store, where Bones ran a numbers book; or at Tuffy La Marche's cigar shop, where he ran an around-the-clock poker game. To pass the time, these guys would kibbitz, play gin rummy, poker, pool, bunker (a dice game), liar's dice, or bet on the nags (horses), athletic games, or boxing matches. They would bet on almost anything, including the weather—or even which way a bird sitting on a telephone wire would fly!

Most of the guys had monikers. There was my dad, "Little Louie," Tuffy La Marche, Sam "Potatoes" Papata, Charlie "Bones" Bennett, "Two Shirt" Sam, Billy "The Belly" Grubowsky, Johnny "The Nose" Suzor, and Big Rollie. Because my last name was House, all of the guys with whom I hung out would refer to me by a number of monikers, such as "Domicile Dan," "Sammy

Shack," "Izzy Igloo," "Gabby Garage," "Railroad Terminal Tom," or my favorite, "Tony Tepee."

Two Shirt Sam got his moniker because he always wore a light blue shirt and brown trousers. We all assumed that he had at least two shirts, and that they were the same. One day, Potatoes visited Two Shirt at his apartment. He opened the closet to find that Two Shirt actually had fifteen identical blue shirts and six identical pairs of brown trousers. He said it made life simpler for him in the morning. Everyone liked Two Shirt Sam, so the way he dressed didn't make much difference. From Two Shirt I learned that it was important and satisfying to "be yourself."

One day when the family was vacationing in Florida, Charlie Bones and Tuffy La Marche came to visit in Charlie's big yellow Cadillac convertible. We all piled into his car for a ride. As we were going down the road, parallel to an intercostal canal, a speedboat passed us by. Tuffy said, "Charlie, I'll bet you $500 you can't beat the boat to the bridge." Charlie said, "I'll bet you this car against your boat." Tuffy said, "You're on," and Charlie hit the accelerator. My mother screamed, "Don't do this, you damn fools, we have two kids in the car." My sister and I yelled in excitement, "Go Charlie, Go!" I'm sure my memory is tainted by retrospective enhancement, but I can recall my sister and I looking over the backseat of the car as we cleared the bridge. I swear we just made it. The overhanging gate was coming down, and the back wheels of the car cleared the bridge by about five feet before the drawbridge opened!

The next day, Charlie came to visit again. He said, "Let's go for a ride. I swear I'll behave." We went down to the dock where Tuffy's boat, which Charlie Bones had just won, was moored. There was a man there with a blow torch. He said, "OK, Mr. Bennett?" Bones said yes, and the man proceeded to remove the names "Fluffy and Tuffy" from the stern of the boat. Fluffy was short for Florence, Tuffy's girlfriend. Tuffy and Bones remained lifelong friends. From this incident, I learned how important it was to make good on your wager and not take a loss personally.

My father always told us not to gamble. He said you can never beat the house. However, he did not discourage me from betting on skill. He taught me to shoot pool when I was about twelve years old. After I learned how to hold a cue, line up the shot, draw, follow, and put a little spin on the ball, he told me he didn't want to catch me playing pool unless I played for at least a quarter or so a game. I said, "But dad, you always tell us never to gamble." He said, "You'll never be a good pool player if you don't play for money. If you don't have a little something on the game, you'll never know whether or not the other guy is really trying. If he's not trying, there's no satisfaction in winning. You're betting on your skill. Gambling is betting on the horses, the numbers, dice or the roulette wheel." Further, he said, "Outwardly, you've gotta be graceful when you lose, but deep down you have to feel it. You show me a good loser and I'll show you a loser."

At that time, men either wore suits, sweaters, or sport shirts. Sports jackets and blazers had not come into style yet. Dad said, "If you're in a strange town, and you want to find the racetrack, look for a guy whose jacket doesn't match his pants. Follow him and he'll take you to the track. He can afford to bet on the nags, but he can't afford a full suit." From these incidents I learned the importance of developing skill and not wishing or hoping fruitlessly that "one day my horse will come in a winner."

One day I went to the barbershop. The barber, Floyd Newmeir, told me a story about my dad's diamond ring, a rock of about a carat and a half in size. He said, "You know, Bob, your dad told me he's gonna leave his ring to you." I told him I was aware of that. He then told me that when times were rough, in the early days, my dad came to his barbershop and said, "Floyd, I need to borrow fifty bucks to buy a new slot machine. The syndicate has busted up one of my machines and it has to be replaced." Floyd said, "What do you have for collateral?" My dad gave him the diamond ring. About a month later my dad came back and paid off the fifty dollar loan and retrieved the ring. I still have the ring. I don't wear it very often because it's quite ostentatious. However, it sure has sentimental value. That ring was the collateral that allowed my dad to turn his business around. It was his venture capital. Clearly, this was a vivid example of persistence and risk taking, backed up by confidence and hard work.

Bones was a legend for practical jokes. He called up 30 tuba players and told them he wanted to hire them for a Saturday afternoon gig. He asked them to meet him at Flat Iron Park, which was a small triangular park in south Toledo. They all gathered in the park, banging their tubas against each other. There wasn't room for 10, let alone 30, tubas. Bones drove by in his yellow Cadillac convertible waving and saying, "Let's hear some music, fellas." He drove around the park and returned with a hot-dog vendor and three kegs of beer. They all had a free lunch and a party, but they never accepted another invitation from Charlie Bones. Since then, I've always enjoyed the fine art of a good but benign practical joke, which I still try to practice when I get the chance. Interestingly, many of my academic colleagues don't know when I'm being serious or "putting them on." Most, however, can take a practical joke in good humor.

Gert, a young woman on whom Charlie Bones had a crush, made beer in her apartment during the Prohibition era. One night, the beer was bottled and stacked in her bathroom. Evidently, she didn't have the formula right. The beer fermented and dripped into the apartment below. The tenants called the police and Gert was arrested. Bones bailed her out to the tune of much razzing, hooting, and laughing from the cops and clerks at the police station, even though he didn't really have to do it. "Hey, Charlie, doesn't your girlfriend even know how to make hooch?" That's when Charlie won Gert's heart. The lesson I learned from this was that loyalty and friendship are not only of value in their own right but sometimes also get rewarded. Loyalty and friendship paid off for Charlie.

HOLTZ'S POOL HALL

My first real accomplishment came at the age of sixteen. I won the Toledo Junior Pocket Billiards Championship. One of my best friends, Bill Murphy, was the runner-up and almost beat me in the finals. Murph (known as "the Thermometer" because he was six-three, skinny, and occasionally wore a red tie) was a better pool player than me. I remember how I won it, however. First, I practiced hard, so I knew my game was as good as it could be at the time. I concentrated hard on every shot; I would make sure that my stance and my bridge (the hand that supports the cue stick) were just right. I lined up the ball carefully, took several practice strokes, calculated the weight of the stroke—that is, how hard to hit the ball—and the position on the table where I wanted the cue ball to stop after sinking the object ball. For a really good pool player, all of this wouldn't be necessary. Pool players like "Fast Eddie" in *The Hustler*, or his opponent, "Detroit Fats" (the real character after whom the fictional character "Minnesota Fats" was named) would do all of this intuitively and quickly. I learned a lot from that experience. Do your homework (practice), stick with the fundamentals, and concentrate.

Let me tell you how this all came about. The pool hall proprietor and owner was Huey Heal. Huey had been the three-rail billiard champion of the world in 1932. Three-rail billiards is not a hustler's game. It's a gentleman's game. The game requires a player to hit three rails with the cue ball before completing the shot by hitting two object balls. This is a very difficult game requiring a mastery of angles, English (spin), and geometry, as well as having a very powerful stroke and a good eye.

When Huey took over Holtz's pool hall, the tables sat on a cold cement floor. The paint was peeling off the walls, and the place was generally run-down. Only the tables were kept in good condition.

Holtz's Pool Hall was a sleaze box if there ever was one. The regulars that hung out there were among the worst of the hustlers. If it hadn't been for Huey Heal,[1] my friends and I might have come under the influence of these people. Fortunately, a few months after we started visiting Holtz's Pool Hall, Huey took over as proprietor.

Huey said to my friends and me, "This is going to be a gentleman's billiard parlor. No foul language, no irresponsible behavior, and no spitting on the floor." He then spat on the floor and said, "That's the last goober you'll ever see on this floor." Soon after, he installed floor tiling, painted the walls, put in a lunch counter, and hired two women to cook and serve short-order meals. He said that when you're in the presence of women, you behave like gentlemen.

He then made his deal. He said, "If you young men will live up to these standards, I'll teach you how to be first-rate pool players." For us, this was like a dream come true—having a former world billiards champion for your coach.

He replaced several of the straight pool and snooker tables with billiard tables. Soon we noticed a change in clientele. The rummy hustlers who previously spent time at Holtz's were gone. Their behavior wasn't appropriate and they couldn't take the cleanliness of the place. I think it made them nervous. In their place were a number of elderly gentlemen, usually around fifty years of age or older, who were well-dressed and mannerly. They were frequently accompanied by their wives, who would watch them play in the tournaments that Huey established. Consequently, a significant part of my adolescent environment was changed for the better, due to Huey Heal. Huey diverted me from an ill-spent youth to a misspent youth.

GETTING AN EDUCATION

My parents stressed that it was important for us to get a good education. While they were good role models when it came to the values of honesty and hard work (and play), they were understandably not good academic role models. While they would tell us to study, they didn't sit down and help us study. While they read the newspaper daily, there were few books in the house. Because there were so many other interesting things to do, I seldom studied. In high school, I spent most of my time in the poolroom, hanging out at Bone's or Tuffy's cigar shops, drinking 3.2 beers, and partying with the other kids whose fathers were in the gambling business. I didn't change my habits when I went to the University of Detroit. Consequently, just prior to the last semester of my senior year, I was informed by the registrar that if I didn't get a solid B average, I wouldn't graduate. I had not gotten one A or one F, but I had a long string of D's. I needed a B average in the last semester to bring my grade-point average up to a flat C, which was required for graduation. Henry Tosi and I joke about being members of a select group who obtained baccalaureate degrees with low C averages only to become Ph.D.'s and professors. Who would have ever "thunk it?" For the first time in my life I studied hard, and ended the semester with four A's and a B. What a revelation! It was fun to learn. I hadn't known what I'd been missing.

After graduation from college, I worked nights on the assembly line at Chrysler while trying to figure out what I wanted to do with my life. My father wanted me to go into his business but I saw that it was too rough a life. The constant bargaining and haggling, the tough competition, and the uncertainties were not for me. While working evenings, I interviewed for jobs in the daytime. I interviewed for most of the jobs that appeared in the want ads that required a college graduate. I didn't know what I wanted to do and thought this would be a good way to find out what kinds of jobs and careers were open to me. It was a good way to get career advice. After about six months on the assembly line, I took a job as a management trainee at Chrysler. After about six months in a job-rotation training program, I was assigned to a personnel research group under the supervision of Ed Harris and Jim Frey, industrial psychologists with Ph.D.s. Both were scholars at heart. Later, Ed was to become a Professor of Management at Wayne State University in Detroit. My exposure to Ed and Jim had a profound effect on the rest of my life. They introduced me to the logic of experimental design and analysis of variance. I was awed by the intellectual power of this kind of analysis.

At this time, I was taking night courses at the University of Detroit, and eventually was admitted to the MBA program. My motivation for taking these courses was to make up for the learning I had not obtained while partying my way through undergraduate school. I felt I had shortchanged myself in undergraduate school by not studying.

In 1957, there was a major downturn in the automotive market. By then I had accumulated about half the credits necessary for an MBA. I enjoyed learning, and my grades were good. I could see that I was going to be laid off as a result of the economic downturn.

By this time I was married and had one child. I knew I did not want to spend the rest of my life working in a large bureaucracy. I thought I might want to be a teacher, but I was concerned that I couldn't support a family on an educator's income. My advisor at the University of Detroit informed me that a full professor could make as much as $10,000 a year. This was in 1957. I applied for admission to Ph.D. programs at several universities and was rejected by all except Ohio State University. However, even Ohio State would not provide funding because my undergraduate academic performance had been so bad. I sold the small house we had in Royal Oak, Michigan, and took the equity, my wife and my son Danny, to Columbus, Ohio, where I completed my Ph.D. I enrolled in September 1958, and completed my Ph.D. in June 1960. Ohio State gave me credit for experience and accepted my MBA credits toward the Ph.D. degree. So you see, ironically, I got a Ph.D. and subsequently became a professor as a result of having been such a poor undergraduate student.

While in my Ph.D. program at Ohio State, I worked as a pharmaceutical detailer for a few months, did some grading for professors, taught a number of introductory business courses to undergraduates, worked at the post office during Christmas season, and studied pretty hard.

After completing my prelims in June 1959, I worked for North American Aviation, Inc., in Columbus, Ohio, as a management training specialist for one year. I collected the data for my dissertation by conducting short management communications programs thirty hours per week. My dissertation design involved two comparison treatments. The first was straight classroom training. The second involved classroom training plus follow-up with the managers whom I counseled with respect to their communication and delegation practices. I believe mine was the first empirical dissertation to have been conducted in the business school at Ohio State University. It was also the shortest—100 pages.

Since the chairman of my dissertation committee, Mike Jucius, was not an empirical investigator, I obtained advice from Cal Shartle, who was a professor of industrial psychology. Cal was one of the original founders of the Ohio State Leadership Research Program. Ed Harris, for whom I had worked at Chrysler, was a graduate of the Ohio State industrial psychology program and had done his dissertation, together with Ed Fleishman, on the effects of management training on managerial leader behavior. Ed Harris and Ed Fleishman were among the first generation of Ph.D.s who graduated after the initiation of the Ohio State Leadership Program. Bernard Bass, whose work was to impress and influence me significantly, was also a member of the same cohort. Like Ed Harris, Cal was a role model and source of inspiration for me. Thus began my interest in leadership, which continues to this day.

EARLY CAREER DEVELOPMENT

My employment at North American Aviation paid off in three ways. First, it provided a family income while writing my dissertation. Second, it provided me the opportunity to collect data for the dissertation. Third, and perhaps most importantly from a career perspective, it provided me with valuable experience concerning how large, complex government contractors with large research and development units are managed—the forerunners of large, modern, high-tech companies. Perhaps a major insight I obtained is that scientific or engineering training, while providing the basis for rigorous intellectual and logical thinking, provides very few answers for the issues faced by middle- and upper-level R&D and engineering managers. My position as a management training specialist brought me in contact with managers at all levels. I consulted with them on the design, implementation and evaluation of management training programs. As a result, they shared many of their experiences and problems with me. One of the major insights I drew concerns Karl Weick's theoretical speculations concerning loose coupling. There is inevitably a lot of slack and loose coupling in technologically driven organizations.

After leaving North American Aviation I was hired as a consultant to design and conduct a management training program for the top management team of the Research, Development, and Engineering Division at North American. As a result of this experience, plus a short period of rather intensive reading of the psychological literature, I was able to write a number of papers on management development efforts as they relate to organizational contexts. These papers were published in respectable managerial-oriented journals and thus encouraged me to continue doing research and writing.

One of the middle managers in the R&D Division of North American who participated in the management education seminars I conducted was Vaughn Beals, to whom I would later consult when he became Vice President of Research at Cummins Engine Company and yet later President of Harley Davidson.

As a result of the North American Aviation project I was hired at NCR (then National Cash Register Inc.) by Hugh Stephenson to design and conduct a management development program for their research and engineering division. It was during this period of time that I wrote the paper titled, "A Commitment Approach to Management Development." What I was trying to do in both the North American and NCR projects was implement a top-down management education program in which there would be consistency of concepts taught across organizational levels. Policies would be formulated by a top management team and communicated downward together with the necessary education to implement them.

My cumulative experience at Chrysler, North American Aviation and NCR was beginning to make me doubtful of the workability of such an approach. There was just too much slack between levels, too many different perspectives with respect to any given topic, a fair amount of suspicion (common in hierarchical organizations), and too many people set in their ways. It was these insights that caused me to think of management development in context and led me to write the papers referred to above. Looking back, it is interesting to note that at that time I still believed that "rational decision making" and top down education could be effective.

Upon receiving my Ph.D. in June 1960, I was offered a job as an Assistant Professor at Ohio State. The salary was $6,720 per year. My second son, Tim, was born the morning of my oral exams. I took written comprehensive exams in my major field, management, and in my minor, finance. Tim was born at 4 a.m. The exam was held at 10 a.m. I drove my wife to the hospital at 11 p.m. the prior evening. The doctor told me to go home and that he would call me when the baby was ready to be delivered. They called me at about 3:15 a.m. and I was there at the time of the delivery. I visited my wife at her bedside after she gave birth. I then went back home and slept until about 9 a.m. I was fully refreshed for the exam. However, I didn't inform my examining committee of this. I merely said that my son was born at 4 a.m. and passed out cigars.

I wasn't nervous during the exam, probably because of my experience during the last year as an instructor of managers. The exam went well and, afterward, Mike Jucius said to me, "You sure talk better than you write."

In my early career, writing was very difficult for me. Someone told me the best guide to good writing is to make sure you write in a way that no one can misunderstand you. That's a challenging standard, and one to which I try to hold to this day. While I think my writing is clear (you be the judge), I tell my colleagues that it's the kind of writing that once you put it down you never want to pick it up again—a sure cure for insomnia. Actually, this autobiography is my first attempt at journalistic writing.

At the beginning, it was a drop of sweat for every word and a drop of blood for every sentence. The knowledge I gained about writing clearly madeth a bloody entrance. However, with practice and exposure to the writing of others, I developed the ability to write quite easily. I have heard that the better scholars are also very lucid writers. Some writers can make forceful arguments, deliver a complicated and abstract theoretical story, and make it so easily understood that you can't misinterpret it. Five such writers stand out in my mind, although there are many others: Herbert Simon, James March, Victor Vroom, Anatol Rappaport, and C. West Churchman.

My Ph.D. education consisted of courses in classical management which stressed the rational functions of managers: plan, organize, coordinate, direct, and control. It also consisted of several courses in functional areas such as personnel, production inventory and control, finance, and the like. It included no education in the behavioral sciences, statistics, research design, or methodology. Consequently, I was educated in one of the schools that came under heavy criticism by the Ford and Carnegie Foundation reports published in 1957-1958. In these reports, the state of the American business school was criticized as being atheoretical and lacking an empirical foundation, based largely on casual observation, memoirs of executives and "armchair theorizing." It was correctly alleged that business education in the United States consisted predominantly of requiring students to memorize long lists of factors and related information that had little empirical validity.

The Ford Foundation, through its prestige and resources, successfully encouraged a rather radical change in the educational practices of American business schools during the 1960s. The Ford Foundation encouraged many schools to recruit to their faculties social scientists, mathematicians and statisticians, and operations researchers who were eventually to become known as systems analysts or decision scientists. Many of the more prestigious schools (Harvard, Stanford, MIT, Carnegie-Mellon, Berkeley, Purdue, and Northwestern) were allocated large institutional grants by the Ford Foundation. This money was used to recruit disciplinary-based scholars into business school faculties.

Thus, the attainment of my Ph.D. in 1960 was a photo finish with my obsolescence. I'm still running this race and hope that with the help of colleagues I can avoid obsolescence before retirement. In the mid-1960s, the editorial review boards of the journals reflected the new wave of rigor that was becoming pervasive in U.S. business schools. The writing was on the wall. I either had to retrain or resign myself to being a second-class academic from the outset.

While at Ohio State, I had the good fortune of being exposed to Ralph Currier Davis in my Ph.D. program and to Ralph M. Stogdill when I subsequently became an assistant professor. While I didn't have much contact with either of these two scholars, I read Davis's *The Fundamentals of Top Management* (1954) at least three times. I also read Stogdill's *Individual Behavior and Group Achievement: A Theory, and the Experimental Evidence* (Oxford University Press, 1959) at least as many times. I read Jim March's *Handbook of Organizations* (Rand-McNally, 1965) from cover to cover. Other books that greatly influenced me in my early career were March and Simon's *Organizations* (Wiley, 1958), Ernst Nagel's *The Structure of Science* (Hackey, 1961), Sherman Krupps' *Pattern in Organizational Analysis* (Holt, Rinehart, & Winston, 1961), Michael Argyle's *The Scientific Study of Social Behavior* (Methuen, 1957), Amitai Etzioni's *Complex Organizations* (1961), and all of the monographs in the Ohio State Leadership Series. This literature had a great influence on my thinking and early development as a social scientist. All of these are still on my bookshelf, sitting proudly dog-eared.

I chose to retrain. Collaboration with Alan C. Filley on a book which was to be published in 1969, titled *Managerial Process and Organizational Behavior*, became the vehicle by which this retraining would be accomplished. Alan was to become one of my most admired and respected colleagues and friends. He now holds an endowed chair at the University of Wisconsin.

Smarting from the criticisms of our educational process and being envious of the better-trained social scientists who were encroaching upon our turf, we decided that a defense of the principles of classical management was in order. Further, we believed that classical management theory could be integrated with social science theory to produce a useful textbook. In those days, good textbooks were regarded as highly as scholarly books, monographs, or refereed publications. The idea was that we would subject each of the major principles and each of the perspectives of classical management to critical review. To accomplish this we would bring to bear social science knowledge relevant to each classical principle or perspective.

For example, the validity of the principle of unity of command was assessed by consulting the literature on role conflict and ambiguity. Implicit in the principle of unity of command was the notion that subjecting one individual to directions from more than one person would result in what psychologists termed role conflict. This is not a new idea. Jesus Christ said, "No man can have two masters: for he will hate the one, and love the other . . ." (Matthew, 6:24). Thus, by consulting the role conflict literature, which deals with the effects of conflicting directions imposed on individuals from multiple others or "role senders," the validity of the principle of unity of command could be inferentially assessed. Another example of our strategy concerns the principle of span of control. The validity of this principle was to be assessed by consulting the literature on small group size and process. The span of control principle asserts that an individual can supervise only a limited number of individuals, and beyond that number, intra-unit coordination, accountability and effectiveness will deteriorate. Thus, a consideration of the empirical findings on optimal group size, under various conditions, could be used to inferentially assess the validity of this principle.

About 1962 we began the project with a substantial advance from Scott, Foresman and Co. Little did we know what an arduous task it was going to be. We began writing the book in 1963 and completed it about 1968. In addition to chapters dealing with management, the management functions, organization design and selected classical principles of management, we also included chapters on behavioral science topics such as decision making, motivation, and leadership.

Al and I each wrote half the chapters. The chapters I did constituted a significant part of my education as a social scientist. They were the term papers I wished I had written while in graduate school.

The book sold quite well. Many people thought it was the first integration of the social sciences with traditional management theory. The contents of four of the chapters I wrote were published as four discussion or review papers in refereed journals prior to the publication of the book. My first refereed publication in a rigorous, scientifically-oriented journal was "T-Group Education and Leadership Effectiveness," published in 1967 in *Personnel Psychology*. This was a review article that critically assessed the effects of sensitivity training on attitudes and behaviors of participants. I was somewhat critical of the sensitivity training movement, but also recognized that it had some merit under selected conditions. I argued that the effects of sensitivity training were conditioned on, among other variables, the work context of the trainees. This, together with the papers I had written on management development for managerially-oriented journals (*Business Horizons, California Business Review, Harvard Business Review*) stressed the importance of organizational context as a moderator of the effects of management development endeavors. This concern of micro-issues in organizational context was to be characteristic of my theoretical and empirical work throughout my career. Both the T-groupers and the anti T-groupers were upset with the article, so I thought it must have been fairly evenhanded.

Back in 1962, Al and I had decided to test some of the classical management principles as well as some hypotheses concerning the effects of leaders on followers. Not being trained in research methodology, we made several errors that resulted in the temporary abandonment of the project in about 1964.

We collected questionnaire and interview data from engineering and research and development employees at National Cash Register and Phillips Petroleum.

In addition, Ralph Stogdill gave us data that he had collected at North American Aviation. We asked the interviewees to tell us how many people reported to them, and to how many people they reported. Unfortunately, we didn't standardize the interview. One of us (I can't remember who) accepted reports of informal reporting relationships, while the other accepted reports of only formal relationships. There were a number of other differences in our interview procedure. The result was that the data were inconsistently collected and consequently didn't make much sense. Further, we used Ralph Stogdills' standard coding manual to score the questionnaire responses concerning leader behavior and member satisfaction. Unfortunately, Ralph failed to tell us that he had changed the coding procedure with respect to the North American data. Consequently, the data were not comparable, and this resulted in very strange findings.

I spent the summer with Al in Wisconsin in 1964 analyzing what were essentially meaningless data. One day riding home in his MG with the top down, a bird dropped on Al's forehead. At this time we were both very frustrated. I offered Al a Kleenex and he said, "There's no use wiping it off, we'll just get dropped on again." We both laughed.

At Ohio State I had the good fortune of having several scholarly and competent colleagues. Notably among these were Henry Tosi, Robert Buzzell, Lou Stern, Frank Bass, and Ralph Stogdill. Henry, Bob, Lou, and Frank went on to become chaired professors at prominent universities. Ralph passed away about eight years after I left Ohio State. Henry Tosi, who is not a bad pocket billiards player, was my first research assistant. I claim credit for Henry's going into the academic world; however, while I had some influence on his career, he had as much on mine. To this day, Henry and I work together. Recently, Henry, Bernie Bass, and I founded a new journal, *The Leadership Quarterly*. Bernie was the Executive Editor and took the lead in organizing the editorial board, finding a publisher and managing the first two years of the journal's operation—a big job, which he, characteristically, did very well.

In 1963 I left Ohio State to join McKinsey and Company, Inc., a consulting firm where I was the Executive Director for the McKinsey Foundation for Management Research.

McKinsey served the largest corporations in the U.S. The McKinsey consultants looked and played the part of successful businessmen. Their dress was conservative, as were their mannerisms. My job at McKinsey was primarily to administer funds which were allocated to university professors. These funds were used to support research or conduct workshops that would result in edited books and bring McKinsey a high degree of visibility in elite management circles. We instituted the McKinsey award for the best research design. The McKinsey Foundation also had the practice of giving an award for best articles in the *Harvard Business Review and Business Horizons*, and an award for the best book of the year written for management practitioners. It was my responsibility to coordinate these programs. To administer these awards, a number of prominent scholars served as judges. Consequently, I came into contact with many of the leading scholars of the day.

While at McKinsey I continued to be active in the Academy of Management. In 1969, at the annual meetings in Chicago, I introduced to the Academy the first session consisting of competitively selected papers. This got me into a lot of trouble with the older, well established members of the Academy. Up to that time, selection of individuals to participate in Academy programs was based on referrals by the well-known senior members of the Academy. Consequently, who one knew and the school from which one graduated played a major role in determining who was invited to be on the program. Competitive selection based on anonymous review threatened the established social influence network. Several of the older members admonished me, accused me of being arrogant (which I was), and tried to shut me out of subsequent participation in both the governance of the Academy and also program participation. Fortunately, the idea of competitive selection caught on and the amount of program time devoted to competitively selected papers grew rapidly. Thus, I was able to be on the program every year since then based on competitively selected papers. I've participated on the program of every meeting since 1958, except two which I did not attend.

Over the years, the older members faded out of the Academy action and I became more accepted in Academy circles. I have served on the Board of Governors for two terms, was a Vice President of the Eastern Academy of Management and, after two nominations, was eventually appointed to the status of Academy Fellow, over the objection of some of the older members. I also served as the Chair of the Academy Awards Committee which, to me, was a great honor. Further, I had the honor of being a cofounder of the Organizational Behavior Division of the Academy. This came about at the 1970 meetings of the Academy in San Diego between 1:00 and 3:00 a.m. in my hotel room.

The cofounders, who were present, were Larry Cummings, Al Filley, Jack Miner, Lyman Porter, Henry Tosi, and Steve Caroll. We debated intensely over the governance structure that the OB Division was to have. We agreed on democratic election of officers and a program policy requiring that the majority of program time (I think 80%) be allocated to competitively selected papers and symposia. This was an exhilarating and heady time. All of the founding members eventually were elected to the chairmanship of the OB Division. Port, Jack and Larry were eventually to be elected presidents of the Academy and Jack and Larry were eventually appointed to the editorship of the Academy's *Journal*. Perhaps more than any other editors, Jack and Larry elevated the *Journal*'s standards of intellectual rigor and scholarship. Their contributions were institutionalized and are still in place today. Port was elected President of the Industrial/Organizational Psychology Division of the

American Psychological Association and was subsequently (in 1985) granted the first Distinguished Scholarly Contribution Award by the Academy—the ultimate award in our field.

While at McKinsey I had a large consulting contract with Cummins Engine Co. Vaugn Beals, who had been a middle manager at North American Aviation and attended the management development sessions there, had, as mentioned, become the Vice President of Research and Engineering at Cummins Engine. The objective of the consulting was to streamline the management practices and improve the organizational performance of the Research and Engineering Division. John Rizzo also participated in the consulting engagement. I had known John as a graduate student while at Ohio State. John had a Ph.D. in organizational psychology and a solid knowledge of research methodology, as well as good insights into people. I learned a great deal working with John, a valued colleague and friend. We conducted about 70 interviews with members of the Research and Engineering Division and members of the corporate staff at Cummins. On the basis of these interviews, we designed a questionnaire and administered it to all of the salaried employees in the Research and Engineering Division. We used the questionnaire results to confirm and refine our interview findings. We also used the questionnaire results for our own research purposes. Subsequently, we published two papers on role conflict and ambiguity as critical variables in a model of intra-organizational functioning.

We developed the role conflict and ambiguity scales, together with several scales that measured organizational practices, by consulting the current literature as well as using our interview findings. We also pulled a few questionnaire items "out of our ears." We expected the role conflict and ambiguity scales to be useful for our purposes at Cummins but did not expect them to have wide generalizability.

Our first publication of the role conflict and ambiguity scales was in *Administrative Science Quarterly* (1970). In that paper we reported the development and psychometric properties of the scales. In a subsequent paper in *Organizational Behavior and Human Performance*, we reported the use of the scales to test the model we had constructed. Again, this was a model of micro behavior within organizational contextual variables.

As it turned out, the scales were widely cited and used by many other investigators. This came as a great surprise to us. Subsequently, there emerged a controversy over the validity of the scales. Further, Tracey and Johnson[2] argued that the scales contained a number of response biases and that they didn't really measure what they were supposed to measure. Two critical papers were published in the 1970s. In response, Randall Schuler, Eli Levononi, and I published a paper based on data collected by Randall. We defended the construct validity of the scales and thought that the matter was an open-and-shut case from then on. However, subsequently, authors of two additional papers further criticized the scales.[3] Then, Kelloway and Barling[4] tested for five competitive models that incorporated all of the prior criticisms. They subjected the scales to confirmatory factor analyses using two large and diverse samples of respondents. The findings showed strong support for the initial version of the interpretation of the meaning of the scales and outruled the alternative interpretations that had been leveled in the papers that criticized the scales. Carlla Smith replicated the Kelloway and Barling findings with three additional demographically heterogeneous samples. I think these recent two studies finally resolved the controversy. As a result of the widespread use of the scales plus the controversy, John Rizzo and I have enjoyed numerous citations in the industrial psychology and organizational behavior literature. *Scientific Citation Classics* has requested us to write a retrospective reflection on these scales because of their many citations by other writers.

The experience with these scales illustrates an interesting point. While they were not designed for general use, several researchers used them because it was convenient to do so. This widespread use, plus the controversy, brought us a fair amount of serendipitous recognition. I think we were very lucky. I think the general use of the scales also reflects the fact that researchers in the field are frequently unwilling to do their own scale development, but would rather take the easy way out—use scales that are readily available even if they are not necessarily appropriate for their research question. As you will see, I too am guilty of this criticism.

While at McKinsey, I decided to take another crack at analyzing the data that Al Filley and I had collected earlier. I hired Sid Lirtzman as a consultant to help me with the re-analysis. At that time Sid was working for Control Data Inc. as Research Director. With his help we identified all the measurement problems and scale anomalies. Subsequently, Al Filley and I published two papers based on these data, one in the *Administrative Science Quarterly* and one in the *Journal of Applied Psychology*. In the *Journal of Applied Psychology* paper we tested for interactions between upward influence possessed by the leader and the effects of various leader behaviors. To do this it was necessary to use hierarchical regression analysis and employ dummy variables. This was a new procedure at that time and was seldom used in the applied psychology or organizational behavior literature. While I knew that this method was appropriate, I was not competent to carry out this kind of analysis. Domino ("Domo") Gujarti of the Statistics Department of the Bernard Baruch School of Business Administration conducted the statistical analysis and thus gained coauthorship.

Here we see the beginning of a practice that I was to continue throughout my career. Because I had no methodological and little statistical training, I solicited the help of others to apply the most current and sophisticated statistical methods of analysis. Actually, I have taken only one course in statistics in my life. It was an undergraduate course at the University of Detroit. I received a grade of D−. Outraged, I went to the professor with fists clenched and veins protruding in my forehead and asked with great indignation, "Why did you give me a D-?!" He looked up from his reading, coolly removed his glasses and said, "I didn't want to discourage you." I never complained about a grade after that.

There are lessons to be learned from our experience with the paper that was eventually published in the *Journal of Applied Psychology*. First, the paper would not have been written without the help of Sid Lirtzman and Domo Gujarati. Second, persistence pays. The paper was first rejected by two other journals. The first journal's reviewers criticized the paper on the basis of failing to control for common method and common source bias. Since there was nothing we could do about this problem, we modified the paper to recognize this limitation and sent it on to a second journal. The single reviewer for the second journal said that the paper tested an "old hypothesis" and therefore was not of much interest. The paper presented a test of Rensis Likert's linking-pin hypothesis. This hypothesis is central to Likert's theory presented in his book, *New Patterns of Management* (1962). While this hypothesis is based on earlier empirical work by Donald Pelz, it had never been subjected to a critical test.

It seemed to us that since this hypothesis had never been tested, and since it was central to Likert's theory, which was very popular at the time, it would be worth testing. Since the reviewer offered us no methodological criticism, we sent the paper off to the *Journal of Applied Psychology*, for which Ed Fleishman was the editor. Ed was, and still is, a longstanding and knowledgeable contributor to the leadership literature. The *Journal of Applied Psychology* accepted the paper without revision. Ed wrote me a letter admonishing me for sending the paper to him without following the APA format. He said, however, that because he thought it was a significant contribution, he was going to have the copy editors correct the format so that he could publish it directly.

The third lesson to be learned from all this is that there is a great deal of uncertainty and controversy, and consequently an element of a lottery, in the editorial review process. Acceptance depends in part on the reviewers to whom a paper is sent. If you are operating at the edge of the state-of-the-art, there is bound to be controversy. I concluded from this experience that if people have confidence in their own work and it is turned down, they should take seriously the criticisms of the reviewers, do what they can to deal with those criticisms, and send it on to another journal.

At the same time, this notion of the review process as a "lottery" was reinforced by another experience. I had the good fortune of meeting Eric Trist, one of the heros of our field, at a meeting. We discussed a particular concept about which I had been writing. I sent him an article expressing my views on this concept. I also submitted the same article to one of the more prominent journals. About the time that I received the letter of rejection of that article,

I also received a letter from Eric, who was then the editor of *Human Relations*, informing me that my paper was accepted for publication. While I had not submitted the article for possible publication, Eric obviously interpreted it as such. My co-author, Mahoud Wahba, and I were delighted to publish in *Human Relations*. So you see, in my early publication endeavors I have been both persistent and lucky. I think luck carried the day.

The findings resulting from the research by Al Filley and me were somewhat contradictory to prior findings concerning the effects of leader initiating structure on follower satisfaction. Whereas earlier researchers found a negative relationship between these two variables, we found a rather strong positive one. While these findings were interesting, they were also perplexing. Why should we have contradictory results? A 1970 paper in *Organizational Behavior and Human Performance* by Martin Evans, titled, "The Effect of Supervisory Behavior on the Path-Goal Relationship," stimulated my thinking about this issue and led to the development of the Path-Goal Theory of Leadership Effectiveness. Martin found that his predictions with respect to the effect of initiating structure on follower responses held in one organization but not in another.

His results suggested that initiating structure would be most effective under conditions in which individuals experienced ambiguity with respect to their role demands. Our findings indicated that initiating structure had a positive relationship with follower satisfaction. Our findings were all based on salaried employees in research and engineering divisions, who had unstructured jobs and little direction from standard operating procedures. It occurred to me that initiating structure was most appreciated under conditions in which individuals needed guidance to clarify their role demands—a marvelous grasp of the obvious! This insight, stimulated by Martin's research, resulted in the development of the Path-Goal Theory of Leadership.

The Path-Goal Theory of Leadership essentially argues that followers need from their leaders motivational incentives, support, and clarification of role demands which the formal system does not provide. Thus effective leaders enhance followers' expectations of success by initiating psychological structure through coaching and direction. When a system does not provide sufficient support or clarity of contingencies, it is the role of a leader to supplement it. If a leader can make rewards contingent upon follower goal accomplishment, and at the same time help a follower accomplish the organizational goals, a leader will be effective not only in motivating individuals to accomplish their goals, but also helping them to do so.

I called Martin on the telephone that morning. I told him I thought I might have a theory of leadership that would reconcile prior discrepant findings. I asked him if it would be disturbing to him if I wrote a theory derived from these insights. He stated that he "did not really have a theory." He was very supportive and encouraged me to develop my theoretical ideas. Thus was born the Path-Goal Theory of Leader Effectiveness. Here again we see the role of serendipity. I was working in the same vineyard as Martin. It just so happened that our findings and his prior arguments came together to stimulate an insight that was to result in the formulation of the Path-Goal Theory of Leadership— a new bottle for old wine.

To test this theoretical notion (at this point it was only a notion or a hunch) I used some data collected by Lawrence Wigdor, who was the first person to obtain his Ph.D. at the Baruch School, and some data collected with John Rizzo while consulting for Cummins Engine Inc. I had the good fortune of being Larry's dissertation advisor. Analysis of his data revealed qualified support for the theory. I used these data, together with additional data from the Cummins' project, to present a plausible case for the Path-Goal Theory. I didn't really think this was a big deal. I merely thought I had another potential publication. Sid Lirtzman told me this might be the most important thing I had ever done. Sid had insight! The paper was accepted by the *Administrative Science Quarterly* and subsequently has been frequently cited, included in reviews of almost every organizational behavior and industrial psychology textbook, and reprinted in about 25 anthologies. It brought me recognition that I had not anticipated. I have been requested to write a retrospective commentary on this theory for *Scientific Citation Classics*, as it is one of the more frequently cited papers in the organizational behavior literature.

There are some lessons to be learned from this experience. First, I was lucky to have been able to connect the findings of my research with those of Martin Evans—the timing was right and Martin's conceptualizations and data were serendipitously available. I was fortunate to have the data made available by Larry Wigdor's dissertation efforts and the data that John Rizzo and I had collected at Cummins' Engine, Inc. In essence, I had tested a theory based on data collected earlier without collecting any new data specifically for the purpose of testing the theory.

Unfortunately for the field, I made use of secondary data without developing and validating measures of the theoretical constructs myself. While the data I presented in the article were consistent with the Path-Goal Theory, the data were not collected explicitly for the purpose of testing it. The leader behavior measures were the early Ohio State measures of leader consideration and initiating structure.

It would have been better to have measures of contextual variables and leader behavior that directly affects path-goal relationships. However, what I actually did was infer that leader behavior as measured by the initiating structure scale was equivalent to path-goal clarification, a central construct of the theory. I did this because initiating structure data from the Cummins study and from Larry Wigdor's dissertation were available. Here again we see the practice of using available scales rather than developing scales specifically to measure the constructs of a theory, a practice followed by many people in the field, including myself. The findings were consistent with the theory for all three samples. Following my lead, a disservice to the field, others who subsequently tested the theory also used leader initiating structure in lieu of a specific measure of path-goal clarification. It was not until Chet Schriesheim developed such measures in his O.S.U. dissertation that adequate instrumentation was available to test the theory. Unfortunately, to my knowledge, no one has used the Schreishiem measures to test Path-Goal Theory.

A number of tests of the theory were conducted by various investigators. In all of these studies, with the exception of Ralph Katz's experimental study reported in *Organizational Behavior and Human Performance*, and Gary Dessler's doctoral dissertation (a field study), some form of the initiating structure scales was used as one of the independent variables.[5] The dependent variables measured in these studies were follower satisfaction, follower expectations that effort would lead to performance, and follower expectations that performance would lead to rewards. In a few studies, performance was measured as a dependent variable.

Follower satisfaction, valences and expectations are appropriate dependent variables. However, because follower self-reports of expectations and satisfaction, together with follower reports of a leader's behavior, potentially involve common-source, common-method bias, follower reports are problematic. Performance is somewhat problematic in that it could be determined by factors other than leadership.

As of about 1976 the results of approximately 15 studies were mixed; approximately half supported the theory and half did not. Interestingly, not a single study has investigated the effects of leaders on follower valence, to my knowledge. This is most likely due to the fact that I did not investigate valence in my initial tests of the theory and also that the measurement of valence is very problematic. The nonsupporting studies could be attributed to a number of methodological flaws such as inappropriate measurement, restriction of range or sampling on the dependent variable. However, the supporting studies also had the same flaws. Most of these flaws can be attributed to the fact that the studies roughly followed the procedures I employed in the initial test of the theory. Here we see a rather widespread tendency of individuals in the field to imitate the work of others rather than improve upon it. I, too, was guilty of intellectual laziness when choosing to use the leader initiating structure scales early in my career.

Later, while at the University of Toronto, I was visited by an elderly gentleman who was very high up in the government of the Peoples Republic of China. His position was something like the equivalent to that of the head of the National Science Foundation in the United States. When he met me he stated, "I've been looking forward to meeting you because there are so few Marxists in the field of organizational behavior." I asked, "Whatever led you to believe that I'm a Marxist?" He said, "The Path-Goal Theory. It is a theory of the people—in your theory it is the needs and the conditions of the people that determine the behavior of the leaders. It is clearly a Marxist theory." I now wonder what he would say about the 1976 Theory of Charismatic Leadership, which is clearly a theory about how leaders *change* people rather than respond to them.

Shortly after joining Baruch, we offered a Ph.D. program in organizational behavior. The program had been approved in principle prior to my arrival. To staff the Ph.D. program, we hired Sidney Lirtzman and Mahmoud Wahba. Both Sid and Mahmoud have become treasured life-long friends. When it came to research, Mahmoud and I were like a couple of kids. We wallowed in our data, discussed our findings and shared successes and disappointments. I can recall one day when we had just received our printouts from the computer center and were about to look at the results of our analysis. Mahmoud said, "Isn't research exciting!" Sid and John Rizzo, with whom I also worked at that time, while actively interested in the research projects we did together, were more mature and less excitable. They did, however, take great pleasure in doing good work and insisted on high-level scholarship.

I am very proud of the students who obtained their Ph.D.'s in the Baruch program: Gary Dessler, Steve Kerr, Sam Ryan, John Turner, Elmer Waters, and Larry Wigdor. Larry was the first person to receive a Ph.D. in the Baruch School. He was an executive during the program and has gone on to be an even more successful executive. All of the others have had successful careers in the academic world. I'm also very proud of David Herold who was my research assistant at Baruch and went on to obtain his Ph.D. at Yale. I feel honored that I had the opportunity to work with these people at Baruch. It was an exciting time of my career and I profited immensely, both in terms of personal and professional development from both my colleagues and students.

About two years after the Path-Goal Theory of Leadership was published, I began a rather ambitious consulting project for a large auto parts manufacturer in Detroit. The company was family owned and managed by a number of long-tenured executives. It had a patent monopoly on its products and therefore had faced little competition in the past. It had prospered, but the patent had run its course and was about to expire. Consequently, the company was going to have to face tougher competition in the near future. The management style was what Robert Blake calls "country club" management, rather lethargic and complacent. After conducting approximately 25 interviews, I concluded that the company executives needed more achievement motivation.

I subcontracted David Berlew, of McBer and Co., to conduct achievement motivation training for the top management team. The training program consisted of having the executives participate in a number of exercises which were derived from the original achievement motivation laboratory experiments, and use the results of their efforts as feedback, introspection, and group discussion. The program was conducted in a large hotel in Detroit. I can recall the expression of surprise and amazement of a maid who came into the hotel room only to find a group of upper-middle age, generous-bellied executives playing ring toss.

Having been a student of David McClelland's about twelve or so years earlier, Dave Berlew had naturally mastered McClelland's theory of personality. According to this theory, the psychological nature of human beings can be explained fairly well by the operation of three needs, or motives: achievement, affiliation, and power. These needs are conceived as nonconscious motivators which can be aroused by a select set of stimuli relevant to each need.

I had read this literature prior to meeting Dave. I was impressed with the achievement motivation training that had been conducted by McClelland in India. Dave and I had many long discussions concerning the McClelland theory of personality. Dave is a good friend and valued colleague. He is a masterful behavioral science consultant. Dave believed that effective leaders empower followers by building their sense of self-efficacy.

From my discussions with him, I concluded that effective leaders also arouse motives that are relevant to particular followers' tasks. Thus, effective military combat leaders arouse the power motive; effective leaders of social groups arouse the affiliative motive; and effective leaders of salespersons, profit center managers, and scientists and engineers arouse the achievement motive.

Motive arousal is equivalent to powerfully enhancing valence (attraction) of particular kinds of outcomes. As a result of motive arousal, the intrinsic valence of such outcomes is substantially increased. From this line of reasoning, I developed the theoretical notion that Path-Goal Theory needed to be supplemented with a set of propositions concerning how leaders empower followers and how leaders arouse motives to enhance intrinsic valences.

If an image of such a leader is formed in the mind's eye, that image is likely to be strikingly similar to the stereotypic charismatic leader. Leaders who enhance follower self-esteem and arouse follower motives appeared to me to be similar to charismatic leaders as commonly perceived. I learned a great deal from my conversations with Dave. He was a major influence on my thinking and the stimulus for the development of the 1976 theory. Thus, the 1976 Theory of Charismatic Leader was conceived. It had yet to be nurtured and brought to birth.

In 1975 I spent three months as a Visiting Professor at Florida International University with Gary Dessler, a former student and a valued friend. During that period I spent most of my nonteaching time in the library reading sociological and political science literatures concerning charismatic leaders. From this literature I gleaned a number of statements concerning the theoretical behavior and effects of charismatic leaders. I then went to the empirical social science literature, primarily personality theory and social psychology, to determine whether or not any of the conclusions drawn from the political science and sociological literatures had been subjected to empirical tests. Sure enough, a number of the statements made by political scientists and sociologists had been supported in laboratory experiments and field surveys by psychologists. These statements became the basis of the propositions advanced in the 1976 Theory of Charismatic Leadership.

From this story, one can see how Path-Goal Theory led to Charismatic Theory. Donald O. Hebb, a famous psychologist, stated that "A good theory is one that holds together long enough to get you to a better theory."[6] Clearly, Path-Goal Theory held together long enough (in my mind) to set the stage for Charismatic Theory. Whether Charismatic Theory is a better theory is still an open question. However, our recent research, and that of at least forty other investigators, much to my pleasant surprise, shows rather strong, if not profound, support for the theory.

THE MIDDLE YEARS

In 1972, I was appointed to the Shell Oil Company Chair at the University of Toronto, and in 1983 to the Secretary of State Professorship in Organizational Behavior at the University of Toronto.

As a result of a divorce, along with some serious eye problems, I was quite unproductive for about eighteen months during 1976 and 1977. Further, I had difficulty concentrating intensively and was not creatively productive for an additional two years or so. Consequently, during that period of time I did not do any serious research on Charismatic Theory. However, with the support of several colleagues who covered for me, I continued to teach, work with graduate students, and did a number of research projects which were not very ambitious. Surprisingly, most of these came to fruition and were published in good journals, thanks to my coauthors, Richard Field, Eli Levononi, and Randall Schuler.

A number of people provided me with support during these troubled times. The support of five people was especially relevant to my work life: Edith Kosow, formerly my secretary, Hugh Arnold, Martin Evans, Randall Schuler, and Ron Valency. To these people I am tremendously indebted for their help and support throughout this very difficult period in my life. I am also indebted to my two sons, Dan and Tim, and my daughter, Mary Kay, for unselfish support in my private life. There are several others who provided support in my private life whose names I will not mention. While at the University of Toronto I also had the professional and personal pleasure of having Steve Motowidlo, Jitendra Singh, Myron Gordon, Suresh Sethi, and Andy Mitchell as colleagues. I shared values and had many discussions with these scholars and profited from them not only in terms of friendship but also intellectually.

At the University of Toronto, Martin Evans and I founded the Ph.D. program in organizational behavior. Hugh Arnold, Steve Motowidlo, and Jitendra Singh were heavily involved in the Ph.D. program and gave unselfishly of their time to the Ph.D. students. Throughout the sixteen years that I was there we had several fine students from whom I learned more than I taught. I had the honor of being the major advisor of Blake Ashforth, Bill Cooper, G. Richard Field, Barry Gibbs, Stan Hamilton, Michael Howe, Eli Levononi, Oli Oliver, Robert Oppenheimer, Mary Purbhoo, Bryan Smith, and Ron Valency. In addition, I had the privilege of having somewhat less direct influence on a number of other students. Notable among these were Joel Baum, Swee Goh, Heather Haveman, Moses Kigundu, Mike MacColl, Tina Madin, Christine Oliver, Alan Sax, John Usher, and Glen Whyte.

I spent the first sabbatical I had in my career, (1979-1980), as a Visiting Scholar at Stanford University. During that year I sat in on seminars offered by Albert Bandura, Walter Mischel, Jeffrey Pfeffer, and an introductory graduate organizational behavior course taught by Jim March. March taught his course at 8:00 a.m. I lived in San Francisco and commuted to Palo Alto. To attend Jim's course I had to get up at 5:00 a.m. It was well worth it; he is a master teacher as well as one of the great thinkers in our field. He also writes poetry in his leisure hours and has published two books of poetry. He laces his lectures with humor and actually has participation with an auditorium full of students. During that year I pretty well mastered social learning theory, the Carnegie School of Organizational Behavior, and Pfeffer's unique perspective on organizations. Stanford is the mecca of the situationalist perspective in organizational behavior and cognitive social psychology. While I came to appreciate these perspectives, I have never been convinced that situational forces are so strong that individual differences do not make a difference, nor that human beings are cognitive information processors without emotions and enduring traits and motives.

One day Jeff Pfeffer, whom I greatly admire and respect, told me proudly that he was appointed to the Dean's Search Committee. I said, "Jeff, since you don't think that leaders make a difference, why are you spending your time on this?" He answered, "Just in case."

While at Stanford I met Jitendra Singh, who was a Ph.D. student in organization studies. He and I played tennis together frequently, had long discussions, and became very good friends. Upon returning to Toronto, we were successful in recruiting Jitendra to our faculty. At that time, David Tucker had collected a substantial amount of data relevant to the population ecology of approximately 270 voluntary social service organizations in the Toronto area. When Dave and I designed the research project, we included a provision for the collection of measures of a large number of variables. We both carefully read the population ecology literature and collected data on everything that had been found to be significant or relevant in past research. We also collected measures of additional variables that we anticipated to be relevant, even though they had not been studied previously. However, neither Dave nor I were competent in doing the sophisticated modeling required of event history analysis, the conventional method of analyzing population data. We invited Jitendra to join the research team. He soon became the intellectual leader of the project. Jitendra not only had a command of event history analysis, but he also developed several theoretical notions that could be tested with the use of the data. The project became tremendously successful and we enjoyed the publication of several papers in first-rate journals.

Again we see a similar pattern. By working with others I was able to broaden my perspective to include population ecology, and to bring to bear sophisticated modeling procedures. Further, the result of this endeavor was the formation of two valued friendships that continue to this day.

In 1983 I began exploring the possibility of using U.S. presidents as a sample of leaders to test the 1976 Theory of Charismatic Leadership. Jim Woycke worked for me initially as a research assistant and soon became a colleague and co-author. Jim's training is in political history. He and I examined the possibility of using original papers written by U.S. presidents as information that might be content analyzed to disclose their motives and behavior. We also considered using presidential biographies and a host of other archival data. After about a year and a half of frustrating exploratory investigation, we concluded that presidential papers were inadequate for the task because the writing style of presidents changed radically over the years, and because the amount of information available for each president varied widely.

We decided to use the biographies of presidential cabinet members to infer both presidential behavior and the psychological effects that presidents had on their cabinet members. Jim Woycke extracted excerpts from the cabinet members' biographies, which described presidential behavior and effects on the cabinet members. Each excerpt was approximately one to three paragraphs long. In total he extracted about 1,200 such excerpts. Nan Weiner developed a rigorous coding scheme to categorize the information from the cabinet members' biographical excerpts. Under Nan's supervision, coders categorized the excerpts according to the variables of the 1976 theory.

Based on these codings, each president was given a quantitative measure for each behavior and each effect specified in the theory, adjusted for the number of biographies. We polled political historians and asked them to categorize presidents as charismatic, noncharismatic or in-between. We analyzed the biographies of the cabinet members of the six most charismatic and the six least charismatic leaders. A definite pattern emerged and we were encouraged.

I contacted Eugene Fodor and requested that he code nineteenth-century presidential inaugural speeches to infer presidential motives. I became aware of Eugene by reading his research reports in *Personnel Psychology*. Eugene, a first-rate psychologist, trained his son, Eric, who was a history student with a particular interest in nineteenth-century America. Eric coded the inaugural addresses, meeting the conventional standards for coding. David Winter and Richard Donley had published codings of the inaugural addresses of twentieth-century presidents, which we used. When we compared the least and most charismatic presidents' motive scores based on our codings of nineteenth-century presidents, and Winter and Donley's codings of twentieth-century presidents. We found a clear pattern: charismatic leaders scored significantly higher on the achievement and power motives than did noncharismatic leaders. The differences were large and the pattern was striking.

My coauthors and I then had a major setback. Jim Woycke, Eugene Fodor, and I wrote a paper describing the presidential findings. I was ready to submit the paper for publication when a paper by David Winter appeared in the *Journal of Personality and Social Psychology*. This paper reported new motive scores, and a statement that the earlier motive scores were invalid. Just like that, all the work we did on U.S. presidential motives was shot. However, as it turned out, there was a silver lining to this depressing cloud.

We felt that we shouldn't publish our motive data, because if House and Woycke presented findings that were in disagreement with Winter, and Winter was in disagreement with Winter and Donley, we would only add confusion to the literature. I phoned David Winter, whom I had never met, and told him of the research we had done on U.S. presidents. I suggested that if we could pool our data we could conduct construct validity tests of the original Winter and Donley scores and the new presidential scores he reported in his most recent paper. He sent me his entire data set, which was based on 25 years of research, together with papers reporting construct validity tests of the new scoring system. These papers convinced me that the new scores were indeed better than the original Winter and Donley scores, so there was no need for additional validation tests.

Winter graciously told me to keep his data set and use it for whatever research I might do. Shortly thereafter, Jane Howell, whose Ph.D. dissertation was an experimental test of the 1976 Charismatic theory, began discussing the possibility of doing some joint research on the 1976 Theory. Jane and I visited Bernie Bass at SUNY-Binghamton. Bernie and his colleagues had been doing research on transformational leadership for some time. There I met Don Spangler. Don is the "compleat" psychologist. He conducts field, lab and archival studies with a high level of scientific rigor. Don suggested that we collect data on all of the U.S. presidents to supplement the data Jim Woycke and I had collected on the six most and six least charismatic presidents. I agreed and Don collected the additional data. We then combined our data sets and added data on several variables taken from the Winter data set that I then possessed.

Don and I developed a model which integrated the McClelland Leader Motivation Theory and the 1976 Theory of Charisma. With the use of Don's newly collected data, some of Winter's data, and some of the data collected by Jim and me, we found strong support for the integrated model as well as McClelland's Leader Motive Theory. Two papers reporting our findings were subsequently published in *Administrative Science Quarterly* and the *Journal of Personality and Social Psychology*. The *ASQ* paper won the 1991 Best Paper award conferred by the Organizational Behavior Division of the Academy of Management.

We have now developed a technology for retrieving archival presidential data. The nice thing about studying U.S. presidents is that their lives are so well-documented. We know their height, their heritage, and even the number of mistresses they had, if any. Jane Howell, Don Spangler, and I plan to test several other models concerning leadership issues based on our combined data sets. This is one of the most exciting streams of research in which I have ever been involved. Thus the original set-back due to the change in presidential motive scores by Winter not only resulted in gaining use of Winter's data, but also stimulated a whole new area for investigation. *Quite a silver lining!*

Despite our earlier setback, with the help of Eugene, Don and Jim, our work finally saw the light of publication. The punch line is first perish (almost) then publish.

THE MORE RECENT YEARS

The last few years have been especially good to me. I have been fortunate in having had the opportunity to be a Visiting Professor at the Sloan School of MIT, Suffolk University, the University of Southern California, The European Institute of Business Administration, the Vrije University of Amsterdam, and the University of Maryland where where I met and enjoyed relationships with many fine colleagues. I am also fortunate to have joined the Wharton School faculty as a chaired professor.

For reasons I cannot fathom, I have had the privilege of doing joint research with a number of colleagues who are somewhat younger than I am: Michael Arthur, Ahmed Ashour, Ann Howard, Jane Howell, Don Spangler, Boas Shamir, Jitendra Singh, David Tucker, and Gordon Walker. These people have brought to our joint research efforts modern day knowledge concerning high-tech computer applications and sophisticated statistical modeling. Further, Chanoch Jacobsen recently introduced me to the use of dynamic simulation. We are now constructing a simulation model to test the most recent extension of The 1976 Theory of Charismatic Leadership: the emergence, rise and fall of charismatic leaders. I am very excited about the progress we have made so far. Perhaps what surprises me most is that these younger colleagues do much more than their fair share of the work. These collaborative relationships have worked out extremely well and resulted in several successful research projects, many of which are coming to fruition at this time.

Today I find the field of organizational behavior to be as challenging, stimulating and exciting as ever. The field is more theoretically driven and scientifically rigorous than it has ever been. With the help of these people and with the modern methods of simulation and statistical modeling, I find developing and testing theory less difficult and more rewarding than ever. This is because the field is more well-developed and there are many more people interested in theoretical development, empirical testing, and the development of technology to implement theory in practice.

I have one major concern about the future of the field of organizational behavior. It seems to me that we may be in grave danger of becoming too psychological and ignoring the context in which our psychological theories play out. Theories of cognitive processes, motivation, decision making, cognition, conflict, attitudes, learning, and the like are not really theories of organizational behavior phenomena but rather theories of the basic psychology of human beings. Unless we are able to show how these psychological processes are affected by, and affect, organizational contextual variables, it is my opinion that research and theorizing in these topic areas would be best left to individuals in psychology departments. Take Valence-Expectancy Theory, for example. This theory becomes organizationally relevant when one specifies the contextual conditions that lead to increases or decreases in expectancies or valences. Without such contextual linkages, expectancy theory is a theory of human decision making and motivation in general.

I do not intend to demean micro-organizational behavior. However, in my opinion, micro-organizational behavior scholars could best spend their time working on issues and topics that are unique to organizational behavior. For example, topics such as task design, organizational citizenship behavior, leadership, or socialization are uniquely organizationally relevant micro-organizational behavior phenomena. Once the underlying fundamental processes involved in these issues become theoretically articulated and tested, I believe they should then be placed within the context of organizations, and organizational factors should be specified as causes, effects or moderators of the micro-processes.

Let me illustrate this concern further. In 1987 I attended a meeting of the Society of Organizational Behavior. This is an organization comprised predominantly of prominent industrial-organizational psychologists. At that meeting a panel discussion was conducted, titled "Organizational-Individual Difference Interactions." I looked forward to this discussion because I thought I would find some enlightenment concerning the relationship between the two sets of variables. One speaker talked about reinforcement scheduling and how individual differences moderated the effects of various kinds of reinforcement schedules. A second talked about personality theory and how broader, contextual variables affect the way personality plays out, but with no mention of organizational variables. A third member of the panel presented a statistical model for testing interactions.

From the floor I asked, "What happened to the 'organizational' in industrial-organizational psychology?" I made the assertion that we have a body of literature consisting of contextual variables relevant to behavior in organizations: environment, structure, informal processes, distributions of power, hierarchical stratification, looseness of coupling, technology, and the like. My comment fell on deaf ears. There was not a single response. It was definitely a "plop."

As a result of this experience I decided that it would be useful to form a group to further meso research. I defined meso research as the simultaneous study of two or more levels of analysis wherein at least one level involves organizational processes or variables, and at least one level involves individual or small group behavioral variables. One could study the effect of organizations on groups or individuals, or the effect of individuals and groups on organizations, within this framework.

I contacted a number of the more prestigious people in the field and asked them if they would join me as founding members. These people are Larry Cummings, Richard Hackman, Don Hambrick, Jim March, Jeff Pfeffer, Jerry Salancik, Barry Staw, Michael Tushman, and Karl Weick. These founding members nominated others who had demonstrated a strong interest in conducting MESO research, and the organization was founded. We held our first meeting in 1990 at Wharton and will be holding our fourth meeting in 1993 at the University of California, Irvine.

It seems that the heartland of organizational behavior is MESO. Until we are able to give reasonable accounts of the interaction between behavioral and organizational variables, I don't see how we will be able to have a coherent theory of intra-organizational behavior. I am optimistic that we will see, within the next ten years or so, a theory that integrates macro- and micro-organizational behavior with a number of linking propositions. I have advanced a MESO theory of the distribution and exercise of power in complex organizations, published in the *Leadership Quarterly* in 1991. I am looking forward to testing several of the propositions of this theory.

I am also looking forward to continuing work on Charismatic Leadership Theory. In the recent past, Mike Arthur, Jane Howell, Chanoch Jacobsen, Boas Shamir, and Don Spangler have advanced a number of propositions that link charismatic phenomenon to organizational and environmental contextual variables. I look forward to testing these propositions.

In 1991 I was granted the Irwin Career Award for Distinguished Scholarly Contribution to Management which is conferred by the Academy of Management. Persistance, a lot of help from my friends and colleagues, and a little luck paid off for me.

I somewhat immodestly tell my friends that while I'm in my prime I am not yet at my peak. Hopefully, if all goes well, my retirement (heaven forbid) will be a photo finish with my obsolescence. I plan to open a ladies and gentleman's billiard parlor for serious players when this happens.

PUBLICATIONS

1962

With L. Peters, and H. Stephenson. Criteria for the determination of management compensation and organizational status. In D. MacFarland (Ed.), *Proceedings of the National Convention of Academy of Management.*
An experiment in the use of management training standards. *The Journal of the Academy of Management* (April).

1963

With and H.L. Tosi, Jr. An experimental evaluation of a management development program. *Journal of the Academy of Management* (December).
Management development is a game. *Harvard Business Review, 41*(4), 130-143.
Methodological requirements for research contributions to the development of management theory. In *Proceedings of the National Convention of the Academy of Management.*

1965

A commitment approach to management development. *California Management Review, 7*(3), 15-28.

1966

With H.L. Tosi, Jr. Continuing management development beyond the classroom. *Business Horizons, 9*(2), 91-98.

1967

Management development: Design, implementation and evaluation. Ann Arbor, MI: Bureau of Industrial Relations, University of Michigan.
T-Group education and leadership effectiveness: A review of the empiric literature and a critical evaluation. *Personnel Psychology, 20*(1), 1-32.

With L. Wigdor. Herzberg's dual factor theory of job satisfaction and motivation: A review of the evidence and a criticism. *Personnel Psychology* (Winter), 369-387.

1968

With L.A. Wigdor. A reply to Winslow and Winsett (proponents of the Herzberg Theory). *Personnel Psychology, 21*(1), 58-62.

Leadership training: Some dysfunctional consequences. *Administrative Science Quarterly, 12*(March), 556-571.

Sensitivity training: A review of the issues and the evidence. In *Management Education and Development.* Princeton, NJ: Educational Testing Service.

1969

T-Group training: Good or bad? *Business Horizons, 12*(6), 69-71.

With A.C. Filley. *Managerial process and organizational behavior.* Glenview, IL: Scott Foresman.

With J.M. Miner. Span of control-group size interaction. *Administrative Science Quarterly, 14*(3): 451-464.

With G. Dessler. Integrating the social psychological resources of merged companies: Some applications of recent behavioral science findings to management of mergers. In B.E. Fox & E. Elanore (Eds.), *Corporate acquisitions and mergers* (Vol. 1). New York: Matthew Bender.

1970

Scientific investigation in management. *Management International Review, 19*(4/5), 139-150.

With J.R. Rizzo & S.I. Lirtzman. Role conflict and ambiguity in complex organizations. *Administrative Science Quarterly* (June), 150-163. [Scientific Citation Classic]

Role conflict and multiple authority in complex organizations. *California Management Review, 12*(4), 53-60.

With L.M. Wigdor & K. Shulz. Supportive leadership as a moderator of the relationship between leader structure and subordinate satisfaction and performance. In W. Frey (Ed.), *Proceedings of the Eastern Academy of Management Meetings.* Boston: University of Massachusetts.

With A.C. Filley. Management and the future. *Business Horizons, 13*(2), 7-20.

With S. Thune. Where long-range planning pays off: Some research findings. *Business Horizons 13*(4), 81-87.

1971

With S. Kerr. Some moderators of the relation between managerial practices and subordinate performance and satisfaction. In *Proceedings.* Williamsburg, VA: Eastern Academy of Management.

With A.C. Filley & S. Kerr. Consideration as a moderator of the relations between leader initiating structure and the satisfaction of R&D Personnel. *Administrative Science Quarterly, 16*(1), 19-30.

A path goal theory of leadership. *Administrative Science Quarterly, 16*(3), 321-338.

With A.C. Filley, & D.M. Gutjarati. Leader hierarchical influence and subordinate satisfaction. *Journal of Applied Psychology* (October), 22-23. [Scientific Citation Classic]

1972

With H.L. Tosi, Jr. & M.G. Dunnette. (Eds.). *Managerial compensation and motivation.* East Lansing, MI: Bureau of Business Research, Michigan State University.

With J.R. Rizzo. Role conflict and ambiguity as intervening variables in a model of organization behavior. *Organizational Behavior and Human Performance, 7*(3), 467-505.

With H.L. Tosi, Jr. Organizational reinforcement of executive development. In E. Burack & J. W. Walker (Eds.), *Manpower planning and programming.* Boston, MA: Allyn and Bacon.

With J.R. Rizzo. Toward the measurement of organizational practices: A scale development and validation. *Journal of Applied Psychology, 56*(2), 378-386.

1973

With J. Turner, & A.C. Filley. *Readings in managerial process and organizational behavior.* Glenview, IL: Scott Foresman.

With S. Kerr. Organizational independence, management practices, and subordinate satisfaction and performance. *Journal of Applied Psychology, 58*(2), 173-180.

An instrumentality perspective of work group cohesiveness under conditions of stress. [Review of *The Impact of Group Cohesion*]. *Contemporary Psychology, 18*(8), 370-371.

1974

With G. Dessler. The path goal theory of leadership: Some post hoc and a priori tests. In J.A. Junt & L.L. Larson (Eds.), *Contingency approaches to leadership.* Carbondale, IL: Southern Illinois University.

With M. Wahba. Expectancy theory of work and motivation: Logical and methodological issues. *Human Relations, 27*(2), 121-147.

With H.J. Shapiro & M. Wahba. Expectancy theory as a predictor of work behavior and attitude: A re-evaluation of empirical evidence. *Decision Sciences 27*(2), 121-147.

With T.R. Mitchell. Path goal theory of leadership. *Journal of Contemporary Business* (Autumn), 81-87.

The quest for relevance in management education: Some second thoughts and undesired consequences. *Academy of Management Journal, 18*(2), 323-333.

1975

The ugly orange exercise. In D.T. Hall, D.D. Bowen, R.J. Lewicki, & F.S. Hall (Eds.), *Experiences in management and organizational behavior.*

Leader behavior questionnaire. In D.T. Hall, D.D. Bowen, R.J. Lewicki, & F.S. Hall (Eds.), *Experiences in management and organizational behavior.*

Etzioni's theory of organizational compliance. In H.L. Tosi, Jr. (Ed.), *Theories of organization.*

With A.C. Filley. A summary of Stogdill's theory of individual behavior and group achievement. In H.L. Tosi, Jr. (Ed.), *Theories of organization.*

1976

With A.C. Filley, & S. Kerr. *Managerial process and organizational behavior* (rev. ed.). Glenview, IL: Scott Foresman.

Schriesheim, C., & S. Kerr. Leader initiating structure: A reconciliation of discrepant research results and some empirical tests. *Organizational Behavior and Human Performance, 15*(2), 297-321.

1977

A 1976 theory of charismatic leadership. In J. Hunt & L. Larson (Eds.), *Leadership: The cutting edge* (pp. 199-272). Southern Illinois University Press.

The situation is not what it seems to be. [Review of *Personnel management: A situational approach*]. *Contemporary Psychology, 22*(3), 226-227.

1978

With K.D. MacKenzie. Paradigm development in the social sciences: A proposed research strategy. *Academy of Management Review* (January), 7-24.

1979

With M.L. Baetz. New directions in leadership research. In B. Staw (Ed.), *Research in organizational behavior* (Vol. 1, pp. 341-423). Greenwich, CT: JAI Press.

With M.G. Evans & M. Kiggundu. A partial test and extension of the job characteristics model of motivation. *Organizational Behavior and Human Performance, 24*(December), 354-381.

Experiential learning: A sad passing fad. *Exchange, Organizational Behavior Teaching Journal, 4*(3), 8-12.

With J.R. Rizzo. The C company I & II. In R.S. Schuler & E.F. Huse (Eds.), *Case problems in management.* New York: West.

Retrospective comment on the path goal theory of leadership. In D.D. Bowen and L.E. Boone (Eds.), *The great writings in management.* PPC Books.

1980

With H.J. Arnold, & M.G. Evans. Productivity: A psychological perspective. In S. Maital & N.M. Meltz (Eds.), *Declining productivity growth: Causes and remedies* (pp. 131-186). Cambridge, MA: Ballinger.

With H.J. Arnold. Methodological and substantive extensions of the job characteristics model of motivation. *Organizational Behavior and Human Performance, 25*, 161-182.

With H. Kolodny. Donny is my leader. *Exchange: The Teaching of Organizational Behavior, VI*(2).

1982

Experiential learning: A social learning theory analysis. In G. Cooper & R. Freedman (Eds.), *Management education and development* (pp. 23-43). Englewood Cliffs, NJ: Prentice-Hall.

With J.R. Rizzo. The organizational practices scale. In H.L. Tosi, Jr. & J. Young (Eds.), *Management: Experiences, projects, and demonstrations.* Irwin.

1983

With R.S. Schuler & E. Levanoni. Role conflict and ambiguity scales: Reality or artifacts? *Journal of Applied Psychology, 68*(2), 334-337.

1984

[Review of *Judgement Calls in Research*]. *Academy of Management Review, 9*(1), 161-163.

Commentary on management research. In A.P. Brief (Ed.), *Productivity research in the behavioral and social sciences* (pp. 268-282). New York: Praeger.

1985

With D.J. Tucker, J.V. Singh, & A.G. Meinhard. Resource environment, organizational form, and the founding of voluntary social service organizations. *Proceedings, The Administrative Science Association of Canada.* [Best Paper Award of Excellence]

1986

With J.V. Singh, & D.J. Tucker. Organizational change and organizational mortality. *Administrative Science Quarterly, 31*(4), 587-611.
With J.V. Singh, & D. J. Tucker. Organizational legitimacy and the liability of newness. *Administrative Science Quarterly, 31*(2), 171-193.
Charismatic and exchange theories of leadership. In G. Raber (Ed.), *Handworterbuck de Fuhrung [Encyclopedia of Leadership].*

1987

With J.V. Singh. Organizational behavior: Some new directions for I/O psychology. *Annual Review of Psychology, 38*, 669-718.
Theory testing in organizational behavior: A review essay. Administrative Science Quarterly, 32(3), 459-464.

1988

With J. Woycke & E. Fodor. Charismatic and noncharismatic leadership: Differences in behavior and effectiveness. In J. Conger & R. Kegundo (Eds.), *Charismatic leadership and management.* San Francisco, CA: Jossey-Bass.
Some overlooked, forgotten, or ignored findings concerning leadership research and theory. In J.G. Hunt (Ed.), *Emerging leadership vistas.* Elmsford, NY: Pergamon Press.
Power and personality in complex organizations. In B. Staw & L.L. Cummings (Eds.), *Research in organizational behavior.* Greenwich, CT: JAI Press.
The ugly orange exercise. In J. Wohlberg & T. Head (Eds.), *Experiencing organizational behavior* (2nd ed.). Houghton Mifflin. (Originally published in 1975)
With F.E. Fiedler. Leadership. A report of progress: Theory and research. In G. Cooper & I. Robertson (Eds.), *International review of industrial and organizational psychology.* Greenwich, CT: JAI Press.

1989

With D.J. Tucker, J.V. Singh, & A.G. Meinhard. Ecological and institutional sources of change in organizational populations. In G.R. Carroll (Ed.), *Ecological Perspectives on Organizations*. San Francisco, CA: Jossey Bass.

1990

With D. Spangler & J. Woycke. Charisma in the U.S. Presidency. In *Best Paper Proceedings*, Academy of Management.

With R. Field. An investigation of the validity of the Vroom-Yetton model of decision making. *Journal of Applied Psychology, 75*(3), 362-366.

With J. Baum. Comment on the maturation and aging of organizational populations. In J. V. Singh (Ed.), *Organizational evolution: New directions*. Beverly Hills, CA: Sage.

Power and personality in complex organizations. In B.M. Staw & L.L. Cummings (Eds.), *Personality and organizational behavior*. Greenwich, CT: JAI Press. (Originally published in 1988)

With J. Woycke & E. Fodor. Charismatic and non-charismatic leadership: Differences in behavior and effectiveness. In B.M. Staw (Ed.), *Psychological dimensions of organizational behavior*. Scott Foresman.

1991

With A. Howard & G.A. Walker. The prediction of managerial success: A competitive test of the person-situation debate. *Best Paper Proceedings*, Organizational Behavior Division, Academy of Management.

With D. Spangler. Presidential effectiveness and the leadership motive profile. *Journal of Personality and Social Psychology, 6*(3), 439-455.

The distribution and exercise of power in complex organizations: A meso-theory. *The Leadership Quarterly, 2*(1), 23-58.

With D. Spangler, & J. Woycke. Personality and charisma in the U.S. Presidency: A psychological theory of leader effectiveness. *Administrative Science Quarterly, 36*(3), 364-396.

With M. Purbhoo. The RDT case. In R. Schuler (Ed.), *Case problems in organizational behavior* (4th ed.). St. Paul, MN: West.

With M. Purbhoo. Teaching note: A theoretical analysis of the RDT case. In R. Schuler (Ed.), *Case problems in organizational behavior* (4th ed.). St. Paul, MN: West.

The Magna Case. In R. Schuler (Ed.), *Case problems in organizational behavior* (4th ed.). St. Paul, MN: West.

Charismatic leadership in service organizations. In C. Wilderom (Ed.), *Way is Leaderschap/Management in Diestrvelenede Organisaties*. Economic en Sociaal Instituut, Vrije Universiteit, Amsterdam.

With T. Mitchell. Path goal theory of leader effectiveness. In H.L. Tosi (Ed.), *Organizational behavior and management: A contingency approach.* Boston: Wadsworth. (Originally published in 1974)

1992

The nature of power in complex organizations. In H.L. Tosi (Ed.), *The environment/organization/person contingency model: A meso approach to the study of organizations.* Greenwich, CT: JAI Press.

With J. Howell. Personality and charismatic leadership. *Leadership Quarterly, 3*(2), 81-108.

1993

With B. Shamir & M. Arthur. The transformational effects of charismatic leadership: A motivational theory. *Organizational Science.*

With B. Shamir. Toward the integration of transformational, charismatic, and visionary theories. In M. Chemmers & R. Ayman (Eds.), *Leadership theory and research: Perspectives and directions.* San Diego, CA: Academic Press.

Epologue. In R.L. Phillips & J.G. Hunt (Eds.), *Strategic leadership: A multiorganizational-level perspective.* Westport, CT: Qurom Books.

With P. Podsakoff. Leadership theory and research: Past, present, and future. In J. Greenberg (Ed.), *Organizational behavior: The state of the science.* Lawrence Erlbaum Associates.

NOTES

1. Huey Heal's name is not disguised.

2. L. Tracy & T.W. Johnson. (1981). What do the role conflict and role ambiguity scales measure? *Journal of Applied Psychology, 66,* 464-469.

3. L.A. King & D.W. King. (1990). Role conflict and role ambiguity: A critical assessment of construct validity. *Psychological Bulleting, 107,* 48-64; G.W. McGee, C.E. Ferguson, & A. Steers. (1990). Role conflict and role ambiguity: Do the scales measure these two constructs? *Journal of Applied Psychology, 74,* 815-818.

4. E.K. Kelloway & J. Barling. (1990). Item content versus item wording: Disentagling role conflict and role ambiguity. *Journal of Applied Psychology, 75,* 738-742.

5. R.C. Katz. (1977). The influence of group conflict on leadership efectiveness. *Organizational Behavior and Human Performance, 20,* 256-286; G. Dessler. (1973). *An investigation of a path-goal theory of leadership.* Ph.D. disseratation, The City University of New York.

6. D.O. Hebb. (1969). Hebb on hocus pocus: A conversation with Elizabeth Hall. *Psychology Today* (November), p. 21.

Understanding Work Motivation and Organizational Effectiveness: A Career-Long Journey

EDWARD E. LAWLER, III

It was almost exactly thirty years ago that I began to seriously consider an academic career. I was a graduate student in experimental psychology at the University of California, Berkeley and had the good fortune to come in contact with three important figures in the field of industrial psychology and wonderful human beings, Mason Haire, Edwin Ghiselli, and Lyman W. Porter. Although they differed in their interests, they all had a sense of excitement about research and a commitment to understanding organizational behavior that made a lifelong impression on me.

Looking back upon my decision to choose an academic career, I feel extremely fortunate. Since my decision I have had the chance to do research in hundreds of organizations and have literally seen thousands of jobs. I have seen none that I would rather have. For me an academic career has been very satisfying, and I feel it fits the abilities that I have. When I think of some of the career options I considered (industrial sales, personnel management, general management) I wonder at my naivete and still have anxiety attacks about how I would have performed in them. Frankly, I don't think they would have been motivating or satisfying nor would I have been terribly successful doing them.

Particularly with respect to personal autonomy and the ability to pursue what interests me, I know of no setting other than perhaps being an entrepreneur which matches the academic world. For me the academic world has provided entrepreneurial opportunities as well as considerable support for a safe landing when my entrepreneurial activities have not worked out. It also has allowed me to have a career of intellectual self-indulgence. I have been able to pursue issues that interest me, create organizational units that are targeted at the kind of issues I think are important and, finally, gain some personal visibility by sharing my thoughts, ideas, and research findings with others. I have been very fortunate in my career to be associated with an extraordinarily large number of very talented individuals and to hold positions at outstanding universities. Thus, as I go through a chronological history of my career you will notice a strong emphasis on how individuals and institutional settings have influenced me and shaped my career. This reflects the reality of what has impacted upon me and the extreme good fortune that I have had.

PRE-HISTORY OR GETTING TO GRADUATE SCHOOL

During my days as an undergraduate at Brown University it was definitely not clear that I would end up in graduate school. My main interests were playing sports and getting by academically. I had similar interests during my years at a small prep school in Virginia where I spent my high school years. The most complex organization I gave any thought to there was our six-man football team.

I became interested in psychology during my junior and senior years at Brown. Originally, I was a history major, but after I had the chance to work with an experimental psychologist, and to do some "rat research," I decided to be a psychology major. Thanks to the small university nature of Brown, I was able to run my own experiment and actually found some interesting results. I also found myself tied to the eating cycle of rats and, frankly, did not enjoy my all too regular interactions with them. In most cases they turned out to be rather nasty creatures who tried to bite and scratch me. I suppose this should not be surprising since most of the studies I did involved electrical shock and hunger.

When my senior year arrived, it became clear that I would have to make a career choice. As did most of my fraternity brothers, I signed up for job interviews through the career placement office. At this point I was interested enough in psychology to think that I might be a good personnel administrator. I targeted job interviews that would help me obtain a position in personnel management. However, I quickly found that most organizations did not hire directly into the personnel function and that if I wanted to have credibility in this field I needed a graduate education. Several of my professors in psychology suggested that I go to graduate school. This, combined with the message I was getting from the job market, led me to send out applications to a number of schools which were seen by the psychology faculty at Brown to be strong in industrial psychology. In retrospect the list was a pretty good one, it included Minnesota, Michigan, Berkeley and other traditional, industrial psychology-oriented schools. My thought was to get a masters degree and again try to find a job in personnel administration. Since I was not at all sure that I could get into a graduate program, I continued my interviewing and ultimately was offered a job in the management training program of New England Telephone. About the same time I was offered a job by New England Telephone I received a blitz of rejection letters from graduate schools, not surprising given my less than outstanding grade-point average. Finally two schools offered me admission—Berkeley and Wayne State University. The interesting thing about my admission to Wayne State is that I applied to the University of Michigan but was rejected. However, my application was forwarded to Wayne State which was more favorably disposed.

Faced with a choice between a career at New England Telephone and an academic career, I opted for the easy way out. I chose graduate school. I was a bit intimidated by the thought of having to work in a real job and adapt to the structure of the telephone company. Besides, I had never been to Berkeley and I was intrigued by the idea of living on the West Coast. My interest was increased further when, as a member of the Brown varsity track team, I went to Berkeley in May of my senior year for the NCAA championship track meet, and fell in love with the Bay area.

I arrived at Berkeley in September 1960, ready to pursue a masters degree in industrial psychology. I quickly discovered that masters degrees were consolation prizes for those who did not get their Ph.D., and that the industrial psychology program was not interested in students until they finished their first two years of general psychology. To say that this news was a bit disconcerting would be an understatement. I quickly received another disconcerting piece of information. No financial support was available for me because I was ranked last (someone has to be) among the sixty-plus entering graduate students.

Quickly, however, things took a turn for the better. I found two jobs, refereeing intramural sports (my first assignment was volleyball—not a good place to start in California if you are from the east and have never played the game) and grading child psychology papers for Richard Alpert (now Baba Ram Das). I was able to take one course in industrial psychology during my first year and to run some further experiments in rat psychology! Like most first year graduate students I found the year stressful, but in many respects rewarding. I made my first contacts with the trio of Porter, Haire, and Ghiselli. My contact with them convinced me that I did want to be in industrial psychology (at this point some people were trying to change its name to Industrial-Organizational psychology) and that I probably should try to get a Ph.D.

Once I made the decision to get a Ph.D., the final three years of my graduate education went smoothly and swiftly with one exception. I had great difficulty learning enough German and French in order to pass the foreign language requirement. My grade-point average in both high school and college was devastated by my problems with French and Spanish so it was not surprising that I had more "language problems" in graduate school.

Porter, in particularly took me under his wing and introduced me to survey research. At the time, he was doing his survey research on managerial satisfaction and this fit well with my interests. Even as an undergraduate my primary interest was in motivation. Admittedly at that point I was studying rats, but I was really interested in why people engage in certain kinds of activities and what influences human motivation. Given my interest in becoming a personnel manager, it is not surprising that I was particularly focused on work situations and why some people work harder than others.

A variety of summer jobs during my high school and college career made it obvious to me that there were large differences in the effectiveness of employees, and that these were only partly due to capability. It seemed to me that it wasn't simply that some people were inherently more committed or more motivated, there were a host of organizational and personal characteristics which influenced people's work motivation. As my work in the graduate school progressed, I became increasingly interested in identifying the determinants of motivation and performance effectiveness.

Primarily as a result of my working with Porter, I was able to develop a strong publication record as a graduate student and thus began to think more and more of an academic career. Undoubtedly, the most important piece of research that I did during my graduate career was my doctoral dissertation. It formed the basis for a number of articles that I was to write during my first several years as an assistant professor, and was the basis for a book that I coauthored with Porter (1968). It presented what is often called the Porter-Lawler model, although I must admit I prefer to call it the Lawler-Porter model! In this research I collected attitude and performance data from a number of middle managers in seven different organizations. Looking back, it was a rather ambitious field study given the norms about what usually constituted data gathering for dissertations. In many respects, it was indicative of my future research activities since it involved motivation, work organizations and a large data set.

The job search process was a painless one for me. Although I loved California and wanted to stay, there were no jobs open on the West Coast that intrigued me. There was, however, a job at Yale and, being an "Ivy Leaguer," it had a strong appeal to me. Basically, I got my job there as the result of the "old-boy network" operating effectively. Chris Argyris was the leading figure at Yale at the time and he knew Mason Haire. Mason recommended me to Chris and I sent my vita along with my publications. Chris responded by offering me a job. He said that they would be happy to have me come and interview if I needed to gather more data to make my job decision, but that the job was mine. At the time this was an unconventional strategy. Schools usually interviewed applicants before making a job offer! Chris, as I was soon to find out, did not always do business as usual. He valued innovation and was very willing to take risks.

I knew the Yale situation reasonably well and thought that I would be happy there, so I ended up accepting the job at Yale without ever visiting or interviewing. The job incidentally was a joint appointment between what was then called Industrial Administration, later to become Administrative Sciences and still later the School of Organization and Management, and the Psychology Department.

THE YALE YEARS

Four years after I began my doctoral program at Berkeley, I arrived in New Haven ready to begin life as an assistant professor. The program in the Industrial Administration Department was in its infancy at the time of my arrival. It had just left the Engineering School and was getting established as a separate department within the School of Arts and Sciences. The Ph.D. program was still in its developmental stage but was soon to produce a number of outstanding graduates.

At the time of my arrival at Yale, Chris Argyris was very interested in T-groups and interpersonal change processes. Two other faculty members shared his interest, Roger Harrison and Fritz Steele. During my graduate days at Berkeley I had been well-conditioned by Porter and Haire to be suspicious of T-groups and other interpersonal-process training methods. So I arrived sharing their bias that these were not particularly high payoff areas for research and not major contributors to organizational effectiveness. Needless to say my view was not shared by the majority of the faculty in the Industrial Administration Department, but I had at least one supporter in Donald Taylor, a cognitive psychologist who was the department head.

I should note at this point that the Industrial Administration Department at Yale was basically made up of two groups. One was an organizational behavior group and the other was an economics/quantitative methods group. The presence of the second group turned out to be critical in the evolution of the department and in my career at Yale.

My years at Yale were extremely productive and rewarding. The behavioral group grew and quickly gained a national reputation for excellence. During my first few years there we hired Douglas T. Hall, J. Richard Hackman, Roy Lewicki, Gerrit Wolf, and Ben Schneider. We also recruited a large number of extremely talented graduate students including Martin Evans, John Wanous, Corty Cammann, and Clay Alderfer.

My first years at Yale were particularly stimulating thanks to the strong leadership of Chris Argyris. There was a tremendous amount of intellectual debate and excitement. I continued to do much of the same type of research that I had done at Berkeley. I published journal articles based on my dissertation, collected new survey data and did some laboratory research on equity theory and the impact of compensation. During this period I further developed my thinking with respect to expectancy theory and worked with Porter on our 1968 book. I am particularly proud of this work because it went beyond the current thinking with respect to motivation and satisfaction. It provided an integrated model of the relationships between motivation and satisfaction and a useful application of expectancy theory to job performance. My favorite piece of this theory is, not surprisingly, the part that I did the most development work on: the effects of performance on satisfaction and the expectancy equation.

During graduate school I decided that compensation was an area where I could profitably focus some of my research. Mason Haire originally suggested that I focus on compensation. The suggestion was based on his view that there was little behavioral-science oriented research on compensation. I picked up on this idea when I was at Berkeley and continued it during my first years at Yale. At the time I did not want to be known only as a compensation researcher, however. My interests were broader, but I found research on pay a good way to focus my thinking. The absence of psychologically based research on compensation made it a topic where studies could have high impact. It also was an area where motivation and satisfaction could be studied within organizations. Thus, it appeared to be and turned out to be a fruitful area for research.

My research on compensation also offered me the chance to influence practice as well as theory. I found this exciting and, to this day, get as much satisfaction out of influencing practice as I do out of influencing research and theory. As I look back upon my 30 years of research on pay, I derive a great deal of pleasure from the fact that many of the pay practices I studied and advocated a decade or more ago are becoming increasingly popular (e.g., skill-based pay, flexible benefits, open-pay communication, risk compensation, participative-pay system design).

The organizational behavior group at Yale in many respects was very cohesive. We met regularly to talk about research and debate issues. For all of us it was a stimulating, growth-producing experience. It opened my eyes to a set of organizational issues that I had not been exposed to at Berkeley. In some cases I changed my views, but in others I maintained my existing "Berkeley Hard Science" orientation. I have to admit as a result of my first four or five years at Yale few of my assumptions went unchallenged.

Almost from the day of my arrival at Yale, Chris Argyris raised issues with me about the kind of understanding and knowledge that one can gain from survey research and whether it or a more intervention-oriented research style produced the best data and the greatest learning. We had many long and, at times, heated debates about the advantages of action research and survey research. We also debated the relative power of his approaches to organizational change such as T-groups and more structural interventions such as those involving pay system changes. In retrospect it is clear to me that these debates had a tremendous long-term impact upon my thinking. Argyris did convince me that there was a role for change-oriented research and that, in some ways, more could be learned about a phenomena through active intervention than through static measurement and survey research methodologies.

Even though I was interested in influencing practice, I did no consulting and only a little management training during my first years at Yale. There was very little time given my commitment to research and publication and I wasn't sure I had a great deal to offer.

My discussions with Richard Hackman led me to participate with him in my first significant study of job design. For several years I had been interested in the impact of work design on motivation. Further, I was a bit tired of doing research on compensation, at least in part because I found few organizations were willing to try innovative compensation systems. My discussions with Hackman helped both of us to conceptualize how work design characteristics influence motivation. He brought a framework for analyzing work and I brought my motivation theory to the discussion. The result was a large-scale field research study that looked at the relationship between job characteristics and employee behavior. We ultimately published the results of this study in a monograph (Hackman & Lawler, 1971) that has turned out to be a very widely cited and I think an important piece of theory and research. Like my earlier work it stayed within the survey research mode and did not involve action or change.

After completing our initial study of job characteristics, both of us were ready to begin to do change-oriented work. A combination of our backgrounds in experimental psychology and our discussions with Argyris convinced us that the best way to understand job characteristics was to manipulate them and study the impact of the manipulation. This led us to do field-change experiments, in the area of compensation and in the area of work design. These were my first major experiences with the sloppiness, the problems and the adventures involved in doing change-oriented research. I found this type of research to be exciting, challenging and in many respects quite productive. Without question it changed forever my research orientation. Although I have continued to do some non-change oriented survey work it became a much less important part of my research portfolio. I began to see it as less exciting and a less informative way of understanding a phenomenon.

My initial years at Yale were rewarding not only in terms of learning but also in terms of recognition. I was promoted from assistant to associate professor in only three years and thus at age 29 found myself an associate professor at Yale. Needless to say I was very pleased with my career progress and in fact found it hard to believe.

Looking back upon my first six years at Yale I would have to say it was almost a perfect environment for me. Great colleagues, the excitement of creating new programs, an influx of outstanding Ph.D. students and a tremendously collegial and exciting intellectual environment. Unfortunately, this nearly idyllic environment was not to last. Even looking back it is not entirely clear to me what all the forces were that changed the situation.

Part of the change clearly was due to the financial pressures that Yale was feeling in the late sixties. Our department ceased to expand and conflict increased between the two parts.

Although I was an associate professor I did not have tenure since Yale's practice at the time was to separate the two decisions. The department decided to put me up for tenure during my seventh year at Yale and I was pleased by this. The promotion process went smoothly within the department, but it did not proceed smoothly after it reached the university level. Two factors came into play. The first was the university's financial problems which led to a general slowdown in granting anyone tenure and the second was opposition to my promotion by a group of economists who felt my work was too based on the study of attitudinal data. In their research paradigm attitude data were soft data, and did not warrant scientific research. The end result was that my promotion was put off for a year and according to the dean of the graduate school, "It's hard to tell what will happen to it next year."

I was surprised and deeply disappointed by my failure to get tenure at Yale. I could have stayed on and tried for it the next year but, psychologically, I was ready to leave. It coincided with my getting divorced and thus leaving the New Haven area offered the chance to leave behind two painful experiences. I went on the job market and was happy to find two outstanding jobs.

Northwestern offered me a professorship in the business school and Michigan offered me a professorship in the psychology department and a research directorship in the Institute for Social Research. The choice between Northwestern and Michigan was an interesting one, but in the end not a difficult one. There were a number of things about Michigan that made it more attractive.

I was impressed with the senior faculty in the psychology department and in the organizational psychology group. The combination of names like Likert, Katz, Kahn, and Seashore, and the capability of the Institute for Social Research to do large-scale research projects was extremely attractive to me. I also valued the opportunity to be in a psychology department although my major appointment was in ISR. Perhaps because I had the promotion problem at Yale and my ego was a bit bruised, I felt it important to reestablish my scientific and research credibility. In any case, I chose to go to Michigan primarily to work with doctoral students and to begin a research program in the Institute for Social Research.

Before going to Michigan I had the opportunity to spend a semester in Seattle at the Battelle Institute. They gave me a fellowship to continue my research and I spent a very productive half year there. During my time there I came in contact with John Rasmussen, who was in the process of starting a social science contract research organization for Battelle. I spent a great deal of time discussing with him the best ways to start and manage social science research organizations. Ultimately, I got intrigued enough with the opportunities at Battelle to help him start an organizational research unit, which was designed to do applied organizational effectiveness research. This was my first introduction to the world of large research contracts and proved to be a useful learning experience given the world I was about to enter at ISR.

THE MICHIGAN YEARS

I arrived in Michigan in the fall of 1972 with high hopes and considerable anxiety. Not only was this my first living experience in the Midwest, it was my first experience living in a contract research organization. In retrospect, I would have to say I was not fully prepared for either life in the Midwest or life as a contract researcher. Nevertheless, I dove into both and ultimately found them to be rewarding. Since this is an academic autobiography I will focus on my role as a contract researcher, rather than on my problems adjusting to life in the Midwest!

To say the least, life as a contract researcher was never boring. It was always full of challenges, many of which involved finding new sources of financial support for my research activities. In some respects, I was well prepared for the work I was going to do at Michigan. I had increasingly been doing change-oriented research and had identified a number of research areas that I wished to investigate further. What I wasn't prepared for, however, was raising money to support graduate students, secretaries and, of course, data collection efforts.

Fortunately, soon after my arrival I formed a partnership with Stan Seashore and began working on several contracts that were already in place at ISR. I quickly decided I would have to develop my own research thrust if I was going to be successful and happy at Michigan. Together with Stan I formed the Quality of Work Life research group in ISR and began seeking financial support for field research projects designed to change organizations. We were fortunate to attract a very talented group of doctoral students to work in our research group (David Nadler, Dennis Perkins, Phil Mirvis, Doug Jenkins,

Nina Gupta, Mark Fichman, and David Berg). In addition, we hired an assistant professor, Corty Cammann, who had been my student at Yale and who became a key contributor to the program.

The QWL program grew substantially during my stay at Michigan and became a major research thrust within ISR. It did research work in a number of areas, but its major focus was on labor-management cooperative projects. Funding for these projects came from the Department of Health, Education and Welfare, the Ford Foundation, the Labor Department and the Department of Commerce.

We formed an alliance with a retired TV producer, Ted Mills, who was interested in workplace change and national productivity. His interest developed out of a consulting relationship he had with the National Commission on Productivity and its head, Jack Grayson. Together, we undertook what may well be the largest coordinated series of workplace change efforts that have ever been tried. It was intended to produce knowledge about employee involvement and to increase the incidence of labor-management cooperation. It was unique because it included extensive funding for change activities as well as an extensive research effort. At Michigan we took responsibility for raising the funds, managing the overall effort, developing research methods, and studying the actual change programs. Ted Mills took responsibility for managing our Washington, D.C. based National Quality of Work Center, finding change sites and identifying consultants.

The basic model we used in the QWL program was an assessment research one. We spent our initial time developing measures. Later we did in-depth studies of change efforts. During the history of this program, eight labor-management cooperative projects were established around the country. In each case a union and management group agreed to create a joint quality of work life committee, which was to look for ways that the union and management could cooperate to increase organizational effectiveness and improve the work life of employees. Not surprisingly, these projects varied widely in the terms of their success. Several of the change efforts became quite highly publicized and did accomplish the goal of focusing national attention on ways that labor and management can cooperate to improve the quality of work life and productivity. Perhaps the two best-known projects were the one at the Rushton Coal Mine and the one at an auto parts plant in Bolivar, Tennessee. The latter in particular captured national attention because it was visibly supported by the United Auto Workers and, ultimately, contributed to Ford and General Motors establishing their own cooperative quality of work life programs. Research based books were written about four of our eight union-management projects, and a fifth book was written on a related project that involved the startup of a new high involvement plant.

Our quality of work life program was quite successful in supporting labor-management cooperation across the United States. The projects that were started were forerunners of a strong, national movement toward labor-management cooperation as an approach to making industrial organizations in the United States internationally competitive. In one respect the projects may have been too successful. Early in our work, joint labor management steering committees were created not as an end in themselves, but as temporary structures to facilitate change in the workplace. In all our projects, however, they became institutionalized and, in some organizations, multiple levels of joint labor management committee structures were developed. The labor management cooperative efforts of Ford, General Motors, and a host of other corporations have followed this same model. In retrospect, I think this is unfortunate. All too often, there has been more bureaucracy than actual organizational change produced as a result of this "parallel system" approach to cooperation.

I have no question that it is useful to have some labor-management cooperative committees established, but this should be an interim step in an overall change process, not an end result of an change process. In the best of all worlds, these committees would disappear as workplace changes and cooperation become a living day-to-day reality rather than a special activity which takes place in occasional quality of work life committee meetings. If I have one research disappointment about my years at Michigan, it is that no final book was produced that pulls together the enormous amount of effort and activity that went into the quality of work life program. The program produced innumerable articles and eight books. Thus, it was productive by most academic measuring systems. However, it did not produce a final book on labor-management cooperation and what its potential is and its limitations are.

Overall, my experiences with the QWL program at Michigan were extremely satisfying and changed the way I think about organizations. As a result of these large-scale organizational change efforts, I learned a great deal about the complexities of organizations. Prior to these efforts, I was a micro-organizational psychologist with relatively little understanding of organizations. As a result of the Michigan change efforts I gained a much greater appreciation for organizations and how they operate. I also gained a much greater appreciation for the difficulties in changing complex organizations. In fact, these projects stimulated my ongoing interest in organizational change and how it can be understood and produced.

Finally and, in many ways, for me most importantly, the change programs and my overall activities at Michigan stimulated my interest in employee involvement and participative management. When I came to ISR it had a long history of doing research on participative management and thus, thoughts about workplace participation were front and center. The activities of the QWL research program were strongly influenced by the ISR history of research on participation. Indeed, the original idea behind establishing union-management committees was to make the workplace more participative and more democratic. The hope was that through labor management cooperation, work could be restructured and reformed in a way that would make organizations more participative.

During my early years in Michigan I became very involved in new plant "green field" employee involvement efforts. I worked with the General Foods Topeka plant during its start-up period, helped study the start-up of a pharmaceutical plant and became involved in a number of other green field situations. These experiences were extremely impactful upon me because they stood in dramatic contrast to what we were able to accomplish in our union-management QWL change efforts. In the union-management situations, employee involvement was extremely hard to produce and changes came very grudgingly. On the other hand, in green field settings, highly effective participative organizations were "easily" produced; within a few years places like the Topeka plant became models for how to manage in the eighties.

My experiences at Michigan helped stimulate my interest in consulting and also helped me develop my consulting skills. I had the chance to observe and study the work of some outstanding consultants. I also found an increasing interest by companies in my work on pay and my work on employee involvement. Given my interest in management practice, it is not surprising that I began to be an active consultant and, to this day, have rewarding consulting relationships with a number of companies. I have learned a great deal from these relationships and I hope that the companies and managers who have worked with me have learned as well.

My work on the quality of work life program alerted me to the role that the government plays in determining the practices and policies of organizations. One of the most valuable parts of our affiliation with Ted Mills was the interface it provided with various government agencies. I had the chance to interact with people in the Department of Commerce, Department of Labor, and the National Commission on Productivity and the Quality of Work Life. It was an interesting education in how a variety of government agencies shape what happens in the American workplace. Although I have not actively pursued the whole area of legislation, it is one that I consider it to be very important. At some point in the future I expect the government to direct its focus toward legislation that impacts on employee involvement in U.S. corporations. I specifically believe that the government will focus on issues of participation as well as on reward distribution.

During my stay at Michigan I was involved with several efforts to make national change happen. I worked with the National Commission on Productivity which, through the influence of myself and others, was renamed the National Commission on Productivity and the Quality of Work Life. Unfortunately, it lacked a strong mandate and made relatively little difference. Part of its activities, however, continued in the Department of Labor where a labor-management cooperation unit was created. It successfully supported the start-up of many joint labor-management projects.

I was also involved with the Department of Commerce in an effort that focused on measuring the quality of work life within corporations. My idea was to begin a program of corporate reporting in the QWL area. Working with Phil Mirvis I was able to get one corporation, Graphic Controls, in Buffalo, New York to begin issuing an "audited" report on the condition of its human organization. The research we did indicated that this report was well received by shareholders and employees, and I think it represented an interesting first step in the area of QWL reporting. Unfortunately, it ceased when the company was acquired and, to the best of my knowledge, no other corporation has committed itself to this practice. In some respects this is not surprising since it is a risky commitment on the part of any corporation and probably will only be done when there is a government mandate to do it.

There is no single reason why I chose to leave Michigan and join the Business School at the University of Southern California. A number of things converged at the same point in time to stimulate this change. In terms of my work situation, things were winding down with respect to many of our QWL projects. The kind of large, institutional funding that we had prior to 1978 was drying up. Most of the projects were either completed or near completion. I was also recently married to Patty Renwick, a Southern California native. She tested living in Pinckney, Michigan, but found it didn't compare favorably with Newport Beach! I was also ready to venture back to the West Coast, an objective of mine since my graduate student days at Berkeley.

USC, because of the outstanding faculty it had, was a logical choice. I approached USC through Steve Kerr and Larry Greiner, and asked them if they would consider making me a faculty appointment. They indicated that they would and, as a result, I phased out my Michigan activities and started teaching at USC. It wasn't a clean break. For a while I was splitting my time among Battelle in Seattle, where I was still working with the organizational research unit I started, Ann Arbor, where I was completing project work, and USC where I was teaching. In 1981, I moved 100 percent of my work activities to the USC School of Business Administration.

USC AND CEO

Moving to USC represented a number of firsts for me. It was the first time that I had ever been associated with a business school and it was the first time in a number of years that I had a "regular" faculty position, although I should add I was not given tenure and still don't have it. At this point I assume I could receive tenure if I wanted to. I have not asked for it because I don't think it is an appropriate reward-system practice. It is in conflict with my writings which stress the importance of having performance-based rewards. I should add I also did not have tenure at the University of Michigan. I must also admit that some of my dislike for the tenure systems may have its roots in my experience at Yale.

Soon after I arrived at USC and began teaching I realized that I did not want to be a "regular" faculty member. That is, I did not want to teach my two courses a semester and do an occasional article and research study. My years at Michigan had changed me. I wanted to do large-scale research and be involved in action. The opportunity to do this at USC appeared quickly after I arrived. A number of members of the Organizational Behavior Department were interested in setting up a research center that would relate to organizations and do action research. I "volunteered" to start this research unit which, thanks to Larry Greiner, was named The Center for Effective Organizations or CEO.

In many respects the early decisions I made about the structure of CEO were heavily influenced by what I had learned and done at Michigan and Battelle. I wanted it to do large-scale research projects. My experience at Michigan taught me that involvement by faculty members on a part-time basis was not enough to support large-scale change projects. Thus I convinced the school to let me hire full-time "research scientists." I also felt that the opportunities for research funding from government agencies and large foundations were not going to be good during the eighties. Thus, I decided to depend on corporate support for CEO.

To facilitate corporate support we created the concept of a corporate sponsor relationship and proceeded to recruit companies who would make an annual contribution. We also decided to charge organizations for any research that we did. The decisions to hire a full-time staff and to rely on private sector support, I believe, have turned out to be wise. CEO has grown over the last decade into a productive, vibrant, self-funding research unit of the School of Business Administration. In many respects it is an entrepreneurial venture since, although the school gave us a few thousand dollars of start-up money and some continuing support, it has grown because of external support. At various times it has been rated as one of the top two or three research organizations in the business school world and it has spawned similar units at other universities.

Although at times it has been difficult to implement the idea of having full-time researchers at CEO, the concept has worked out well. CEO has been able to attract an extremely talented group of researchers and to draw upon the very talented faculty in the USC business school (e.g. Kerr, Greiner, Cummings, Bennis, O'Toole, Birnbaum-More, Nathan, and Bowen). My first hire in the center was Monty Mohrman; subsequent to that, Susan Mohrman, Gerry Ledford, Jay Galbraith, Morgan McCall, and Susan Cohen have joined the CEO staff. All have excellent research track records and have given CEO a group of nationally known researchers who can do field research and relate effectively to both the academic and corporate world.

Support for CEO has grown from three corporate sponsors in its first year of operation, to over 40. At any one point in time, CEO is likely to be doing research projects with 10-15 corporations. CEO published hundreds of articles and ten books during its first decade of operation.

For me, helping CEO grow and develop has been very rewarding. It has also helped me further my research interests. As a result of being associated with outstanding researchers, I have been able to continue my work in the area of pay systems and to expand and develop my thinking about them. I now see them as a key strategic factor in organizational effectiveness. My book, *Strategic Pay* (1990), captures the evolution of my thinking with respect to pay systems. My earlier research essentially focused on its ability to impact individual behavior while my recent book places it in an organizational context and talks about how pay policies can complement particular organizational strategies and contribute to organizational effectiveness. Much of this thinking of course is based on my early expectancy theory work on how pay influences individual behavior. To me this theory is the basic building block in understanding how organizations can administer pay in ways that further their performance objectives.

My CEO work has allowed me to develop and further my work in the area of participative management and employee involvement. When CEO started in the late seventies, few organizations were interested in employee involvement practices, but today the situation is radically different, partly as a result of our early CEO work. CEO is well established as a major research entity in the area of employee involvement and participative management. As a result of this we have been able to do important work on quality circles, self-managing teams, and union-management quality of work life efforts.

My 1986 and 1992 books on high involvement management summarize a great deal of my work on involvement and put it into an organizational effectiveness context. In many respects it represents what I think is the kind of knowledge generation which can best be done by a center like CEO. Such a center can produce knowledge which is drawn from organizational experience, but is looked at from a theoretical perspective and validated by empirical measures of effectiveness and impact. My CEO research has enabled me to go beyond generalizations like participative management leads to higher satisfaction. I have been able to document the organizational impact of a variety of employee involvement practices.

During the 1970s and late '60s, I reduced the amount of research I did on pay systems because organizations simply weren't willing to change their pay practices. As a result of their unwillingness to change, it was impossible for me to learn about the impacts of many pay practices that I felt needed to be studied in order to further develop our understanding of how pay effects behavior. Simply stated, in the absence of organizations being willing to install a practice, it was impossible to determine the impact of the practice. I could talk as much as I wanted about the theoretical advantages of paying for skills, open pay, participation in pay system design and a whole host of other issues. Without the chance to actually experiment with them it was difficult to provide evidence that these were good or bad practices and it was difficult to further develop theory concerning pay.

The same thing was true for my interests in employee involvement and participation. Few organizations were willing to change their practices. Theoretical work was possible, but empirical validation was not. For me that limited the amount of theoretical development of which I was capable. My best conceptual thinking comes about as a result of my being able to see organizations experiment with new and different practices. I learn from their experiences, but I can only learn if they do things which are new and different and which challenge the existing order.

By getting involved in long-term data gathering activities with organizations, I and other people at CEO have been able to follow and measure the impact of specific organizational change efforts. This has allowed us to produce the kind of knowledge that simply is not obtainable through survey research methods, or even laboratory experiments. It has made me even more of a believer in the old statement that the best way to understand something is to try to change it. I would add to this, it helps if you can measure its condition and the effects it produces during the change process. Finally, it also helps understanding if one enters the change process with a conceptual model that tells one where to look for change and a set of measures that can measure change.

As a result of my CEO activities I have become increasingly intrigued by organizational change efforts and models. In particular I have developed an increasing interest in why organizations change the way they manage and in different strategies for producing change. In many respects, my interest in these issues stems from my own efforts to install new pay practices and new work designs in a wide range of organizations. In many respects, the 1980s were and, I believe, the 1990s will be great years in which to study organizational change and management. There is simply a growing flexibility and willingness to change organizations. This undoubtedly comes from the performance problems that many organizations have experienced and probably will continue to experience. In any case, it has made my research life much more interesting and exciting.

Because organizations are now doing new and different things, I have been able to further develop my own thinking about organization design, reward systems, organizational change and employee involvement strategies. What excites me most now is the opportunity to influence how organizations operate, and the opportunity to gather good data about the impact of any changes which are made. As long as I have the opportunity to be involved in situations where significant change is taking place and research on the change is possible, I think I will be a productive researcher and will forward my career long search for an understanding of motivation and organizational effectiveness.

PUBLICATIONS

1963

With L.W. Porter. Perceptions regarding management compensation. *Industrial Relations, 3*, 41-49.
Age and authorship of citations in selected psychological journals. *Psychological Reports, 13*, 537.

1964

With L.W. Porter. The effects of "tall" vs. "flat" organization structures on managerial job satisfaction. *Personnel Psychology, 17*, 135-148.
How long should a manager stay in the same job? *Personnel Administration, 27*, 6-9.
With C.O. Lawler. Who cites whom in psychology. *Journal of General Psychology, 73*, 31-36.

1965

Secondary reinforcement value of stimuli associated with shock reduction. *Quarterly Journal of Experimental Psychology, 17*, 57-62.
With C.O. Lawler. Color-mood association in young children. *Journal of Genetic Psychology, 107*, 29-32.
With L.W. Porter & E.E. Lawler. Properties of organization structure in relation to job attitudes and job behavior. *Psychological Bulletin, 64*, 23-51.
Should managers' compensation be kept under wraps? *Personnel, 42*, 17-20.
Managers' perceptions of their subordinates' pay and of their superiors' pay. *Personnel Psychology, 18*, 413-422.

1966

Ability as a moderator of the relationship between job attitudes and job performance. *Personnel Psychology, 19*, 153-164.
Managers' attitudes toward how their pay is and should be determined. *Journal of Applied Psychology, 50*, 273-279.

The mythology of management compensation. *California Management Review, 9,* 11-22.

With L.W. Porter. Predicting managers' pay and their satisfaction with their pay. *Personnel Psychology, 19,* 363-373.

1967

Secrecy about management compensation: Are there hidden costs? *Organizational Behavior and Human Performance, 2,* 122-142.

The multitrait-multitrater approach to measuring managerial job performance. *Journal of Applied Psychology, 51,* 403-410.

How much money do executives want? *TRANS-ACTION, 4,* 23-29.

Attitude surveys as predictors of employee behavior: The missing link. *Personnel Administration, 30*(5), 22-24.

Post-doctoral training for industrial psychologists. *The Industrial Psychologist, 4,* 34-40.

With L.W. Porter. The effects of performance on job satisfaction. *Industrial Relations, 7,* 20-28.

Management performance as seen from above, below, and within. In *Evaluation of executive performance.* Princeton, NJ: Educational Testing Service.

Antecedent attitudes of effective managerial performance. *Organizational Behavior and Human Performance, 2,* 122-142.

1968

With L.W. Porter. *Managerial attitudes and performance.* Homewood, IL: Irwin-Dorsey.

With L.W. Porter. What job attitudes can tell us about employee motivation. *Harvard Business Review, 46*(1), 118-126.

Does money make people work harder? *Yale Alumni Monthly, 31*(3), 40-43.

With E. Levin. Union officers' perceptions of members' pay preferences. *Industrial and Labor Relations Review, 21,* 509-517.

With E.A. Koplin, T.F. Young, & J.A. Fadem. Inequity reduction over time in an induced overpayment situation. *Organizational Behavior and Human Performance, 3,* 253-268.

With L.W. Porter & A. Tannenbaum. Managers' attitudes toward communication episodes. *Journal of Applied Psychology, 52,* 432-439.

Motivation and the design of jobs. *ASTME VECTORS, 3,* 14-21.

Effects of hourly overpayment on productivity and work quality. *Journal of Personality and Social Psychology, 10,* 306-314.

Equity theory as a predictor of productivity and work quality. *Psychological Bulletin, 70,* 596-610.

1969

Job design and employee motivation. *Personnel Psychology, 22,* 426-434.
Pay, promotion and motivation. *ASTME-VECTORS, 4,* 4-11.
Money as an (expensive) communication device. *Innovation, I*(3), 48-56.
With D.T. Hall. Unused potential in R. and D. Labs. *Research Management, 12,* 339-354.

1970

With I. Wood. The effects of piece rate overpayment on productivity. *Journal of Applied Psychology, 54,* 234-238.
Accounting data and behavior in organizations. In T.J. Burns (Ed.), *The behavioral aspects of accounting data for performance evaluation* (pp. 275-284). Columbus, OH: Ohio State University.
With D. Hall. The relationship of job characteristics to job involvement, satisfaction and intrinsic motivation. *Journal of Applied Psychology, 54,* 305-312.
Job attitudes and employee motivation: Theory, research and practice. *Personnel Psychology, 23,* 223-237.
With D.T. Hall. Job characteristics and job pressures and the organizational integration of professionals. *Administrative Science Quarterly, 15,* 271-281.

1971

With J.R. Hackman. Employee reactions to job characteristics. *Journal of Applied Psychology, 55,* 259-286.
The changing role of industrial psychology in university education: A symposium. *Professional Psychology, 2,* 2-22.
With B. Schneider & R.E. Carlson. Hickory dockery dick, Let's get off the stick. *Professional Psychology, 2,* 232-234.
Compensating the new life-style-workers. *Personnel, 48,* 19-25.
With K.C. Scheflen & J.R. Hackman. The long-term impact of employee participation in the development of pay incentive plans: A field experiment revisited. *Journal of Applied Psychology, 55,* 182-186.
With D.T. Hall. A positive view of job pressure. *American Scientist, 59,* 64-73.

1972

Secrecy and the need to know. In H. Tosi, R. House, & M. D. Dunnette (Eds.), *Managerial motivation and compensation* (pp. 455-476). East Lansing: Michigan State University Press.

With J.R. Hackman. Corporate profits and employee satisfaction: Must they be in conflict? *California Management Review, 14*, 46-55.

With J.L. Suttle. A causal correlational test of the need hierarchy concept. *Organizational Behavior and Human Performance, 7*, 265-287.

With J. Wanous. Measurement and meaning of job satisfaction. *Journal of Applied Psychology, 56*, 95-105.

With C. Cammann. What makes a work group successful? In A.J. Marrow (Ed.), *The failure of success* (pp. 122-130). New York: Amacom.

1973

Motivation in work organizations. Monterey, CA: Brooks/Cole.

With C. Cammann. Employee reactions to pay incentive plan. *Journal of Applied Psychology, 58*, 163-172.

With L. Suttle. Expectancy theory and job behavior. *Organizational Behavior and Human Performance, 9*, 482-503.

With J.R. Hackman & S. Kaufman. Effects of job redesign: A field experiment. *Journal of Applied Social Psychology, 3*, 49-62.

With J. Rhode. Human resource accounting: Accounting system of the future. In M. Dunnette (Ed.), *Work in the year 2001* (pp. 153-177). Monterey, CA: Brooks/Cole.

With J.E. Sorensen & J.G. Rhode. The generation gap in public accounting. *Journal of Accountancy, 136*(6), 42-50.

Quality of working life and social accounts. Chapter in M. Dierkes & R.A. Bauer (Eds.), *Corporate social accounting* (pp. 154-165). New York: Praeger.

1974

For a more effective organization—Match the job to the man. *Organizational Dynamics, 3*(1), 19-29.

The individualized organization: Problems and promise. *California Management Review, 17*(2), 31-39.

With D.T. Hall & G.R. Oldham. Organizational climate: Relationship to organizational structure, process and performance. *Organizational Behavior and Human Performance, 11*, 139-155.

1975

With L.W. Porter & H.R. Hackman. *Behavior in organizations.* New York: McGraw-Hill.

With W.J. Kuleck, J.G. Rhode, & J.E. Sorenson. Job Choice and post decision dissonance. *Organizational Behavior and Human Performance, 13*, 133-145.

Participation and pay. *Compensation Review, 7*(3), 62-66.

With G.D. Jenkins, D.A. Nadler, & C. Cammann. Standardized observations: An approach to measuring the nature of jobs. *Journal of Applied Psychology, 60,* 171-181.

Pay, participation and organizational change. In E.L. Cass & F.G. Zimmer (Eds.), *Man, work and society* (pp. 137-149). New York: Van Nostrand Rienhold.

Measuring the psychological quality of working life: The why and how of it. In L.E. Davis & A.B. Cherns (Eds.), *The quality of working life* (Vol. 1, pp. 123-133). New York: The Free Press.

With J.G. Rhode, & G.L. Sundem. Contabilization del valor de los recursos humanos. *Administracion de Empresas, T.VI,* 465-479.

1976

With J.G. Rhode. *Information and control in organizations.* Pacific Palisades, CA: Goodyear.

With J.G. Rhode & G.L. Sundem. Human resource accounting: A critical assessment. *Industrial Relations, 15,* 13-25.

With M.W. McCall. High school students' perceptions of work. *Academy of Management Journal, 19,* 17-24.

Control systems in organizations. In M. Dunnette (Ed.), *Handbook of industrial and organizational psychology* (pp. 1247-1292). Chicago: Rand-McNally.

Comments on H. H. Meyer's, "The pay for performance dilemma." *Organizational Dynamics, 4,* 23-75.

Should the quality of work life be legislated? *The Personnel Administrator, 21,* 17-21.

Conference review: Issue of understanding. In P. Warr (Ed.), *Personal goals and work design* (pp. 225-234). New York: Wiley.

Humanizing organizational behavior. In H. Meltzer and F.R. Wickert (Eds.), *Humanizing organizational behavior* (pp. 201-210). Springfield, IL: Thomas.

New approaches to pay: Innovations that work. *Personnel, 53*(5), 11-23.

Effective pay programs. *Compensation Review, 8,* 14-24.

Comment. In M. Schiff & G. Sorter (Eds.), *Proceedings of the conference on topical research in accounting* (pp. 44-48). New York: Ross Institute of Accounting Research.

With J.E. Sorensen, T.L. Sorensen, & J.G. Rhode. A behavioral study of staff retention in the profession of public accounting. In *Symposium on Auditing Research* (pp. 89-135). Urbana-Champaign, IL: Department of Accounting, University of Illinois.

With J.G. Rhode & J.E. Sorensen. An analysis of personal characteristics related to professional staff turnover in public accounting firms. *Decision Sciences, 7*(4), 771-800.

1977

With J.R. Hackman & L.W. Porter. (Eds.). *Perspectives on behavior in organizations.* New York: McGraw-Hill.

Reward systems. In J.R. Hackman, & J.L. Suttle (Eds.), *Improving Life at Work* (pp. 163-226). Santa Monica, CA: Goodyear.

With J.G. Rhode & J.E. Sorensen. Sources of professional staff turnover in public accounting firms revealed by the exit interview. *Accounting, Organizations and Society, 2*(2), 153-164.

Developing a motivating work climate. *Management Review, 66*(7), 25-38.

With R.N. Olsen. Designing reward systems for new organizations. *Personnel, 54*(5), 48-60.

With J.A. Drexler. A union-management cooperative project to improve the quality of work life. *Journal of Applied Behavioral Science, 13*(3), 373-386.

Administering pay programs. *Compensation Review, 9*(1), 8-16.

With P.H. Mirvis. Measuring the financial impact of employee attitudes. *Journal of Applied Psychology, 62*(1), 1-8.

Workers can set their own wages—responsibly. *Psychology Today, 10*(9), 109-112.

Adaptive experiments: An approach to organizational behavior research. *Academy of Management Review, 2*, 576-585.

1978

The new plant revolution. *Organizational Dynamics, 6*(3), 2-12.

With J. Kane. Methods of peer assessment. *Psychological Bulletin, 85*(3) 555-586.

With J. Drexler. The dynamics of establishing cooperative quality of work life projects. *Monthly Labor Review, 101*(3), 23-28.

With P.A. Renwick. What you really want from your job? *Psychology Today* (May), 53-65.

With R.J. Bullock. Pay and organizational change. *Personnel Administrator, 23*(5), 32-36.

1979

With D. Nadler & J. Hackman. *managing organizaitonal behavior.* Boston: Little, Brown.

With J. Kane. Performance appraisal effectiveness. In B. Staw (Ed.), *Research in organizational behavior* (Vol. 1, pp. 425-478). Greenwich, CT: JAI Press.

With P.S. Goodman. Etats unis [United States]. In *Les Nouvelles Formes D'organisation du Travail* [*New forms of work organization*] (pp. 167-207). Geneve: Bureau international du travail.

With L. Ozley. Winning union-management cooperation on quality of work life projects. *Management Review, 68*(3), 19-24.

Performance appraisal and merit pay. *Civil Service Journal* (April/June), 14-18.

1980

With D. Nadler & C. Cammann. *Organizational assessment.* New York: Wiley Interscience.

Task design. In B. Karmel (Ed.), *Point and counterpoint in organizational behavior* (pp. 95-107). Hinsdale, IL: Dryden.

With V.G. Nieva & D. Perkins. Improving the quality of life at work: Assessment of a collaborative selection process. *Journal of Occupational Behavior, 1*, 43-52.

With D.A. Nadler & M. Hanlon. Factors influencing the success of labour-management quality of work life projects. *Journal of Occupational Psychology, 1*, 53-67.

With R.J. Bullock. Incentives and gain-sharing: Stimuli for productivity. In J.D. Hogan (Ed.), *Dimensions of productivity research.* Houston, TX: American Productivity Center.

Motivation: Closing the gap between theory and practice. In K.D. Duncan, M.M. Grunberg & D. Wallis (Eds.), *Changes in working life* (pp. 539-550). London: Wiley.

With J.S. Kane. In defense of peer assessment: A rebuttal of brief's critique. *Psychological Bulletin, 88*, 80-81.

1981

Pay and organization development. Reading, MA: Addison-Wesley.

With G.D. Jenkins. Impact of employee participation in development of a pay plan. *Organizational behavior and human performance, 28*, 111-128.

With P.A. Renwick & R.J. Bullock. Employee influence on decisions: An analysis. *Journal of Occupational Behavior, 2*, 115-123.

With J.R. Hackman. Quality of work life in the 1980s. In *Working: Changes and choices.* New York: Human Science Press.

Merit pay: Fact or fiction. *Management Review, 70*(2), 50-53.

With J.A. Drexler. Entrepreneurship in the large corporation: Is it possible? *Management Review, 70*(4), 8-11.
With P.H. Mirvis. How graphic controls assesses the human side of the corporation. *Management Review, 70*(10), 54-63.

1981

With G.E. Ledford. Quality of work life programs, coordination, and productivity. *Journal of Contemporary Business, 11*, 93-106.
Strategies for improving the quality of work life. *American Psychologist, 37*, 486-493.
With G.E. Ledford. Productivity and the quality of work life. *National Productivity Review, 1*(1), 23-36.
Entwicklung and Anwendung von Bewerlungsmabstoben fur das Humankopitol in Organisationen. In H. Schmidt (Ed.), *Humon Vermogens Rechming* (pp. 191-222). Berlin: Grugter.
Creating high involvement work organizations. In E. Flamholtz (Ed.), *Human resource productivity in the 1980's* (pp. 216-239). Los Angeles: Institute of Industrial Relations, University of California.
Quality of work life: An overview. *Transamerica* (1), I-III.
Increasing worker involvement to enhance organizational effectiveness. In P. Goodman (Ed.), *Change in organizations* (pp. 280-315). San Francisco: Jossey-Bass.

1983

With S.E. Seashore, P. Mirvis, & C. Cammann. *Assessing organizational change.* New York: Wiley-Interscience.
With D. Perkins & R. Nievaf. *Managing creation: The challenge of building a new organization.* New York: Wiley-Interscience.
With J.R. Hackman & L.W. Porter. (Eds.). *Perspectives on behavior in organizations* (2nd ed.). New York: McGraw-Hill.
With P.H. Mirvis. Systems are not solutions: Issues in creating information systems that account for the human organization. *Accounting, Organizations and Society, 8*, 175-190.
With D.A. Nadler. Quality of work life: Perspectives and directions. *Organizational Dynamics, 11*(3), 20-30.
With A.M. Mohrman. Motivation and performance-appraisal behavior. In F. Landy & S. Zedeck (Eds.), *Performance measurement and theory* (pp. 173-189). Hillsdale, NJ: Erlbaum.
Human resource productivity in the 80's. *New Management, 1*(1), 46-49.
With S. Mohrman, T. Cummings, & E. Lawler. Creating useful research with organizations: Relationships and process issues. In R. Kilman, K.

Thomas, D. Slevin, R. Nath, & S. Jerrell (Eds.), *Producing useful knowledge for organizations* (pp. 613-624). New York: Praeger.

1984

With A.M. Mohrman & S.M. Resnick. Performance appraisal revisited. *Organizational Dynamics, 13*(1), 20-35.
With R.J. Bullock. Gainsharing: A few questions, and fewer answers. *Human Resource Management, 23*(1), 23-40.
With P.H. Mirvis. Accounting for the quality of work life. *Journal of Occupational Behavior, 5,* 197-212.
With S.A. Mohrman. Quality of work life. In K. Rowland & G. Ferris (Eds.), *Research in personnel and human resources management* (Vol. 2, pp. 219-260). Greenwich, CT: JAI Press.
Whatever happened to incentive pay? *New Management, 1*(4), 37-41.
Qu'en est-il aujourd'hui du salaire au rendement? In M. deMontmollin & O. Pastre (Eds.), *Le Taylorisme* (pp. 287-300). Paris: Editions La Decouverte.
With A.M. Mohrman. A review of theory and research. In F.W. McFarlan (Ed.), *The information systems research challenge, proceedings* (pp. 135-164). Boston: Harvard Business School Press.
The strategic design of reward systems. In C. Fombrun, N. Tichy & M. Devanna (Eds.), *Strategic Human Resource Management* (pp. 127-147). New York: Wiley.
Leadership in participative organizations. In J. Hunt, D. Hosking, C. Schriesheim, & R. Stewart (Eds.), *Leaders and managers* (pp. 316-332). New York: Pergamon Press.
Human resource productivity in the eighties: A critical analysis of trends. In E. Flamholtz & T. Das (Eds.), *Human Resource Management and Productivity* (pp. 9-26). Los Angeles: University of California Press.

1985

With A.M. Mohrman, S.A. Mohrman, G.E. Ledford, T.G. Cummings & Associates. *Doing research that is useful for theory and practice.* San Francisco, CA: Jossey-Bass.
The new pay. *New Management, 3*(1), 52-59.
Making performance pay. *Enterprise, 9*(5), 23-25.
Education, management style, and organizational effectiveness. *Personnel Psychology, 38*(1), 1-26.
With S.A. Mohrman. Quality circles after the fad. *Harvard Business Review, 85*(1), 64-71.

With A.M. Mohrman. The diffusion of QWL as a paradigm shift. In W.G. Bennis, K.D. Benne, & R. Chin (Eds.), *The planning of change* (pp. 149-161). New York: Holt.
With G.E. Ledford. Skill based pay. *Personnel, 62*(9), 30-37.
Participation to involvement: A personal view of work place change. *O.D. Newsletter* (Winter), pp. 4-50.

1986

High-involvement management. San Francisco, CA: Jossey-Bass.
Scap merit pay, focus on team performance. *Los Angeles Times* (March 2).
Profit sharing plans lack key motivation. *Los Angeles Times* (December 7).
Managers must share power with employee. *Daily News* [Los Angeles] (April 7).
Gainsharing: It works. *Commitment Plus, 2*(2), 5.
What's wrong with point-factor job evaluation. *Compensation and Benefits Review, 18*(2), 20-28.
Reward systems and strategy. In J.R. Gardner, R. Rachlin, & H. W. Sweeny (Eds.), *Handbook of strategic planning* (pp. 10.1-10.24). New York: Wiley.
With S.A. Mohrman, G.E. Ledford, & A.M. Mohrman. Quality of worklife and employee involvement. In C.L. Cooper & I. Robertson (Eds.), *International review of industrial and organizational psychology* (pp. 189-216). London: Wiley.
With J.B. Prince. Does salary discussion hurt the developmental performance appraisal? *Organizational Behavior and Human Decision Processes, 37*, 357-375.

1987

The design of effective reward systems. In J.W. Lorsch (Ed.), *Handbook of organizational behavior.* Englewood Cliffs, NJ: Prentice-Hall.
Paying for performance: Future directions. In D.B. Balkin & L.R. Gomez-Mejia (Eds.), *New perspectives on compensation* (pp. 162-168). Englewood Cliffs, NJ: Prentice-Hall.
With S.A. Mohrman. Quality circles: After the honeymoon. *Organizational Dynamics, 15*(4), 42-55.
Paying for organizational performance. *Business and Economics Review, 1*(1), 12-19.
Pay for performance: A motivational analysis. In H.R. Nalbantian (Ed.), *Incentives, cooperation and risk taking* (pp. 69-86). Totowa, NJ: Rowman and Littlefield.

Transformation from control to involvement. In R.H. Kilman, T. J. Covin & Associates (Eds.), *Corporate transformation* (pp. 46-65). San Francisco, CA: Jossey-Bass.

With S.A. Mohrman. Unions and the new management. *Academy of Management Executive, 1*, 293-300.

Pay and organization development consultation. *Consultation, 6*, 281-283.

1988

Rehire the air controllers Reagan fired in 1981 strike. *Los Angeles Herald Examiner* (February 25).

Global competitiveness—Will you be ready? *Tapping the Network Journal* (Winter), pp. 20-28.

Human resources management: Meeting the new challenges. *Personnel, 65*(1), 22-27.

Choosing an involvement strategy. *Academy of Management Executive, 2*(3), 197-204.

Substitutes for hierarchy. *Organizational Dynamics, 17*(1), 4-15.

Pay for performance: Making it work. *Personnel, 65*(10), 68-71.

Gainsharing theory and research: Findings and future directions. In W.A. Pasmore , & R. Woodman (Eds.), *Research in organizational change and development*, (Vol. 2, pp. 323-344). Greenwich, CT: JAI.

With G.A. Ledford & S.A. Mohrman. The quality circle and its variations. In J.P. Campbell, R.J. Campbell, & Associates (Eds.), *Productivity in organizations* (pp. 255-294). San Francisco, CA: Jossey-Bass.

With S.A. Mohrman. Participative managerial behavior and organizational change. *Journal of Organizational Change Management, 1*, 45-59.

1989

With S.A. Mohrman. Champions of change. *Executive Excellence* (April).

Employee involvement: New challenges. *Letter: American Productivity and Quality Center, 9*(4), 4-5.

With A.M. Mohrman & S.M. Resnick-West. *Designing performance appraisal systems.* San Francisco, CA: Jossey-Bass.

With G.E. Ledford & S.A. Mohrman. *Employee involvement in America.* Houston, TX: American Productivity and Quality Center.

With A.M. Mohrman, S.A. Mohrman, G.E. Ledford, T.G. Cummings, & Associates. *Large-scale organizational change.* San Francisco, CA: Jossey-Bass.

Participative management in the United States: Three classics revisited. In C.J. Lammers & G. Szell (Eds.), *International handbook of participation in organizations* (Vol. 1, pp. 91-97). New York: Oxford.

Pay for performance: A strategic analysis. In L.R. Gomez-Mejia (Ed.), *Compensation and benefits* (pp. 136-181). Washington: BNA.

With S.A. Mohrman. High-involvement management. *Personnel, 66*(4), 26-31.

With S.A. Mohrman. Parallel participation structures. *Public Administration Quarterly, 13*, 255-272.

1990

Let the workers make white-knuckle decisions. *Fortune, 1212*(7), 49.

Making your firm more competitive. *Executive excellence* (November), pp. 9-10.

Strategic pay. San Francisco, CA: Jossey-Bass.

The new plant revolution revisited. *Organizational Dynamics, 19*(2), 4-14.

Executive behavior in high-involvement organizations. In R.H. Kilmann, I. Kilmann, & Associates (Eds.), *Making organizations competitive* (pp. 176-194). San Francisco, CA: Jossey-Bass.

Achieving competitiveness by creating new organization cultures and structures. In D.B. Fishman, & C. Cherniss (Eds.), *The human side of corporate competitiveness* (pp. 69-101). Newbury Park, CA: Sage.

With D.J.B. Mitchell,& D. Lewin. Alternative pay system, firm performance and productivity. In A.S. Binder (Ed.), *Paying for productivity: A look at the evidence* (pp. 15-94). Washington, DC: The Brookings Institution.

1991

The organizational impact of executive compensation. In F.K. Foulkes (Ed.), *Executive compensation* (pp. 129-151). Boston, MA: Harvard Business School Press.

Employee involvement and pay system designs. In M.L. Rock & L.A. Berger (Eds.), *The compensation handbook* (pp. 592-603). New York: McGraw-Hill.

Participative management strategies. In J.W. Jones, B.D. Steffy & D.W. Bray (Eds.), *Applying psychology in business* (pp. 578-586). Lexington, MA: Lexington.

Paying the person: A better approach to management? *Human Resource Management Review, 1*, 145-154.

The new plant approach: A second generation approach. *Organizational Dynamics, 20*(1), 5-14.

Executive behavior in high-involvement organizations. In R.H. Kilman, I. Kilman, & Associates, *Making organizations competitive* (pp. 176-194). San Francisco, CA: Jossey-Bass.

1992

With D.E. Bowen. The empowerment of service workers: What, why, how, and when. *Sloan Management Review, 33*(3), 31-39.

With S.A. Mohrman & G.E. Ledford. The Fortune 1000 and total quality. *Quality and Participation, 15*(5), 6-10.

With D.E. Bowen. Total quality-oriented human resources management. *Organizational Dynamics, 20*(4), 29-41.

With J.D. Jenkins. Strategic reward systems. In M.D. Dunnette & L.M. Hough (Eds.), *Handbook of industrial and organizational psychology* (2nd ed., pp. 1009-1055). Palo Alto, CA: Consulting Psychologists Press.

With A.M. Mohrman & S.A. Mohrman. The performance management of teams. In W.J. Burns (Ed.), *Performance measurement, evaluation, and incentives* (pp. 217-241). Boston, MA: Harvard University Press.

Pay systems must support quality. *TQM, 2*(5), 248-250.

With S.G. Cohen. Designing pay systems for teams. *ACA Journal, 1*(1), 6-19.

With S.A. Mohrman & A.M. Mohrman. Applying employee involvment in schools. *Educational Evaluation and Policy Analysis, 14*, 347-360.

With G.E. Ledford. A skill-based approach to human resource management. *European Management Journal, 10*(4), 383-391.

With C.G. Worley & D.E. Bowen. On the relationship between objective increases in pay and employees' subjective reactions. *Journal of Organizational Behavior, 13*, 559-571.

With S.A. Mohrman & G.E. Ledford. *Employee involvement and total quality management: Practices and results in Fortune 1000 companies.* San Francisco, CA: Jossey-Bass.

The ultimate advantage: Creating the high-involvement organization. San Francisco, CA: Jossey-Bass.

1993

With G.E. Ledford & L. Chang. Who uses skill-based pay and why? *Compensation Benefits and Review, 25*(2), 22-26.

With J.R. Galbraith & Associates. *Organizing for the future: The new logic for managing complex organizations.* San Francisco, CA: Jossey-Bass.

Doing Problem-Oriented Research:
A Daughter's Interview

PAUL R. LAWRENCE with ANNE T. LAWRENCE*

A: *I want to start by asking you about something I heard you say once: that your research has been largely problem-oriented. Is that true?*

P: I think that is a fair way of describing what's motivated the research I've done over the years. I've kept looking for important problems where research might contribute to a solution as well as contribute to theory. But you have to realize it's not always just a question of identifying a problem and then setting out to find an answer. Often times there is a bit of luck or serendipity involved. You have to seize opportunities that may present themselves unexpectedly. And it certainly helps to be working in a congenial setting. I've been lucky to have been based at the Harvard Business School [HBS] all these years. There's a strong problem-solving orientation at HBS and I've been given support and encouragement all along the way.

---

* Anne T. Lawrence is Associate Professor of Organization and Management at San Jose State University. She holds a Ph.D. in sociology from the University of California, Berkeley, and did two years of postdoctoral study in organizations and mental health at Stanford University. This interview was originally conducted as a gift for her mother, Martha Stiles Lawrence, on the occasion of her parents' fortieth wedding anniversary. It has been significantly extended and edited for this volume.

A: *Let's talk about your latest research interest, Soviet management practices. Was the research that led to the book,* Behind the Factory Walls, *motivated by concern with a problem?*

P: It certainly was. By spring 1987, signs of important change were manifest in the Soviet Union. Like most people, I was keenly interested in what was going on. And, being me, I wondered about changes related to my particular area of interest, organizations. Even though no one knew much about Soviet management practices, it was pretty obvious that the magnitude of change that would have to take place would dwarf the change we normally study in organizational behavior. I began reading everything I could lay my hands on, and I was becoming more and more intrigued.

And then, enter the serendipity factor. One Charalambos Vlachoutsicos, a person I'd never met before, hadn't even heard of before, came to my office one afternoon in April 1987. A 1954 graduate of the Harvard Business School, he runs a family trading business in Greece and has for many years done business in the Soviet Union. Wanting to get more background on the changing circumstances in the USSR, he had taken a leave from his company to become a Research Fellow at the Russian Research Center at Harvard. He sought me out with the idea that with *glasnost* the conditions might be favorable for doing some intensive research on Soviet management. We talked and talked that afternoon. We agreed that the success or failure of the reform effort in the USSR would clearly have significant consequences throughout the world. We each wished we might make some constructive contribution. We sensed right away that we would make a good team. He knew his way around the USSR, and I knew about doing research. When I told your mother about the conversation that night, she responded enthusiastically, "Go for it!" So that's how the project came into being.

A: *Briefly, what was the project?*

P: It was a comparative study of management decision making in the United States and USSR. We undertook it because we thought that joint ventures were important and for them to have any hope of success each "side" would need to know how the other managed. We put together a bi-national, bi-lingual team of scholars, and did intensive field work in four U.S. factories and four roughly matched Soviet factories. It really represented the first time Western scholars have had a good inside look at Soviet management culture. It was interesting that we found more management commonalities than we might have expected. But as you might imagine, there were important differences too, differences that managers of joint ventures will need to consider seriously.

A: *Interesting. Now, before I ask you about other research you've done, let me probe a bit into how you happened to land at the Harvard Business School in the first place, doing the kinds of things you've done these past forty-odd years.*

EARLY YEARS

A: *The story in the family is that originally you thought of being a Methodist minister. Is this true?*

P: Not really. There was some family conversation about it when I was young. My grandfather was a Methodist minister. He picked me out among his grandchildren as the one who might turn to the ministry. My mother echoed that in conversations with me.

A: *Why do you think your grandfather and mother singled you out as the child of your generation most suited to the ministry?*

P: I never thought about that. I suppose it was because I was really studious. I did go to church and Sunday school. I was fond of my grandfather, and he used to talk to me about his days in the ministry. That was all part of my upbringing.

A: *At what point did you make a definite career decision?*

P: There really wasn't any special point. When I went to [Grand Rapids, Michigan] Junior College, there was some family discussion about whether I should go into a pre-med program, but I never enrolled in it; I took straight liberal arts. When I went to Albion College two years later, I thought about pre-law, but in fact I took a dual-major in economics and sociology.

A: *You left Albion to go to the Harvard Business School. What brought that about?*

P: Through my older brother, who had graduated earlier from the Harvard Business School, I found out about a special program HBS had initiated immediately after Pearl Harbor to take a number of students who had finished three years of college and put them directly into the master's program. At the time, I was nineteen years old and was just finishing my junior year. I expected to have one more year of education before I went into the service, and I thought it would be more interesting at HBS than at Albion. I remember thinking explicitly that I wasn't going there in order to go into business.

A: *What influence did your parents have on these decisions?*

P: My father had a remarkable career. In spite of the fact that his schooling stopped after high school, he entered banking, moved into finance in industry, entered the top levels of state government, and wound up as the CEO of a paint manufacturing company. He was always very active in community affairs. My mother had been a teacher before her marriage. Both my parents had a strong commitment to higher education. Of the six children, all of us finished college and five of us earned higher degrees.

A: *At the time you entered HBS, what were your thoughts about a career?*

P: Around the time I moved from the small town of Ionia to Grand Rapids as a teenager, I remember being very interested in all the labor strikes we had at that time. This was when there were the sitdown strikes in Flint; John L. Lewis had just founded the Committee for Industrial Organization which eventually became the CIO. These strikes were drawing a lot of national attention. The Governor, Frank Murphy, was asked to call up the National Guard to suppress the sitdown strikes and to defend property rights. He refused to do it. That gave the union a chance to persist and eventually led to the unionization of the auto industry. That impressed me very much. I was sympathetic to the unions, but not anti-management. I remember thinking that there should be some way to settle these fights. I had a strong sense that I wanted to prepare myself to do something useful about these conditions.

A: *So was there a carry-over from your Methodist upbringing?*

P: I suppose I was born and bred to be concerned with social problems.

A: *When did you go into the service?*

P: I arrived at HBS in May 1942, and I left in May 1943. Meanwhile, I had signed up for the Navy, and they gave me a leave from active duty to finish my first year of business school. I suppose they thought this schooling would help me do my supply corps job better. I was full time in the Navy for three years. The Navy sent me to Wellesley College, of all places, for my officer training, and then I went to the South Pacific.

A: *Do you feel in retrospect that your Navy experience had any impact on your subsequent work?*

P: Yes, definitely. When I was first at Harvard I sought out courses in labor relations and the human aspects of management. I especially liked my courses with the sociologist Pitrim Sorokin, and with Sumner Slichter, my favorite economist. Then, when I was overseas in the Navy, I wrote away and got some books by Fritz Roethlisberger and Elton Mayo and did a lot of thinking and reflecting about all of this. Such books were hard to get in New Guinea, but I did it.

A: *You mean to say you were in effect doing an independent study on the Hawthorne studies in the middle of the New Guinea jungle?*

P: Right. I was also thinking about the human aspects of management as I was carrying out my responsibilities there. I had quite a few people reporting to me in my work in the Navy.

A: *You know, I always assumed that your training was exclusively academic—that you had no hands-on management experience. But in a sense you did have management experience—in the military.*

P: Actually, that's right. Considering my age, I had major responsibilities. At one time or another, I had two or three hundred people reporting to me. I had a bunch of equipment and facilities, and the things that go with that.

A: *What happened after your discharge?*

P: I got out of the Navy in June 1946 but couldn't return to HBS for my last MBA term until that fall. So I spent that summer in Detroit working on the assembly line at Chevrolet. I decided to do that because it was something I had never done, and I felt it would be a good education.

A: *What do you remember of that experience?*

P: I was at Chevrolet Gear and Axle, working with brakes. I remember it as a pretty tough experience, with a lot of very routinized work. There was high turnover. People were constantly being moved around. You never knew who your boss was. Actually the union provided more continuity than management did. At Chevrolet, I learned all about "work restriction" and about how to play various games so management didn't "take advantage" of you. I wrote a case about that.

A: *What case was that?*

P: It was called "Jim McFee." We used that case for many years at HBS. I was Jim McFee. It was very amusing to teach that case year after year. I had to keep my role a deep, dark secret, because the case always elicited a good deal of criticism of Jim McFee.

DOCTORAL STUDIES AT HBS

A: Let me interrupt here. Now we have you at the point of returning to HBS after your Navy service. At what point did you make a decision to do graduate work beyond the MBA?

P: When I came out of the service, I thought I might go for a Ph.D. in sociology. That summer I went to the University of Chicago and talked with the people there about signing up for the Ph.D. program. I wound up talking to Burleigh Gardner, who had done some of the early human relations work. He had been associated with the Harvard Business School for a while. I told him I wanted to study industrial sociology. When he heard that, he said, "What do you want to come to Chicago for? Go on back to Harvard. Some of the best work in the field is being done right now at the Harvard Business School. You've already got a running start at it. Why don't you go back and finish there?" So I returned to HBS and started right in letting the human relations people know that I was interested in switching over to the doctoral program and applying for a job as a research assistant. At that time people got research assistant jobs after they finished their MBA by being tapped by some professor. Nobody asked me, so I just went out and knocked on doors and asked them. It was an unorthodox approach, but it worked.

During my last semester in the master's program, I took a course from Fritz [Roethlisberger]. I got to know Fritz some that way, so I applied to be a research assistant for his course. He didn't have anything available. The first thing that turned up was a chance to go to work for the production people. So I went to work writing production cases, with the understanding that I would switch into human relations or labor as soon as something opened up. Later I went to work for George Lombard, who was in charge of case writing for the required Administrative Practices course, under the general leadership of Ed Learned.

A: *How did you learn to write cases?*

P: Well, by the time you get a Harvard MBA, you've read a lot of cases. And then you get some coaching by whoever you're working for. At that time, George and Ed believed in a kind of total immersion in field work. You were expected to hang around your field site, talk with people and find out what was going on, and out of that eventually you would get some interesting cases.

A: *Did you find that as a research assistant at the Harvard Business School you generally had access to research sites, or was that a problem for you?*

P: Well, you couldn't take it for granted, you did have to search around and negotiate, but it turned out not to be too big a problem. Early on, we got into an electronics division of a major company that was producing an experimental product. In fact, they were doing early work on transistors and computers, so it was an exciting mix of R&D and production work. That turned out to be where I did the research for my doctoral thesis.

A: *When you took these research and case-writing jobs at the Business School, were you concurrently enrolled in the doctoral program there?*

P: Yes, in a way, although I was not officially admitted until a little later.

A: *As you proceeded through the doctoral program, who were the instructors who influenced you the most?*

P: I would say Fritz Roethlisberger and George Lombard primarily. I overlapped with Mayo for a very short period. My actual graduate activity was supervised primarily by George, but I got a great deal of valuable guidance from Fritz.

A: *Do you believe that any of these men saw you as a protégé or in any sense as a special student?*

P: Well, Fritz said that a number of years later, but I don't remember it being that way at the time.

A: *My childhood recollection is that Fritz was very much of a personal friend to our family as well as a mentor and colleague of yours.*

P: Yes, that is certainly true.

A: *Were there aspects of your relationship with Fritz that you would consider problematical or difficult?*

P: Not really. I remember feeling afterwards that he had not steered me to some of the relevant literature. But he was very supportive and generous with his time and ideas.

A: *Was your doctoral dissertation important to your subsequent intellectual development? Was it of significance to you beyond being merely a requirement for the degree?*

P: Absolutely. It was an intensive study of intergroup conflict. The groups I was studying were mostly engineers and technicians, although I also worked in a secondary way with production teams. These groups were involved in intense conflicts—turf battles—that were a tremendous handicap to their doing what they were supposed to be doing, which was developing new products and getting them into production successfully. I was interested in the dynamics of the conflict and what it would take to get reasonable integration between the groups' perspectives and interests. You might say that the thesis provided the problem on which I based some of my later thinking on differentiation and integration.

A: *My impression from hearing you talk about your graduate work is that you did not receive training in what we would today call quantitative methods—that is, statistical analysis of data.*

P: Certainly not much. We had to take a course in statistics and a seminar in field methods. Of the various disciplines, anthropology had the strongest influence. I had a little exposure to the methodology of psychology, although I got most of that back in my undergraduate days at Albion. You know, this was all before the days of computers, and people weren't thinking about models and modeling. The only statistical tests were simple chi-squares and straight linear equations under very simple assumptions. And we didn't even do much of that.

A: *At what point along the way did you decide on an academic career? Can you even state that?*

P: Well, I had set my sights on that by the time I came back from the Navy.

A: *I am trying to form an image in my mind of how you visualized yourself. Did you think of yourself as becoming a professor of sociology in a liberal arts setting? Or by the time you made the decision to go back to HBS did you see yourself as teaching in a professional business school setting?*

P: Well, as I said, at that time I wanted to be an applied industrial sociologist, and when I looked around I didn't see a better setting for that work than HBS. I mean, the field called organizational behavior didn't exist at that time. Very shortly after I finished my doctoral work in 1950, the Business School instituted a doctoral program in organizational behavior. It actually consisted of exactly the same courses and exams I had taken. Organizational behavior was a post-war product, a discipline that really got started within a business school context, much of it at the Harvard Business School. So the field developed, and I was in the right place to develop with it.

A: *When, in fact, was the department founded at Harvard?*

P: It occurred in multiple steps. In the early 1950s, HBS set up the so-called area structure. Joe Bailey was the first organizational behavior chairman. This is an interesting historical footnote. The chair I eventually got was the Donham Professor of Human Relations. When I assumed that position in 1967 after Fritz Roethlisberger's retirement, it seemed entirely natural to rename it the Donham Professor of Organizational Behavior.

A: *Turning to another issue, can you explain to me your transition from graduate student to faculty member? At some point your status was elevated. How did that come about?*

P: In those days, we didn't have many doctoral courses. I took courses in business history and economics, and some basic theory courses. Aside from that, it was just a kind of tutorial which always involved being an RA to somebody about something. You worked as a research assistant, then as a research associate, then as an instructor. I worked up through those three steps.

A: *Let me backtrack a minute. In other words, everyone who was enrolled in the doctoral program at that time could have expected an appointment to instructor?*

P: If they wanted it and if all went well, yes.

A: *So your key promotion was not to instructor but to assistant professor.*

P: That's right. That's when I actually got onto a tenure track.

A: *What was the nature of the process that led to your selection?*

P: It was sort of curious. There were three of us who were RAs together in organizational behavior. The other two were both having some thesis problems—in fact, they never did get degrees. I got my degree in June 1950. I had qualified for it in February, and I started teaching fulltime that spring. In July, I got appointed assistant professor. Actually, I never went off the payroll.

A: *I want to push you further on your transition from graduate student to faculty member status. It seems to have been a very gradual, almost indistinct, transition for you. Do you recall that you ever actually applied for or were interviewed for a job on the Business School faculty?*

P: Not really. There was no interview process, there was no job talk, there was no sense of—you know, there are two openings, and you are one of a certain number of candidates—none of that.

A: *In fact, did the Business School ever hire from the outside at that time?*

P: They mostly hired from the inside.

A: *Did you ever think about who it was who chose you, who made that decision? I get the impression from your comments that Fritz and George must have pushed you as their candidate.*

P: They probably did, but personally I think the person who was probably the most influential was Ed Learned. He was in charge of the Administrative Practices course, and so he had a lot to say about who was going to get hired. Actually, I hadn't worked that closely with him. At one point, he had asked me to be his RA on a research project that he was undertaking, but I declined. I would describe the situation as a gradual apprenticeship program in which you kept climbing to the next step, and other people kind of dropped off along the way to do other things. It was the same way for me through the different steps of the promotion ladder, too. There were a number of assistant professors there when I was who didn't stay on, but it was never too clear to me exactly what the tenure and promotion process was, or what decided it.

TEACHING

A: At this point, I'd like to depart from the chronology of your career and ask you some more general questions. First, how did you learn to teach?

P: I never had any formal courses in pedagogy. HBS has its own somewhat special teaching methods, and you learn them by observation and apprenticeship. We do have a tradition at Harvard of experienced teachers sitting in on classes of the less experienced teachers and giving them critiques and feedback, so that you have an opportunity to get that kind of guidance. We take teaching meetings very seriously and spend a lot of time planning our teaching sessions and reviewing each other's work as a group, so that there is a lot of coaching and mutual aid that way.

When I started teaching at Harvard, we were very much caught up in a trend at the time called nondirective teaching. This was considered a superior method of teaching.

A: How would you describe the nondirective method?

P: There was no lecturing. We were expected to engage students in a process of questioning and to reflect back to them their assumptions and feelings. We were supposed to draw the students out and use this dialogue as the sole basis for education. We literally ran our courses in those days entirely, one hundred percent, with cases. There was absolutely no text material in any form. We were expected to figure out how to make it work, and it was taken very seriously.

It was quite a demanding thing to make it work. The students often went through a stage of rejecting the whole process. The instructor had to articulate that feeling and develop something constructive out of it. Over the years, the purist attitude about nondirective teaching has dwindled. I have stayed with the trends of the times, you might say, and become more expository in my teaching. I am probably still more nondirective than the average HBS professor today, though, because I was brought up in that school.

A: *It strikes me that for a young starting assistant professor that this would have been a challenging if not intimidating teaching technique to use, because you have so little control in the classroom with nondirective techniques.*

P: That's true. You sort of depended on a daily miracle that it would come out correctly. But, the whole theory of motivation and self-development behind it gave you confidence to proceed, and of course we had a teaching group that could support you through periods where you were getting negative feedback.

A: *What do you see as your strengths and weaknesses as a classroom teacher?*

P: I think maybe my greatest strength is that I can be a very effective listener. I can be very tuned into what's going on and really kind of crawl inside the perspective of a student and reach a seriousness of discourse that can be a very positive experience. I think I have a number of shortcomings: one, I don't have a very keen sense of humor, two, I ....

A: *Let me ask you about the first point. You say you don't have a very keen sense of humor. I certainly don't consider you a joke-cracker, but I think you have a wry and amused view of the world. In what sense do you say you don't have a sense of humor, do you mean that you aren't a slick joke teller in the classroom, or something else?*

P: Well, if you compared the number of belly laughs in my classes with those in the classes of many of my colleagues, mine would be on the low end, there's no question about that. And the other thing I was going to say—I think one's ability to be an effective, nondirective teacher is to some extent handicapped the more one feels one knows about his subject matter.

A: *That's intriguing. Do I understand you correctly to be saying that as you have gained experience, not only do you have a lot to say, but the students know you have a lot to say, so they feel you are holding out on them if you don't give them "The Answer"?*

P: That's right. I feel I was a more effective nondirective teacher when I was younger and less well informed. Perhaps a third weakness is that my response time in the classroom isn't as fast as it might be. For some people, my pacing is about right. For others, it's too slow.

A: *How do you think the students evaluate your classes relative to those of other faculty members?*

P: I think I am considered a good strong teacher, but certainly not—to use a term that we sometimes use around our place—a world-class teacher.

A: *World class! That is a formidable standard. Tell me, in general, have you found your teaching to be an activity that has enhanced your research or simply been another track that has competed for your time and attention?*

P: Well, I like to think there has been a beneficial relationship, but when you get right down to it, and look backwards, there probably wasn't all that much. It's not that I haven't learned a lot from the students. I have always found it particularly fascinating to talk with those in executive programs about their businesses and the problems they run into. I get a big kick out of recognizing certain classic problems they are struggling with and helping them gain a perspective on these problems. I'm sure there's a real relationship between teaching and research, but I'm having trouble finding examples of it.

A: *What about your doctoral students? I've always had the impression that you found teaching doctoral students very gratifying and rewarding. Is that accurate?*

P: Yes, that's very true. And I have done a lot of it. I must have taught a doctoral seminar every year for about thirty years. I've served on at least sixty doctoral thesis committees. So these things represent an important part of my career. A few years ago, I also worked with Harrison White and Freed Bales to start up a joint Ph.D. program in Organizational Behavior between HBS and the sociology and psychology departments at Harvard Arts and Sciences. That is now off to a strong start.

A: *My impression is that you are very gifted at advising doctoral students. What is it about you that makes you good at that?*

P: I think I am most effective in helping them on their theses. I like research and enjoy thinking through the various alternative ways of going about it— finding creative ways to get evidence, ways of sharpening the question and clarifying the design. The best intellectual fun I have had over the years is that kind of one-on-one exchange with doctoral students where we kick various possibilities back and forth.

A: *To inject an observation of my own here, I think one of the reasons that you are good at that is that you are a good listener and you don't necessarily impose your own research agenda on a student. There are a lot of professors who encourage students to carve out a piece of their own research projects or who impose their ideas about research design and theoretical formulations. I think you have a wide ranging intellectual curiosity, and you are very good at getting inside your students' frameworks and helping them do what they want to do in the best possible way. From my own experience as a graduate student, I would say that is quite unusual.*

Before we leave the subject of teaching, do you think during your time at HBS you made any innovations or particular contributions to pedagogy there?

P: Yes, I can think of a couple. I had a hand in one big curriculum reform the School went through about 1959. I was on the key committee and probably contributed some creative thinking.

A: *What was your contribution?*

P: We were responding to a critique of business schools by the Carnegie and Ford Foundations, and the Dean felt we ought to have a very thorough review. What we were trying to do was find ways to more creatively combine functional problem-centered areas of study like marketing, finance, and production with more discipline-based areas of study, such as economics, statistics, and organizational behavior. That was the major theme in that reform. We changed the schedule around and introduced a couple new courses. One was in managerial economics, or applied decision theory, and another in organizational problems.

A: *Were you involved in any subsequent curriculum changes at the School?*

P: I was instrumental in starting up our required first-year course in Human Resource Management and also in a major reform of our only required second-year course, Managing Policy and Practice. I also helped introduce sequential cases to get more dynamics into case discussions.

A: *Is there anything else you want to add about teaching?*

P: There's one other thing about my teaching career that probably ought to be in the record. After coming on the faculty, I taught in the first year MBA program for 18 consecutive years. There can't be too many people at the school who have done it longer. So I have done a lot of teaching, just in terms of sheer numbers of students. We used to have 90 to 100 per section often, with two sections, each meeting 60 to 70 times per year. I have no regrets about leaving all those bluebooks behind.

ADMINISTRATION

A: *Let's turn now to the administrative duties you have had over the years.*

P: I'll try to tick off the list of them quickly. My first administrative responsibility was as course head for a required MBA course, Administrative

Practices. I did that for a number of years. Then I was the first head for a new required course called Organizational Problems. I was area chairman twice, the first time for five years, the second time for four years. That was another major administrative responsibility. The first time through I didn't enjoy it very much, but the second time through, I really did. By that time I had figured out a lot more about how to do the job right, and I had a few more breaks in terms of the general morale, relationships with the front office and so forth.

A: *What were your insights that helped you do a better job as chairman the second time?*

P: I think I did a better job of holding area meetings that developed a sense of group goals and purposes, so there was more unity. Also, I had improved my skills in organizing a careful search and review process for new faculty.

A: *What other administrative roles have you played?*

P: As far as other things go, I spent one year as chairman of the MBA program. I was briefly chairman of the Advanced Management Program. I didn't enjoy that too much because a lot of it was ceremonial. I'm not too good at welcoming and graduation exercises and things like that. I did have a couple of interesting committee chairmanships, most recently on the issue of outside activities.

In the late sixties, I was head of a committee to plan for HBS in the seventies, what should be the agenda, and how we were going to respond to the need for change and so forth. We had a lot of group sessions on that, subcommittees, and lots of discussion and papers. I think it did do some good in terms of just plain stretching people's thinking and getting them more generally alert to the times, but it didn't produce much concrete change. We did sponsor some new forms of course development and helped give students more voice in the system.

Then in 1969 and 1970 I was chairman of one of the key subcommittees in a university-wide process that was triggered by the University Hall occupation and the general student unrest. I was in charge of the subcommittee that developed a document on the purposes of the university. In general, committee work wasn't great, but it was important, and it usually went well.

CONSULTING

A: *Now let me ask you about consulting. My understanding is that consulting work was considered part of the professional work of faculty members at the Harvard Business School. How much consulting did you do?*

P: Most people outside the School would probably think that I have done more than I actually have. I am probably in the lower quartile of our faculty in the amount that I have done. I have never seen it as a very important part of my professional life. I haven't given it very high priority either in terms of professional development or learning about organizations.

The assignments I have liked the best are those where I have been able to have an ongoing relationship with a company over a period of years, where I could deal with issues I felt were matters of substance, you know, something of significance to the firm. In those instances, I tried to develop a comprehensive, diagnostic understanding of the organization. I have developed such a relationship only three or four times in my career.

A: *With what firms?*

P: The first one I developed that kind of relationship with was Alcan, the Canadian aluminum producer. I worked with them for many years. Later on, I had that kind of relationship with Coca Cola. Also in that category was General Motors, and to a lesser extent, AT&T.

A: *How were these relationships initiated? Did these companies approach you personally, did they approach Harvard Business School, or did you seek them out as settings for research?*

P: In all these cases, they approached me directly, not through the School per se.

A: *Did your consulting jobs significantly influence your intellectual work?*

P: They taught me a lot about the difficulties involved in pulling off significant organizational change—the sources of resistance and the practical problems involved. In this sense, they certainly did. But I wouldn't say they were primary sources for my more important research ideas.

A: *I have always been interested in where you got data. For example,* Organization and Environment *looks at firms in three different industries. Were the companies you studied ones with which you had a consulting relationship?*

P: No. Really, none of the companies I did consulting with figured much in my research. I did go back to Alcan once after I had been in there to consult and asked them for research access to a particular site, but that was not a big deal. Some of my work with General Motors was explicitly designed to be action research, but as research it didn't work all that well. A lot of people speak very highly of action research as a primary research vehicle, but I haven't found it to be very workable.

A: *Why not?*

P: I think the action part of action research tends to dominate the need to properly document events. Often the client is fairly uncomfortable with the research aspect of the relationship and comes to question whether or not they are getting their consulting money's worth, or whether they are perhaps being the target of an academic experiment.

A: *What you are saying surprises me somewhat. You've said yourself that your intellectual creativity has been driven by the stimulation of real events and real problems.*

P: Well, I certainly hope it has.

A: *But isn't that statement contradictory to what you just told me?*

P: No, I don't think it is at all. I mean, I have done a lot of field research where you do get involved in real problems and issues, out of which come certain insights and observations that lead to some general findings. But for me, this has rarely happened as part of a consulting situation.

A: *That's a helpful clarification. Considering, then, that you found consulting to be a less than an ideal setting in which to develop research insights, what was your primary motivation for taking on consulting jobs? Was it financial or professional or something else?*

P: I thought it was kind of fun and interesting to do, and it was also financially rewarding. It also provided the kind of experience that sometimes found a useful carryover to teaching.

A: *Did you often relate stories from your consulting experiences in the classroom?*

P: Actually, not very often. I know a lot of teachers are good at that, but I'm not. For me, it usually took the form of being able to help make a case come alive to the students, by the way I would interpret it and the way I would talk about it.

RESEARCH AND PUBLICATIONS

A: *We've talked about teaching, administrative work, and consulting. I'd like to focus now on your research and the intellectual contributions you have made to the field of organization and management theory. Why don't we get a handle on that by going through a list of your publications chronologically. My guess is that we'll find some interesting diversions, so don't worry about my bombarding you with a strictly 1-2-3 approach.*

I'd like you to give me a sense of the motivation of the various studies that you undertook, what you saw as their key contributions, and also what the transitions were from one set of intellectual questions to the next. I'd also like to get some feel for how it happened that your work has covered such a wide range of issues and settings.

P: My first book, *Management Behavior and Foreman Attitude*, was written with Don Booz and Dave Ulrich. At the time, the three of us were graduate students and working on cases for the Administrative Practices course. We produced a long series of cases called Flint Electric which were used for many years at the School. They basically described the communications process up and down the chain of command, and all the various kinds of distortions and confusions that occurred. After we did those cases, we had the idea for this book, which told the story of the foreman who was caught in the middle between upper management and the work force. It was a topic book that grew out of case research.

A: *So you were a graduate student at the time that book was written and published?*

P: That's right. I wrote my second book, *Administering Changes*, with Harriet Ronken. It included a major rewriting of my doctoral dissertation and was based on research she and I did in the same "Flint" plant. Harriet and I spent months in there keeping daily journals on what was going on. We did long interviews with all of the principals. After we got to know them well, we would simply drop back every day and get an update on what was going on. It got so that we could tap into any place in the organization at any time. This technique evolved from the Western Electric studies. It's a very time-consuming way to study a situation, but you really achieve an in-depth understanding that you can't get any other way. The book focused mainly on conflict and collaboration between engineers and manufacturing people in the production of a new product. Essentially, Harriet wrote the first half of the book, and I wrote the second.

A: *Tell me more about the research question you were interested in.*

P: At the time, this firm was having a lot of trouble getting coordination among the various functions, and all sorts of intergroup conflict were going on. One of the things that generated the most conflict was that a new product had been invented and initiated by the "wrong" set of engineers. It was done by industrial engineers, instead of development engineers, and the latter were the stronger group in the factory. The development engineers just never could seem to make that product work for them, until they redesigned it completely to their specifications. So the problem was not so much a technical one as an organizational one.

A: *But let me backtrack for a minute. You said your first two books were based on that one enterprise, and you have described how you used intensive anthropological field research methods. To what extent would you characterize this work as theoretically informed or theoretically driven?*

P: Theory was a term that we practically never used in those days. We didn't think in terms of theory. Our basic assumption was that we were studying a phenomenon in all its complexity, and that even to talk about theory would be pretentious and misleading. We talked only about having a conceptual scheme to help guide our observations. No, our work was not particularly theory-informed. Anyway, at that time there really was very little organizational theory to build on.

A: *The research model taught today is a more positivist one: master the theory, develop propositions based on the theory, and then go out and test them empirically.*

P: Even at that time we were aware of that research model, but we thought that at such an early stage in the development of our understanding of organizations, using that model would amount to an inappropriate aping of the natural sciences.

A: *Very interesting. Let's move on with the chronology now. Can you make some links between that early work which grew out of a body of fieldwork, and some of the next steps you took?*

P: *The Changing of Organizational Behavior Patterns* was the next book I got involved in. It was the only book I ever solo-authored. Jim Clark helped me with the field work. This book looked at a supermarket chain's attempt to introduce more decentralized, participative management methods. I heard that the company was involved in this change effort, so I approached them and got permission to study the process. I made detailed observations over time and interviewed managers. I also tried some more systematic data collection that could lend itself to quantification. My basic research method was to travel with a district manager from store to store, calling on store managers, and as soon as their dialogue started, I got out my notebook and started with my little system to code the conversation—who was talking and for how long, what were the topics, whether it was a question, a direction, an explanation, or what. I then categorized the dialogue between superior and subordinate, in this case the district manager and the store manager, to see if there was a change in actual behavior over time. Different district managers had quite different management styles. These were clearly related to the success of the decentralization effort. If orders and instructions were all one-way, the store manager was unlikely to take more responsibility for making decisions on his own. I restudied the same managers two years later to record the actual change in their behavior.

I think I learned a lot from that study about why organizational change is so difficult. Although it didn't make a particularly big impression on the literature at the time, this book has recently been selected for republication as a classic.

A: *How did you explain the variation in behavior among the district managers? Did you have an organizational, or essentially a psychological, explanation for it?*

P: Well, the explanation wasn't exclusively one or the other. I attributed it both to organizational pressures and to people's self-concepts. One key manager had as part of his basic beliefs about himself that he could learn and change with the times, so he had a certain predisposition to change that the other managers really didn't seem to have.

A: *To depart from your storyline for a moment, you mentioned that this was the only book that you published on which you were the sole author. All the rest of your books have been written collaboratively. I wonder if you could say a few words about why you have chosen to work collaboratively rather than as sole author in most of your work.*

P: Well, I thought it was a more effective way to get the job done. Exchanging observations about what we were studying and getting insights into what was going on—I think it speeds up the process. You learn more from what you are doing because you can talk it over with somebody, exchange views.

A: *Did you find it harder to write this particular book, for which you were sole author?*

P: I don't remember that it was harder, but it took longer.

A: *You certainly have had a lot of collaborators. Most people probably know you have worked extensively with Jay Lorsch, but probably fewer know that you have co-authored books with—by my count—36 different individuals. It's apparent to me that you have been open to working successfully with people who bring a variety of different theoretical perspectives and research talents.*

P: I've never thought about that, but I do think it's true. One trend I see in my younger colleagues at Harvard—and I don't think it's much different from any place else—is that very few of them do collaborative research these days, and most of it seems to be for what I consider to be the wrong reasons. They seem to assume that solo work will better meet promotion requirements and help them achieve professional recognition.

A: *By comparison, was there a certain norm at the Harvard Business School in 1950s that not only permitted, but actually encouraged collaborative intellectual endeavors?*

P: Oh, absolutely. That was part of the tradition, going back to the Western Electric studies, which were of course a collaborative effort. It was taken for granted—we want to study something, we'll put a team in there. It wasn't true just at Harvard either; it was true at places like the University of Michigan and Columbia, too. Intensive fieldwork studies take more than one person to be done well. You just can't do as careful and thorough a job working on your own.

A: *Do you advocate reforming the tenure and promotion process today, to give greater weight to collaborative endeavors?*

P: I wish we could. But I'm not sure what can be done about it. Young people feel they must develop a solo track record so they can be viewed as excellent in a number of different institutional settings, and the dominant style is positivistic, quantitative, hypothesis-testing research. This has had a lot of consequences. It tends to preclude intensive fieldwork and qualitative, longitudinal, or exploratory research. It means that people are driven to study issues that are less critical and less important so they can formulate the question in a way that lends itself to quantification and hypothesis testing.

A: *Yes, I agree with that. Let me ask you a couple of other questions that come to mind about the book you are talking about now. The methodology you used was very time-intensive—you travelled around with the district managers, observed meetings, and conducted what we today might call conversational analysis or ethnomethodological fieldwork.*

I am trying to imagine you as an associate professor. You published this book in 1958. I was seven years old, my brother was one. You had just bought a new house that needed fixing up. Presumably you were teaching first year MBA courses and had a fairly heavy volume of daily classroom responsibility, administrative duties, and so forth. I am trying to visualize actually how you structured your life to spend hours every week travelling around with these district managers.

P: I recall clearing my calendar for two days a week to do research. On non-teaching days I would just get up in the morning and go off and do my research.

A: *So this means you had to concentrate all your teaching related responsibilities, not just classroom work, but grading papers, preparing lectures, and so forth, on those days in which you actually had classroom duties?*

P: Yes, that's right.

A: *I get the clear sense that doing research for you meant going out into the field, not reading in the library or writing something up in your office.*

P: As I remember, I did my analysis and writing more in the summer time, but I did the actual data collection during the school year.

A: *There's one other question I want to ask you. It applies both to this early work and to much of your subsequent work as well. Most of your books have been published by the Harvard Business School's Division of Research. Was it fairly routine in those days for the Harvard Business School to publish in-house any qualified work by its own faculty? Did you ever debate taking your work to a commercial or other academic press?*

P: Well, publishing in-house was the accepted thing to do. I'm not sure that it was too smart. The Research Division in those days was not very well organized to market its publications. But we sort of assumed that since Harvard Business School research funds were behind the research, that it should be published in-house. I don't believe we ever got any royalties. We sold mostly to academics, and the market for organizational research was nothing like it is today.

A: *Listening to you, I get the sense that you never really suffered much anxiety about getting your work published. Is that a correct assessment?*

P: Well, a panel of three people read everything for the Division of Research and decided whether or not to publish it. Occasionally they said no or sent it back to be rewritten. So it wasn't completely a sure thing. On the other hand, we didn't face the test of some publisher's saying if it won't sell a certain number of copies, it won't be done.

A: *Let's move on.*

P: My next book was *High Level Administration in a Large Organization,* written with Jack Glover. This book was an anthropological study of change in the Pentagon. Jack had the idea for it. It grew out of his long association with Gene Zuckert, who at the time was Assistant Secretary of the Air Force. Now, Jack had an awful lot of energy and a lot of enthusiasm for doing research. He really believed in very careful, rigorous fieldwork. We would spend all day interviewing and observing, and all night recording and reflecting on the day's events. We had a great time wandering around the halls of the Pentagon. I think we did a good job of identifying well the complexities of bringing about change in a big federal bureaucracy.

The next one was the case and textbook, *Organizational Behavior and Administration.* I was the senior author of that one. It went through three editions, and at one time I think it was the principal text in that area.

A: *Did that book grow out of the collaborative process of developing the Administrative Practices course at HBS?*

P: Right, and it came out not too long after I became course head.

A: *To make a general observation here, I get the sense that a lot of your intellectual work can be seen as a reflection of the organizational structure and norms of the Harvard Business School. For example, the Administrative Practices course at HBS was taught collaboratively, so you wrote a collaborative casebook with seven other authors. HBS encouraged collaborative field research, so you co-authored several studies based on intensive anthropological studies of individual organizations.*

P: That's all very true. Now, the next book was *Industrial Jobs and the Worker.* Ever since my doctoral days, I had wanted to test the idea that the content of industrial work influences workers' responses in terms of satisfaction, turnover, and absenteeism.

Art Turner and I wrote the book together. We spent a lot of time trying to conceptualize what we were trying to study and how it could be measured. We worked hard thinking through the attributes of work that are closely associated with human responses, and did some preliminary fieldwork to try and figure that one out. We came up with a system for measuring job variety, autonomy, interaction, knowledge, skill, and responsibility. Then we went to factory after factory to gather data. Then came a lot of numerical analysis, using very primitive technology—punched IBM cards in the basement of Baker Library.

A: *What were the conclusions of the study?*

P: Well, we went in there with the hypothesis that the more the work engaged a person's intellect or capacity for assuming responsibility and the more it required collaborative relationships with other people, the more positively people would respond to their work. We thought there would be an association between what you might call work "complexity" and a positive response to work. But, as a general proposition, that didn't turn out to be the case.

A: *What did explain the positive response to work?*

P: The social needs and subcultural conditioning of the workers seemed to make the difference. People with certain backgrounds responded very positively to responsibility, complexity, and the chance to make intellectual inputs into the work, and so forth. For another set of workers, though, that just seemed to add burden and make the job less attractive. Their ideal job was one where they could just put in their time, go through it pretty mechanically, and be thinking about something else.

A: *Did you look for the origin of these differences among workers?*

P: Our study wasn't designed to trace that very far. We did tease out of our data some city versus small town contrasts. There was some evidence it was associated with religion.

A: *Our family spent the summer of 1961 in London, where you were working with some colleagues at the Tavistock Institute. I later learned that those individuals were at that time involved in developing the theory that we now call the sociotechnical systems approach. Your book with Turner was published in 1965. Can you say something about the influence of the sociotechnical model on that work and on your subsequent work?*

P: Well, I was influenced by the early Tavistock coal and textile studies that were available at the time. I remember when I first began to think about designing that study, I went to Eric Trist and asked him what he thought of the research, and he gave me a good deal of encouragement, so clearly I was thinking of this work in connection with Tavistock. However, these ideas also came out of the earlier Hawthorne studies. I remember when I first started thinking about a dissertation topic, I almost chose to write on this same topic.

A: *You are probably best known for your theoretical ideas about contingency, that is, the idea that different organizational forms are appropriate under different circumstances. Am I correct that these ideas evolved, in some respects, from this work with Turner?*

P: Yes. The contingency idea started very much as a spin off from *Industrial Jobs and the Worker*. We argued in that book that to design jobs well, you have to look at people's predispositions as well as at technologies. Right away I started thinking about further organizational research along these lines. I actually persuaded Art to guide the book through publication, so I could get on with my next study.

A: *It strikes me as interesting that the contingency idea in* Industrial Jobs and the Worker *has to do with the relationship between individual predispositions and certain kinds of work. But the contingency idea that you became famous for is very different—it involves the relationship between environmental uncertainty and organizational structure. It's the same conceptual package, one thing is contingent on another, but the pair of variables was completely different in the two studies.*

P: Well, yes and no. In *Organization and Environment* we discussed people's predispositions as an environmental variable. So, it's in there, along with technology and the market, as another external element, although we didn't measure it or emphasize it in that study. Jay Lorsch did that in his subsequent book with John Morse.

A: *We seem to have moved on to* Organization and Environment. *It strikes me that for one reason or another this book came along at a time when the organizational behavior community was ready for a new idea. To make a generalization, I would say that much of organization theory before that date looked for systematic regularities in administrative behavior. Your book in a very clear way made the argument that there is no one best way to organize. That is, that organizational practices are contingent on environmental factors. This idea really turned the field intellectually.*

P: Well, I think that's right. The fact that the book has been so well received is probably a function of our having had the right idea at the right time. To tell you the truth, when Jay and I were about halfway through the manuscript, I remember saying to him that I didn't think it was likely that either of us would ever again come up with an idea with as much leverage and timeliness.

A: *To return to the question I began to explore earlier, can you make any further generalizations about how and why you got the idea at that time?*

P: When we were doing our fieldwork for *Industrial Jobs and the Worker,* it was clear that quite different organizational forms seemed to be working. For example, the lowest job complexity we found anywhere was in a plant in Montreal that made cans. We just couldn't find any jobs that scored any lower than that. It was the bottom. But the amazing thing was that this plant was tied for the top score on employee satisfaction.

I thought, what's going on here? The technology hadn't changed for decades, the market was very predictable, and the jobs were very routinized. Decisions were highly centralized, and the hierarchy was clear and strong. People were treated in a perfectly hygienic way—they had lots of baseball teams and things like that, and they had good job security. Oh, there was some pressure to get results, but all they had to do was keep the machines running and not flagrantly goof off or try to sabotage things. The hourly employees were urban French-Canadians with strong extended families. Well, they thought it was great. There was absolutely no intellectual content or concern, no responsibility, nothing. But, given this market, this technology, and this workforce and their predispositions, how can we knock it? Who was I to say that they had gotten it all wrong?

So, here was a complete organizational system that seemed to fit its particular environment. It was completely different from what we saw in specialty paper plants, for instance.

So, the contingency idea didn't come out of reading the literature or looking at theory. It came directly out of field observations.

A: *The initial insight may have come out of your field research, but I think in your book you were able in very ingenious ways to ground your notion of contingency in prior theoretical literature. In other words, you were able to build a theoretical case for an idea that apparently came out of fieldwork.*

P: Well, that's right. We did a lot of thinking about that, getting our points written up in a way that grounded them in the literature. But the fact was, that analysis took place after we had finished our fieldwork. It didn't come at the front-end, it came at the back-end.

A: *That's fascinating. Now, how would you describe the division of labor between you and Jay on the book?*

P: I designed the study and laid out what I wanted to do and then I went out and looked for a research assistant to help me do it. Jay at that time was a very bright doctoral student with great promise. I offered him the job, and he went to work with me on it. He was very effective. He and I shared the field work and the writing.

A: *Did you start with the six-fold matrix at the outset of the study?*

P: No, we built it up over time. We didn't get to the food companies until we had done the plastics and the container industries, for example.

A: *But didn't you have the key questions before you selected your sites?*

P: Yes, that's right, but the actual terms *integration* and *differentiation* didn't come to us until we were about half way through. These concepts helped us characterize what we were seeing.

A: *I want to ask about that. Did you draw these concepts from calculus?*

P: No, we got them from biology. Of course, those terms pop up in different fields, but we were thinking of the basic physiology of biological systems that have differentiated organs and integrative mechanisms like the nervous system and the circulatory system, and how with evolutionary advances more differentiated forms appeared but they could only persist as the integrative organs became more sophisticated.

A: *Were either you or Jay reading biology at the time? Literally, what made you think of the differentiation and integration analogy?*

P: I don't really know. Of course, as part of our whole tradition, we read biology, so it wasn't strange to us. I don't know exactly where the terms came from. I was rereading *Management and the Worker* not too long ago, and I was surprised to find those terms in there. They are not highlighted, but they are in there.

A: *One thing that I have always observed about you is that you have a wide-ranging intellectual curiosity about many fields and have a keen interest in many scientific areas that are not immediately related to your discipline. You are interested in biology, history, and so forth. From what we know about the history of science, often times new ideas come from the juxtaposition of two disciplines in a time of intellectual ferment when people are looking for new sets of organizing concepts. I feel that you are very good at that, because you are quite conversant with other schemas, other ways of looking at the world. This has always greatly intrigued me because I think that your formal education was actually really quite narrow and limited.*

P: Limited, perhaps, but not narrow. I was exposed to many disciplines.

A: *Turning back to your work, what came next?*

P: Jay and I did two books as direct follow-ups to *Organization and Environment*; one, *Organizational Systems*, was a compilation of follow-up studies with doctoral students and the other, *Developing Organizations: Diagnosis and Action*, was written more as a how-to book for practitioners.

Then there was a book, *Behavioral Science Concepts in Case Analysis*, with Tagiuri, Barnett, and Dunphy. This book consists of a detailed behavioral sciences analysis of some rich teaching cases. It helped clarify the linkage between theory and practice.

Then I did two chapters for a book called *Social Innovation in the City*: "Organization Development in the Black Ghetto" and "The Uses of Crisis: Dynamics of Ghetto Organization Development." Those two articles represent the only written output—a rather small amount, actually, considering the amount of time I put in—based on research I did in black and underprivileged neighborhoods. I was working with others in a project called Society and Technology that IBM funded. This was the time of the riots in major cities like Newark and Detroit. We were trying to understand and perhaps facilitate efforts to create "community business organizations," which were hybrid community organizations and commercial enterprises. Anyway, we spent time interviewing in places like Bedford-Styvesant, Newark, and ghetto areas of Boston and Cleveland. I started an elective MBA course, Organizational Development in the Inner City, at that time.

A: *This work was motivated by your concern about race relations—certainly one of the major social concerns of the time. Does this reflect a general pattern of motivation for your work?*

P: Yes, I think it does. As I said when I was talking about my childhood, I seem to have been born and bred to be concerned with social problems. My earlier work was really dictated by a generalized notion about the possibilities of improving the quality of work. These interests surfaced later in work I did on a human resource management course and a book I wrote with Dick Walton. At one time I spent quite a bit of time in medical schools and hospitals. That was motivated partly by the obvious difficulties those organizations were having in delivering good care in a cost effective manner. My current work on organizations in the Soviet Union comes out of my strong concern about international tensions and the need to reduce the nuclear hazard. Another topic I have been interested in right along is labor relations, with the idea that there must be ways of organizing to share power to improve the labor-management relationship. And then there's the issue of national competitiveness. Do we as a society have the capacity to organize to achieve both efficiency and innovation?

If we want to talk in general terms, I guess this is good evidence that my work has been primarily problem-oriented rather than theory- or methodology-driven, and that the problems that engage me are often social ones.

A: *The breadth of your social concerns strikes me as quite remarkable. I find it interesting to think about how different issues you have addressed in your career have reflected historical events. For example, your interest in race relations and inner-city organizations was raised at a time when those issues were on the historical agenda. Your concern with the Soviet Union coincided with reform there and the subsequent breakup of communism in Eastern Europe.*

P: I do think that I have gotten into some of those issues in a fairly timely way, almost in anticipation of what was to become "hot." I have always had a feel for topics of growing importance. A principle of organizational change that I learned early on is that you can often use the energy that comes from discontent to engage in restructuring and reform work. You can't really change things without a sense of crisis. Many crises come and go, however, without constructive results, because people weren't ready to steer the energy with some carefully developed ideas.

A: *That raises another question for me. I think your politics could be described as liberal. Some of the issues that you have become interested in intellectually reflect your political orientation. How did your views, for example on race relations or disarmament, fit in relative to the spectrum of opinion at the Harvard Business School? Did that create any problems for you?*

P: I think I was probably a little naive about that, but it was really never a problem as far as I could tell. The few polls that have been taken at HBS show that the student body is usually more conservative than the faculty. Also, I found that for many of these issues, focusing on organizational issues became—well, sort of an apolitical way of getting at important topics. For example, with the Soviet Union, it is possible to discuss these organizational issues without delving very far into some of the ideological differences that are more divisive. So, to answer your question, I guess that it didn't make that much difference.

A: *Let's return to the subject of urban issues.*

P: I brought my study of urban issues to a close with my research with John Kotter on mayors and city government. This work was another effort to broaden our understanding of different types of organizations. *Mayors in Action* was a good book, if I do say so myself. We emphasized the concepts of the managerial agenda and networking.

Well, moving right along. I was involved with others in putting out a whole series of smaller case books focused on special topics. As an aside, I might add that in my career I probably worked on over 200 teaching cases.

Well, then there was *Matrix*, written with Stan Davis and published in 1977. I saw that as an extension of contingency theory. At the time, the matrix organization was quite popular. That book was written especially for practitioners, and it sold very well. It had quite an impact, and I think it still represents a fairly definitive statement about that organizational form.

A: *When did you become interested in health care delivery and organization?*

P: In 1978, Marv Weisbord and Marty Charns and I wrote "Three Dilemmas of Academic Medical Centers." This article summarizes a series of articles the three of us wrote from research on medical schools and teaching hospitals done under sponsorship of the National Institutes of Health. These organizations were fascinating to study. In essence we found they had gone overboard for differentiation with virtually no integration. Little wonder they were not cost effective.

This work led directly into a study of NIH itself and Bell Laboratories, which came out in a 1981 book called *Managing Large Research and Development Programs*, written with Harry Lane and Rod Beddows. It never drew much attention, but I find that whenever I get involved in a conference on R&D work—for example, a recent seminar on biomedical research—I keep pulling out those ideas and using them with various audiences, and I find that they seem to go over very well.

A: *How did you come to undertake the project that resulted in* Renewing American Industry?

P: This book represents my interest in the problem of organizational adaptation and industrial competitiveness. It was for me a major work, at least six years in the making. I found a historian to help me with it, Davis Dyer. We worked intensively together on the fieldwork and writing for about two years. We tracked the long-term history of seven major U.S. industries: autos, steel, farming, coal, construction, hospitals, and telecommunications. It was written as a scholarly book for a general audience. The book sold reasonably well but I think the theory it proposes—a new, extended version of contingency theory—has been underappreciated.

When we started the project, I thought I was doing more of what I usually do—organizational level analysis. But I found as I analyzed the data, I was drawn almost in spite of my intentions into seeing implications more for public policy than for managerial practice. That book pulled me for the first time into addressing public policy issues. Essentially the book was about industrial policy, although it's politically unpopular to use that term.

I have written a couple of follow-up articles. I find it a particularly interesting topic and may write some more about it in the future under the general rubric of socio-economics. I believe we still do not have adequate theory to address the issue of sustaining a healthy economy.

A: *It seems to me that your ideas in* Renewing American Industry *reach over into a variety of other disciplines and fields, particularly economics and public policy. But because of the extreme segmentation of disciplines in our academic institutions, economists and public policy experts are not likely to read your work. Isn't that true?*

P: Unfortunately, yes. The same has been true of political scientists in regard to our work on mayors and city government.

A: *After the work on adaptation, you returned to some of your earlier interests in labor and human resource management issues.*

P: Yes, then I worked on *HRM Trends and Challenges*, a human resource management book edited with Dick Walton. I feel pretty good about that material. I think we helped reconceptualize the field of human resource management as a subject matter in the curriculum, and in particular helped make HRM issues more accessible to people from a general management orientation. *HRM Trends and Challenges* added to that literature by putting those issues into an historical perspective and highlighting the notion of mutual commitment. I think it has had some influence on how that material is being taught now.

A: *More recently, you've taken a look at networks among organizations.*

P: Yes, in an article with Russell Johnston, "Beyond Vertical Integration: The Rise of the Value-Adding Partnership." We described an important trend in industry not only in America, but also worldwide, that has been little recognized in the literature.

A: *Can you describe what a value-adding partnership is?*

P: Well, in a nutshell it's a relationship between two or more firms that, while independent in terms of ownership, have entered into a long-term, enriched relationship. Essentially, it's a relationship between a supplier and an industrial customer that then goes on to involve mutual help and information exchange on many other things. For example, the firms might collaborate on product design, quality improvement, or strategic planning. A lot of these things used to be considered trade secrets. It's very different from vertical integration where you get coordination through ownership, or from an alliance where one party is completely dominant.

A: *Finally, there is the US-Soviet research that led to the publication of* Behind the Factory Walls. *We started the interview talking about it. My goodness, we have come to the end of the publications list.*

P: Not quite. There's still a book I co-edited with Amitai Etzioni, *Socio-Economics: Toward a New Synthesis* that came out in 1991.

CONCLUSION

A: *Before we quit, I want to talk a little bit about writing. When I think about your writing, I think of it as being a fairly easy process for you. Do you want to make any general comments about the actual craft of writing?*

P: Well, I have never pretended to be a particularly gifted writer, but I can get my thoughts on paper, and I can grind out passable prose. You know, I've never felt I had to turn out a literary masterpiece in order to go to press. I don't do endless fine-tuning. Perfectionism is just not one of my characteristics.

A: *So that's one explanation for your extraordinary productivity. Any other secrets?*

P: I've always had a lot of curiosity and energy. There's always something I'm eager to do next. And I can keep quite a few balls in the air at one time. I must confess I have taken pride in the sheer quantity of things that I have been able to accomplish in my career.

A: *Well, we've talked about all kinds of things. Now I want to share some reactions I've had to what you've said. As I listen to you, I am developing a rudimentary theory of my own about the evolution of your work. I'd suggest to you that your work has been driven by three different influences. One is social problems that you perceive as important and that you believe organizational analysis can illuminate in some way. Second, there has been an internal unfolding of ideas, that is, some logical sequence of concepts. Questions emerged in one research project that led to new questions and subsequent projects. The third influence, it seems to me, is the case work and curriculum development you have carried out as an instructor at the Harvard Business School. Certain issues are raised in the context of the curriculum development process that then drive your work.*
    I believe your best work, the most exciting work, has come from projects where two or more of these influences come together simultaneously, ones

where you take an important insight gleaned, say, from earlier research that suddenly can be brought to bear on a new social problem that is rising in significance. You produce your best work when you are able to synthesize these motivations. Does this sound accurate to you?

P: Well, that's an interesting observation. You know, after *Organization and Environment* was written, those materials were built right into the new macro OB course. That represented one of those junctures. The idea gave a fresh impetus to the macro OB topic generally, not only at Harvard. OB up until that time had really mostly been micro, more concerned with interpersonal and small group behavior and personality theory, and was dominated by the contributions of psychologists. That book put sociology into OB in a more serious way. Subsequently, HRM has come forward as part of organizational behavior, where I think it belongs. HRM needs to address organizational arrangements for coping with significant numbers of people and the policies and frameworks under which that proceeds.

A: *Given the great variety in your work in terms of the topics you have covered and the methodologies you have used, are there any common themes you see that tie the body of your work together?*

P: I believe that organizations can best be understood as complex, dynamic systems, and that in order to advance our general knowledge of them we need to study them as systems. Different studies, of course, focus on different variables, different levels of analysis, different time slices, and so forth. I think we have advanced the field by going around the horn on various variables, doing the best we can on them, studying first this topic for a while and then that topic for a while and then recycling. I see myself working on organizations, a few pieces at a time, in order eventually to better understand the whole beast.

A: *It looks as if we've come to The End. And now, how about retirement? Knowing you, Dad, I suspect you always have some projects up your sleeve.*

PUBLICATIONS

1950

With D. Booz & D. Ulrich. *Management behavior and foreman attitude.* Cambridge, MA: Division of Research, Harvard Business School.

1952

With H. Ronken *Administering changes.* Cambridge, MA: Division of Research, Harvard Business School.

1958

The changing of organizational behavior patterns. Cambridge, MA: Division of Research, Harvard Business School.

1960

With J. Glover. *High level administration in a large organization: A case study.* Cambridge, MA: Division of Research, Harvard Business School.

1961

With J. Bailey, R. Katz, J. Seiler, C. Orth, J. Clark, L. Barnes, & A. Turner. *Organizational behavior and administration: Cases, concepts, and research findings.* Homewood, IL: Irwin. (Revised 1965; 3rd revision with J. Lorsch & L. Barnes, 1976)

1965

With A. Turner. *Industrial jobs and the worker: An investigation of responses to task attributes.* Cambridge, MA: Division of Research, Harvard Business School.

With J. Lorsch. Organizing for product innovation. *Harvard Business Review* (January-February).

1967

With J. Lorsch. *Organization and environement: Managing differentiation and integration.* Cambridge, MA: Division of Research, Harvard Business School. (Reprinted: Irwin, 1969; Harvard Business School Press, 1987)

With J. Lorsch. Differentiation and integration in complex organizattions. *Administrative Science Quarterly* (June).

1968

With R. Tagiuri, R. Barnett, & D. Dunphy. *Behavioral science concepts in case analysis.* Cambridge, MA: Division of Research, Harvard Business School.

1969

With J. Lorsch. *Developing organizations: Diagnosis and action.* Reading, MA: Addison-Wesley.

How to deal with resistance to change. *Harvard Business Review* (January-February).

Organization development in the black ghetto. In R. Rosenbloom & R. Marris (Eds.), *Social innovation in the city*. Cambridge, MA: Harvard University Program on Technology and Society.

The uses of crisis: Dynamics of ghetto organization development. In R. Rosenbloom & R. Marris (Eds.), *Social innovation in the city*. Cambridge, MA: Harvard University Program on Technology and Society.

1970

Edited with J. Lorsch. *Studies in organizational design*. Homewood, IL: Irwin.

With G. Dalton & L. Greiner. *Organizational change and development*. Homewood, IL: Irwin.

With G. Dalton & J. Lorsch. *Organizational structure and design*. Homewood, IL: Irwin.

With G. Dalton. *Motivation and control in organizations*. Homewood, IL: Irwin.

1972

With J. Lorsch. *Organization planning: Cases and concepts*. Homewood, IL: Irwin.

With J. Lorsch. *Managing group and intergroup relations*. Homewood, IL: Irwin.

1974

With J. Kotter. *Mayors in action: Five approaches to urban governance*. New York: Wiley.

1975

Individual differences in the world of work. In Cass & Zimmer (Eds.), *Man and work in society*. New York: Van Nostrand Reinhold.

1977

With S. Davis. *Matrix*. Reading, MA: Addison Wesley.

With H. Kolodny & S. Davis. The human side of the matrix. *Organizational Dynamics* (Summer).

1978

With S. Davis. Problems of matrix organizations. *Harvard Business Review* (May-June).
With J. Sonnenfeld. Why do companies succumb to price fixing? *Harvard Business Review* (July-August).
With M. Weisbord & M. Charns. Three dilemmas of academic medical centers. *The Journal of Applied Behavioral Science, 14*(3).

1981

With H. Lane & R. Beddows. *Managing large research and development programs.* Albany, NY: SUNY Press.

1983

With D. Dyer. *Renewing American industry.* New York: Free Press.

1984

With M. Beer, B. Spector, Q. Mills, & R. Walton. *Managing human assets.* New York: Free Press.

1985

With M. Beer, B. Spector, Q. Mills, & R. Walton. *Human resource management: A general manager's perspective.* New York: Free Press.
Edited with R. Walton. *HRM: Trends and challenges.* Cambridge, MA: Harvard Business School Press.
The HRM futures colloquium: The managerial perspective. In R. Walton & P.R. Lawrence (Eds.), *HRM: Trends and challenges.* Cambridge, MA: Harvard Business School Press.
The history of human resource management in American industry. In R. Walton & P.R. Lawrence (Eds.), *HRM: Trends and challenges.* Cambridge, MA: Harvard Business School Press.

1987

Historical development of organizational behavior. In J. Lorsch (Ed.), *The Handbook of organizational behavior.* Englewood Cliffs, NJ: Prentice-Hall.
Competition: A renewed focus for industrial policy. In D. Teece (Ed.), *Strategy and organizations for industrial innovation and renewal.* Cambridge, MA: Ballinger.

1988

With R. Johnston. Beyond vertical integration—The rise of the value-adding partnership. *Harvard Business Review* (July-August).

1989

Why organizations change. In A. Mohrman, S. Mohrman, G. Ledford, T. Cummings, & E. Lawler (Eds.), *Large-scale organizational change*. San Francisco, CA: Jossey-Bass.

1990

With C. Vlachoutsicos, I. Faminsky, E. Brakov, S. Puffer, E. Walton, A. Naumov, & V. Ozira. *Behind the factory walls: Decision making in Soviet and US enterprises*. Cambridge, MA: Harvard Business School Press.
With C. Vlachoutsicos. What we don't know about Soviet management. *Harvard Business Review* (November-December).

1991

With A. Etzioni. *Socio-Economics: Toward a new synthesis*. Armonk, NY: M.E. Sharpe.

Edmund P. Learned

Reflections on Leadership, Teaching, and Problem Solving Groups

EDMUND PHILIP LEARNED

The Learned family in America was founded by Benjamin Learned who came to the Massachusetts Bay Colony in 1630. My Father was born in Maine and came to Kansas in the early 1880s. He had seven years of apprentice-journeyman training in Maine and lived with the merchant's family who trained him. He had no more formal training but had a very successful career as a merchandise manager and first floor supervisor in a department store.

My Mother, Alice Preisach Learned, was born in Lawrence, Kansas in 1861. Her parents had come from France to Indiana where they were neighbors of the Studebakers. They moved to Lawrence late in the 1850s. She graduated from high school and went to work in the same store that my Father first joined.

Both parents proved to be very bright people who were determined that their children should have a good college education or more. Beginning in the 5th grade of elementary school, I began to receive high grades and received responsible assignments from principals. I was tied for the top of my class in high school and was the ranking student in the Economics Department of the University of Kansas in Lawrence.

My parents deserve credit for making their sons "achievers" in any opportunity that became available to them. Salaries were low in Lawrence. My parents offered housing and food while sons were in college, but we had to earn our college expenses. At age 13, I earned $27 for three months work on a farm, the next year $15 a month, and the third year $35 a month. When the United States had joined World War I, Camp Funston was being built at Fort Riley, Kansas, and I worked as a laborer building warehouses. I

151

worked seven days a week for $30 a week. I had also worked one summer on a 12-hour night shift at the local corrugated box factory at 17½ cents an hour. I earned enough to pay part of my college expenses.

While in college I had several jobs, some of them simultaneously. I worked in the College Library paging books (a great learning experience) and at the circulation desk, earning 25 to 35 cents per hour. I was brakeman on the printing press of the local paper, and I also wrapped magazines that the newspaper published for an insurance company. Finally I graded papers for courses in Economic History of England, Economic History of the United States, and Money and Banking at 75 cents an hour.

I never expected to be a professor. I had taken Spanish in order to be eligible to be employed by National City Bank, now Citicorp. For several years it had been employing the ranking student in economics. However, the 1920-21 depression put a stop to that. I therefore took courses in education to qualify for a State Teachers Certificate. Without experience in teaching, I was given an offer to teach at a Kansas City, Missouri high school. I was given a slight raise at the Library while I waited for the formal high school offer at $1,400 a year.

Early in July, the head of the Department of Economics asked me to teach the introductory economics course in the Summer School and said he would ask the University to make me an Instructor in Economics beginning in September. If the Kansas City offer came first, I felt an obligation to accept it. Fortunately the University offer came first and my academic career began. I taught there for three years and four summers before going to Harvard. My initial salary was $1,800, which was increased each year, and was finally $2,300. I married Zella Rankin (Kansas University AB '21) of Albuquerque, New Mexico, on August 30, 1922. For almost 63 years she was my strong supporter in many opportunities that no one could foresee. These proved to be the basis of any contributions to various areas of management that I may have made.

During my teaching years at KU, I taught a course in Economics each term in different combinations with courses in Industrial and Commercial Geography, Accounting I and lab, Accounting II, and Elements of Economics (in the School of Engineering). The Geography course proved of great value when I taught in Hawaii, Japan and Europe. An undergraduate course in European Industry and Commerce had later value when I taught in Europe. Our readings on Russia provided background for understanding the Russian revolution and the tactics of Stalin during World War II. Little did I ever expect this course to be useful when I was on the Headquarters Army Air Force staff in charge of Program Control in World War II.

My Master's thesis was on Gasoline Taxes and was the first book published under my name. It was also the first book on that subject. I concluded that a tax of over 3 cents might reduce demand; up to that point demand was inelastic. In the 1980s taxes of 9 cents, after allowing for inflation, were lower than the 1920 tax of 3 cents.

Courses in Political Science and Psychological Sociology proved very useful in understanding people and organizations at work.

Junior professors or instructors in economics and accounting discussed course content, choice of teaching materials and/or texts as well as student reactions. This teamwork approach was later used at Harvard Business School and in the consulting jobs or government work in which I was involved.

I had originally planned to go to the University of Chicago for graduate work in economics but several KU professors who had attended the Harvard Business School urged me to go there, and I took their advice.

I took the required first-year courses of Marketing, Finance, Industrial Management, Statistics, and Auditing (a second-year course). At the end of the first term, as one of three with the highest grades in my class, I was elected to the Student Board of the Harvard Business Review Board. Other ranking students were added to this Board at the end of the year and together we prepared the student section of the Review. I was made editor of the Legal Section.

We had some great teachers in our first-year and outstanding lectures by Dean Wallace Donham, and Visiting Lecturers such as Mr. Elton Mayo, Mrs. Lillian Gilbreth, and two Presidents and other representatives of the so-called Taylor System of Management. We had 28 written reports during the year based upon case studies prepared by the various courses, but we had limited instruction in report writing.

In the second year the two-term Business Policy I course was a required course. Business executives presented cases, and a report by students was directed to each executive. Many students dreaded the experience, but it turned out to be very valuable in their future jobs.

Another required second year two-term course was Business Policy II. The first term was Business History and the second term was Business Economics. By the second half year, the impact of the historical perspective became evident in both class discussions and written reports.

As a member of the Student Board of the *Harvard Business Review* Board, I was limited to four courses per term for credit, rather than the fifth required of other students. I took two other two term courses for credit in the second year: one in Industrial Accounting and one in Advanced Principles of Accounting. In addition I audited a course in Banking for the full year and frequently visited a course in Retailing.

With a solid training in Accounting and Finance, I thought I might be chosen by Goldman Sachs, who employed high ranking students during the summer of the first-year and chose most of them as permanent employees. However, with a wife and two small children, I could not leave for New York and instead took a summer job with Hood Rubber Company that involved auditing branch accounts. Many of the auditors seemed to be afraid to ask their boss a question and came to me instead. That situation made me think about superior/subordinate relations about which more will be said later.

Early in the second year, Associate Dean Biddle asked me not to accept a job on graduation without first consulting him. The faculty had voted to expand the first-year entering class from 400 to 600, and one new professor would be needed in each first-year course. The heads of the first-year finance, accounting, and marketing courses asked that I be appointed as an instructor beginning September 1, 1927. I accepted an appointment in Marketing at $2,000, with expected raises of $200 each year for the next three years. When Dean Biddle made the offer, he also warned me that I would need at least $500 more to cover living expenses. I borrowed from my father and my wife's father as needed. By 1939, I had paid back all I owed.

I turned down an Antioch College offer of an Associate Professorship in Accounting and a second offer as Assistant to the President at $3,500. One other Business School made an offer of $6,000. A second Business School made an offer after I had accepted the Harvard Business School offer, and the Gillette Razor Company of Boston offered me a position which I declined.

The first year as instructor in Marketing, I attended the classes of Professor Copeland and Professor Lewis in order to observe their different teaching styles and to better supervise the grading of Marketing reports and interviewing of students. The second year I taught two sections while Professor Copeland was on leave of absence. The second term I concentrated on my doctoral dissertation on "Quantity Buying from the Seller's Point of View" and continued supervision of the graders in Marketing. The third year I was made an Assistant Professor at $4,500 a year and taught two sections of Marketing each term. Professors rotated sections so that until 1935 I had been exposed to nearly all the first-year class members.

Dean Donham called me to his office after my doctor's degree was awarded. He described the ten greatest books in his law profession and urged me to do research in the marketing field for as long as 15 to 25 years, after which I should write one of the "great" books in the field. However, he later gave me many other assignments that spoiled this objective.

Professor Copeland asked me to direct three Marketing research assistants in the preparation of case materials for his third edition of "Problems in Marketing." Research assistants collected the data by interviews. The cases revealed the main problems to be solved by management, the ones we expected our students to solve before coming to class or in their reports. Possible solutions management was considering and any differences of opinions of members of management or possible customers were presented in the cases. Our method of research was inductive in character. Generalizations were tentative and revised as more data and experience so justified.

By the time I was an associate professor, I was drafted by my senior colleagues and the Dean to head the Marketing course. When I took over, I asked the teaching group to meet together weekly to review cases and our class discussion experiences. My senior colleagues had fun initiating me, and new younger professors had an opportunity to learn from the group interaction. Thereafter, the first Learned edition of "Problems in Marketing" was produced.

The booming stock market of the late 1920s and the long depression of the 1930s had a major impact on the Harvard Business School. I was one of those who disapproved of the questionable tactics of Investment Bankers that gave a selected few a chance to buy new issues at lower than the public offering price. Such views contributed to the decision to establish an elective course in Business Ethics. The founder of that course invited professors from the Economics and Government Departments of Harvard College, the Law School, the Divinity School, and the Business School to attend monthly discussions led by a member who chose the topic of the meeting. Topics included social and economic issues such as labor relations, the National Recovery Act, collapse of commodity prices, hunger, and so forth.

Mr. Hugh Cabot gave up teaching and sponsored a discussion group of guests from selected major companies in the United States. This group met once a month on Friday, Saturday, and Sunday mornings. Topics varied from month to month. Speakers made remarks designed to stimulate thought on public policies and business policies that would affect the recovery period and lead to constructive action by companies. After the passage of the anti-trust Robinson-Patman Act and its enforcement by the Federal Trade Commission, Cabot asked Professor Isaacs and me to conduct one Saturday morning session.

In another joint venture, I was one of four Business School professors who had School appointments in both the Graduate School of Business Administration and the Littauer School of Public Administration (now known as the Kennedy School of Government).

In September 1939, when I was made a Professor of Marketing, I was asked to reorganize the first-year Statistics course with the help of the current course faculty. I worked with them until the United States joined World War II.

Next the faculty established the Industrial Administrator (IA degree), a three-term program. Dean Donham gave me a directive to establish the Management Control course that would merge the human relations concepts of Professor Fritz Roethlisberger and the control concepts of Professor Ross Walker. Our outline for the course, sources of existing cases, and plans for new ones were established with the help of two excellent research assistants.

In less than two months, General Marshall, in a secret letter of September 1941, invited me to attend the first two-month Civilian Orientation Course at the U.S. Army Command and General Staff School at Fort Leavenworth, Kansas. I graduated with a superior record the day before the Pearl Harbor disaster. Robert Stevens (later Secretary of the Army), Lt.Col. McNarney of the New York National Guard, and I reported to General Marshall the following Monday (December 8) to provide reactions to the program. He informed us there would be later requests for our services. General Staff doctrine and command relationships we learned at Leavenworth had many implications for managing organizations.

The Management Control course at the Business School had a successful first run. Fritz Roethlisberger and I were also able to adapt it to a Retraining Program for Executives whose businesses were practically shut down because of materials shortages or who were willing to leave their businesses, to join some of the many war agencies or the armed services.

Thus, by January-February 1942, I was involved in Statistics, Management Control, and the first Retraining Program. I was also Chairman of the Committee on Instruction, Chairman of a Special Committee of seven Professors to recommend to the Dean program changes required by the War, and had begun, with Mr. Cecil Fraser, negotiations with the War Department for a Statistical Officer Candidate School at the Harvard Business School.

On May 8, 1942 Lt. Charles B. Thornton, Chief of the Statistical Control Staff in Headquarters Army Air Forces asked the Harvard Business School to bring a group to Washington to plan a program and curriculum for the Statistical Officer Candidate School that was to begin in June. Major John F. Heflin was named Military Commander and I was named Director of Training. The objective of the School was to train officers to be capable of providing facts and analyses of operations so that commanders of combat, training, transport, and materiel units at various levels could exercise command intelligently.

The statistical reporting system eventually developed by the Statistical Control Division of Headquarters Army Air Forces also required reports from overseas commands. Data in these reports and analyses thereof by the Division were available to the units under the Assistant Chiefs of Staff for planning or operating decisions.

All the young men on the original teaching staff were appointed as Special Consultants to Statistical Control, at $10 a day plus travel, in order to gather data at the field command level on the possible use of the statistical reports about to be designed. In fact senior officers in the Statistical Control Division (recruited from business) and instructors from the Statistical Officer Candidate School (in their late 20s or early 30s) together wrote directives in their areas of acquired expertise. I went to Washington once a week as a Special Consultant to the Statistical Control Division to coordinate the work of the Stat School and Headquarters.

There are two histories of the Stat School on file at Harvard Business School archives, one by me and one by Dan Smith, who became the second Director of Training.

There were several other opportunities to serve in government. In 1941, before I became Director of Training at the Stat School, the Department of the Interior under Secretary Harold Ickes had chosen me as Gasoline Administrator. While negotiating for the Stat School, I received a phone call from a former student, Colonel Bobrink of the Quartermaster Corps offering an appointment as a Lt. Colonel in charge of Military Requirements. I was unable to accept either of these jobs at the times they were offered.

In December 1943, Dean David received a phone message from General Giles (a copy of which was sent to me) as follows:

> This is General Giles, Chief of Staff, Army Air Forces, calling for General Arnold in his absence. We have a big job which calls for the service of one of your men. I am calling you to ask for immediate concurrence in the AAF drafting Dr. Edmund Learned immediately.
>
> As you may know, the overall Program of the AAF is an extremely complex problem. For the past two years, we have been trying to control the widely diversified phases of the program, and we are still having difficulty. The job of pulling the various parts of the program together calls for a top-grade, control-minded officer, who has vision and the understanding necessary to keep all of the many factors in balance.
>
> I have been told that there is only one man who can fill that job, and that is Dr. Learned. His contribution to the AAF and to the war effort could be no greater in any other area than in helping us establish and maintain effective program control.
>
> We realize that it means a considerable sacrifice on your part, but we are counting on your assistance in making Dr. Learned available to the Air Force. We shall commission him a full colonel immediately, and we are preparing the necessary directives to give him full authority. He will have my backing in getting this job done.

General Giles wrote a Memorandum to the Assistant Chief of Air Staff, Operations, Commitments and Requirements (OC&R) on the subject of Program Control as follows:

> It is directed that you establish immediately a Deputy Chief of OC&R for Program Control with full authority and responsibility for the establishment, maintenance and control of the Army Air Force Program in all its phases. This will be the single agency for control of the program, and no other Army Air Forces Office or agency will take action affecting the program without the coordination and concurrence of the Deputy for Program Control.
>
> At the earliest practicable date, the Deputy for Program Control will prepare, in book form or other suitable method, an adequate presentation of the Army Air Forces Program which will reflect the plans, requirements, and progress of its various components, and will maintain such a presentation on a current basis.
>
> The Deputy for Program Control is further charged with the responsibility of defining for all agencies affected, all quantitative requirements for recruitment, procurement, production, allocation and movements necessary for the implementation of the Army Air Forces Program as established by decisions of the Commanding General. The Deputy for Program Control will work in close conjunction with Statistical Control to assure the availability of accurate data reflecting the status of the Army Air Forces at all times.
>
> It is further directed that immediate action be taken to carry out the provisions of this directive, and that a written report of actions contemplated and accomplished be forwarded to this office.

The above directive became the effective basis of the Offices of Program Control and Program Monitoring (Office of Chief of Staff) which I headed from December 13, 1943 to August 31, 1945. However, by my choice, I served as a civilian rather than a commissioned officer.

The Assistant Chief of Staff for Operations, Commitments and Requirements, as well as his operating deputy, said the above directive exceeded their power. I therefore proposed that my title be Adviser for Program Control. Later when General Ira Eaker became Deputy Commanding General, he moved my office to the Office of the Chief of Staff and called it Office of Program Monitoring. I am omitting detail descriptions of these offices. However, it is important to note that I was able to exercise the power of the original directive since I reported to the Commanding General of the Air Forces as well as to the Assistant Chief of Staff for Operations. I told the Assistant Chief of Staff and his Deputy that I would prepare directives and procedures prescribed by my office and send them to their office for official signature. Within three months they told me to sign my own directives, but it was necessary for me to use my academic title, Dr. E.P. Learned since the title *Mr.* would have indicated a military rank of Warrant Officer.

My major problem was how to enlist the support of the Assistant Chiefs of Staff. I asked each of them to nominate an officer for appointment to my staff who would then communicate back to them. In my opinion this arrangement was the perfect example of task force management.

Air Force Colonel Johnson was doing excellent work with a contractor that had been employed by the White House to find out what was wrong with the Army Air Force Program. I took over the management of this contract and supervised its completion. The initial output was 450 pages in three volumes. At one Air Staff meeting a representative of the Joint Production Survey Committee demanded to see the books at once at the White House. My superior officers told me to present and explain the books but not to surrender them. The presentation was well received by the Committee. I appeared many times as a witness before them, largely to inform the other services of Air Force procedures. We made periodic revisions of the Program Books.

Air Force Commanding General Arnold loaned a copy of the Program Books to General Marshall, Commanding General of the Army. He, in turn, gave a copy to his Deputy Chief of Staff, General McNarney. McNarney suggested to me that Air Force Program Control should sponsor a manpower study. The Air Force Chief of Staff turned to me, and said, "That is an order." We did produce manpower studies, and the net result of the periodic Program and Manpower Books was a saving of 200,000 spaces (men). Later some of these spaces were used when the number of B-29 bomber groups was increased.

Assistant Secretary of War Lovett asked me to visit the Training Command Headquarters and The Third Air Force to obtain from their commanding generals information that should improve the programming process. Both commanding generals gave helpful information.

The Commanding General of the Training Command reported conflicting requirements submitted by Air Staff/Personnel and Air Staff/Training. On return from the Training Command at Fort Worth I asked a colonel from the Assistant Chief of Staff/Personnel and one from the Assistant Chief of Staff/Training to join with one of my staff members and me to review the differences pointed out by the Training Command. We met all day every day for a week until the two colonels came to agreement on each difference, and that was accomplished at noon on Saturday. This meeting convinced me that I should establish a consolidated training directive with elaborate procedures to result in an agreed upon training program to be signed jointly by the Assistant Chief of Staff/Training and the Assistant Chief of Staff/Personnel.

The results of joint planning by Program Control and its Air Staff counterparts were illustrated in the meeting of the Air Staff Requirements Board of March 1944. In February 1944 the AAF had its largest loss of bombers, far exceeding established planning factors. Even so, Program Control proposed reducing procurement by 4,000 bombers because of a change in planning factors.

I had asked a major on my staff to make the presentation to the Board. I did not attend the Board meeting because I wanted to test if the careful preparation of data would stand up before a board of general officers. The major returned with a long face and said, "We lost. General Giles asked where you were. He said that henceforth you would be a full member of the Board sitting with the generals and making recommendations for the numbers in the Aircraft Program." The Assistant Chief of Staff/OC&R confirmed this officially. Thereafter, two majors, one from Program Control and one from the Requirement Division of Operations, Commitments and Requirements, sat behind me at meetings of the Board and were prepared to answer in detail any questions asked by a Board member.

The savings resulting from aircraft program planning were phenomenal by 1940 values. Bombers then cost about $250,000 each. A total of 14 billion dollars in authorized expenditures and 9 billion dollars in appropriated funds was saved between February 1944 and August 1945.

Secretary of War Lovett had to approve the Board's recommendations. He approved the aircraft cutbacks but not the corresponding cutbacks in crew personnel. His reply was that bombers can be produced in about three months, but pilots take over two years to train. The result of this decision was best illustrated in 1945 at one air base where 30,000 pilots were competing for flying time necessary to maintain their efficiency.

The preparation of the Manpower Books provided good training for the Air Staff and the Commands. Working out detailed responses to the directive and showing complete programs for 12 months ahead in printed books did much to clarify the missions and schedules of the various Commands. Cooperation of Commands was generally good, with two exceptions. One Command was informed their figures were unacceptable because they had added to their manpower requirement 30,000 more persons than were really needed.

The Transport Command made no response to the directive. The Assistant Chief of Staff/Air Staff/OC&R called the Commanding General of the Transport Command who asked for a conference with the Program Control Office. Then the Commanding General asked his Chief of Staff whether the Command had received the directive. The reply was yes. The Commanding General said "Why in the hell didn't you respond? Get going on it, and do a first class job." The young captain assigned the task of preparing the book, using guidance and resources of Program Control, completed the task and later received a Legion of Merit in which the citation referred to the Manpower Book.

Program Control had a wide variety of tasks, only a few of which will be mentioned hereafter. In August 1944 General Arnold stated that the Joints Chiefs of Staff thought there was a possibility that the war in Europe would end November 1, 1944. The end of the Japanese war was projected for December 1946. He predicted that the Training Command might be reduced to 40% of its current size and said, "Now you go out and find out if this is correct." The subsequent analysis confirmed General Arnold's intuitive estimate of the necessary reduction. From this point on monthly updates on aircraft requirements were produced. Two sets of figures were produced—one front (Japan) and two front (Europe and Japan). Field actions, particularly the Battle of the Bulge, made changes necessary in projected dates and requirements. After the Battle of the Bulge we also made 10-day running estimates of Air Force aircraft and personnel losses. I was informed by the Air Staff Plans Office of changes in end of war dates. When any major changes were made, I also informed 25 officers on my key task force, so that our projections could be promptly updated.

In March 1945, after General Eisenhower estimated the end of the European war, we stopped all current planning and began planning only for the one front war on Japan. As an example of the role of the Program Office, information came to me that the Chief of Staff had approved bomb requirements which I knew were too high. He had asked for 350,000 tons of explosive bombs and 60,000 tons of incendiary bombs per month. The Air Force had never dropped more than 100,00 tons of bombs per month in Europe. I asked a group of officers to develop a better answer, and told them that it would be my job then to convince the Chief that his figures were too high. The answer was provided and the Chief accepted it.

A few more significant actions taken by the Program Office follow. Secretary Lovett gave me a week to save a billion dollars. Cooperation of a key office enabled me to save a total of $1,400,000,000. By spring 1945, it was obvious to all of the armed services that the Japanese war would be ending soon, well before the originally projected date. (This conclusion was reached when the successful test of the atomic bomb was reported to headquarters.) The Program Office immediately began planning for demobilization and for a change from a one front war to a postwar Air Force, recommended to be 105 groups. Program books for this plan were published in July 1945.

At the end of the Japanese war, General Arnold asked for the discharge of one million men before Christmas. He said, "The wives and sweethearts want these men back, and the men want the women. Why not save the government the expense?" A point system had been established for eligibility for discharge. However, the Air Forces had a surplus of men eligible for discharge, and I offered to the commanding generals of the Ground Forces and the Service Forces whatever number of these surplus officers and enlisted men they could use, and that offer was accepted.

Judge Patterson, Under Secretary of War, and I made presentations before the Joint Business Labor Advisory Council to explain the approved personnel cutbacks in the Army Forces (Ground, Air and Service Forces). Justice Byrnes, on leave from the Supreme Court and acting virtually as deputy to the President, presided at the meeting. The meeting was a great success. Labor leader Gompers asked no questions, but Philip Murray not only asked good questions but stated that he had learned what he needed to know to prepare his union for the readjustment period.

On October 5, 1945 Secretary Lovett sent a memorandum to General Arnold on the Need for Improved and Increased Business Management Procedures and Solutions Through Establishment of Office of an Air Comptroller General. Secretary Lovett believed that "the Office of Air Comptroller General should include the functions of the Office of Program Monitoring, the Office of Statistical Control and the Budget and Fiscal Office. These offices could perhaps become divisions of the new Staff Agency." No action was taken immediately.

The new Secretary of the Air Force Symington demanded action, and Deputy Commanding General Eaker asked my advice. He had provided for such advice in a directive relieving me from full time assignment of Chief of the Office of Program Monitoring and reassigning me for duty as special consultant to the Commanding General, AAF, on a part time basis. My general responsibility was to be: "a. General supervision for the Commanding General, of program monitoring and related activities; b. Periodic review of AAF programs and planning procedures with a view to recommendations for changes or improvements; c. Special assignments as directed by the Commanding General or Deputy Commanding General."

Several key recommendations I made to General Eaker will be stated here. I agreed that the proposed Air Comptroller Office should be established, and

I recommended that it should report directly to the Commanding General. I listed the qualifications which I recommended for the chief of the office, and at the same time warned against filling the chief's position with a military officer who happened to be available but did not have the qualifications needed. I suggested that a better title for the office should be chosen. I indicated that the purpose of Secretary Lovett's memo was to give the Commanding General of AAF, who in business terms is the chief executive of the AAF, the same kind of advice and technical assistance that the chief executive of a large business organization has available. The Air Comptroller would provide that assistance and coordination to the Commanding General but would not be charged with any of the command functions of the AAF.

Over the years of consulting with the Air Forces Comptroller's Office I helped them define their mission. I advised on special problems and projects on request, working with several different comptrollers and Assistant Secretaries.

General Rawlings was the first Air Force Comptroller after the Army Air Force became the United States Air Force. Later, when he became head of the Air Force Material Command, he invited me to work with him and his staff to improve planning and programming practices.

In 1949 Congress established the position of Comptroller in the Department of Defense, to be a civilian Assistant Secretary. Before the effective date, Department of Defense Secretary Forrestal appointed a Board of Accountants (known as the Vorhees Board) to give him advice in making this new position fully effective.

Air Force Secretary Symington asked the Vorhees Board to appear before the Department of Defense Secretaries and the Chiefs of the three services. The Board recommended a strong comptroller of the Department of Defense and a civilian comptroller with a military deputy in each department. I expressed opposition to the proposal as far as the Air Force Comptroller's Office was concerned.

Secretary Symington asked me to meet with the Vorhees Board in New York to explain why I was opposed to following their recommendation for Air Force Comptroller. The experience in the Air Force with a military comptroller and a civilian deputy had been very successful. I made no recommendation for other Defense departments. The Board did not disagree with me.

My recommendation to Secretary Symington was that an agreement should be reached between the Secretary of the Air Force and the Comptroller of the Department of Defense (and if necessary with the Secretary of Defense) that the comptroller should be regarded at headquarters and at command level, as a member of the military staff team and should receive and accept military orders consistent with the technical directive of the Defense Department.

I returned to full time active duty as a civilian on the Air Staff January 1951. I was a Special Consultant to General Vandenberg, the Commanding General of the Air Force. This time I was also assigned as Special Assistant to the Deputy Chief of Staff/ Materiel. The third role was to guide Harvard Business School personnel on contracts between Harvard and the Air Force.

During this Korean War period we kept a log of all the offices with which I had contacts or involvement, and it is extensive and broad but too numerous to list. It included two special projects for the Training Programs, advice to seven Air Force offices and commands (both headquarter and field), and consultation on 13 subjects which involved more than one office. A few of these will be highlighted.

I was made chairman of a group which worked on an Air Force manpower study. The minimum statement of resulting savings was 260,000 in personnel for a savings of $854 millon annually.

In an Air Materiel staff meeting I heard a figure, concerning the number of aircraft required on the ground for every aircraft in the air, which seemed excessive to me. I decided to investigate and formed a task force to do that. I asked one depot commander if engines could be flown to a base instead of shipped by freight, and he said yes. The estimated savings of $1.5 billion in two fiscal years were used to buy additional aircraft for a larger air force.

At one point Commanding General Vandenberg was dissatisfied with the staff work. On a Friday he met separately with three different groups of colonels, described how staff work was done when he worked at that level, and asked their assessment of what was currently wrong. Their responses convinced him that some action was needed. On Monday morning he called his Assistant Deputy Chief of Staff McKee and me in, reported his Friday meetings, and gave us till afternoon to give some recommendation on what to do. General McKee and I recommended that a one-week orientation course be developed, required for all officers (including generals) reporting for duty, and offered once a month. This recommendation was accepted and implemented.

The goal of the course was to improve staff work. The content included the perspectives of the Air Force Secretaries and key units of the Air Staff, as presented by them, and The Theory and Philosophy of Staff Procedures and Operations, as presented by me in a long speech. I attended every session of the course offerings, and on the next to last day I answered questions from the participants. The course closed with a final speech by the Vice Chief of Staff. Air Staff work did improve. It also resulted in several additional courses being offered at George Washington University, many of which I taught. One of these was a course specifically designed for Wing Commanders. General Vandenberg required all the Wing Commanders to attend one of the multiple offerings, and he spoke at the first one.

In February 1954 one general asked me for suggestions regarding changes in planning procedures. He said that several Air Staff officers had developed a weapons system concept. He felt that there was an urgent need for one central office in Air Staff to control the entire AAF program, on a weapons system basis. I agreed on the centralization issue and suggested that the choice for that responsibility be between the Assistant for Programming or in a new small office under the Assistant Vice Chief of Staff. I recommended the latter. When General White became Chief of Staff, he settled this issue by creating a Deputy Chief of Staff for Plans and Programming. This move recognized the long interrelationship between the functions of planning and programming and accomplished the centralization at a higher level in the Air Staff.

Secretary of Defense McNamara and Secretary of the Air Force Zuckert were both former students of mine and also had been instructors in the Army Air Force Statistical Officers Candidate School. Air Force Chief of Staff McConnell and I first met during the negotiations for the foregoing school. As a result of these prior contacts, there were many demands during the Kennedy and Johnson administrations for my consultation on a wide variety of subjects. Most of them are too technical to mention, but I will mention one interesting incident.

I refer to an interview at the Harvard Business School with an Air Force colonel who arrived at my office carrying a machine gun. He had with him on his back, a 2-foot-high stack of papers. These included highly classified war plans against an enemy country, as supporting documents for a request by General LeMay, Air Force Chief of Staff, for *one billion dollars* for B-1 bombers.

I knew Secretary McNamara would never approve such a sum. Neither would I, and without my approval, Secretary Zuckert would also disapprove. It should be noted that LeMay's proposal for a B-1 bomber was very important to him. He was near retirement and wanted to insure that a first class weapon system would replace the aging B-52s. I called the Vice Chief of Staff on my private line to find out how much I could say to the colonel. He indicated I should give him honest opinions and follow up by mailing him a top-secret statement of these by registered mail. In a humorous vein, I said the proposal looked as if some officer was trying to win a promotion by his staff study. I asked the colonel if he would return to my office with a revision, and he agreed. Three weeks later, without machine gun, he came with a request for *two hundred million dollars.* I agreed. Secretary Zuckert and Secretary McNamara agreed, and put it in the budget request. Senator Proxmire, a former distinction student of mine, managed to kill the proposal in the Senate. His argument succeeded because of the high cost of the Vietnam War.

Throughout my Air Force full time headquarters and my consulting years, I tried to introduce the best methodology of business. I did not hesitate to be very frank and very firm. I demanded high standards and usually was pleased with the responses. There were no dollar limits on faculty earnings from consulting (only limits on hours away from Business School work). The $25 to $75 per day consulting fees for my Air Force consulting were far less than the fees for business consulting. However, I never regretted giving up lucrative business consulting to serve as an Air Force consultant.

I had the greatest respect for the general officers, and for other officers and civilians I worked with on task forces, and I learned a lot from them which I was able to use in the Air Force and later at the Harvard Business School. Only two generals that I dealt with could be considered close to incompetent. I enjoyed the Washington experience and found the appearances before Congress and at the White House truly rewarding. I had pride in my contributions to better organization and communications. I think my greatest satisfaction was in the proof of the value of task force management to problem solving and in the resulting enormous dollar savings in government spending, some of which have been indicated in this manuscript.

Just before the Germans surrendered in Europe, Dean Donald David of the Harvard Business School called me in Washington and ask me to return to the school. He offered me a choice of becoming Associate Dean (which had already been approved by President Conant and the senior faculty) or heading a new course in the first-year of the postwar M.B.A program. Since I knew that General Arnold would not release me until the war with Japan was over, I urged the Dean to appoint Stanley Teele, Associate Dean, since he was the Dean's other choice for these two positions. Moreover, I was genuinely interested in the new course and was challenged to lead a group of instructors in its development. The new course was part of a full-year program called Elements of Administration. It was called Administrative Practices and was a blend of administration, management problems, and human relations.

The book *Executive Action* (1951) was based on material from Administrative Practice cases and field research by the authors and Kenneth Andrews and John Sensibaugh.

First, executives who are concerned about building organizations that will operate effectively and also provide people with satisfying activities need to recognize that the process is a continuous one.... No one organization plan.... will suffice to solve the problem once and for all. Second,...the task of top management was no longer a one-man job.... Most executives underrated the need for securing the participation of men from other departments and staff groups in working out problems of common interest. (p. 209)

Many department heads and vice presidents believed they had not been consulted enough by their equals. Third,... in many companies executives could have placed a great deal more faith in the capacity of their subordinates to assume greater responsibility. Fourth, there is no substitute for face-to-face contacts as a means of insuring adequate communication in an organization. (p. 210)

The leader of a unit has a dual responsibility: for transmitting instructions and information to his group and for transmitting information, ideas, and attitudes from his own group to his own equals and superiors in the organization. He should know the members of his group well enough personally so that he can gauge with some accuracy how they perceive what is going on around them, and so that they can in turn know what his point of view is.... Each individual has a unique perception of the goals of the business and the requirements of his particular position, and he attaches his own values to them. His capacity to hear and understand instructions is conditioned by his background, training, and experience. It may also be affected by the beliefs and codes of the group to which he belongs.... Unless he (the administrator) understands people as individuals and realizes their expectations, as well as those of the group as a whole, he will not have defined the limits or the opportunities of his work. (p. 211)

In 1954 at the request of the junior professors in Business Policy, I became head of this second-year required course when my predecessor chose to take a leave of absence and an assignment in the doctoral program.

Professors met weekly to discuss their pedagogical problems, the content of cases, and the objectives of the course. To begin with, I presented an outline of the major topics considered in one company where I had advised top officers for over ten years. I had attended meetings of Board of Directors. Sometimes, the chairman, president, vice presidents, or outside members of the Board asked me to present my views on controversial issues, either before, at, or after the meeting.

Each professor had an opportunity to present his views on what part of my foregoing company outline belonged in the Business Policy course. The contributions of Professors Christensen and Andrews regarding corporate strategy and its implications were notable and later were fully developed under their leadership.

Problems of General Management was published in 1961. Its cases were based on seven companies. Two editions of *Business Policy: Text and Cases* followed in 1965 and 1969. The text in the 1969 edition by Andrews was an important addition and was helpful to students and others interested in general management. It will be reflected later in charts, diagrams, and my discussion of the role of general management was published.

In 1961-62, I spent a year in Lausanne, Switzerland at the IMEDE Institute of Management Development (initially founded and financed by the Nestle Corporation of Switzerland). I taught a 9-month course in Business Policy and General Management to 48 middle management executives from 11 countries (7 different languages represented). Fifteen of the class were from the Nestle international organization. My two research assistants, who were fluent in several European languages, and I prepared cases and studied intensively the chemical and electronic industries of Europe. Other faculty did case research with us on a French company. I also organized for Nestle executives from all over the world a two-month course that involved Nestle business policies and practices. The class included 15 men from the 9-month program. In 1963 *European Problems of General Management.*

On return from Europe, I planned to devote full time to final research and writing a book titled *The Role of General Management.* I withdrew from teaching M.B.A. classes and was asked to teach Business Policy in five sessions of a 13-week Advanced Management Program (AMP) for vice presidents and major department heads of leading corporations in the United States and several foreign countries. I had previously participated in seven such programs between 1946 and 1960.

Members of AMP classes were recommended by their companies. They were considered promotable individuals who should profit from the broadening experience they received in before-class discussion groups and the class interaction between groups and the professors. I opposed reducing the program to 10 weeks because it took so long for men to overcome the experience they brought to the program. A chief executive who was visiting the Harvard Business School for a year of independent study attended the course in Business Policy in both the AMP program and my M.B.A class. He decided to drop AMP attendance because the M.B.A. students more quickly came to grips with the real issues of the case under discussion than the AMP's did, and in his opinion, often showed more imagination regarding solutions. His observation reinforced the need to keep the length, and not shorten the length, of the AMP program. The AMP students did profit from the program and most received substantial promotions—even to the presidential level. We professors learned an enormous amount from our AMP students about management problems and the role of general or top management that we put into published articles or books.

I was not able to complete *The Role of General Management* because of my Air Force duties from 1962-1966. In addition I served two years as Economic Consultant to a Cabinet Committee, appointed by President Johnson, to study need for a supersonic airplane. I also served as Economic Consultant to The Federal Aviation Administration, which conducted all the technical and economic analyses for presentation to the Cabinet Committee.

Before summarizing lessons learned about management and managers in business or government, it is pertinent to refer to other research projects conducted in my 40-year membership in the Harvard Business School faculty.

My first research study was "Merchandising of Cotton Textiles: Methods and Organization." The Textile Foundation with funds from the federal government appropriated $10,000 for this study on marketing methods for an industry in transition.

My research assistant and I did all the fieldwork with companies, north and south. We always approached a company through its Chief Executive and he named persons we should see. Some of the young men welcomed the chance to talk as they were hoping to advance by making suggestions to their managements. This phenomenon of interpersonal reactions was duplicated in fieldwork on case collection for HBS, and on consulting jobs involving many executives at higher levels.

We also studied practices in the silk and wool industries for comparative purposes. One woolen sales agent offered me a position that I refused.

A consulting project in the late 1930s that included McNair, Meriam, Teele and myself with Standard Oil Company (N.J.) required much field research that was done by Teele and me. President Roosevelt had established the Temporary National Economic Committee (TNEC) under the chairmanship of Leon Henderson to investigate the industries that might be violating antitrust acts. The General Counsel of an operating subsidiary prepared a file of books four feet long that gave full details of the policies and operating methods of the company and its operating subsidiaries. The company asked the consultants to verify the accuracy of its statements and was willing to change any policy thought to be indefensible. Only one was so found and it was changed, long before the TNEC hearings and that of a Congressional Committee.

The American Petroleum Institute had decided to have the Chairman of Sun Oil be the first witness before TNEC and Mr. Farish, Chairman of Standard Oil (NJ) the last. The consultants were asked to prepare for Mr. Farish drafts of the final statement and also one on Marketing Practices. Later the Marketing assignment was given to Vice President Sydney Swensrud of The Standard Oil Company (Ohio).

Mr. Farish was so disturbed by the antagonistic attitude and apparent preconceptions of Leon Henderson that he asked me to draft a final additional statement, beyond the formal one already distributed to the Committee. He approved the draft at lunch. I gave him the typed copy in the hearing room 15 minutes before he ended his formal presentation.

As a result of the work of the group, I received an offer to become Controller of Standard Oil Company (NJ) and head of a new Economics Department at two and half times my Harvard Business School salary. In my second year I was to be elected to the Board of Directors. I told the director who made the offer that I should not be called Controller as it in effect would make four Controllers around the world feel demoted. I felt that my seat in the dining room the first-year and at the board table the next would provide all the authority I needed. My management philosophy respects feelings of persons and contributes to teamwork required. I did not accept the offer for family reasons.

Several years later the Chairman of The Standard Oil Company (Ohio) suggested that I write an article for the *Harvard Business Review* on price leadership. I asked him to read the text before publication for accuracy of content. He made no requests to change the text; I would have refused to change factual statements or my interpretations of the company's process of fixing its prices in Ohio. This longest article ever published in that journal was extended, by further research on my part, into a book on gasoline prices in Ohio published in 1951.

In 1950, Mr. Alfred Sloan of General Motors arrived at the Harvard Business School one morning to meet with a group of senior professors to discuss research on the attacks on big business. I was his host because Dean David had asked me to be the leader of the proposed study group. Mr. Sloan said: "The Justice Department had more lawyers spending more time on General Motors than the Federal Trade Commission did. I think those attacks deserve some study." However, he had no intention that the study be restricted to General Motors.

I organized the group and directed their work until January 1951 when I returned to Washington for a year and a half of full-time consulting for the United States Air Force. The scope of the big business study was then narrowed and the research team reduced. Nevertheless, there were several resulting publications mentioned below.

Kenneth Andrews in 1951 wrote an article for the *Harvard Business Review* on "Product Diversification and the Public Interest."

John Glover reviewed the nature of the attacks on big business. He concentrated on economic arguments and those arguments based on social and political grounds and on ethical and moral grounds. His study "The Attack on Big Business" (1954) was widely reviewed in the business and general press.

The second major study to emerge from the so-called Big Business project was a book by Professors John McLean and Robert Haigh titled *The Growth of Integrated Oil Companies*. The *Economist* called it an "outstanding contribution." Those in the industry studied it for keys to competitive strategy as a function of company structure.

I delivered copies of these books to Mr. Sloan in his New York office. From his own experience in writing a draft of the history of General Motors, he said the books by Glover, Mclean, and Haigh appeared to be a result of a lifetime of work. He also told me which former and present executives of General Motors (GM) to interview for my study of the role of general management. They and graduates of HBS working for GM were very cooperative. GM President Cole agreed to speak to students of both the MBA and Advanced Management programs. In turn, I was asked to conduct seminars for GM middle management personnel on organizational relationships.

I will give examples from interviews with executives of the problems they had in fulfilling their roles as presidents, vice presidents, board members, or other high ranking members of general management teams. But first I will summarize my conception of the role of top management and general management personnel in the following paragraphs.

I consider a company as a *System Among Systems*. In simple terms a system is a set of interrelated parts. A social system, whether in the family, a business, or some other organization, involves two or more people who interact and share common goals and beliefs. My concepts of the general manager's role are the result of underlying assumptions about the place of business in society and the social nature of the firm. First, a business unit and its managers should behave as a socially responsible institution. Second, a general manager is exposed to and must reckon with a wide variety of systems both inside and outside a firm. Third, managers should cultivate a sense of history for a firm and its traditions, as well as those of the community, the state, or nation in which it operates. These affect policies and practices that can be successfully adopted by a firm. Fourth, managers must consider the implications of the fact that a firm is among other things, an aggregation of human beings. Skill in human relations is just as important at the executive level in dealing with each other as it is for operating managers in dealing with workers or the lower ranks of salaried personnel.

Chief executives and others have a threefold task: (1) shaping long-run corporate objectives and strategies that will be matched to both company capacities and external realities in a world marked by rapid technological, economic, social, and political change; (2) casting effective well meshed sets of general policies for the pursuit of these strategies; and (3) guiding the organization accordingly.

Top management is thus faced with: the formal subsystems and informal subsystems in and between its organizational units; outside organizations and institutions in the environment such as the press, churches, social organizations, consumer groups, trade associations; other business firms such as customers, suppliers, competitors, and consultants; financial institutions; educational and professional institutions; labor unions, and so forth. In addition the nation, state, and local governments also create a system of responsibilities and constraints that the firm should realize may affect its options or possible success.

In various roles as a professor, researcher, or consultant with a few companies, professional organizations, and government organizations in the United States (including Hawaii), Europe, Australia, and Japan, I interviewed companies that varied in size and scope of activity. They were: (1) companies that had only one or two executives of any kind and no formal functional specialization; (2) companies that had executives in charge of separate functional departments, and a president or chief executive officer; (3) companies that had a top management echelon consisting of an active chairman of the Board, a president and a few vice presidents, plus an echelon of line executives in charge of different divisions (e.g., product line, geographical, or research divisions), plus echelons of functional managers in both headquarters staff and divisions. In some instances group executives were added. Some of these executives were more important to the business than others. These variously styled teams of managers are a resource which the top leaders can neglect only to the detriment of the company.

Some were specialists and played more than one role. Whatever their assignment, it is desirable that they also be generalists. These executives should look beyond their own parochial self-interest to try to assess alternative proposals in light of what seems best for the firm as a whole. Companies where the higher echelons are manned by this type of individual are in a position to make decisions that are likely to be conducive to the health and growth of the firm. Men of lesser vision, no matter how expert in their specialties, often lead to dissension as they rise to higher positions.

I was surprised by some of the examples from my field work that I mention below. Presidents asked questions about their organizations. Presidents also introduced me to key persons to interview and in only one instance restricted contact with a person I wished to interview. Key persons also made suggestions of others to see. They tipped me off, so to speak, on messages or conclusions I should present to top management and that I did present. Chief executives involved in my research or consulting asked me to act as a trainer of some of their staff. Sometimes they revealed their own uncertainties on policies or their leadership style. Two successive chairmen of one company asked me to sit in on board meetings and later named executives whom I helped train, for high positions.

In another company studied by me on a research basis, I was asked to attend board meetings on two occasions. I was offered membership on the board, which I refused as I felt such a position might endanger the frank discussion I was having about the organization. A junior officer who had introduced me to executives began to call me for further interviews, the essential content of which he hoped I would pass on somehow indirectly to the Executive Vice President. The top executive of this company actually came to Washington during the Korean War to seek my advice.

My first consulting jobs in Massachusetts were in small firms. A retail coal distributor sought advice. The woman manager had succeeded her father (at the request of her two brothers) after their father's death, and they now shared ownership with her. The brothers were drawing their share of profits and part of hers, to operate a new trucking company. I interviewed her brothers and found they were taking advantage of new highways between New England and New York. The firm later expanded to cover the east coast. This was my first encounter in consulting with a firm taking advantage of new opportunities. I urged her to increase her investment as much as possible in the brothers' business. Actually her share of company profits offset her losses in the stock market crash.

A partner in the leading investment banking firm in Boston, a generous benefactor of the Harvard Business School, lost $10,000,000 of his $12,000,000 net worth in the October 1929 crash. He decided he should attend my class in Marketing for three hours each week for nine months and thus fill a gap in his knowledge. He later asked me to study a former client's business which was having difficulty, and this was my second consulting project. It was a company manufacturing a line of compasses for ships and boats. Sales through agents had declined from $150,000 to $50,000. The widow of the founder was now its general manager but had no business experience. The secretary of the company kept the accounting records. By interviewing the principal sales agent

I found the company had an outstanding reputation in Europe, so much so that European ships came to New York equipped with temporary instruments and then installed the company's products after arrival. An accounting professor and I analyzed cost records for various models and decided that the company had underpriced some of its most desirable models and overpriced others. A new price list was sent to agents. Foreign buyers, realizing that the company had discovered its errors and fearing further corrections in prices, flooded the agents with orders and the company was saved. Later it was sold at a substantial gain.

Another research project involved two chemical companies that had merged. The two presidents of the merged companies had different management styles. One president sat around a table and discussed with his vice presidents and departments heads any problem or new idea he had, or in turn any problems they had or ideas they wanted to discuss. This was the most informal and participative management style that I have ever seen. The other president and his executive vice president had styles which were quite the opposite. They were on a floor by themselves. To their subordinates they seemed to have favorites among lower ranking executives and were not noted for consultation with subordinates.

Later those three executives, now with different titles asked me to preside at a meeting designed to help them solve their differences and to choose among the two candidates for president of the holding company. The Chairman had dinner with me the night before; the President had breakfast with me; and the Vice Chairman saw me at 10 A.M. At 11:30 A.M. I met with all three, noted their differing positions and made suggestions I wanted them to consider. My recommendation was to have both candidates work together in the corporate headquarters and thereafter to recommend key policies and plans for the merged units to the top three officers. This plan was approved and I was asked to give the message to the two men. None of the three ever told these men why they were to come to Boston to see me. They were told I had important information to give them. When they arrived in Boston, I gave them a quick summary of their future roles that I had recommended. I did not have to tell them this could have a bearing on who would become president eventually. Both expressed disgust that their bosses did not have the guts to tell them. I agreed with their view. I would not have accepted the assignment except for the fact that, I thought that, working together, they would help build better management leadership practice, a better company, and reduce latent bitterness among their superiors. I was right. Each of the candidates eventually served successively as president of the holding company.

I have observed rivalries for position and power in both large and medium size companies. One company founding owner had a vision of new products to meet new trends. He had four key employees who developed the company rapidly according to his objectives. The owner was a real eccentric in his dealings with his executives. He also hired a consulting firm, which warned him of the power of the executive group, who had so well developed his company. The consulting firm even tried to undermine the executive group. The response of the executive group was an offer to buy the company at a very high price. The owner rejected this offer. After unsuccessful concerted efforts by members of the executive group to resolve differences with the owner, they all eventually resigned. They went on to found two companies, one an early conglomerate, and the other a scientifically oriented company. Both companies became very large and successful. This case is an illustration that power struggles may have positive results.

In 1954, I had a unique experience in the indirect use of power of position when I was Director of Training in the first Advanced Management Program at the University of Hawaii. Business leaders financed the program. Chief executives nominated subordinates for the eight-week program. At the end of the program, the faculty invited sponsors and chief executives along with the students to attend a full day's program. I was asked to speak at the dinner. Knowing this, members of the class provided me their views on the deficiencies. and in some cases the strengths, of their top managers. My summary views, considered by me the best talk I had ever made to that date, were warmly received by both students and the guest executives. I was thus able to use my indirect power as Director of Training in the program to communicate in my speech a summary of the views of class members concerning both deficiences and strengths at various management levels within their sponsoring companies. This led to almost immediate management behavior changes in several companies.

Sponsors had also asked me to interview executives of Hawaiian companies. They especially urged contacts with the Chinese and Japanese business leaders who had not been integrated into the major problems of growth and development of industries in the Hawaiian islands. I met with executives as requested, and we identified problems and exchanged ideas about them. The businesses included a variety, such as pineapple, sugar, banks, shipping, and real estate. I had much cooperation from the Chinese business community and limited contact with the Japanese community.

The president of a trust company and controlling stockholder of the Bank of Hawaii later asked me to become Executive Vice President of the Bank, to be promoted to President within a year or two. In his letter, he said: "We do not need a banker, but we do need a leader who understands the community." I was unable to accept the position.

Later the president of the Trust Company offered to nominate as a director of the Bank of Hawaii, a Chinese businessman, who then flew to Boston to consult me. He told me that he did not want to be the only Oriental (though born in Hawaii), to be accepted by the white leadership in Honolulu. I advised him to take the directorship and to state his opinion about the representation of Orientals in the business community. He followed my advice, and eventually Japanese businessmen did serve local institutions.

The foregoing anecdotes show how important interpersonal relations and communication skills are in organizations. Top management must strike a balance among the technical and economic needs of a firm, the social needs of its constituent subgroups, and the psychological needs of its individual members. Rarely, however, is a leader able to satisfy all claimants. In addition there is a need for effective communication up as well as down.

Persons or groups at lower levels can make real contributions to the welfare of a company and to management practice. Leaders can learn from so-called followers; leaders do not have to know all the answers. One executive I met who had a wide variety of assignments during his career in a large company often sought to present problems requiring solution, to what I would call a task force. Members of the task forces varied as the matter under discussion changed. He relied on personnel in other organizational units as well as those on his small staff or from his subordinate operating units. Of course there are many executives who would not be comfortable operating this way as it does not fit their personality or their views of their power. In some such cases, the executive has had a deputy or a favorite officer who performed the function of listening. Unions may sometimes be helpful in upward communications affecting workers. Foremen, factory managers, marketing managers, divisions chiefs, and so forth. may be good at upward communication. Others not possessing communication skills or afraid to express their true opinions may turn to the personnel department for help, or to other men or women they trust to express their views where it may count. At any rate, a company is fortunate if it can keep its channels for up and down communication open so as to tap ability wherever it is.

Edmund P. Learned
passed away on July 29, 1991

PUBLICATIONS

1929

Quantity buying from the seller's point of view. *Harvard Business Review, 8.*
Mergers in the cotton textile industry. *Harvard Business Review, 8.*

1931

Recent books in marketing. *Harvard Business Review, 10.*

1935

The cotton textile situation. *Harvard Business Review, 14.*

1936

With N. Issacs. The Robinson Patman Law: Some assumptions and expectations. *Harvard Business Review, 15.*

1948

Pricing of gasoline: A case study. *Harvard Business Review, 15.*

1949

Problems of a new executive. *Harvard Business Review, 27.* (Reprinted, 1966, vol. 44)

1951

With D.N. Ulrich & D.R. Booz. *Executive action.* Boston, MA: Graduate School of Business Administration, Harvard University.
With M.P. McNair, J. Linter, & E. Bursk. Our economic capacity to meet mobilizaiton needs. *Harvard Business Review, 29.*
Trends in administration. *Harvard Business Review, 29.*

1959

With A.R. Dooley & R.L. Katz. Personal values and business decisions. *Harvard Business Review, 37.*

1961

With C.R. Christensen & K.R. Andrews. *Problems of general management business policy–A series casebook.* Homewood, IL: Irwin.

1963

With C.E. Wilson, F.J. Aguilar, & R.C.K. Valtz. *European problems in general management.* Homewood, IL: Irwin.

1965

With C.E. Wilson, C.R. Christensen, G.F. Barker, Jr., K.R. Andrews, & W.D. Guth. *Business policy.* Homewood, IL: Irwin. (Revised 1969)

1966

With A.T. Sproat. *Organization theory and policy: Notes for analysis.* Homewood, IL: Irwin.

Harry Levinson

Teacher as Leader

HARRY LEVINSON

In the course of writing *The Exceptional Executive* (1968), I came across an article by L.S. Ewing[1] in which he reported a phenomenon that fascinated me. When he paired male cockroaches against each other in combat, up to 80% of the losers died from injuries, most of which seemed not to be serious enough to cause death. The moral of that research seemed to be that even among primitive insects defeat has powerful psychological consequences.

Fred E. Fiedler[2] had reported on the significance of intergroup competition on the adjustment of group members so the sequelae of defeat among humans was already established in the management literature, but the Ewing study indicated how far below man in organic complexity that experience was to be found. It is highly unlikely that cockroaches have enough of a brain to entertain such a concept as self-esteem, but, clearly, something goes on in the head of a cockroach that has the same ramifications as what goes on in the head of a human being. And the fundamental nature of that "something" is powerfully significant for understanding both motivation and stress. Ultimately, it became the core of my teaching and consulting about management.

The Exceptional Executive was an effort to integrate all of the then contemporary theories of motivation in management under a psychoanalytic umbrella. It was the culmination of 14 years of effort in creating and developing the Division of Industrial Mental Health at The Menninger Foundation. I had begun that task on January 1, 1954, when Dr. William C. Menninger asked me to undertake a project that would do something about keeping well people functioning well. He himself had been chief of U.S. Army psychiatry in World War II, and had had significant success in modernizing the Army's psychiatric practice, but he recognized the need for prevention. In fact, he said[3] that psychiatry was at a crossroads: it had to apply its knowledge beyond the treatment of individual people for the good of all. Now he was inviting me to give body to his conception. Naturally, if one is to do something in a public health sense about keeping people well, that is most easily done through social systems and primarily, therefore, with those institutions in which people work, inasmuch as their work is of great psychological significance to them.

IN THE BEGINNING...

Neither he nor I knew what to do. I spent about 18 months reading the literature of management and industrial psychology (organization development was still a long way off), and traveling the country and talking to people in personnel, occupational medicine, executives, those few psychiatrists who were working in industry, faculty members, industrial psychologists, and others whom I thought to be knowledgeable. I discovered that what we thought we had to know about how to treat people who are mentally ill, namely, a comprehensive conception of human personality, was almost totally unknown in management circles.

Dr. Will provided the financial support to get me started. Subsequently, he took my proposal for a Division of Industrial Mental Health to the Rockefeller Brothers Fund which supported the first three years of an effort to establish a mode of promoting mental health in industry with a grant of $105,000. I became director of the Division of Industrial Mental Health at The Menninger Foundation in July 1955 and served in that capacity for 14 years.

Beginning this new task, I was faced with the fact that I knew nothing about management or industry. I knew of no good public health examples of prevention. Therefore, I had to learn about management, as well as to develop knowledge and create principles for carrying out a preventive activity. After my 18-month exploration, I concluded that there were many data in the literature, but there was no information. By that I mean, despite many studies, there was no systematic way of diagnosing problems in organizations, nor was there any systematic logic for psychological intervention.

Clinically, one learns that there are treatments of choice, namely, "What do I do with this problem, in this person, under these circumstances, with this history, with my own assets and limitations and those of the client?" The industrial psychology literature and that of contemporary organizational behavior is still largely an ad hoc literature, odds and ends and bits and pieces of various kinds of short-term research, based on a reward-punishment psychology of conscious motivation, uninformed by a comprehensive systematic theory of personality. The conclusions from the research are usually too limited to permit systematic generalizations. There were two implications for me: (1) I had to learn about organizations firsthand; and (2) I had to combine what I knew from psychoanalytic theory and my clinical training together with what was in the literature into a systematic way of working with organizations.

Step One

I thereupon laid out a three-step program. The first step, to begin to learn about organizations, was to undertake an exploratory study in the Kansas Power & Light Company (KPL). I assembled a team of colleagues—a sociologist (Charlton R. Price) and a psychiatrist (Dr. Kenneth J. Munden)— and undertook a two-year study. Two other psychologists (Dr. Harold Mandl and Dr. Charles M. Solley) joined us after the fieldwork.

In effect, this task was an immersion, a kind of psychological anthropology. We were concerned not only with how people felt, but also with the context in which they were working. In fact, we felt we could not do an adequate sampling because so many of the communities in which the company's offices and services were located (scattered over one-third of the state) were significantly ethnic and we did not know to what degree they differed from each other culturally, historically, and socioeconomically. Furthermore, we couldn't use a formal research design because so much of what formal questionnaires yield does not lend itself to understanding in depth how people feel about themselves and their experiences. How people feel is the core of a clinical approach.

We interviewed some 874 people in open-ended discussions on which we dictated notes. Then two members of the team independently read all of the transcribed interviews in each location, abstracted the dominant themes, and wrote a comprehensive essay on the themes. These essays became the basis for a book, *Men, Management, and Mental Health* (1962). For reasons of confidentiality, we could use only a small part of the data. But we succeeded in becoming thoroughly immersed in the organization, having spent the better part of two years in the field, sweating profusely in the hot Kansas summers or shivering in sometimes bitter winters as we accompanied the crews in the cities and gas fields. It was more comfortable interviewing the officers in their respective offices.

The field experience became a context of reality, a frame of reference for understanding the interview data, for getting a sense of the impact of work on people who were doing it and, in turn, their impact on the organization. A number of powerful ideas resulted.

One of these was the concept of the "psychological contract." We came to understand that people unconsciously chose organizations to meet their psychological needs and support their psychological defenses. Organizations, in turn, chose people who would meet the organization's often unstated needs and defend it in multiple ways. When these needs were being met mutually,

one could speak of reciprocation. Subsequently, I formulated a questionnaire—Levinson Reciprocation Scale—to measure the degree to which the
psychological contract is being fulfilled for employees. In addition, the
firsthand immersion provided a baseline for putting the literature into context.
It also served as a frame of reference for judging others' findings and theories,
as well as calibrating my own.

But another important issue became clear. In his military work, Dr. Will
had been responsible for moving psychiatric treatment services close to the
front so that soldiers could be quickly treated for psychological trauma and
returned to their units. Previously, moved far to the rear, they became chronic
psychiatric casualties. He noted the work of earlier psychiatrists who had called
for "emotional first-aid stations" in industry and the classical counseling
services that resulted from the Hawthorne studies in Western Electric.[4]
Menninger and I had written an article (1954) calling for just such programs,
predecessors of today's Employee Assistance Programs in employment
organizations.

However, the most important lesson I learned in the KPL study was that
when an organization is managed well, namely, for its own perpetuation, that
is good for the people in it because "managing well" means management must
strive to make maximum use of their skills, talents, and abilities. When an
organization is managed expediently, namely, for short-term gain, that is not
good for the people in it because usually it means that employees are exploited
for the gain. That discovery led me into studying management per se, and
leadership in particular.

Perhaps that turn of events was not solely the reason for my interest in and
concern with management. In fact, my own psychoanalysis with Dr. Gertrude
R. Ticho shed considerable light on my choice of occupational direction, as
I note later.

Step Two

While the KPL study was under way, I undertook the second step in the
program which I had outlined for myself: to do something about the lack of
understanding in organizations of unconscious psychological dynamics, the
finding of my initial inquiry. Therefore, in January 1956, I undertook the first
of what has since become a 37-year experience with seminars for executives
on psychological aspects of leadership and the management of change. Using
psychoanalytic theory as a base, I evolved a structure for teaching the theory
at a layman's level and translating it into management problems on the
assumption that greater insight into fundamentals of motivation would lead
executives to think about themselves, as well as their employees, and of the
impact of their management practices on others.

In addition, I undertook a parallel series of seminars for physicians who practiced in industry to help them become more aware of and alert to psychological and psychiatric aspects of their work. Those seminars were also successful. As a result, I became involved in some of the activities of the Industrial Medical Association and various other groups which had to do with occupational health. I got an award from the *Journal of Occupational Medicine* for a paper on the future of health in industry (1960). (Later I learned I was not given first prize because I was not a physician.)

I was a consultant to the Committee on Psychiatry in Industry of the Group for the Advancement of Psychiatry, and to the Committee on Industrial Psychiatry of the American Psychiatric Association. Part of my task in both of those committees was to stimulate them to a broader vision and a greater publishing initiative. As a product of those activities and the seminars for occupational physicians, I was later asked to serve on the Joint Committee on Mental Health in Industry of the American Medical Association and on the board of the *Archives of Occupational Health*. I was also awarded an honorary membership in the American Medical Association. Meanwhile, I sought kindred souls in psychological and management organizations as well.

Those activities were consistent with the example I cited in the beginning as illustrative of the sustaining trend of my intellectual curiosity, namely the recognition that the fundamental biological reaction is against helplessness, even the sense of helplessness or the threat of helplessness. There is much evidence about the meaning and consequences of defeat, ranging from the studies of pecking orders among animals, to the experience of male mice pitted against each other in combat. In that experiment, the winners then will drop feces all over the cage floor as usual, but the losers will urinate only in the corners.[5] Sociobiologists have concluded that such competitive behavior is intended to pass on the genes of the victors at the expense of those of the losers (Barash, 1982). Discussion of stress, motivation, or of defensive behavior all seem to come back to the same core. I have conceptualized the experience of stress as contingent on self-esteem as a product of the gap between the self-image (the mental picture one has of self at any given time) and the ego ideal (the mental picture of oneself at one's future best):

$$\text{Self-Esteem} = \frac{1}{\text{Ego Ideal} - \text{Self-Image}}$$

The lower the self-esteem, the greater the stress (the greater the feeling of helplessness), resulting in more intense angry pressure on self to attain greater self-esteem. The pressure on self to attain greater self-esteem by achievement or mastery can have many positive consequences. Without a high ego ideal there would be little wish to achieve. Frequently, however, there are other consequences: the effect of the spillover or displacement of that hostility onto others; greater effort to control the rage (the most primitive form of aggressive impulse from which anger is derived) by personal constraint, resulting in psychophysiological symptoms; or the attack on self in the form of self-defeat and self-destruction.

I conceive of people as being rooted in their social environment as trees are rooted in the ground. Trees obtain water and nutrients from the soil. The wider and deeper the range of roots, the greater the stability and the more sources of input. Similarly, people obtain affectional input from their relationships with others and their environments. The greater the affectional input, the greater the support for the self-image and the easier it is for people to cope with the harsh self-criticism that is the inevitable sequence of a significant gap between the ego ideal and the self-image. Simultaneously, the more psychologically solid the range of such relationships in which people are rooted, the greater their personal stability.

When individuals or groups or nations experience defeat, they nurse their depressive anger for even centuries and vow to attain revenge so that they will not be always those who are the more helpless.[7] When people experience drastic change, as in merger or the reorganization of corporations or loss of jobs, then the sense of helplessness is exacerbated and the depression somehow must be alleviated to allow for successful readaptation to occur. Without relieving that rage, levels of depression and, therefore resistance to change, vengefulness, and distrust remain.

These external processes that influence behavior occur in a context of unconscious feelings and thoughts, and are given meaning by different people according to their psychological development. People respond less to life events themselves than to the meaning they give to those events. Therefore, it is important to understand that meaning if one is to discern motivation, alter organizations, or relieve stress. Thus, the central issue of striving toward one's ego ideal in coping with the sense of helplessness is the core of my professional theoretical thinking, conceptualization of problems in organizations and in society, and in consultation.

My psychoanalytic framework ranges from earliest drive theory to include Eriksonian developmental theory,[8] object attachment theory,[9] ego psychology,[10] and elements of self-psychology.[11]

Step Three

The third major step was to become involved in organizational consultation and public education. I found that if I were to teach myself, to integrate the data from industrial psychology, sociology, anthropology, and other fields, I would do so best by writing about how managers might solve psychological problems. I also found that many topics which were of particular relevance in management, such as the influence of unconscious guilt on performance appraisal and self-defeat, were not being dealt with in traditional industrial psychology or organizational behavior.

BEFORE THAT....

Like so many other immigrant fathers, David Levinson was a poorly educated Polish Jewish tailor. His family had been farmers in the area of Lodz. He was one of a large family of a twice-married father. Apparently, he did not get along well with his stepmother, for he was apprenticed and subsequently left for the wider world. At first, that meant London, which he felt to be too damp. He went to New York where he worked in sweat shops that made men's suits. Apparently, he didn't like the incarceration of the big city, having been influenced by a wellness movement among young Polish Jews similar to that which characterizes many contemporary young people. After traveling to the West Coast, stopping in Chicago (where he had a brother), Denver (too many consumptives), and Los Angeles, in 1911 he settled in Port Jervis, New York, a small railroad town about 80 miles northwest of New York City at the junction of New York, New Jersey, and Pennsylvania. Ten years later, he married my mother, Gussie, who was only three weeks off the boat. She was the uneducated daughter of a Polish Jewish tailor who also had a large family by three wives. Fearful of pogroms, her father had sent her and her younger stepbrother to the United States to join three other sisters. Quickly married off to what she had been told was a prosperous man, she found herself a total stranger in a foreign culture with a language that she never really did learn to speak.

My father was an extremely conscientious family man and an excellent tailor. His high standards applied both to suit making and personal behavior. He was contemptuous of men who appeared on the streets drunk and those who did not do good work. He was not orthodox in his religion, nor a significant participant in the affairs of the local Jewish community, but was certainly identified with it and also suffered the discrimination that was less virulent than in Poland, but, nevertheless, followed him in America. For a few years, he began to prosper, but the Depression ended that. Although, fortunately, he had saved enough money to be able to buy his own home for $1,500 in 1929 before the Depression hit, he remained essentially a poor man, rarely making a suit in that lower class workingman's town, but reduced to repairs, cleaning, and pressing by hand. (He wouldn't use a pressing machine because he felt the steam wasn't good for the cloth. I think he didn't want to see himself as a presser which was a lowly unskilled role in clothing factories.) When he bought his home in an Irish-Catholic neighborhood, he lost as customers several men who lived in that neighborhood.

Discrimination was a fact of life. As a kindergartner, I heard from my peers that Jews killed Christ, something about which I had no previous inkling, nor could possibly understand. Shortly thereafter, I saw a cross burning at night on a mountainside on the Pennsylvania side of the Delaware River. The KKK was active even that far north. That kind of hostility, together with the acute sense of being poor (we were the poorest in the Jewish community), was my constant companion for many years thereafter. Misery is less painful when shared: it was good that for me there were many other people in that town who also were poor. Many were on the Roosevelt era make-work projects, but my father was too proud to accept help.

My father seemed to accept his fate as a poor tailor with considerable equanimity. He never complained. He did not envy other people's attainments or wealth. He was his own man who had a well-defined lot in life and did the best he could with it. My mother, however, was not satisfied with that position, which, she often complained with painful frustration, was hardly better than what she had left in a small town called Kremienicz in southeastern Poland. Many loud arguments ensued, some very bitter and angry, and, indeed, some frightening to a small child. I trace my interest in making organizations better to my wish that I might have been able to make my family better. As later became more apparent in my own analysis, the unconscious wish to reform my own family became one of the major roots of my interest in social and organization reform.

I earned my first money at the age of nine by polishing a neighbor's furniture. I bought my mother five pounds of tomatoes with my 25 cents. Then I sold Watkins products from a catalog to earn a pair of roller skates. In my junior high years, I started to work regularly selling shoes, later in high school managing a dairy and delicatessen shop, and working in other stores. When I attained 13, in the Jewish tradition, I became bar mitzvah. There was enough cash among the gifts that I could buy a balloon-tired Columbia bicycle with which I could deliver groceries and a small Philco table radio for $20. Up to that point, we had not had a radio. We never did have a car.

Our four-room ground floor apartment was heated with a coal stove in the living room. We children rushed toward it on cold mornings to dress, and then I would often sit in the corner reading, a practice that ultimately led to my being somewhat round-shouldered. I practically devoured books. Since then, I've always read widely, particularly about current events, biography, and history. In my high school days, I also wrote a column for the high school newspaper, a practice which later led to my doing additional writing, both in college and subsequently. Even today, I publish a newsletter that requires that I read widely.

THEN, THE TEACHERS

Since my parents were uneducated immigrants who nevertheless valued education, certain teachers became significant agents of my socialization. Sara Haney Zeh, my fourth grade teacher, took a special interest in me, although I had a hard time trying to understand what she meant by being "saved" and why she kept asking me whether I had achieved that state of bliss. She was the first of what subsequently became a series of teachers who were supportive identification figures.

My parents could not tell me much about the educational world or aspirations which could lie beyond it. But I never knew a time when I did not expect to go to college. Even as a small child I would scribble my name with a Ph.D. after it. I had no idea what a Ph.D. was or even where I got that notion. Despite the fact that he had little money, my father bought a Metropolitan Life endowment policy for $7.53 per quarter, so that I could ultimately have $500 for college. He could not afford similar policies for my sister, Mildred, and later my brother, Samuel, younger by 18 months and 7 years, respectively.

Then came Isabelle M. DeWolfe, in the seventh grade. She was a woman of considerable dignity who enunciated impeccable English, rather old-fashioned in her appearance, with silver-rimmed glasses and a bun in the back of her black hair. She led me to believe that I was going somewhere. I did not know where, nor did she specify, but somewhere. She took great pride in my progress, and we remained close until her death.

I won a silver medal from the local chapter of the Daughters of the American Revolution for a seventh grade essay. I had great difficulty trying to figure out what to do with the medal. I never did find out whether I was supposed to wear it or hide it. Nobody else wore medals to school, so I left it in a drawer. It is still there.

In high school, I was involved in a wide range of activities: orchestra (violin), band (bass drum), debate, newspaper, German Club, and others that I have long since forgotten. I wrote some short stories and poems and began to struggle with what I wanted to be: a journalist or a teacher? My choices were complicated by the fact that I could not expect to get a teaching position in New York State outside of New York City because of discrimination, so, although I was admitted to the New Paltz State Normal School, there seemed to be no point in going there. My grades were not high enough to compete for scholarships. The family hassles were not conducive to studying. I knew nothing about the outside academic world or how one would pursue it. Besides, I had no money other than the $500 that my father had saved for me.

After I graduated from high school, I resigned myself sadly to working in a factory that made braid for furniture trimming. My task, reknotting the ends of spools of thread that had almost run out so that the odds and ends could be used, quickly became boring nearly to the point of torture. I was earning the grand sum of $14 a week. I knew I could not continue doing that, nor would I last long in similar factory jobs. That year (1939), the local high school recruited a guidance counselor for the first time. Her name was Leone Johnson and she came from Salina, Kansas, having gotten her master's at Columbia. Although already out of high school, I went to see her.

She suggested that I go to Kansas where, she said, everybody worked, the cost of living was low, and I would find no discrimination. I wrote for the catalogs of the three teachers' colleges in Kansas, having decided I wanted to be a teacher, and now a guidance counselor. Two of the colleges required ROTC, which did not interest me. The third, that accepted me, was in Emporia, a name familiar to me because I had heard of William Allen White. My father had tears in his eyes as he put me on a Trailways bus on January 14, 1940, for the 36-hour ride to Kansas. I had never before been more than 50 miles west of the Delaware River. Who knew what Indians lay in wait out there!

My college experience was warm and fruitful. The campus in those days was like something out of a movie set. Once again I was quickly involved in many extracurricular activities (they still took precedence over studying) and soon found three faculty members who became particularly important to me: Edward W. Geldreich (psychology), whose major avocation was trying to broaden students' minds by provoking them to think of such issues as socialism and communism and other radical points of view; M. Wesley Roper (sociology), a tall, kindly, white-haired, slow-moving man; and George R. R. Pflaum (speech), who coached debate.

The first two were intellectually stimulating and the third became something of a father figure for the four poor boys who comprised the debate team. It was with George Pflaum that we began to explore the world beyond the campus by going on debate trips by train, north to Minneapolis, south to Durant, Oklahoma. Those trips included eating in the dining car—a great privilege (as well as an educational experience) when dining car service was at its formal best.

Leone Johnson was right. The cost of living was low, everybody worked. My job (at 25 cents per hour, 40-hour limit, $10 a month), paid for by the National Youth Administration, involved digging ditches, shoveling snow, and other such menial tasks. That part of my life would have been easier if my father had taught me tailoring, but he had never encouraged me to learn from him. Later, I wrote press releases and edited the college newspaper.

I also became involved in campus politics. As on most campuses, there were fraternities and sororities, and the rest, the *hoi polloi*, the whole group of independents. I was not particularly happy about that social class distinction, particularly since the Greek front controlled the campus political offices. I organized another political party and headed it for three years, managing to win elections consistently and placing obscure farm kids in campus political positions.

Then came World War II. Soon, my fellow male students were leaving the campus. Those of us who remained in the Army Reserve drilled with wooden rifles and awaited our turns. I went into the Army Specialized Training Program in July 1943, and was assigned for basic training to Fort Hood, Texas, even though I had already just graduated from college. When that fact was discovered after basic training, I was reassigned to the infantry and went overseas to Italy.

Ultimately, for reasons I would never either know let alone understand, I wound up in the 178th Field Artillery Battalion, then dug in in the Apennine Mountains between Florence and Bologna, which was comprised of Tennessee and South Carolina National Guardsmen. Many of them could not read, and even some of those who drove trucks could read only one word, "mines." For unfathomable reasons, the job to which I was assigned in that outfit, which had been in the lines since the North African invasion, was that of parts clerk. It was my job to get parts and equipment for the big 155 mm. howitzers, the tractors that pulled them, and the six-wheeled trucks that carried both ammunition and personnel, as well as the smaller vehicles. I could not even drive, let alone know one part from another. I learned to drive on those snow-covered Italian mountainside roads. Among other things, I started a little news bulletin by typing a page of items that I then tacked to a bulletin board near our headquarters which was in the basement of an old farmhouse. I also tried (not very successfully) to teach some of the illiterate men to read by candlelight.

THE TURNING POINT

When I returned from military service in January 1946, I married Roberta Freiman in New York. I was torn between wanting to go to the Columbia Graduate School of Journalism and going on with psychology. At the urging of my new wife, we went back to Emporia where I was once more enrolled, now in a master's program. Then, the Veterans Administration announced that it was opening clinical psychology training programs in its hospitals, including one in Topeka in association with the University of Kansas and The Menninger Foundation. I applied and was accepted.

That, too, was a major turning point. At the time, I was debating whether to continue in psychology or go into speech correction, since my master's dissertation had been on stuttering. I had applied to the University of Minnesota for speech correction. My acceptance by the University of Kansas came the day before that of the University of Minnesota. So, off to Topeka we went, Roberta into a secretarial job in the VA Hospital to help support us.

The Topeka clinical psychology program was directed by the late Dr. David Rapaport, who was probably the single most significant person in my career choice, in my identification with psychoanalytic psychology, and for my professional standards. He was the closest thing to genius that I have ever known. Unlike most clinical Ph.D. programs, comprised of two or three years of academic work and then a year of internship, with Dr. Rapaport's imagination, the twenty psychology interns started the first day on the wards of the Winter VA Hospital. We rotated every six months through the various sections of that hospital, taking courses concurrently both there and in Lawrence, twenty miles away where the University of Kansas was located. That hospital experience enabled us to see clinical phenomena firsthand, to learn diagnostic psychological testing and psychotherapy, as well as research methods, and then contrast what we had seen with what was in the textbooks. It was an eye-opening experience to discover how little in the academic psychology texts related to the phenomena with which we were dealing. It was also an immersion experience, the prototype for the immersion experience in the KPL, and for the immersion process I used subsequently to teach my organizational diagnosis students.

The psychology department at the University of Kansas was headed by Roger Barker, who had assembled an outstanding group of Kurt Lewin adherents. They provided insights into Gestalt psychology and social psychology, both of which complemented my psychoanalytic base.

In the summer of 1948, I was enrolled in a sociology class on the community. As part of our clinical training, we had been assigned to a two-week stint at the Topeka State Hospital, which was across town from the Veterans Hospital and only half a mile from The Menninger Foundation. There had been practically no contact between those two institutions. What I saw appalled me. Patients sat in long lines of rocking chairs among ferns on locked wards in old three-story limestone buildings. My paper for that course was comprised of abstracts from all of the state hospital reports from the first in 1868. I picked the repetitive themes from those reports and put them together in pamphlet form titled *A Study in Neglect* (1948). The instructor sent it to Dr. Karl A. Menninger, who headed the VA Hospital and The Menninger Clinic. He scribbled on it in large letters, "Should be published and widely distributed." Overnight I became an authority on the state hospital, which then led to my becoming involved in its reformation.

One of my old debate colleagues, John P. McCormally, was elected to the Kansas legislature and was simultaneously a reporter for the *Emporia Gazette.* He lived with Roberta and me while he was in the legislature and not only introduced me to many legislators and members of the press, but also undertook a series of exposes which culminated in the legislature's voting significant appropriations to reform the hospital system.

When, a year later, not much had happened and the legislature was getting restless, Dr. Karl asked me to go to the state hospital and see what I could do. I was called coordinator of professional education. My ostensible task was to set up and coordinate training programs in psychiatry, social work, psychology, and adjunctive therapies. My first office was a corner of a large room used as the hospital's post office. But, actually, a major part of my self-determined task was to develop a public relations program for the hospital and to help deal with the legislature.

Dr. Karl himself became the next significant model. I worked with him closely over a three-and-a-half-year period and absorbed some of his zeal for the reform of those institutions that dealt with the most difficult problems in our society, the mentally ill and the imprisoned. He had established tremendously high standards for professional performance at The Menninger Clinic, which then had been transformed into application in the VA Hospital and the Topeka State Hospital. Both were firmly anchored in psychoanalytic theory, with a concomitant emphasis on the therapeutic environment. Between Dr. Rapaport's extraordinarily high conceptual and professional standards and Dr. Menninger's equally high professional standards and involvement in the social change of public institutions, I developed a strong identification with psychoanalytic theory, the importance of the nurturing environment, and the need for social institutional reform. Now, I was in full swing, both trying to improve society and organizations.

THE CHALLENGES

My involvement in the reform of the Kansas State hospital system was the most unusual and important challenge I have ever experienced. That seemed to be an almost hopeless situation: 1,500 terribly sick people imprisoned in obsolete massive limestone warehouses, cared for by untrained staff, with totally inadequate budgets. From that experience I learned that when one took a corner of a problem, no matter how hopeless it seemed, and started to work, it ultimately took shape. But one could gauge one's progress only by looking backward. Depending on retrospection made it possible to tolerate the responsibility and ambiguity of that task, as well as the seemingly impossible odds.

I had started in that effort in June 1950, not yet having my Ph.D., which I finally got in 1952, having previously flunked my first comprehensive examination. (I have always had a poor memory.) By the end of 1953, the job was pretty well done. The old snake pit was now among the best state hospitals in the country. It was time to think of another kind of challenge.

Because of my experience with the public, the press, and organizational reform, Dr. Will then asked me to undertake the project that I referred to above. He became the next model. He had a remarkable capacity for enlisting the aid of state legislatures in the mental health movement. In fact, he had spoken before 43 of them before the end of that phase of his effort. In the process of fund-raising among major corporate management leaders, he had generated considerable interest in mental health issues. Karl and Will Menninger came out of a rich religious tradition that undergirded their conception of public service. That, too, was part of my identification, an identification with teachers that derived in part also from that vicarious identification with the sages of the Old Testament.

I spent seven years developing the Division of Industrial Mental Health without a clear conception of where it was going to come out. I was trusting to my psychoanalytic orientation, my clinical base, and my immersion experience to help me establish a frame of reference with which I could work. In addition to the KPL study and beginning consultation with management, my self-teaching writing began to include what I was learning from the executive seminars that now provided my Division's financial support. I wrote *Emotional Health in the World of Work* (1964) for managers. The first four chapters on psychoanalytic theory had already appeared in the *Harvard Business Review* (*HBR*) (1963). Fifteen years later that article was reprinted as an *HBR* Classic, reflecting the demand for some 45,000 reprints. Chapter 18, "Management by Guilt," had appeared in IBM's *Think* (1964). That remains the only paper in the management literature on that topic. The seminars were also attracting increasing attention from managements and growing in number and acceptance. I was never able to interest union leadership, despite active effort.

The seminars, by the way, were, and still are, week-long sessions on the application of psychoanalytic theory to leadership and the management of change. They are comprised of lectures and small group discussions around cases prepared by the participants. The larger plenary groups are divided into small groups of seven, each led by a clinical psychologist or a psychiatrist, to discuss those cases and to tie the theory to the cases, to resolve the case problems, and to clarify the conceptual presentations if necessary.

REGENERATION

After some seven years of this, the late Douglas McGregor invited me to MIT for a year while Warren Bennis was at IMEDE in Switzerland. There I taught graduate students organizational diagnosis and Sloan Fellows leadership. That also was my first exposure to academic programs in organization development, to McGregor's work, to his T-group orientation, and to the atmosphere of a nationally recognized business school. I found it stimulating and highly gratifying. However, I discovered also that much of what I had developed myself was not yet included in the MIT teaching or anybody else's academic program. Although both McGregor and Bennis had been psychoanalyzed, and some of that experience was reflected in their interest in the innovative group psychology of the British psychoanalyst, Wilfrid R. Bion, they had not pursued psychoanalytic theory in greater depth. In a certain sense, I was then conceptually ahead of where they were, although considerably behind in terms of group process activity.

After my 1961-62 academic year at MIT, having gone back and forth to Topeka to conduct seminars, I returned to Topeka determined to devote intensive effort to writing. By now there had been significant political changes at The Menninger Foundation. The painful rivalry between the brothers Menninger had become exacerbated. (I had become a displacement object for Dr. Karl, which was one of the reasons I went to MIT.) Dr. Will had withdrawn from Menninger Foundation activities other than fund-raising and general policy making, and my Division now reported to Dr. Karl through an intermediary department head. I was learning firsthand the problems of: (a) family businesses; (b) entrepreneurial behavior; (c) a mercurial leader who chose, manipulated, and rejected favorite sons. It was not without direct experience that I became an authority on family businesses, entrepreneurs, and leadership.

Nevertheless, I needed to accomplish two major tasks. The first was to undertake my own analysis which I had postponed in the interest of the activities I was developing. The second was to write a number of articles and books that were simmering in my head and that I needed to write to integrate my own thinking. I returned to Topeka and wrote like mad.

In those Topeka years I had the gratifying support of Deane E. Ackers, who was then CEO of KPL; Robert K. Greenleaf, then nominally the director of personnel research at AT&T, but far more influential in management education circles than that title suggested (Greenleaf has suggested me to Douglas McGregor); and Dr. Alfred J. Marrow, then CEO of the Harwood Co., and a pioneer of group dynamics and the application of group processes to management; Earl Scott, then an executive with Tektronix; and Claude R. Miller, formerly CEO of Comet Rice Co. They remained important friends until each died.

In the spring of 1965, there was a palace revolt at The Menninger Foundation, as a consequence of which Dr. Karl retreated to Chicago for an extended period and Dr. Will took charge. Unfortunately, nine months later he developed cancer of the lung (he had been a three-pack-a-day smoker) and died at the age of 66 in 1966.

That precipitated a major political decision at The Menninger Foundation, namely, was it going to become a collegial institution, or continue as a family business? The upshot of many conflicting efforts was that it continued in the direction of a family business. As a result, several of us who had come to Topeka in 1946 and had remained for 22 years now chose to go elsewhere.

HARVARD

I was invited to the Harvard Graduate School of Business in 1968 for a four-year period as the Thomas Henry Carroll—Ford Foundation Distinguished Visiting Professor. I had sent earlier the manuscript for *The Exceptional Executive* (1968) (McKinsey Foundation, Academy of Management, and American College of Hospital Administrators Awards). In that book I advanced the concept of the employing organization as a learning institution and the executive as a teacher. I also formulated the concepts of ministration, maturation, and mastery needs as critical elements to be met at work. A series of articles in IBM's *Think* became the basis for *Executive Stress* (1970).

When I moved to Boston, I brought with me the manuscript for *Organizational Diagnosis* (1972). I had been frustrated during the KPL study and subsequently because I could not find a mode for assessing organizations comprehensively. Stemming from my clinical days, I believe one should diagnose before intervening. Otherwise, interventions are ad hoc and assumptions remain obscure. Ideally, consultation should be scientific: diagnosis is always hypothesis to be tested in practice. When assumptions are stated, they are conscious and testable. If they prove untenable, one can formulate others so that there is a rational, rather than trial and error, basis for consideration. After much abortive effort, I finally found the answer to that problem under my own nose. I adapted Dr. Karl's open-system model for formulating a psychiatric case study method[12] to an organizational case study outline that became the basis for *Organizational Diagnosis*, written with the help of Andrew G. Spohn and Janice Molinari. This highly detailed outline instructs a student or consultant how to enter an organization, what kinds of data to seek, how to organize those data in a logical and systematic way, and then how to arrive at diagnosis and prognosis. It is still the preeminent volume of its kind. It recognizes diagnosis as hypothesis and leads the consultant or the student from fact to inference to interpretation with the understanding that diagnostic hypothesis needs constantly to be amenable to revision and reformulation and that the internal logic of diagnosis must be readily apparent so that one may evolve interventions of choice.

Such a conception is critically important because much of what has come to be called organization development is little more than a series of ad hoc methods for bringing people together in organizations without defining the nature of the problems, the resources, history, character, demographics, and limits of the people in a given organization and the organization as a whole.

Meanwhile, I continued to write articles for the *Harvard Business Review* (at this writing 18 in all), of which "On Being a Middle-Aged Manager" (1969) and "When Executives Burn Out" (1981) won McKinsey Foundation Awards. A number of those articles became the basis for *The Great Jackass Fallacy* (1973), and much later for *Designing and Managing Your Career* (1989).

Subsequently, I wrote *Psychological Man* (1976b); *CEO: Corporate Leadership in Action* (1984) (James A. Hamilton-Healthcare Executives 1986 Book Award); and *Ready, Fire, Aim* (1986). *CEO*, comprised of interviews with Thomas J. Watson, Jr., of IBM; Ian K. MacGregor of AMAX; John W. Hanley of Monsanto; Reginald H. Jones of GE; Arthur O. Sulzberger of the *New York Times*; Walter B. Wriston of Citicorp; and a half dozen subordinates of each; was an effort to describe the behavior by which each led his organization.

The invitation from Harvard resulted significantly from my many *HBR* articles that translated clinical thinking and orientation into management conceptions and management application. At Harvard, I was asked to try to help reformulate the first-year Business School teaching in organizational behavior by introducing psychoanalytic theory. This I tried to do by teaching some of the faculty, helping them rethink and revise cases, and introducing some theoretical considerations into what previously had been open-ended case discussion in which every student's opinion about the case was as good as every other's. Such a discussion was as if to assume that there was no conceptual knowledge, no body of experience in dealing with human behavior and motivation. It was also much like having eighty first-year medical students determine whether the patient had a brain tumor, and, if so, what to do about it.

In the second year of my stay there, I introduced a "Seminar on Organizational Diagnosis" (1981) for the second-year MBA students which I continued for the next 14 years. In that seminar, limited to 15 students, I divided the students into groups of five and arranged for each group of five to spend an academic year in an organization—business, religious, medical, or educational—for an immersion experience. I introduced them to the chief executive, they then had to introduce themselves all the way down in the organization, and then prepare a study plan based on my book, undertake the study, and then finally feed back a summary of what they had found in the same order as they had come into the organization. The intensive experience was described by many of the students as the best course they had taken at Harvard. And parallel with the field experience, I introduced them to my version of psychoanalytic theory and provided consultation to them on the process of their diagnostic study, using some of my clinical colleagues as coaches for each of the teams.

I found efforts to teach faculty in the Business School psychoanalytic theory not particularly successful. No doubt, much of the problem lay with me. I was disappointed in the absence of critical intellectual discussion in the Business School. I had expected the same vigorous debate I had been accustomed to in Topeka. My own strong positions came across as arrogance. Tenured professors saw no need to learn more, and their juniors depended on them for their promotions. Although I created an opportunity for counseling/

training in one of the local hospital outpatient departments, no one really wanted to take advantage of it. Besides, I was fairly outspoken about what I thought about T-groups and other then-popular techniques in organizational behavior and some of the faculty were quite unhappy that I was running The Levinson Institute independently.

When I came to Harvard, I set up The Levinson Institute privately because I did not want to lose the seminars that I was conducting for executives and that would have had no formal place in any of the Harvard activities. That work continues. By this time the staff includes 25 clinical psychologists and psychiatrists, most of whom have Harvard appointments and all of them continue to be engaged in their own clinical practices. The Institute also consults on organizational change and leadership problems, and has long-term relationships with a number of major business organizations.

Unfortunately, in 1970, Roberta and I divorced. We had four children: Marc, Kathy, Anne, and Brian. All of them are now adult. At this writing, I have four grandchildren, Aaron, Rebecca, and Deborah, children of Marc and his wife, Kay; and Kathy's daughter, Reade.

Following my tenure in the Business School, I was invited by Dr. Gerald Caplan to take part in the Laboratory for Community Psychiatry and appointed a lecturer in the Harvard Medical School as a member of that organization. I also taught a course in the Boston University School of Business (on whose advisory board I served) for a year. In addition, I was invited to teach in a new master's program in business administration for managers at AT&T General Offices in New York that was then being evolved by Michel Beilis of AT&T between that company and Pace University. Each year 40 managers were appointed to that program. Pace managed it to meet its standards, but the company was allowed to select some outside instructors of sufficient repute and experience to be respected by the managerial students. I undertook to teach the two courses in Organizational Behavior and Organizational Problems. This two-course sequence had to be taught in 12 days, each course taking a full six days in order to get the 36 hours required for the equivalent of a semester-long program. That required going back and forth to New York and subsequently to New Jersey, but provided some pioneering opportunities.

Before the first time I was to teach the course on Organizational Behavior, I asked that the spouses of the participants be invited. They were. After initial doubt, the spouses found the course to be particularly helpful. First, for a change, they were being invited to share something with their company-employed spouses, rather than having those partners expected to do something that demanded more time away from them. Second, they had the opportunity to discuss cases with their spouses before class, and in their class, which enabled them to keep up with their spouses. Third, and most important, both spouses were learning the same psychological concepts. If there were marital or family problems that needed attention, they could more easily talk about them and, if necessary, undertake referral, which a number have done. In the subsequent years, every time I am invited to speak at a business organization meeting, I have continued to ask whether spouses can be involved.

Affiliation with the Laboratory for Community Psychiatry enabled me to continue teaching my seminar on Organizational Diagnosis which was open to students in all the Harvard graduate schools. Since the School of Education was closer to my home and the student participants were more often drawn from education, arts and sciences, and sometimes divinity, as well as business and public health, it was easier to do the actual teaching in one of the classrooms at the Ed School. As a result, I was appointed a member of the faculty at the School of Education and that seminar was also formally designated as part of the School of Education curriculum.

There are six Departments of Psychiatry in the Harvard Medical School, all of whose psychology is psychoanalytically oriented. The Laboratory for Community Psychiatry was part of the Massachusetts Mental Health Center, so, officially I became a member of that Center. Subsequently, I was named head of its Section on Organizational Mental Health and clinical professor of psychology in the Department of Psychiatry.

Dr. Ralph G. Hirschowitz, then in the Laboratory, and Dr. Miles F. Shore, head of the Massachusetts Mental Health Center, became close friends and supportive colleagues. Ralph taught me much about group processes and Miles about the complex problems of leadership of a state-owned institution embedded in a medical school. Dr. Elliott Jaques, a seminal thinker, with whom I frequently did collaborative seminars, had a significant influence on my thinking about organizations.

RETROSPECTION

After I lectured once on stages in adult development and their implications for the major decisions managers had to make about their own lives, the floor was thrown open for questions. The first question threw me temporarily: "What accounts for your own success?" I replied that I was fortunate enough to have been in the right place at the right time on several different occasions that became turning points in my life. That, indeed, is true, but certainly it isn't the whole story, nor can I take the Skinnerian position that it was all a matter of rewarded responses. In fact, I'm sure much of it was a matter of responding to hostile and painful events with a kind of intensity and dogged determination that in themselves created particular problems for me.

The shape and development of my professional life is one of continuing growth. Although often guided by the unexpected, by chance, or by some streak of good fortune, like being in the right place at the right time, generally I have followed an evolving pattern: identification with my parents' values; the wish for an education; identification with my teachers; the choice of vocational guidance in secondary schools as a career direction; the recognition that there was greater sophistication in psychology than that level; the opportunity for clinical psychology training when I might easily have gone off in the direction of journalism or speech correction; the continued recognition that working with individuals was not enough, although the underlying theoretical base provided for greater understanding and effectiveness and therefore sustained my community work in dealing with the Kansas legislature and the community of Topeka and its problems; the shift to working with organizations based on a preventive conception.

While the several roles seem to differ widely, there was no drastic shift in my career from one role to another, only broader scope and increasing sophistication. The same is true with respect to psychoanalytic theory. Although I was firmly anchored in it in my training days and continue to be, I had to simplify it and make it much clearer for teaching psychiatric aides in the Topeka State Hospital. Doing so, in turn, made it easier for me to integrate innovative conceptions in the theory and apply the theory, coupled with other knowledge, to specific managerial problems. Later, managers were able to find in what I wrote ways of coping with specific problems that seemed to be more effective than their previous methods. The task of communicating my mode of thinking to professionals in clinical and organizational practice followed. In addition to providing insights for them and to legitimizing avenues through which clinically trained and psychoanalytically prepared clinicians could use their knowledge in a broader scene, my intention is to increase the level of psychological sophistication of managers and executives, particularly top management and those in human resources.

From a historical perspective, I think I have made a number of contributions: first, recasting psychoanalytic theory as it was evolving into forms that could be used by lay people and professionals alike in working with organizations; second, conceptualizing the ego ideal/self-image relationship; third, evolving the diagnostic process in *Organizational Diagnosis* to provide a systematic way of studying organizations; fourth, developing a model for teaching consultation; fifth, integrating the various concepts of motivation in management under a psychoanalytic umbrella; and, sixth, concurrently, developing the concept of the executive as a teacher inasmuch as the business organization inevitably must be a learning organization.

By utilizing people most effectively, an employing organization ideally not only enhances their mental health, but also encourages their continued maturation, and mastery. My seventh contribution was to advance the concepts of ministration, maturation, and mastery as three stages in development. Eighth, I gave particular meaning to the concept of the psychological contract in its unconscious form. In furthering this mode of thinking, I have been something of an iconoclast, arguing vehemently against psychologically naive assumptions, limited concepts, and part theories. Further, I have been critical of the failure of so many in organizational behavior and management to recognize unconscious motivation.

For me, science means organizing experience into theoretical formulation, testing that theoretical formulation by repetitive observation and other forms of gathering data, making certain that there is a clear line from fact to inference to interpretation, and making public the methods for arriving at conclusions. By that criterion, management is not yet a science, despite the proliferation of measurement.

Obviously, management, like any other mode of thinking or action, must assume responsibility for the outcomes of what it conceptualizes and how it encourages, instructs, and causes people to behave. With respect to their presence in a society, managers have not only individual responsibility as citizens, but also group responsibility for making clear to others their way of understanding and resolving social problems so that they can be tested in the broader social arena and, if found useful, redound to the advantage of the society as a whole.

Certainly, conceptions by which people manage presumably have explanatory power. Managers can explain why they choose to do what they do. Unlike astronomy or abstract mathematics, their observations and conclusions for the most part are verifiable in everyday observation. Even if some of their conceptions do not explain behavior adequately, nevertheless they are subject to correction and modification. Therefore, ultimately much of managerial practice can become part of a science, rather than merely a tacit belief system.

The concept of immersion was tremendously important and helpful to me, as I have already indicated several times. One can contrast this method with the usual modes of learning— questionnaires, attitude surveys, or other typical methods that result in limited circumscribed information and journals clogged with unimportant information. As a result of the immersion experience, my students never again had to be afraid of entering an organization for whatever kind of consultation they would undertake. Consequently, I heartily endorse the immersion phenomenon, accompanied by intellectual or conceptual input and careful supervision, as a basic method of teaching students to understand organizations. Students become responsible for both gathering data and verifying data, for organizing their information systematically, for reporting it back, and for maintaining successful relationships with the management of the organization so that the organization is not harmed by their work, but ideally is advanced by it. Beyond the practical education, the broader the range of liberal arts, the greater the understanding of community context and history and culture, the more effective a student of management psychology can be both in his or her research and in whatever intervention or management he or she undertakes.

My advice to every novice is exactly as I have indicated above, as an undergraduate not to substitute training for education, but to get as broad an education as one can. Then, I suggest, get a solid psychological base for whatever direction one wants—whether research, consultation, or management. Unless the student gets a comprehensive conception of unconscious motivation and how it functions, much of what he or she will do will be a self-limiting exercise.

Any young person who thinks of entering management or management education and consultation should first get some experience as a supervisor and manager in a business organization. He or she should learn what goes on in organizations and be recognized by others for competence as a manager. Following that experience, a person should undertake graduate level courses in clinical psychology with ancillary work in organization development. The clinical psychology should be psychoanalytically based. Those who would be involved in consultation should get formal psychoanalytic training. That does not mean the person has to practice psychoanalysis, but would be in a more sophisticated position to apply psychoanalytic theory to understanding organizational and managerial processes.

As higher-level management becomes increasingly psychologically sophisticated and has to deal with greater complexity both inside and outside the organization, it will lean more heavily on professionals to be more knowledgeable than they are now. Neither the theories on which most human resources activities are based, nor the knowledge or skill one acquires along the way to do them, will be sufficient to be accepted by the highest levels of management as skilled and knowledgeable professionals.

One of the major outstanding unresolved issues in our discipline is the reluctance to take into account the validity of unconscious thoughts and processes. The discipline is geared very heavily to the motivational influence of external forces. From time to time there is talk of intrinsic motivation, but what constitutes intrinsic motivation is never clarified. It is as if one were trying to understand the functioning of the human body by describing the various forms of behavior people engage in without taking into account anatomy and physiology. As a result, research papers are long on correlations, but short on organizing from those data significant meanings that give rise to one or another form of behavior. So often, the best one can say is "Variable X occurs in association with Variable Y." Such a conclusion does not leave the scholar with much depth of understanding, or the manager-executive, who presumably is to apply such findings, with anything that he or she can do systematically to resolve problems. One can argue that the same kind of research goes on in genetics, microbiology, and other medical disciplines, but these take place against a basic understanding of anatomy and physiology and their findings can be fitted into an already established frame of reference.

A secondary major area that needs much attention is conceptual development. Only the work of Elliott Jaques[13] has given us a systematic way of viewing the relationship of conceptual development to the selection of managerial and executive candidates, to their assignment to roles that are consistent with their conceptual development and their further development, and to an organizational structure based on human capacity. Instead, we have selection methods based on psychological tests that frequently do not have adequate norms for higher-level roles, nor are they necessarily highly correlated with given tasks, since so often they are taken from the shelf. Competency models work well for lower- or middle-management roles, but are less useful at higher level executive roles where greater sensitivity to people is involved in idiosyncratic ways.

If perpetuation of the organization is fundamental, then it follows that a key task of all executives and managers is the development of their subordinates. In turn, that requires a highly detailed behavioral job description for each role,[14] and significant incident feedback,[15] as well as teaching skills. These have to be incorporated into performance appraisal and compensation schemes. Most often they are not and, therefore, such efforts are honored in the breach. Formal management and executive development programs cannot take over the responsibility that should be fulfilled by individual executives any more than school can take over the functions of the parent.

These are three major issues that will have to be dealt with, particularly the recognition that we are always dealing with some assumptions about human behavior and those assumptions should be made clear. Anyone who would be involved in study of organizational behavior should be particularly knowledgeable about his or her assumptions about basic motivation.

It follows that the experimental scientific approach has serious limits as a means of understanding and knowing persons and groups. The futility of so much of what is already in the organizational behavior literature is testimony to the that fact. A simple example comes from studies of stress. There are many such studies. They are often collected together in the form of odds and ends of recommendations about what to do about stress. Most of them refer to stressors and most of the recommendations have to do with relaxation, usually in the form of some kind of self-hypnosis. As a matter of fact, stress is significantly a product of the gap between the ego ideal and the self-image. Anything that tends to lower the self-image or raise the ego ideal to astronomical proportions will be stressful. With that concept, one can organize a whole range of research results that presently are only odds and ends. Using such a conceptual framework would obviate the need to do a wider range of bits and pieces of stress research, each of which presumably then will stand on its own, without being part of a broader picture. If all those were integrated as I suggest, then one could look at what goes on in organizations that diminishes the self-image on the one hand, and artificially pressures the ego ideal demands on the other. In short, one could look more closely at more comprehensive organizational practices and policies, at organizational structure and processes, to see what they then do to give emphasis to either end of this continuum. We need a broader model, a more comprehensive paradigm, as Kuhn[16] would have it.

We know more about human motivation than most people think. We do not all know it equally well, nor do we apply what we know equally well. As in any other discipline, only a very few have comprehensive exceptional knowledge; much of what followers practice then is relatively mediocre. We are becoming increasingly knowledgeable about research methods. There is much more opportunity to observe behavior, ranging all the way from that of animals, to infant and mother interactions, to interaction in managerial meetings, and so on. With the use of videotape and other forms of data gathering, one can observe firsthand rather than infer from questionnaires and other sources of information that may be one or more steps removed from the actual behavior. Of course, there is much we don't know, and, particularly, we don't know as much as we should about how the brain functions. But imaginative insights are coming from neuroscience, as well as from genetics and in microbiology. We are in an era that is weighted in the direction of psychobiology and neurobiology. However, much of what is presently alleged to be genetic in origin or product of brain functioning alone, will turn out to be inadequately explained by findings from those disciplines. We will then see the pendulum swing once more to psychological explanations.

My philosophy of life is reflected in my behavior. It includes a number of significant elements. The first of these is preoccupation with and concern about my family. I am pleased that I was able to take care of my aging parents in a manner that ensured their well being, although I had to institutionalize both of them. I am also pleased that my four children have carried on my values. Each is identified with an aspect of my own occupational interests in writing, business, and public service. Each has been constructive and creative in his or her own right and has not destructively exploited other people.

I believe firmly in and support humanitarian causes, no doubt significantly out of a Jewish tradition and its concern for others both individually and collectively.

That same tradition has held out the value of learning and, therefore, fundamental to my own activity is continuous learning, which means also readiness to change one's perception and point of view when new evidence and social changes require it.

I value careful critical examination of phenomena and practices. I think one can do something to change aspects of society and that a good citizen is a continuous goad to such changes.

I think also it is important for one to use one's role, position, function, skill, competence, and resources to help other people grow and develop, for only by doing so can one continue to grow and develop himself. Such a philosophy assumes a sense of fair play and integrity. No doubt that is what being a teacher is all about, which is where I started.

PUBLICATIONS

1943

With G.S. Phillips & H.E. Schrammel. *P-L-S journalism test.* Emporia, KS: Bureau of Educational Measurements.

1948

With V.L. Norris & H. Moore. *A study in neglect.* Topeka, KS: Kansas State Board of Health.
Mathematics aptitude. In O.J. Kaplan (Ed.), *Encyclopedia of vocational guidance* (Vol. 2). New York: Philosophical Library.

1949

With J.T. Dickson, I. Stamm, & A. Leader. The contribution of social workers to the interviewing skills of psychologists. *Journal of Social Case Work* (October).

1950

Behind these walls. Topeka, KS: Shawnee County Association for Mental Health.

1952

Doors are to open. Topeka, KS: Topeka State Hospital.

1953

State hospitals are different now. *Menninger Quarterly, 7*(2), 7-12.

1954

When is it sick to be sad? *Menninger Quarterly, 8*(2). 16-20.
With W.C. Menninger. The machine that made pop. *Menninger Quarterly, 8*(3), 20-26.

Industrial mental health: Observations and perspectives. *Menninger Quarterly,*
8(4), 1-31.

1955

Consultation clinic for alcoholism. *Menninger Quarterly, 9*(2), 19-21.
Of gifts and givers. *The Campfire Girl, 34*, 3.

1956

Why work? *Personnel Service* (January-February), 1-7.
Employee counseling in industry. *Bulletin of The Menninger Clinic, 20*(2), 76-
84.
Experimental seminars in industrial mental health. *Menninger Quarterly,*
10(2), 21-23.
A significant decade. *Menninger Quarterly, 10*(3), 6-8.
Seminars for executive and industrial physicians. *The American Journal of*
Psychiarty, 113(5), 451-454.
We are the learners. *Menninger Quarterly, 10*(4), 11-14.
Toward understanding men. Topeka, KS: The Menninger Foundation.

1957

The illogical logic of accident prevention. *Menninger Quarterly, 11*(1), 19-26.
Review: Industrial mental health. *Menninger Quarterly, 11*(2), 17-21.
The next step. *Menninger Quarterly, 11*(2), 22-24.
Social action for mental health. *Mental Hygiene, 41*(3), 353-360.
Emotional first aid on the job. *Menninger Quarterly, 11*(2), 17-21.
Alcoholism in industry. *Menninger Quarterly, 11*(Suppl.).
With W.C. Menninger. *Human understanding in industry.* Chicago: Science
Research Associates.
Toward understanding men (2nd ed.). Topeka, KS: The Menninger
Foundation.

1958

With H.C. Modlin. What you can do about stress. *Nation's Business, 46*(June),
34-35, 90-95.
Know yourself. *Supervisory Management, 3*(September), 32-29.
The nature and genesis of prejudice. In G. Noar (Ed.), *Proceedings of the Plains*
States Conference on Human Relations Education (pp. 6-10). Omaha,
NE: University of Omaha.

What makes us work safely? *President's Conference on Occupational Safety* (U.S. Department of Labor Bulletin, No. 196, pp. 71-73). Washington, DC.

1959

New way to fight tension. *This Week* (March 15), pp. 21, 23.

Open letter to my son. *National Jewish Monthly, 73*(6), 26.

The psychologist in industry. *Harvard Business Review, 37*(September-October), 93-99.

Executive awareness and health. In *Readings in management planning and principles*. New York: Corn Products Co.

1960

Dilemmas of the occupational physician in mental health programming: Part II. *Journal of Occupational Medicine, 2*(May), 205-208.

First aid for worried workers. *Nation's Business, 48*(9), 54-55, 58, 60, 61.

Industrial mental health: Progress and prospects. *Bureau of Industrial Relations* (University of Michigan) (October).

1961

Cause and cure of personality clashes. *Nation's Business, 49*(4), 84-86, 88-89.

Interdisciplinary research on work and mental health: A point of view and a method. Topeka, KS: The Menninger Foundation.

1962

Seminars for executives and occupational physicians. *Bulletin of the Menninger Clinic, 26*(1), 18-29.

The executive's anxious age. *Think, 28*(7), 22-25.

A psychologist looks at executive development. *Harvard Business Review, 40*(5), 69-75.

With H.J. Mandl, C.M. Solley, K.J. Munden & C.R. Price. *Men, management, and mental health.* Cambridge, MA: Harvard University Press.

1963

What killed Bob Lyons. *Harvard Business Review, 41*(1), 127-144.

Men, management, and mental health. *Menninger Quarterly* (Spring), 19-25.

The executive and his teenage children. *Think* (May-June), 29-5, 26-30.

Work and mental health. In *Encyclopedia of mental health*. New York: Franklin Watts.

1964

What work means to a man. *Think, 30*(1), 7-12.
Anger, guilt and executive action. *Think, 30*, (2), 10-14.
Turn anger into an asset. *Nation's Business, 52*(5), 82-86.
The changing meaning of the organization. In *Fifth Annual Personnel Officers Seminar: A Report*. (Special Report #128, pp. 27-35). Lawrence, KS: Governmental Research Center, University of Kansas.
[Review of *The act of creation*]. *National Observer* (October 27).
Why women work. *Think, 30*(6).
With C. Price. Work and mental health. In A.B. Shostak & W. Gomberg (Eds.), *Blue collar world: Studies of the American worker* (pp. 397-405). Englewood Cliffs, NJ: Prentice-Hall.
Participant in *Human Needs in Housing: Report on a Round Table Conference*, Occasional Paper No. 4, U.S. Savings & Loan League, Chicago, IL.
Emotional health in the world of work. New York: Harper & Row. (Rev. ed, 1980).

1965

The problems of promotion. *Think, 31*(1), 7-10.
Reciprocation: The relationship between man and organization. *Administrative Science Quarterly, 9*(March), 370-390.
Stress at the bargaining table. *Personnel, 42*(2), 17-23.
What is mental health. *Think, 31*(2), 24-28.
How to get out of a dead-end job. *Popular Science Monthly, 186*(4), 104-105, 194.
The future of health in industry. *Industrial Medicine & Surgery, 34*(April), 321-334.
Do you look for culprits—Or causes? *Think, 31*(3), 14-18.
[Review of *Organizational Stress*]. *Administration Science Quarterly, 10*(June), 125-129.
What an executive should know about scientists. *Think, 31*(5), 6-10.
Who is to blame for maladaptive managers? *Harvard Business Review, 43*(6), 143-158.
Foreword. In C.A. Ferguson et al. (Eds.), *The legacy of neglect* (pp. vii-viii). Fort Worth, TX: Industrial Mental Health Associates.

1966

What ever happened to loyalty? *Think, 32*(1), 8-12.
How to undermine an organization. *Think, 32*(4), 15-19.
The high return on enlightened giving. *Think, 32*(5), 21-24.
[Review of *The executive in crisis*] *Administrative Science Quarterly, 11*(11), 297-299.
Service is management's responsibility. *Cooking for Profit* (November).
With P. Tournier, V.E. Frankl, A. Thielicke, P. Lehmann, & S.H. Miller. *Are you nobody?* Richmond, VA: John Knox Press.
The changing meaning of the organization. In T.O. Wedel & R.P. Scherer (Eds.), *The church and its manpower management.* New York: Department of Ministry Vocation and Pastoral Services, National Council of Churches of Christ in the U.S.A.

1967

Problems that walk in your door. *Think, 33*(1), 13-16.
Mentally ill puzzle industry. *Menninger Quarterly, 21*(Spring), 7-13.
[Review of *Mental health with limited resources*]. *Archives of Environmental Health, 15*(July), 134.
George R.R. Pflaum. In R.L. Roahen (Ed.), *Qualities of greatness II.* Emporia, KS: The Kansas State Teachers College Press.
[Review of *The anarchist movement and the T-Groups: Some possible lessons for organizational development*]. *The Journal of Applied Behavioral Science, 3,* 232-233.

1968

Is there an obsolescent executive in your company—Or in your chair? *Think,* 34(1), 26-30.
[Review of *A psychiatrist for a troubled world–Selected papers of William C. Menninger, M.D.*]. *Archives of Environmental Health, 16*(2), 296-297.
[Review of *The job hunt: Job-seeking behavior of unemployed workers in a local economy*]. *Archives of Environmental Health, 16*(2), 296-197.
What an executive should know about his boss. *Think, 34*(2), 30-33.
The trouble with sermons... *The Journal of Pastoral Care, 22*(2), 65-74.
Psychiatric consultation in industry. In W.M. Mendel & P. Solomon (Eds.), *The psychiatric consultation* (pp. 159-180). New York: Grune & Stratton.
Some responses from outside the company: The exceptional executive. In *Managing organizational stress* (pp. 135-178). Proceedings of The Executive Study Conference, Educational Testing Service, Princeton, NJ.

The exceptional executive. Cambridge, MA: Harvard University Press.

1969

[Review of *To work is human*]. *Industrial and Labor Relations Review, 22*(2), 303.
Technology: Human challenge. *The McKinsey Quarterly, 5*(Spring), 4, 41-52.
[Review of *The case of the alcoholic employee*]. *Harvard Business Review, 47*(3), 14.
[Review of *Work and human behavior*]. *Contemporary Psychology, 14*(7)), 367-368.
On being a middle-aged manager. *Harvard Business Review, 47*(4), 51-60.
Emotional toxiocology of the work environment. *Archives of Environmental Health, 19*(2), 239-243.
[Review of *Motivation through the work itself*]. *Monthly Labor Review, 92*(10), 68-69.
Seminars for executives and occupational physicians. In R.T. Collins (Ed.), *Occupational psychiatry*. Boston, MA: Little, Brown.
The exceptional executive. In *Proceedings of a Symposium, The Exceptional Executive*. Athens, OH: Division of Research, College of Business Administration, Ohio University.
Managing executive stress. *Panhandle Magazine, 4*(2), 16-19.

1970

A psychologist diagnoses merger failures. *Harvard Business Review, 44*(2), 139-147.
Management by whose objectives? *Harvard Business Review, 44*(4), 125-134.
Executive stress. New York: Harper and Row.
With L. Weinbaum. The impact of organization on mental health. In A.A. McLean (Ed.), *Mental health and work organizations*. New York: Rand-McNally.

1971

Conflicts that plague family businesses. *Harvard Business Review, 45*(2), 90-98.
Various perspectives on managerial theory and practice on motivation in industry. *Archives of Environmental Health, 22*(May), 612-618.
Psychiatry in industry. *Psychiatric Annals, 1*(2), 60-71.
[Review of *Work, creativity and social justice*] *Bulletin of the Menninger Clinic, 35*(6), 488-490.

With C. Petrow, & T. Stern. The quiet revolution at foggy bottom. *Management Review, 60*(12), 4-14.

1972

The clinical psychologist as organizational diagnostician. *Professional Psychology, 3*(1), 34-40.

Comments on What should you know about the working wife and mother? *Occupational Mental Health, 2*(1), 8.

Management by objectives: A critique. *Training and Development Journal, 26*(4), 3-8.

Critique of Motivation and management. In J.W. McGuire (Ed.), *Contemporary management: Issues and viewpoints.* Englewood Cliffs, NJ: Prentice-Hall.

With A.G. Spohn & J. Molinari. *Organizational diagnosis.* Cambridge, MA: Harvard University Press.

Problems that worry executives. In A. Marrow (Ed.), *The failure of success.* New York: American Management Association.

An effort toward understanding man at work. *European Business, 33*(Spring), 19-29.

Easing the pain of personal loss. *Harvard Business Review, 50*(5), 80-88.

1973

The great jackass fallacy. Cambridge, MA: Harvard University Press for The Division of Research, Graduate School of Business Administration.

Asinine attitudes toward motivation. *Harvard Business Review, 51*(1).

A psychoanalytic view of occupational stress. *Occupational Mental Health, 3*(2).

[Review of *Victims of success: Emotional problems of executives*]. *Contemporary Psychology, 19*(5), 400-401.

[Review of *Mental health in the world of work*]. *Administrative Science Quarterly, 19*(2), 260-262.

1974

On leadership. *Pegasus* (Mobil Services Co. Ltd.).

Don't choose your own successor. *Harvard Business Review, 52*(6), 53-62.

1975

On executive suicide. *Harvard Business Review, 53*(4), 118-122.

Motivating administrators and organisations for change. In H.M. Mathur (Ed.), *Development policy for change.* Jaipur, India: HCM State Institute for Public Administration.

1976

Psychological man. Cambridge, MA: The Levinson Institute.
The conceptual context for compensation. In E.L. Cass & F.G. Zimmer (Eds.),
    Man and work in society. New York: Van Nostrand Reinhold Company.
Appraisal of *what* performance? *Harvard Business Review, 54*(4), 30-46.
The changing role of the hospital administrator. *Health Care Management
    Review, 1*(1).

1977

[Review of *Knowledge in action*]. *The Bulletin of the Menninger Clinic, 41*(3),
    291.
How adult growth stages affect management development. *Training, 14*(5), 42-
    47.
Managing psychological man. *Management Review, 66*(6), 27-28, 37-40.
[Review of *Systems of organization: Management of the human resource*].
    Administrative Science Quarterly, 22(2), 362.
[Review of *A general theory of bureaucracy*]. *The Columbia Journal of World
    Business, 12*(3), 132-136.
Oedipus in the board room. *Psychology Today* (December), pp. 44-46.

1978

Being good isn't good enough. *Bell Telephone Magazine, 57*(1), 25-26.
The mid-life crisis—And how to make the best of it. *New Jersey Bell
    Magazine, 2.*
Office politics—A path to success. [Interview with Harry Levinson]. *U.S. News
    and World Report* (March 27), pp. 75-76.
The abrasive personality at the office. *Psychology Today* (May), pp. 78-84.
The abrasive personality. *Harvard Business Review, 56*(3), 86-94.
In search of a mentor. *MGR, 4.*
Is HRD a hoax or a necessity: Answers from an organizational psychologist
    and a no-nonsense executive. *Training* (October), pp. 52-54.
Organizational diagnosis in mental health consultation. In T.E. Backer & E.M.
    Glaser (Eds.), *Proceedings of the Advanced Workshop on Program
    Consultation in Mental Health Services* (pp. 23-50). Los Angeles, CA:
    Human Interaction Institute.

1979

[Review of *Consulting with human service systems* and *The consultation process
    in action*]. *The Journal of Applied Behavioral Science, 15*(2), 239-243.
Picking up the pieces. *Manager* (Southwestern Bell), 10-13.

Commentary on: Sexual dysfunction in the 'two-career' family. *Medical Aspects of Human Sexuality* (January), pp. 16-17.
At their own hands. *Executive* (Cornell University), (March), pp. 30-33.
[Interview]. In T.E. Backer & E.M. Glaser (Eds.), *Portraits of 17 outstanding organizational consultants* (pp. 79-105). Los Angeles, CA: Human Interaction Research Institute.

1980

An overview of stress and satisfaction: The contract with self. In L.A. Bond & J.C. Rosen (Eds.), *Competence and coping during adulthood* (pp. 224-239). New England, Vermont Conference on the Primary Prevention of Psychopathology.
Motivational issues and compensation: An integrative overview. In D.J. McLaughlin (Ed.), *Executive compensation in the 1980s* (pp. 144-163). San Francisco, CA: Pentacle Press.
Power, leadership, and the management of stress. *Professional Psychology, 11*(3), 497-508.
Criteria for choosing chief executives. *Harvard Business Review, 58*(4), 113-129.
Choosing your successor. *Chief Executive Magazine, 14*(Winter), 29-33.

1981

Deskbound managers on the way out. *InterNorth/81*, 2(February).
When executives burn out. *Harvard Business Review, 59*(3), 73-81.
Comments on The failing company: In the long run, consultation doesn't help. *Consultation, 1*(1).
Seminar on organizational diagnosis. *Consultation, 1*(1), 45-47.

1982

The need for comprehensive performance appraisal. In *Executive compensation and performance* (pp. 81-124). Proceeding of the Second Pentacle Conference on Executive Compensation, New York. New York: Pentacle Press.
Professionalizing consultation. *Consultation, 1*(2), 38-41.
[Review of *The stress check* and *The work stress connection: How to cope with job burnout*]. *The Journal of Applied Behavioral Science, 18*(2), 239-245.
Diagnosis and intervention in organizational settings. In H.C. Schulberg & M. Killilea (Eds.), *The modern practice of community mental health* (pp. 289-311). San Francisco, CA: Jossey-Bass.

1983

Clinical psychology in organizational practice. In J.S.J. Manuso (Ed.), *Occupational clinical psychology* (pp. 7-13). New York: Praeger.

After the change. *Long Lines, 63*(1).

Intuition vs. rationality in organizational diagnosis. *Consultation, 2*(2), 27-31.

A second career: The possible dream. *Harvard Business Review, 61*(3), 122-129.

Getting along with the boss. *Across the Board, 20*(6), 47-52.

Consulting with family businesses: What to look for, what to look out for. *Organizational Dynamics* (Summer), pp. 71-80.

1984

Executive selection. In R.J. Corsini (Ed.), *Encyclopedia of psychology* (p. 460). New York: Wiley.

Organizational diagnosis. In R.J. Corsini (Ed.), *Encyclopedia of psychology* (p. 473). New York: Wiley.

With S. Rosenthal. *CEO: Corporate leadership in action.* New York: Basic Books.

A psychologist looks at executive development (Insights on Business Management cassette series). The Consolidated Capital Foundation.

[Review of *The psychoanalysis of organizations*]. *Journal of the American Psychoanalytic Association, 32*(3), 704-706.

1985

Invited commentary: Consultation by cliche. *Consultation: An International Journal, 4*(2), 165-170.

With M.F. Shore. On business and medicine. *The New England Journal of Medicine, 313*(5), 319-321.

Is entrepreneurship an effective tool for social change? *The Tarrytown Letter, 53*(November), 16.

Fate, fads, and the fickle finger thereof. *Consulting Psychology Bulletin, 37*(3), 3-11.

1986

How to handle troublesome people [Interview]. *Boardroom Reports, 15*(14), 13.

Ready, fire, aim: Avoiding management by impulse. Belmont, MA: The Levinson Institute.

The dark side of entrepreneurial personalities. *The President* (July/August), p. 1.

Architects of transcendent purpose. *Healthcare Executive* (September-October), pp. 30-35.

1987

Psychoanalytic theory in organizational behavior. In J.W. Lorsch (Ed.), *Handbook of organizational behavior* (p. 51). Englewood Cliffs, NJ: Prentice-Hall.

Panel on organizational consultation. In J. Krantz (Ed.), *Irrationality in social and organizational life* (pp. 44-51). Washington, DC: A.K. Rice Institute.
How they rate the boss. *Across the Board, 24*(6), 52-58.
Trends in consulting practice. *Managerial Consultation Division Newsletter, 15*(7).

1988

To thine own self be true: Coping with the dilemmas of integrity. In S. Srivastva and Associates (Eds.), *Executive integrity: The search for high human values in organizational life.* San Francisco, CA: Jossey-Bass.
Organizational psychology. In G. Dixon (Ed.), *What works at work: Lessons from the masters* (pp. 278-287). Minneapolis, MN: Lakewood Books.

1989

To see ourselves... *Intrapreneur* (September).
Designing and managing your career. Boston, MA: Harvard Business School Press.

1990

The case of the perplexing promotion. *Harvard Business Review, 68*(1), 11-21.
Consultant's casebook—The "Me, me, me" manager. *Working Woman* (June).
Freud as an entrepreneur: Implications for contemporary psychoanalytic institutes. In L. Lapierre (Ed.), *Clinical approaches to the study of managerial and organizational dynamics.* Proceedings of the fourth annual symposium of the International Society for the Psychoanalytic Study of Organizations, Ecole des Hautes Etudes Commerciales, Montreal, May.
Leadership anyone? *Consulting Psychology Bulletin, 42*(3), 1-7.
Can we develop leaders? Paper presented to the Academy of Management, San Francisco, CA, August 13.

1991

Counseling with top management. *Consulting Psychology Bulletin, 43*(1), 10-15.
Diagnosing organizations systematically. In M. Kets de Vries, *Organizations on the couch.* San Francisco, CA: Jossey-Bass.

1992

Fads, fantasies, and psychological management. *Consulting Psychology Journal, 44*(1), 1-12.
Shadow excellence, *Vision/Action, 11*(2).
How organizational consultation differs from counseling. *Consulting Psychology Journal, 44*(2), 21-22.

With J. Sabbath & J. Connor. Bearding the lion that roared: A case study in organizational consultation. *Consulting Psychology Journal, 44*(4), 2-16.

Transformations, from *The Levinson Letter,* December 15. *Management Quarterly,* pp. 27-31.

Career mastery. San Francisco, CA: Berrett-Koehler.

Case discussion, talented or just tempermental? *Harvard Business Review,* pp. 142-143.

1993

Looking ahead: Caplan's ideas and the future of organizational consultation. In W.P. Erchul (Ed.), *Consultation in community school, and organizational practice* (pp. 193-204). Washington, DC: Taylor & Francis.

NOTES

1. "Fighting and Death from Stress in a Cockroach." *Science, 155*(1967), 1035-1036.

2. "The Effect of Intergroup Competition on Group Member Adjustment." *Personnel Psychology, 20*(1, 1967), 33-44.

3. *Psychiatry in a Troubled World.* New York: Macmillan, 1947.

4. *Management and the Worker.* Cambridge, MA: Harvard University Press, 1939.

5. C. Desjardins, J.A. Marvniak, & F.H. Bronson, "Social Rank in House Mice: Differentiation Revealed by Ultraviolet Visualization of Urinary Marking Patterns." *Science, 182*(1973), 939-941.

6. D.P. Barash, *Sociobiology and Behavior* (2nd ed.). New York: Elsevier, 1982.

7. J.V. Montville, "Psychoanalytic Enlightenment and the Greening Diplomacy." *Journal of the American Psychoanalytic Association, 37*(2, 1989), 297-318.

8. E.H. Erickson, *The Life Cycle Completed.* New York: Norton, 1982.

9. O.F. Kernberg, *Object Relations Theory and Psychoanalysis.* New York: Jason Aronson, 1976.

10. H. Hartmann, *Ego Psychology and the Problem of Adaptation.* New York: International Universities, 1958.

11. H. Kohut, *The Analysis of Self.* New York: International Universities, 1971.

12. K.A. Menninger, *A Manual for Psychiatric Case Study* (rev. ed.). New York: Grune & Stratton, 1962.

13. *Requisite Organization.* Arlington, VA: Cason Hall, 1989.

14. H. Levinson, "Behavioral Job Description: How and Why." *The Levinson Addendum,* 1985.

15. H. Levinson, "Performance Appraisal—Too Little, Too Late." *The Levinson Letter Addendum,* 1975.

16. *The Structure of Scientific Revolutions.* Chicago: University of Chicago Press, 1962.

Principled Ambition

EDWIN A. LOCKE

THE ROOTS OF AMBITION

My philosophy of life is best expressed by my favorite novelist and philosopher, Ayn Rand, who wrote in the Appendix to *Atlas Shrugged*:

> My philosophy, in essence, is the concept of man as a heroic being, with his own happiness as the moral purpose of his life, with productive achievement as his noblest activity, and reason as his only absolute.[1]

Ayn Rand had this to say about ambition:

> "Ambition" means the systematic pursuit of achievement and of constant improvement in respect to one's goal. Like the word "selfishness," and for the same reasons, the word "ambition" has been perverted to mean only the pursuit of dubious or evil goals, such as the pursuit of power; this left no concept to designate the pursuit of actual values. But "ambition" as such is a neutral concept: The evaluation of a given ambition as moral or immoral depends on the nature of the goal. A great scientist or a great artist is the most passionately ambitious of men. A demagogue seeking political power is ambitious. So is a social climber seeking "prestige." So is a modest laborer who works conscientiously to acquire a home of his own. The common denominator is the drive to improve the conditions of one's existence, however broadly or narrowly conceived. ("Improvement" is a moral term and depends on one's standard of values. An ambition guided by an irrational standard does not, *in fact*, lead to improvement but to self destruction.)[2]

217

My own ambition was always principled and never blind. Honesty is a quality that I have always valued both in myself and in others. As a child, I could not validate this virtue philosophically, but I made it a point of pride (despite the usual childhood slip-ups) to be honest in everything I did.

The roots of ambition have not been studied by scientists and thus, are not known, but they might lie partly in childhood dreams. Here, I do not refer to night-time dreams but to day-time dreams. For example, Ted Turner said, "I dreamed about world conquest when I was a boy. I was a great fan of Julius Caesar, Alexander the Great, Napoleon. I drew pictures of airplanes and battleships and sailing ships. I wished I was with Horatio Nelson at the Battle of Trafalgar or with Isaac Hull in the frigate Constitution fighting the British. I saw every movie starring Errol Flynn. And I wanted to be a fighter pilot. I dreamed that I was flying a spitfire jet in the Battle of Britain."[3]

I did not have specific, career ambitions as a child, but I did have qualities that might have fostered high achievement later in life. I can think of three. (1) Like Ted Turner, I loved heroes. My first heroes were comic book characters such as Superman, Batman, Captain Marvel, and the like. Later, I learned to love heroes in books. I treasured stories such as *Ivanhoe, Knights of the Round Table*, and the *Adventures of Sherlock Holmes*. When I had to stay home from school due to illness, I would read voraciously, often completing six books in a single day. I also loved movies, especially westerns, and radio shows such as *The Green Hornet* and *The Shadow*.

(2) I wanted to excel at the things that I did if I felt that they were within my capability. I hated to lose, even at cards and was rather bad-tempered when I did lose.

(3) I was generally not a procrastinator. I believe that it is not enough to dream in order to achieve something great; one must work to actualize one's dreams in reality. To actualize one's dreams, one must constantly be taking action. And if one procrastinates, one will not take the needed actions. In school, I turned in assignments on time. In one of my first summer jobs, I worked in an aluminum factory as sort of an all-around clerical helper. At the end of the summer, one of the things my supervisors said that they really liked about my work was that when I was given something to do, I did it and did it immediately. They said, "If you would ever like to work here when you finish school, please come back."

CHILDHOOD AND EDUCATION

I was born in New York City in 1938 and lived most of my early life in New York and Washington, D.C. I would call my upbringing upper-middle class. My father was a bank vice-president; later, a special ambassador to the Middle East for President Truman; and later, a businessman. His business success was never what he wanted it to be. His real dream, which he never achieved, was to be permanently in government service in the role of something like a regular or permanent ambassador or Secretary of State. He was an absentee father. When he was around, which was seldom, he was nice but totally uninvolved in the process of childrearing. Many years later, he told me the motive for this. He feared that if he got involved in child rearing, he would get into arguments with my mother and did not want to get into such arguments— so he simply stayed out of it. I resent this abdication of responsibility to this day, but I suppose it could have been worse. After all, he was not abusive, was not alcoholic, and did not desert the family (though my parents were later divorced).

The burden of rearing three children fell on my mother with the help of various maids, and when we were quite young, governesses. She was the daughter of a fairly wealthy Wall Street broker and a very socially conscious (snobbish) mother. I never agreed with my mother's philosophy, which was Christian with a moderate to heavy dose of martyrdom thrown in, but I do give her credit for taking the role of parent seriously and trying to do the best for us. For me, this included many attempts to find a father substitute for me, for example, trying to get men friends of hers to do things with me after school and sending me to summer camp so that I could be with other boys and men.

She forced me to go to Sunday school, but did not succeed for very long in converting me to her religious views. I began to show considerable skepticism in high school and became an atheist in college. She still resents me for not accepting her philosophy, though for the most part, she has adjusted to it.

I have an older sister and a younger brother; as children, we fought and bickered all the time. I remember being quite jealous of my younger brother who I felt was babied frequently and held to much lower standards of behavior than I was. (We get along well now.) Socially, I was shy but always had a few close friends. I was not a social butterfly and was never in the "in" clique.

I think one of the best things that my parents, especially my mother, did was to see that I went to very good private schools most of my life. From the fourth to the eighth grade, I went to an excellent private elementary school in New York City (Buckley). When I graduated from there, I went to an outstanding boarding school in New Hampshire (Exeter). I then went to Harvard for my undergraduate degree. For graduate school, I went to Cornell (my own choice).

I am very grateful to my parents for their help in sending me to these excellent schools, all of which taught me to meet the highest intellectual and educational standards. Of all of the private schools I went to, the hardest one for me was the elementary school. My high school, in turn, was easier than that. College, in turn, was easier than that. And graduate school, in turn, was still easier. This is an interesting sequence psychologically: to be pressured to accept high standards when you are young so that subsequent standards seemed quite reasonable by comparison.

With respect to grades, my goals were my own. I was not explicitly pressured by my parents to excel, although they did appreciate good performance in school. I personally always took pride in doing well in school as long as the courses were within my capabilities. I basically saw myself as a B to A student, depending on the context. When I first started in elementary school, I earned low Cs, because I had come from a public school in Florida where I had gone for one year. But after a couple of years, I adjusted and was able to get mostly Bs, although I had to work quite hard for them. When I went to prep school, I started with Bs and Cs and ended up with Bs and a few As. When I went to college, I started with Bs and Cs and ended up with straight As. When I went to graduate school, I got all As. So, clearly, the pattern was that each place I went, I did better than the place before. I still attribute this to the high standards of the first good school that I went to.

Occasionally I got side-tracked in my school performance. I remember when I was in my sophomore year in college, I started a small business with one of my roommates, selling paperbacks, candy, and cigarettes outside the dining hall. That semester, I got a couple of Cs, and I was infuriated because my view was that Cs were simply "not me." I was so angry that I immediately quit the business. I told my roommate, "Its yours," and immediately got down to hard work and brought my grades up dramatically the next semester.

I would not call myself, at least before college, an intellectual. When I was in prep school, my mother would often say something on the order of, "You used to be nice before you went to Exeter," suggesting that I had become cynical there. This was probably true, because at Exeter they taught us to question and criticize everything; however, they did not really offer any philosophy to replace those that they taught us to question.

When I went to Harvard, the atmosphere was quite intellectual and we used to discuss ideas quite a bit, especially religion. I remember that one of the most intellectual people I met there was a young man named Dan Frost who was black. I was very impressed that at every meal he would be discussing ideas of some sort, and I am sure he would have become a famous intellectual of some kind if it were not for his tragic death shortly after graduation in a boating accident. (In those days, there was no such thing as the grotesque policy of affirmative action, a thinly disguised form of quotas. There were no double standards for admission. When you saw black students at Harvard, you knew they had earned their way there; they were just as smart as everyone else.)

When I was in college (1956 to 1960) there was some drinking but virtually no drugs, at least of the kind kids take nowadays. The biggest "drug scandal" that I recall was a student who took No-Doz for two nights in a row in order to write a term paper and then fell asleep in class!

One thing I regret about my education is that I went, for a period of nine years (five years in elementary school and four years in prep school) to all-boys' schools. The result was that girls were considered to be a very desirable but very unknown and distant species. The only time you even saw them was for special dances and get-togethers. In college, things were better because Radcliffe students went to classes with the Harvard men.

I was never a great athlete. I won a junior varsity letter in prep school for running the mile (not very fast). When I got to college, some people urged me to go out for coxswain on the crew, because I was one of the smallest kids in the class. The job of coxswain was a good one for me because it required one to do several things at once; namely, steer the boat, keep track of where the boat was in relation to the course, keep track of the other boats, time the number of strokes per minute of our own boat by means of a stop watch, coach the crew, and encourage them. Despite winning a varsity letter and defeating archrival Yale, my proudest moment in crew came in another way. One year, the Harvard coxes challenged the Yale coxes to a four-oared race; that is, with four coxes rowing and one of the oarsmen serving as cox. I was very proud when we crushed them. The next year, they refused to row against us.

My major sport since college has been tennis, which I took up seriously about ten years ago. I approached this sport with the same intensity that I approached my work. I started out being a very poor player but was determined to improve myself, and I worked steadily through lessons and practice for ten years to improve every stroke in the tennis repertoire. I was always surprised that most club players I knew showed no desire at all to improve. Perhaps they got pleasure from simply playing, while I got pleasure from playing well in relation to my ability.

In college, I majored in psychology, and I remember that one of my most interesting courses was one in human motivation taught by David McClelland. He used to say in the class and in various lectures around campus that what we needed was "a good five-cent measure of motivation." I also took courses from other eminent people: leftist economist John Kenneth Galbraith, whom I did not agree with; anthropologist Clyde Kluckhohn, who came out in favor of Zen Buddhism; sociologist Samuel Stouffer; obscure theologian Paul Tillich ("God is one's 'ultimate concern'") who did not convert me. I also took a philosophy course, but found it to be very disappointing because the teacher was just a cynic and gave one nothing to believe in.

One of the two most important things that happened to me at Harvard was to get some *career direction*. I was very unsure in the fall of my senior year about what to do in terms of a career. I had some interest in business, but then I read a book by William H. Whyte titled *The Organization Man*. It somewhat discouraged me because of the stress on conformity that he claimed was endemic to business at the time. At the same time, I liked psychology, but I did not want to make a career out of rat and pigeon psychology.

I went to my advisor, R.J. Herrnstein who, after some discussion, suggested that I combine my two interests and apply to graduate school in industrial psychology. He specifically recommended Cornell because it had two of the leading people in the field, T.A. Ryan and Patricia C. Smith. I had never heard of industrial psychology, but I thought his arguments were sound. So I applied to the industrial psychology graduate program at Cornell and was accepted with an assistantship. I was also accepted at the University of Chicago but decided on Cornell. I will always be very grateful to Dick Herrnstein for his excellent career advice. Just recently (30 years later), I sent him my new goal setting book—*A Theory of Goal Setting and Task Peformance* (1990)—and told him how happy I was that he had pointed me in this direction. He wrote back that he was extremely impressed with the book, and I was gratified that he was.

The second thing of importance that happened to me at Harvard was discovering the work of Ayn Rand. I was writing a paper on business executives for a course, and one evening, quite by chance, I saw a movie on television called *The Fountainhead.*[4] I went to my course discussion leader (whose name I think was Leon Bramson), and said that I had seen this movie and that it seemed of relevance to the paper I was writing. I asked him if he knew whether it was based on a book. To my everlasting gratitude, he said, "Yes. It is a book by Ayn Rand." I immediately obtained a copy and read it and loved it more than any book I had ever read. She projected, in adult form, the heroes that I had admired so much as a child. The theme of the book was individualism vs. collectivism, not in politics but in man's soul.

Later, I learned that she had written another book, *Atlas Shrugged*, and I immediately got a copy of that book and read it. It took me about three days to read it and I was in a state of emotional and intellectual shock the entire time. I had never read anything like it and I never have since. (Its theme was the role of man's mind in existence.) I learned from the book that egoism and capitalism were good rather than evil as I had been told by my professors, that philosophy is important and relevant to this life, and that a rationally defensible system of philosophy is possible.[5] I was especially struck by a line in the book which said, in effect, that each man should strive to achieve the best within him. After reading the book, I thought that nobody on earth could fail to see this book as one of the greatest, if not the greatest, book ever written. I was very disappointed to learn, however, that when I recommended it to my roommates, they either had no interest in it or did not agree with it. It took me some time to realize that most people did not share my premises. Some forty years after reading the book I was happy to be able to write a book review essay about it for the *Academy of Management Review* (1989).

At Cornell, Patricia Smith, who had offered me the assistantship, became my mentor, and I learned a great deal from her. She was somewhat taken aback with me because she kept saying, "You are intelligent and yet you are right-wing." She was quite left-wing in her own politics. Nonetheless, she appreciated my ability and was very supportive of me in the graduate program.

It was a lot easier then—that is, between 1960 and 1964—to go through a graduate program because there was a lot less to know than there is now. For example, I believe that there were only two books written about work motivation at that time: one by Viteles and the other by Herzberg. (Vroom's 1964 book came out during my last year there.) I recall that in *one* doctoral seminar, we covered all there was to know about supervision and leadership, creativity, operations research, moderator variables, and one or two other topics. I worked for several years on the Cornell job satisfaction project, the outcome of which was the "Cornell Job Descriptive Index." Chuck Hulin, now a professor at the University of Illinois, also worked on this project.

I think there were four crucial things that I got out of graduate school over and above the degree:

Publishing. Pat Smith stressed, from the beginning, the importance of publishing. Unlike some of my fellow doctoral students, I took her advice very seriously and published several pieces while I was in graduate school. I liked writing, as I always had, and found that I could do it successfully and without procrastination.

Goal Setting. I first learned about the idea of goal setting as a motivational technique from one of the classic texts in industrial psychology, Ryan and Smith's *Principles of Industrial Psychology.*[6] In one of the motivation chapters was the report of a research finding obtained by C.A. Mace in England in 1935. It showed that specific challenging goals led to a higher level of performance on a learning task than the goals of "do your best." I found this a fascinating finding and it fit in with a point Ryan had made in a couple of articles that he had written—namely, that the most direct determinant of what a person does is what he intends or is trying to do.

At the time that I was in the graduate program, Ryan was writing a book later to be titled *Intentional Behavior* (1970); a number of the doctoral students were allowed to read the preliminary chapters of the book. This got me thinking that using goal setting as an approach to motivation might be a fruitful one, and I decided to do my dissertation on this subject. I will never forget announcing to Pat Smith that I was going to do my dissertation on goal setting rather than on the job satisfaction project. I announced this over the phone one day and I remember there was a long, long silence, during which, I could imagine what she was thinking and could tell clearly that she was disappointed. But to her credit, she accepted it. That was the beginning of my goal setting research, some of which was even included in Ryan's book, which was not published for another six years.

Ambition. In graduate school, I began to concretize my somewhat amorphous ambition by deciding that I wanted to make an important contribution to the field of psychology. At that time, I did not know exactly what it would be, but at least I had focused it on that field. I recall that I used to make long lists of research ideas based on books and articles that I had read. Even though I did not research the ideas that I first wrote down, I was always thinking of interesting projects to do.

Ayn Rand. During graduate school, I began to study the philosophy of Ayn Rand, which she called "Objectivism." The more I studied it, the more sense it made and the more depth that I saw it had. Unlike some theories, philosophies, and treatises, where the more you study them, the less merit they seem to have, the opposite was the case with Objectivism. Further, I observed that when I studied the philosophy and argued the points with other people, they could not refute them. Even though they might call me names and scream, they could not expose any flaws in the actual arguments. Finally, I saw not only that the philosophy applied to the real world but was totally integrated and rational. I am still studying and applying the philosophy today.

WORK HISTORY

When I graduated from Cornell, I considered three job possibilities: the first was at the University of Illinois where Chuck Hulin had gone. This job interview turned out to be an unfortunate one. It was during the Goldwater election and I remember going to a faculty get-together, during which politics naturally came up, and I turned out to be the only Goldwater supporter, I think, in the entire room. The arguments became very heated, and I remember that one professor threatened to punch me out. My argumentativeness and passion did not go over well with the faculty and they announced—not to me, but to others who got back to me—that I was somewhat mentally deranged and would never amount to anything, and that I would undoubtedly use my classes to beat my students over the head with false ideas. They did not make me an offer.

My second interview was with Sears Roebuck. Sears, under Jon Benz, had an outstanding personnel research program, and I seriously considered going there. One question I asked Dr. Benz was, "If I go to Sears, would I work on what I want to work on or what you want me to work on?" He answered that I would have to work on what they wanted me to work on. While I thought that was quite reasonable, I wanted a job where I would have more freedom to choose my own research topics.

Thus, I accepted a job at the American Institutes for Research (AIR), whose Washington office was run by Ed Fleishman. This was a nonprofit research institute where they supported you part of the time but where you were expected eventually to get grants to support your own research. I am especially grateful to Ed Fleishman for hiring me, because at the time I was being interviewed, I said I had certain doubts about whether it was right to take government money to do research. I finally resolved the issue in my own mind and received my first grant or contract from the Office of Naval Research (ONR). This supported my goal setting research for about three years. I hired Judy Bryan as my research assistant. People acquainted with the goal setting literature will recognize many early articles published by Locke and Bryan or Bryan and Locke. The work under the ONR grant convinced me that the goal setting paradigm was a viable one.

I realized during and after graduate school that the dominant paradigm in psychology was behaviorism. I felt virtually alone in opposing this pernicious philosophy. I remember one review of an article I submitted to the *Journal of Experimental Psychology* expressed shock that anyone would do research on something like goal setting and stated, in effect, "Haven't we gone beyond these old-fashioned, mentalistic concepts by now?"

There were only two people in the field that I knew who were even making a pretense at defending consciousness: Don Dulany at Illinois and Charles Speilberger, temporarily visiting at the National Institutes of Mental Health. Despite being in a minority, I was convinced that my cognitive approach was correct. There were two reasons that I was certain of my view: First, the evidence of introspection provided to me an overwhelming refutation of behaviorism. Anyone who looked into his own mind for five seconds could see that what he believed and desired affected his actions. Behaviorists claimed that these experiences were epiphenomena. But they never proved this, and I always found their claim to be arbitrary, as well as self-contradictory.[7] Furthermore, the work of Dulany and others demonstrated that without taking into account what a person thinks, the behaviorists were unable to explain human action.[8]

The second reason I was certain of my approach was the philosophy of Objectivism, which by this time I had studied quite thoroughly and was convinced was valid. Several aspects of the philosophy were relevant here. One was that consciousness was a philosophical axiom and could not be escaped.[9] The second was that free will (volition) was a derivative axiom and could not be denied without self-contradiction.[10] Ultimately volition, like the axiom of consciousness, is validated by introspection.[11]

I tried to do my share to show the fallacies of behaviorism.[12] I think my most important and influential piece was the discussion of Wolpe's method of psychotherapy, which I demonstrated, despite Wolpe's denial, had to involve dealing with the client's consciousness.[13]

Of course, behaviorism soon collapsed as the dominant paradigm in psychology and is now no longer taken seriously by anyone except diehards. But it has still always puzzled me that behaviorism was *ever* taken seriously.

I have concluded that the following factors were responsible for this: First, it had no opposition. At the time the views of its founder, John B. Watson became popular, his only real competitor was William McDougall who argued for a theory of psychology based on instincts. It was not very difficult to expose the fallacies in such a view. Watson also had to fight European introspectionism which came to America mainly via Titchner. But this, too, was a very narrow view because introspectionism only introspected about things like sensory qualities and not about things like motives.

The second reason was poor introspection on the part of psychologists. Many psychologists distrust introspection, claiming that it can sometimes be wrong. But this is an invalid argument. Addition and subtraction can sometimes be wrong also in the sense that one *can* make errors in one's computations, but this does not invalidate mathematics.

The claim that one could not validate introspective reports was unjustified. One validates introspection through observation (through direct awareness of one's own mental contents and processes); in other people introspective reports are validated through inference. It is never possible to do away with inference in any science, including physics and chemistry.

A third factor in the dominance of behaviorism, I believe, was intellectual self-doubt and cowardice on the part of psychologists and, to an extent, philosophers of science who knew better. Philosophically, reason had been attacked and seemingly destroyed by every major philosopher from Hume to the present (except Ayn Rand), so that all we were left with, at best, was simply sense experience. This was the essence of logical positivism and its derivative, operationism (e.g., "intelligence is what intelligence tests measure"). Both of these collapsed in philosophy even before behaviorism did.

The cowardice is exemplified by a statement that a well-known psychologist made to me in the 1960s. He said that he, too, opposed behaviorism but that it was not safe in terms of your career success to speak out too loudly, against it, because it was the dominant view. But, he added, "after you get to be really eminent and secure, then you can speak out." Of course, he never did. I never had any sympathy with such a view and I always was shocked when people who did not agree with behaviorism tried to compromise with it or seemed to go along with it out of fear of being criticized by a dominant majority. I wonder how many wrong paradigms in science have endured over the centuries simply because people who disagreed with them and had good evidence to question them did not have the courage to speak out against them.

What finally destroyed behaviorism was the same thing that finally destroyed communism: It didn't work. Behaviorist (and communist) premises were antithetical to reason and reality and thus could be evaded only so long. As Ayn Rand taught me: "A is A"; reality is inexorable; and the irrational must fail. The irrationality of behaviorism was especially fantastic, because it involved a science rejecting its own subject matter—consciousness. How would the field of biology progress if it rejected the concept of life? How would the field of chemistry develop if it rejected the concept of molecule? How would the discipline of history function if it rejected the concept of the past?

The fourth reason behaviorism flourished for a time was that it made people feel safe by allegedly taking its methodology from the natural sciences. Psychologists have always had an inferiority complex about the fact that psychology was not a "hard" science. So out of a desperate desire to conform to the standards set by the natural sciences, it tried to deal only with those things which were directly observable, such as, stimuli, responses, reinforcements, and behaviors. Aside from this not working, the joke was on the psychologists because even physics and chemistry deal with unobservables through inference. For example, no one has ever directly (with the unaided senses) observed an atom or a quark. I believe behaviorism retarded the science of psychology by at least 50 years. Today, at least, most psychologists, despite many disagreements among themselves, take consciousness seriously and study it as a legitimate enterprise.

(The fundamental behaviorist error was to deny the fact that reality must come first and scientific methods and procedures must adapt to it; thus, if consciousness is the subject matter, suitable methods have to be devised for measuring it. Instead, the behaviorists redefined the subject matter as "behavior" in order to conform to the method they felt safe with, namely, observation of the external world.)

I was treated very well at the American Institutes for Research (AIR) and enjoyed my stay very much. During my third year there, Jack Bartlett, who was doing some work for AIR, was building an industrial/organizational psychology program at the University of Maryland, College Park, and suggested I join him in the program. I thought this was a good opportunity for me, and so I applied for the job and was accepted. I had published extensively by this time and had no trouble getting tenure in 1969, two years after joining the department (in 1967).

Everything went smoothly in the department until I had a run-in with the same Jack Bartlett who had recruited me. I forget the details, but I believe it began in a doctoral pro-seminar which all the faculty and grads attended. Some student asked me why I did not do statistical tests of some ideas that I was discussing. I said that it is not always appropriate to do such tests and asserted (somewhat defensively) that there are people who use statistics as a substitute for thinking. Bartlett, who was in the class, somehow concluded that this was a direct attack on him. Such an attack was in no way intended by me, but it caused a real uproar; and he came back with some insulting comments of his own.

As head of the Industrial Organizational Psychology Program, Bartlett held considerable power and everyone knew it. Just like the power theories would have predicted, graduate students and faculty alike scurried away from me like priests from an atheist, except for one very courageous doctoral student named Norman Cartledge. At considerable risk to himself, he announced that he would continue to work with me and that he did not care what the other people thought. I have always admired him and been grateful to him for this gesture. He graduated from the program with no problems.

A young lady in the program was not so fortunate. She was doing research for her masters thesis with Bartlett and me, and we had had some difficulty resolving a certain statistical problem. After this blow-up occurred, she came to me, obviously frightened, and indicated that she was not sure that she wanted to work with me because she said (to rationalize her fear) that I was dishonest. I asked her the reason, and she said it was because of my approach to the statistical issue in her thesis. I told her that if she believed that, I would not work with *her* anymore. I was subsequently informed that *one year later*, she was told that her thesis problem could not be solved and she left the program.

By that time I, essentially, had left as well. An opening came up in the Business School at Maryland which was just building its management group at that time. Jack Bartlett suggested that maybe it would be a good idea if I took a look at this opening. At that time, Jack Miner was the Department Chair. I did look at it and got an offer to go there on a two-thirds time appointment with one-third of my time remaining in psychology. I thought it looked like a smart thing to do, all things considered, and so I took the offer. It proved to be a very good decision, and I have been there ever since. I am now full-time in the business school and an affiliate in psychology.

Despite the blow-up with Bartlett, I was grateful that he later went to great pains to make sure I got promoted to full professor. One of the reasons I have remained at Maryland was because I was treated very well by business school Dean Rudy Lamone. Rudy was strongly merit-oriented and always rewarded people for their performance, keeping political issues to a minimum. Furthermore, the management group developed into a very fine faculty. For many years, I did not think it was so unusual for a department of ten or twelve people to have every single person be productive and to have no venomous factions among the group; I simply assumed that this was normal. I later learned that this was quite abnormal in terms of what other faculty around the country experienced. So I have been especially grateful to have such an outstanding group of both productive and personable faculty in the department.

One of the most important things that happened to me after I began working was to meet my future my wife, Anne.[14] We met on a tour of Europe. She had all the qualities that I wanted in a woman: intelligence, honesty, beauty, ambition, class, taste, and a sense of humor. She shared completely my philosophy and outlook on life and also tolerated my somewhat compulsive work habits. She, too, was an educator; and in 1977, she opened her own Montessori school in Annapolis which has grown in size from 13 students the first year to 95 (maximum) in recent years. She has made it a brilliant success through her enormous competence and hard work. I would have been loath to move from the Washington, D.C. area, even if I had gotten a good offer, simply because it has taken her so long to build up the school and its reputation. Four years after being married, we were proud to have our first and only child, a daughter, Joanna. Now a college senior, she has turned out to be a very responsible and intelligent young lady.

RESEARCH AND THEORY BUILDING

As noted earlier, I started publishing while in graduate school and have been doing it ever since. There have been several themes in my research, such as, job satisfaction, the fallacies of behaviorism, philosophy of science, participation in decision making, and so forth, but my main focus for the past 25 years has been on motivation through goal setting. This research, which I started in graduate school and continued at the American Institutes for Research and at Maryland, has culminated (for now) in my recent book with Gary Latham, titled *A Theory of Goal Setting and Task Performance* (1990). I believe the keys to the success of this endeavor were the following:

- The *core idea* was powerful and yet, simple; it focused around a main effect, not three-way interactions or multiple contingency factors.
- *Gary Latham*. I met Gary a few years after I began my laboratory research on goal setting. At the time I had certain doubts as to how well the laboratory findings would apply in field settings. Gary's prolific and brilliant fieldwork on goal setting not only assuaged those doubts but made important theoretical contributions in their own right. Gary and I have been collaborating happily now for over 20 years.
- *Persistence*. I stayed in essentially the same research area for 25 years rather than changing topics every two or three years as is quite popular in the field today. I do not believe that one can really understand a phenomenon by studying it for a couple of years; rather, I think one has to study it for decades. In the case of goal setting, even after 25 years, I feel there is a great deal that I need to learn about it.
- To build goal-setting theory, I was constantly *integrating*—not only integrating the findings themselves, but integrating goal setting concepts with other related concepts such as participation in decision making, feedback, and satisfaction. I was also integrating goal theory with other relevant theories, such as expectancy theory and social-cognitive theory.[15] These integrations have not only helped build goal setting theory into a more powerful theory, but also have added to our overall knowledge by showing how the theories complement one another.

It seemed at first that integrating expectancy theory and goal setting theory would be quite a simple matter, but it turned out to be very complex. It took me 25 years to understand how the expectancy aspect alone could be integrated.[16] I am just now learning how to integrate the valence and instrumentality aspects of expectancy theory with goal setting. Some of the preliminary work is in the book,[17] but some of it is still going on.[18] I just recently figured out how to fully integrate job satisfaction with goal setting via the mechanism I call the high performance cycle.[19] I could never integrate goal setting with behaviorism, although I did note in some articles that the methods used by OB Mod are almost identical to the methods used in goal setting, but the behaviorists simply attached other names to these mechanisms.[20]

• I had a certain *attitude toward negative findings* in goal setting. When I went to graduate school, one industrial psychologist's theory was just becoming popular and I observed his very antagonistic attitude, both in personal correspondence with people like Pat Smith and at professional meetings, toward anyone who disagreed with any part of his findings. He would get extremely hostile and contemptuous and the effect of this was simply to make people angry. More importantly, from the point of view of his own theory, it prevented his theory from growing because he was, in effect, building a barricade around himself and shooting anyone that came over it, rather than trying to further develop the theory and correct any flaws that it might have. I always used a basic principle of Ayn Rand's philosophy in dealing with negative findings: Reality first (she called it the "primacy of existence" to distinguish it from its opposite, the "primacy of consciousness," such as, wishes). So I always viewed such findings (if based on valid studies) as something that I could learn from and use to adjust or modify the theory. In fact, I even tried to anticipate situations in which the theory would not come out, such as when there was low commitment to goals or when the task was complex. I learned about things I had overlooked from others. For example, Miriam Erez[21] helped me to understand the necessary role of feedback in the goal-setting process. Bandura's[22] social cognitive theory made me understand the role of self-efficacy, a concept which I later connected with expectancy theory.

Presently, many researchers are studying goal setting on complex tasks, which has proven to be a very complicated issue. But people like Chris Earley (University of Minnesota) and Bob Wood (University of Western Australia) have made important contributions here. Some current work I am doing with Ken Smith (University of Maryland) is also throwing light on this phenomenon.[23]

• A final factor in the success of goal-setting theory was what I call *research networking*. I get a great deal of mail about my research, some of it from young researchers just starting their research careers or planning dissertations. I have always taken pains to reply to these letters or talk to such people on the phone or talk with them at length at meetings on the grounds that the more people doing research on goal setting, the more knowledge we will acquire. I have made it a point to never get angry at such people (with one exception to be discussed below), even when the studies did not come out. I always try to look at their ideas seriously; often, they suggest ideas that I had never thought of. The result of this is that it encourages them to keep in contact with me and to give me ideas in turn. They, in turn, get in touch with others. So it has developed that a very large number of people now are interested in goal setting. Obviously, this is partly because the phenomenon is quite robust and they get good results and can publish them, but I think it is also because they feel that there is a network of people, including myself, whom they can correspond with and from whom they can obtain good insights.

One of the most successful networking projects involved Latham, Erez, and myself. We collaborated in order to discover why Latham's and Erez's studies of participation on goal setting obtained contradictory results. We designed four experiments based on differences in the methods used by Latham and Erez that we thought could have influenced the results. With me acting as mediator, we conducted four new experiments and resolved the disagreements to our mutual satisfaction. We were very gratified when our paper "Resolving Scientific Disputes by the Joint Design of Crucial Experiments by the Antagonists: Application to the Erez-Latham Dispute Regarding Participation in Goal Setting" (1988) won the best paper award from the OB division of the Academy of Management.

The one exception to being very positive toward young researchers involves a small number of people who have taken goal setting theory, relabelled it under new names and then taken credit for it as their own theory. I have little sympathy with such people. I applaud genuinely new discoveries in goal setting and genuinely new insights, but people who simply relabel known phenomenon hold no interest for me.

I attribute the success I have had in my career to four major factors. I am talking here in a wider sense than why goal setting theory became popular. Rather, I am focusing on why, personally, I feel my career has been a successful one. First, *ambition*. I made work achievement a high priority in my life, as did my wife. However, to go back to a comment made at the beginning of this essay, I never followed the policy of success at all costs; it was always success achieved honestly.

Second, *independence*. I have always used my own judgment about what is right and wrong in science, and in my field in particular, and what is important or is not important among the latest fads in the field. When I started doing goal-setting research, nobody was doing it, and many people (although not Pat Smith or Art Ryan) criticized it on the grounds that it was not in the behaviorist paradigm. But since I knew they were wrong, I simply did and said what I thought was right anyway. Despite the dire warnings of those who worried about the penalties of speaking out, I do not believe this has hurt my career in the long run.

Using my own judgment actually has helped by enabling me to know which
strategies work in research and which do not. For example, the standard way
to do theorizing in the field has always been the hypothetical-deductive
approach in which you first look at a phenomenon, after which you lay out
56 hypotheses about it, and then you go and test each in turn.

I never followed this paradigm, because it never made sense to me. How
can you develop a theory in advance of any data? Such a theory simply involves
blind guesswork by ignorant people, including yourself. Furthermore, such
advanced theorizing rigidifies your thinking along a certain track long before
you have any data to suggest in what direction the theorizing should go. Goal
setting theory always grew out of the data and was not the beginning but the
end of the process—completely the opposite of the conventional view.[24]

When I was developing goal setting theory, I did not fully realize the reasons
why the hypothetical-deductive approach could not work, but I think now I
do. Science deals with the discovery of the unknown and it is worse than futile
to pretend you know the unknown before you know it. Thus, trying to develop
a theory before you have any knowledge about the phenomenon seems useless.
It may be no coincidence that very few successful (widely replicable, widely
generalizable) theories have been developed in organizational behavior or
industrial -organizational psychology. One reason might be that people are too
wedded to the hypothetical-deductive approach.

The third element in my career success was *philosophy*. Ayn Rand's
philosophy of Objectivism did not provide, with the exception to be explained
below, the content for my theoretical work, but it did give me the theoretical
base for such work. The proper role of philosophy is not to serve as a substitute
for actual scientific investigation, but rather to form the foundation for it.
Philosophy answers such questions as: Is there a reality? How do you know
it? How do you form and grasp concepts? And so on. From Objectivism, I
knew that reality was real, that objective scientific knowledge was achievable,
and that consciousness and volition were an axioms which were not to be
escaped. So I knew that studying conscious mechanisms in the regulation of
behavior was a valid enterprise in principle despite my minority position in
the field.

Objectivism also demonstrated that independence was a fundamental virtue.
Reason is an activity of the individual mind. Knowledge can be shared by a
group of individual people, but knowledge as such is an individual phenomenon
and no individual can claim knowledge unless he individually goes through
the process of validating it using his own judgment. Thus, I knew that the fact
that a lot of people *believed* something was true had no epistemological
significance whatsoever. It was only the judgment of my own mind which was
important. This does not mean that I would not listen to good advice, but
people had to convince me that their arguments were correct before I would
accept them.

With respect to specific content, Objectivism helped me in one respect. Ayn Rand[25] had identified the fact that emotions stem from one's subconscious value judgments. This was of enormous help to me in developing my theory of job satisfaction which viewed satisfaction as the result of an appraisal of job against one's value standards.[26]

I was very happy to have been able to meet Ayn Rand in the late 1960s. My wife and I took a course on nonfiction writing which she gave at her apartment and also had several paper conferences with her. I was totally awed by her. She was the most reality-focused, logical, and honest person I have ever met—and also the most brilliant. To give one example of the latter: the problem of the nature of concepts (e.g., what is a concept, how do we form them?) had puzzled the greatest philosophers for more than two millennia. She solved it, in essence, in half an hour![27] This was only one of her many stunning philosophical achievements.

The fourth factor that contributed to my career success was *efficient effort.* Here are some of the ways that I think this manifested itself:

- Working on *multiple projects.* When you first start out as a doctoral student or a new professor, you are usually working on one or two projects. But if you are successful and ambitious, you keep widening your scope. It is typical for me today to be working on between seven and ten research projects at one time, typically with other people. These could be fellow faculty, doctoral students at Maryland, or faculty and even students at other universities. I have always found it very easy to think of ideas; I can think of far more ideas than I could ever research. The advantage of having multiple projects is that all projects have "dead" periods during which nothing is happening, and if you do not have something else to put in their place, you are simply wasting time. If you have seven to ten projects going at once, when several are in a "dead" period, you can be working on the others, and this allows you to have higher total productivity.

- *Delegation.* Delegation eliminates unnecessary effort. I never do something myself that I can reasonably delegate. I do not think I have done more than a few minor data analyses on my own since I left graduate school (although, I do supervise them). When I was at the American Institutes for Research, Judy Bryan did all the analyses, although I would check the work at first to make sure it was done accurately. Since I came to Maryland, I have had doctoral students do all my data analyses (under supervision) which saves my time for more useful activities such as planning, supervising and writing.

- *Use of time.* As I mentioned earlier, I am not a procrastinator. This does not mean I do not have to make an effort to get started, but I try not to waste time. One of the things that I do procrastinate on is keeping up with the literature. I am typically about three years behind in reading books and about two years behind in reading journals, because there is only so much time in the day. I might pick out particular books to read or particular articles, but as to really going through the journals (except for articles on goal setting), I am hopeless. Sometimes, after two years delay, I give up and simply put them on my shelf. If you are going to do a lot of research, you have to set your priorities carefully; you can never be fully up to date on the latest research done by others if you spend most of your time doing your own research.

It will surprise some to know that I never use a word processor. I type my first drafts (at home) on either a 30-year-old, electric typewriter (an IBM, bought used, which has never broken down) or (at school) on an ageless manual typewriter. I let the secretaries type the rough drafts onto their word processors. (There is much debate as do whether this *really* saves time or not.)

The one thing I do not delegate, however, is proofreading. To rewrite Will Rodgers, "I never met a proofreader I didn't distrust." Thus, I always do the proofreading of the text and the references myself. I am not perfect, but my error rate seems to be considerably below what it would be if I delegated this procedure.

I also do not do a lot of consulting. And, with respect to teaching, I am conscientious (and have even won awards), but I do not spend the bulk of my time working on my courses. Again, this is an issue of priority and of having limited time in my life. However, my service seems to get greater and greater each year simply because I am senior professor and chairman of my area and am well known as being helpful on committees. This is taking more and more of my time, but Maryland has been good to me and I do not mind helping out.

● The fourth factor under effort is that of distributing the effort among different people through the use of *joint projects.* If each of two people work on two projects instead of each one working on one, they end up with two research projects instead of one research project, and each person learns more that way. Sometimes, we get three, four, or even five people working on a given project. At Maryland, we try to publish with our doctoral students and get them involved in research, because the main way you learn about research is through apprenticeship. This gives them a good background on how research is actually done and also gets them a publication which helps them get a job later when they go on the market.

I have somewhat of a worldwide network and so I keep in touch with people in other countries, such as Miriam Erez in Israel, Bob Wood in Australia, and Tamao Matsui in Japan, as well as with people in the United States such as Gary Latham, Chris Earley, Cynthia Lee, John Hollenbeck, and Howard Klein and others.

Of course, there are costs in making your career your number one priority in life. One of them is that you have less time to spend with your family. My daughter insists that she will not work as hard at her career as her parents have at their careers; yet she expects to be equally successful. I am not quite sure whether she can pull this off or not, but I will be very impressed if she can.

Also, there is less time to do other things. In terms of leisure activities, my major one is tennis and my wife's main one is gardening. When we do things together, it is usually things like going to movies, ballets, or operas. It is fortunate that my wife's and my careers do not require us to travel very much so that, at least, we can see each other in the evening (usually at dinner, which I cook in 30 minutes, and after 10:00 p.m.).

I think making a marriage work successfully is actually more difficult than being successful at one's career; I give my wife a great part of the credit for making our marriage work successfully for a period of 25 years. We are both high-strung and sometimes get on each other's nerves, but our attachment is not based on superficial qualities but on deep-seated sharing of fundamental values and deep admiration for each other's character; this is what has made it work for so long.

CAREER STAGES

Six years ago, when I was delivering a public lecture at the University of Maryland, as a Distinguished Teacher-Scholar Award winner, I semi-facetiously laid out a number of autobiographical career stages, using bird metaphors. These seemed to generate considerable interest, and so I will repeat them here. However, I make no claims for the universality of these stages.

• *Lonely Gull.* There is a drawing of one on the wall of my office. This is the first stage, during which you are the only one doing what you are doing. You go your own way, oblivious to the world. Most people have no idea what you are doing. Some think you are crazy, detached from reality. The pluses of this stage are that you are not bothered by anyone and have little to lose. Of course, there are risks—you could fly over deserted beaches forever and accomplish nothing. But if you pick up enough speed, you become a

• *Roadrunner.* You are going somewhere fast and purposefully. Your accomplishments look promising, although you are not there yet. The positive side of being a roadrunner is that you are "on a roll" and feel a sense of progress. Roadrunners, of course, can run into stone walls. They also can try to go in too many directions at once and end up going nowhere, turning into chickens with their heads cut off. But if the roadrunner gets up enough momentum, he can achieve new heights and become a

• *Soaring Eagle.* A soaring eagle is looked up to with respect. He is asked to fly everywhere, including abroad. He feels on a "high" because he has convincingly made his point. On the negative side, people begin to take cheap, pot shots at him. He becomes a target of bounty hunters and poachers out to make a killing for themselves. Sometimes eagles get shot down. But if they survive, they can become a

- *Mother Hen.* Mother hens hatch their own graduate students who come to them attracted by their bulk and substance. The mother hen helps her brood to grow and prosper, protecting it from hungry hawks. The hen develops a wide circle of correspondents and spreads both gossip and knowledge. Hens feel proud to have large, productive families but have to watch themselves lest they get sluggish and grow in body but not mind. Also the hen must be careful not to overprotect her brood. Eventually, the hen may grow into a

- *Wise Old Owl.* The owl looks with bemused detachment from on high. But unlike the young gull, he looks down, seated firmly on a tree branch. He stays out of the daily struggle but might make occasional midnight raids when hungry for some excitement. He appears to give wise answers to questions. He is rarely hooted at but may hoot at others. He may get told, "I thought you died a long time ago." Younger birds may say, "Who is that old coot?"

Of course, these stages are overlapping so that you may have two and three-headed birds. I will let the reader decide on the usefulness of these categories in career development theories!

If I were starting over, I can think of very few things in my career that I would do differently. I have enjoyed virtually every minute of it and I am very happy with the outcome.

To end, I would like to quote the words which I put into the time capsule which was buried in the foundation of the new University of Maryland Business School building which was completed in 1993. This time capsule will be opened 50 years from now. Inside the capsule is a copy of *Atlas Shrugged* and the following accompanying note:

> The state of the world 50 years from today will depend on the degree to which the countries of the world are acting in accord with the principles articulated in this book, namely: reality as an absolute, reason as man's only means of knowledge, rational egoism as man's guiding moral principle, and individual rights and laissez faire capitalism as the basis for man's political and economic system. If, in the year 2043, the world has descended into war and chaos, it will be because people have rejected the principles of Ayn Rand's philosophy of Objectivism. If, on the other hand, the world has ascended into a state of peace and prosperity, it will be because people have accepted these principles. When this capsule is opened, I will no longer be among the living. But I have enjoyed a great career at the University of Maryland and a great life in the United States of America—the country that came closest to living by the principles in *Atlas Shrugged*. I wish the University and the world well. Don't let them go.

Edwin A. Locke, Professor and
Chair, Management and
Organization Faculty.

PUBLICATIONS

1961

What's in a name? *American Psychologist, 16,* 607.

1962

With C.L. Hulin. A review and evaluation of the validity studies of activity vector analysis. *Personnel Psychology, 15,* 25-42.

1963

The development of criteria of student achievement. *Educational and Psychological Measurement, 23,* 299-307.
Some correlates of classroom and out-of-class achievement. *Journal of Educational Psychology, 54,* 238-248.

1964

With K.D. Locke, G.A. Morgan, & R.R. Zimmermann. Dimension of social interactions among infant rhesus monkeys. *Psychological Reports, 15,* 339-349.
With P.C. Smith, L.M. Kendall, C.L. Hulin, and A.M. Miller. Convergent and discriminant validity for areas and rating methods of job satisfaction. *Journal of Applied Psychology, 48,* 313-319.

1965

With P.E. Breer. *Task experience as a source of attitudes.* Homewood, IL: Dorsey Press.
A test of Atkinson's formula for predicting choice behavior. *Psychological Reports, 16,* 963-964.
The relationship of task success to task liking and satisfaction. *Journal of Applied Psychology, 49,* 379-385.
The interaction of ability and motivation in performance. *Perceptual and Motor Skills, 21,* 719-725.
With A. Zavala, H.P. Van Cott, and E.A. Fleishman. Studies of helicopter pilot performance: I: The analysis of maneuver dimensions. *Human Factors, 7,* 273-283.
With A. Zavala, & E.A. Fleishman. Studies of helicopter performance: II: The analysis of task dimensions. *Human Factors, 7,* 285-307.

1966

The relationship of intentions to level of performance. *Journal of Applied Psychology, 50,* 60-66.

The relationship of task success to task liking: A replication. *Psychological Reports, 18,* 552-554.

The contradiction of epiphenomenalism. *British Journal of Psychology, 57,* 203-204.

Logical relationships of questions to issues in verbal conditioning studies. *Psychological Reports, 19,* 291-298.

With J.F. Bryan. Cognitive aspects of psychomotor performance. *Journal of Applied Psychology, 50,* 286-291.

A closer look at level of aspiration as a training procedure: A re-analysis of Fryer's data. *Journal of Applied Psychology, 50,* 417-420.

With J.F. Bryan. The effects of goal-setting, rule-learning, and knowledge of score on performance. *American Journal of Psychology, 79,* 451-457.

Relationship of task success to satisfaction: Further replication. *Psychological Reports, 19,* 1132.

With R.B. Ewen, P.C. Smith, & C.L. Hulin. An empirical test of the Herzberg two-factor theory. *Journal of Applied Psychology, 50,* 544-550.

With K.D. Locke, & L.R. Dean. A comparison of the attitudes of civil defense directors and community leaders. *Journal of Applied Behavioral Science, 2,* 413-430.

1967

Further data on the relationship of task success to liking and satisfaction. *Psychological Reports, 20,* 246.

With J.F. Bryan. Performance goals as determinants of level of performance and boredom. *Journal of Applied Psychology, 51,* 120-130.

With J.F. Bryan. Goal-setting as a means of increasing motivation. *Journal of Applied Psychology, 51,* 274-277.

Relationship of goal level to performance level. *Psychological Reports, 20,* 1068.

The case against licensing of psychologists. *The Industrial Psychologist, 4*(3), 25-29.

The motivational effects of knowledge of results: Knowledge or goal-setting? *Journal of Applied Psychology, 51,* 324-329.

With J.F. Bryan. Parkinson's law as a goal-setting phenomenon. *Organizational Behavior and Human Performance, 2,* 258-275.

The relationship of success and expectation to affect on goal-seeking tasks. *Journal of Personality and Social Psychology, 7,* 125-134.

1968

With J.F. Bryan. Grade goals as determinants of academic achievement. *Journal of General Psychology, 79*, 217-228.

With J.F. Bryan, & L.M. Kendall. Goals and intentions as mediators of the effects of monetary incentives on behavior. *Journal of Applied Psychology, 58*, 104-121.

Toward a theory of task motivation and incentives. *Organizational Behavior and Human Performance, 3*, 157-189.

With J.F. Bryan. Goal-setting as a determinant of the effect of knowledge of score of performance. *American Journal of Psychology, 81*, 398-407.

With N. Cartledge, & J. Koeppel. The motivational effects of knowledge of results: A goal-setting phenomenon? *Psychological Bulletin, 70*, 474-485.

The effects of knowledge of results, feedback in relation to standards, and goals on reaction time performance. *American Journal of Psychology, 81*, 566-574.

With J.F. Bryan. Knowledge of score and goal difficulty as determinants of work rate. *Journal of Applied Psychology, 53*, 59-65.

1969

With J.F. Bryan. The directing function of goals in task performance. *Organizational Behavior and Human Performance, 4*, 35-42.

What is job satisfaction? *Organizational Behavior and Human Performance, 4*, 309-336.

Purpose without consciousness: A contradiction. *Psychological Reports, 25*, 991-1009.

Reply to Eysenck et al. *Bulletin of the British Psychological Society, 22*, 162.

1970

With N. Cartledge, & C. Knerr. Studies of the relationship between satisfaction, goal-setting and performance. *Organizational Behavior and Human Performance, 5*, 135-158.

Job satisfaction and job performance: A theoretical analysis. *Organizational Behavior and Human Performance, 5*, 484-500.

The supervisor as "motivator": His influence on employee performance and satisfaction. In B. Bass, R. Cooper, & J. Hass (Eds.), *Managing for accomplishment* (pp. 57-67). Lexington, MA: Heath Lexington.

With W.H. Mobley. The relationship of value importance to satisfaction. *Organizational Behavior and Human Performance, 5*, 463-483.

1971

With J. Schneider. A critique of Herzberg's incident classification system and a suggested revision. *Organizational Behavior and Human Performance, 6*, 441-457.

Is "Behavior Therapy" behavioristic? (An analysis of Wolpe's psychotherapeutic methods). *Psychological Bulletin, 76*, 318-327.

1972

Critical analysis of the concept of causality in behavioristic psychology. *Psychological Reports, 31*, 175-197.

In "defense" of defense mechanisms: Some comments on Bobbit and Behling. *Journal of Applied Psychology, 56*, 297-298.

1973

Satisfiers and dissatisfiers among white collar and blue collar employees. *Journal of Applied Psychology, 58*, 67-76.

1974

With R.J. Whiting. Sources of satisfaction and dissatisfaction among solid waste management employees. *Journal of Applied Psychology, 59*, 145-156.

With T.C. Harris. Replication of white-collar-blue-collar differences in sources of satisfaction and dissatisfaction. *Journal of Applied Psychology, 59*, 369-370

Is violence itself necessarily bad? *American Psychologist, 29*, 149.

1975

With G.P. Latham. Increasing productivity with decreasing time limits: A field replication of Parkinson's Law. *Journal of Applied Psychology, 60*, 524-526.

Personnel attitudes and motivation. *Annual Review of Psychology, 26*, 457-480.

Guide to Effective Study. New York: Springer.

1976

The nature and causes of job satisfaction. In M.D. Dunnette (Ed.), *Handbook of industrial and organizational psychology* (pp. 1297-1349). Chicago: Rand-McNally.

The case against legislating the quality of work life. *The Personnel Administrator, 21*(4), 19-21.

With D. Sirota, & A.D. Wolfson. An experimental case study of the successes and failures of job enrichment in a government agency. *Journal of Applied Psychology, 61*, 701-711.

Legislating the quality of work life: Locke's reply to Lawler's rebuttal. *The Industrial Organizational Psychologist, 14*(November), 24.

1977

Comments on I/O Psychology in Sweden. *The Industrial-Organizational Psychologist, 14*(February), 23.

The myths of behavior mod in organizations. *Academy of Management Review, 2*, 543-533.

An empirical study of lecture note-taking among college students. *Journal of Educational Research, 71*, 93-99.

1978

The ubiquity of the technique of goal setting in theories of and approaches to employee motivation. *Academy of Management Review, 3*, 594-601.

With T. Mento, & B. Katcher. The interaction of ability and motivation in performance: An exploration of the meaning of moderators. *Personnel Psychology, 31*, 269-280.

Job satisfaction reconsidered-reconsidered. *American Psychologist, 33*, 854-855.

1979

With D.M. Schweiger. Participation in decision-making: One more look. In B.M. Staw (Ed.), *Research in organizational behavior* (Vol. 1, pp. 265-399). Greenwich, CT: JAI Press.

Myths in "The myths of the myths about behavior mod in organizations." *Academy of Management Review, 4*, 131-136.

Behavior modification is not cognitive—and other myths: A reply to Ledwidge. *Cognitive Theory and Research, 3*, 119-125.

With G.P. Latham. Goal Setting: A motivational technique that works. *Organizational Dynamics, 8*(2), 68-80.

1980

Latham vs. Komaki: A tale of two paradigms. *Journal of Applied Psychology, 65*, 16-23.

Attitudes and cognitive processes are necessary elements in motivational models (Debate). In B. Karmel (Ed.), *Point and counterpoint in organizational behavior* (pp. 17-45). Hinsdale, IL: Dryden Press.

With D. Feren, V. McCaleb, K. Shaw, & A. Denny. The relative effectiveness of four methods of motivating employee performance. In Duncan, Gruneberg, & Wallis (Eds.), *Changes in working life*. London: Wiley.

With A.J. Mento, & N.D. Cartledge. Maryland vs. Michigan vs. Minnesota: Another look at the relationship of expectancy and goal difficulty to task performance. *Organizational Behavior and Human Performance, 25*, 419-440.

Behaviorism and psychoanalysis: Two sides of the same coin. *The Objectivist Forum, 1*(1), 10-15.

With A.S. Mode, & H. Binswanger. The case against medical licensing. *Medicolegal News, 8*(5), 13ff.

[Review of *Mig Pilot*]. *Objectivist Forum, 1*(4), 10-15.

1981

With C. Bartlem. The Coch and French study: A critique and reinterpretation. *Human Relations, 34*, 555-566.

With K.N. Shaw, L.M. Saari, and G.P. Latham. Goal setting and task performance: 1969-1980. *Psychological Bulletin, 90*, 125-152.

Comment on Neider: The Issue of interpretation of experiments. *Organizational Behavior and Human Performance, 28*, 425-430.

With F. White. Perceived determinants of high and low productivity in three occupational groups: A critical incident study. *Journal of Management Studies, 18*, 375-381.

1982

The ideas of Frederick W. Taylor: An evaluation. *Academy of Management Review, 7*, 14-34.

Goal setting. In C. Heyel (Ed.), *Encyclopedia of management* (3rd ed.). New York: Van Nostrand Reinhold.

Licensing. *American Psychologist* (February), p. 239.

With W. Schilit. A study of upward influence in organizations. *Administrative Science Quarterly, 27*, 304-316.

The relationship of goal level to performance with a short work period and multiple goal levels. *Journal of Applied Psychology, 67*, 512-514.

Critique of Bramel and Friend. *American Psychologist* (July), pp. 858-859.

Employee motivation: A Discussion. *Journal of Contemporary Business, 11*, 71-81.

[Review of *Soul of a new machine*]. *Objectivist Forum, 3*(1), 5-9.

Ayn Rand and psychology. *Objectivist Forum, 3*(5), 5-8.

Ayn Rand and psychology cont. *Objectivist Forum, 3*(6), 12-15.

1983

Performance appraisal under capitalism, socialism, and the mixed economy. In F. Landy, S. Zedeck, & J. Cleveland (Eds.), *Performance measurement and theory*. Hillsdale, NJ: Erlbaum.

Joe Morgan-Computer Elements (Case). In National University Consortium, *Systems organization coursebook*. Dubuque, IA: Kendall-Hunt.

[Review of *Handbook of organizational behavior management*]. *Contemporary Psychology, 28*, 681-682.

With W. Fitzpatrick, & F. White. Job satisfaction and role clarity among university and college faculty. *Review of Higher Education, 28*, 681-682.

Eleven entries. In R. Harre, & R. Lamb (Eds.), *Encyclopedia dictionary of psychology*. Oxford, England: Blackwell.

[Review of KGB today]. *Objectivist Forum, 4*(5), 12-15.

1984

With G.P. Latham. *Goal setting: A motivational technique that works*. Englewood Cliffs, NJ: Prentice-Hall.

With G.P. Latham (with Alain Gosselin). *Goal setting for individuals groups and organizations*. Chicago: Science Research Associates.

[Review of *Inside the criminal mind*]. *Objectivist Forum, 5*(2), 8-15.

With E. Frederick, C. Lee, & P. Bobko. The effects of self-efficacy, goals and task strategies on task performance. *Journal of Applied Psychology, 69*, 241-251.

Job satisfaction. In M. Gruneberg & T. Wall (Eds.), *Social psychology and organizational behavior*. Chichester, England: Wiley.

With S. Taylor, C. Lee, & M. Gist. Type A behavior and faculty productivity: What are the mechanisms? *Organizational Behavior and Human Performance, 34*, 402-418.

With E. Frederick, E. Buckner, & P. Bobko. Effects of previously assigned goals on self-set goals and performance. *Journal of Applied Psychology, 69*, 694-699.

Les techniques tayloriennes considerees du point de vue des theories et des pratiques conteporaines. In M. deMontmollin & O. Pastre (Eds.), *Le Taylorisme*. Paris: Editions La Decouverte.

With K.N. Shaw. Atkinson's inverse-U curve and the missing cognitive variables. *Psychological Reports, 55*, 403-412.

1985

With D. Henne. Job dissatisfaction: What are the consequences? *International Journal of Psychology, 20*, 221-240.

With G.P. Latham. The application of goal setting to sports. *Journal of Sport Psychology, 7*, 205-222.
With D.M. Schweiger, & C.R. Anderson. Complex decision making: A longitudinal study of process and performance. *Organizational Behavior and Human Decision Processes, 36*, 245-272.

1986

Generalizing from laboratory to field: Ecological validity or abstraction of essential elements? In E. Locke (Ed.), *Generalizing from laboratory to field setting*. Lexington, MA: Lexington Books.
(Editor). *Generalizing from laboratory to field settings*. Lexington, MA: Lexington Books.
With D.M. Schweiger, & G.P. Latham. Participation on decision making: When should it be used? *Organizational Dynamics, 14*(3), 65-79.
With R.L. Somers, & T. Tuttle. Adding competition to the management basics. *National Productivity Review* (Winter), pp. 7-21.
With D. Henne. Work motivation theories. In C. Cooper & I. Robertson (Eds.), *International review of industrial and organizational psychology*. Chichester, England: Wiley Ltd.
Job attitudes in historical perspective. In D. Wren & J. Pearce (Eds.), *Papers dedicated to the development of modern management* (pp. 5-11). Academy of Management.
With S.J. Motowidlo, & P. Bobko. Using self-efficacy theory to resolve the conflict between goal theory and expectancy theory in organizational behavior and industrial/organizational psychology. *Journal of Social and Clinical Psychology, 4*, 328-338.

1987

[Review of *Social foundations of thought and action*]. *Academy of Management Review, 1*, 169-171.
How to motivate employees. *State Legislatures, 13*(1), 30-31.
With R.L. Somers. The effects of goal emphasis on performance on a complex task. *Journal of Management Studies, 24*(4), 405-411.
With R.E. Wood, & A.J. Mento. Task complexity as a moderator of goal effects: A meta analysis. *Journal of Applied Psychology, 72*, 416-425.
With R.O. Edmister. The effects of differential goal weights on the performance of a complex financial task. *Personnel Psychology, 40*, 505-517.
With M.E. Gist, & S. Taylor. Organizational behavior: Group structure, process and effectiveness. *Journal of Management, 13*, 237-257.
With R.E. Wood. The relation of self-efficacy and grade goals to academic performance. *Educational and Psychological Measurement, 47*, 1013-1024.

1988

With G.P. Latham, & M. Erez. The determinants of goal commitment. *Academy of Management Review, 13,* 23-29.

With G.P. Latham, & M. Erez. Resolving scientific disputes by the joint design of crucial experiments by the antagonists: Application to the Erez-Latham dispute regarding participation in goal setting. *Journal of Applied Psychology, 73,* 753-772.

With C. Lee & P. Earley. Preliminary empirical analysis of a goal setting measure. *Eastern Academy of Management Proceedings,* pp. 128-130.

The virtue of selfishness. *American Psychologist* (June), p. 481.

1989

[Review of *Atlas shrugged*]. *Academy of Management Review, 14,* 100-103.

[Review of *Executive power*]. *Contemporary Psychology, 34,* 259-260.

With T.W. Lee, & G.P. Latham. Goal setting theory and job performance. In L. Pervin (Ed.), *Goal concepts in personality and social psychology.* Hillsdale, NJ: Erlbaum.

With D. Chah, S. Harrison, & N. Lustgarten. Separating the effects of goal specificity from goal level. *Organizational Behavior and Human Decision Processes, 43,* 270-287.

With V. Huber, & G.P. Latham. The management of impressions through goal setting. In R. Giacalone & P. Rosenfeld (Eds.), *Impression management in the organization.* Hillsdale, NJ: Earlbaum.

1990

With C.R. Leana, & D.M. Schweiger. Fact and fiction in analyzing research on participative decision-making: A critique of Cotton, Vollrath, Frogatt, Lengnick-Hall, and Jennings. *Academy of Management Review, 15,* 137-146.

With G.P. Latham. *A theory of goal setting and task performance.* Englewood Cliffs, NJ: Prentice-Hall.

With G. Latham. The high performance cycle. In U. Kleinbeck, H. Quast, H. Thierry, & H. Hacker (Eds.), *Work motivation.* Hillsdale, NJ: Erlbam.

With R.E. Wood. Goal setting and strategy effects on complex tasks. In B. Staw & L. Cummings (Eds.), *Research in organizational behavior* (Vol. 12, pp. 73-109). Greenwich, CT: JAI Press.

With G.P. Latham. Work motivation and satisfaction: Light at the end of the tunnel. *Psychological Science, 1,* 240-246.

With K.G. Smith, & D. Barry. Goal setting, planning and organizational performance: An experimental simulation. *Organizational Behavior and Human Decision Processes, 46,* 118-134.

With M.S. Taylor. Stress, coping and the meaning of work. In A. Brief & W. Nord (Eds.), *The meaning of work in America.* Lexington, MA: Lexington Books.

1991

With C. Lee, P. Bobko, & C. Earley. An empirical analysis of a goal setting questionnaire. *Journal of Organizational Behavior, 12,* 467-482.

With A.A. Chesney. An examination of the relationship among goal difficulty, business strategies, and performance on a complex management simulation task. *Academy of Management Journal, 34,* 400-424.

Goal theory vs. control theory: Contrasting approaches to understanding work motivation. *Motivation & Emotion, 15,* 9-28.

With G.P. Latham. The fallacies of common sense "truths": A reply to Lamal. *Psychological Science, 2,* 131-132.

With S.A. Kirkpatrick & G.P. Latham. *Using goal setting to improve performance.* King of Pressia, PA: Organizational Design & Development.

Introduction to special issue. *Oranizational Behavior and Human Decision Processes, 50,* 151-153.

The motivation sequence, the motivation hub and the motivation core. *Organizational Behavior and Human Decision Processes, 50,* 288-299.

With G.P. Latham. Self-regualtion through goal setting. *Organizational Behavior and Human Decision Processes, 50,* 212-247.

With S. Kirkpatrick. Leadership: Do traits matter? *Academy of Management Executive, 5*(2), 48-60.

Problems with goal-setting research in sports—and their solution. *Journal of Sport & Exercise Psychology, 8,* 311-316.

The essence of leadership. New York: Lexington-Macmillan.

1992

With S.A. Kirkpatrick. The development of measures of faculty scholarship. *Group & Organization Management 17*(1), 5-23.

Reflections on the Latham/Erez/Locke study. In P. Frost & R. Stablein (Eds.), *Doing exemplary research.* Newbury Park, CA: Sage.

With C.D. Fisher. The new look in job satisfaction research and theory. In C.J. Cranny, P.C. Smith, & E.F. Stone (Eds.), *Job Satisfaction.* New York: Lexington-Macmillan.

There can be no balance between animal and human rights. *Psychological Science, 3,* 143.

With A.J. Mento & H. Klein. Relationships of goal level to valence and instrumentality. *Journal of Applied Psychology, 77,* 395-405.

The Linda Gottfredson case. *The Industrial Psychologist, 29*(4), 60-61.

With G.P. Latham. Comments on McLeod, Liker & Lobel, *Journal of Applied Behavioral Science, 28*, 42-45.

1993

Facts and fallacies about goal theory: A reply to Deci. *Psychological Science, 4*, 63-4.

In Press

With S.A. Kirkpatrick. Commentary on Armstrong and Sperry. *Interfaces.*
With T.A. Judge. Effect of dysfunctional thought processes on subjective well-being and job satisfaction. *Journal of Applied Psychology.*
With K.G. Smith, M. Erez, D-OK Chah, & A. Schaffer. The effects of intra-individual goal conflict on performance. *Journal of Management.*
With G.P. Latham. Goal setting theory. In H. O'Neil (Ed.), *Motivation: Research and theory for individuals and teams.*
Goal setting and productivity under Capitalism and Socialism. (To appear in a book edited by Z. Zaleski.)

NOTES

1. *Atlas Shrugged.* New York: Random House, 1957.
2. Quoted in H. Binswanger, *Ayn Rand Lexicon.* New York: New American Library, 1986, p. 12.
3. The Executive of the Year Award speech given by Ted Turner at the University of Arizona, 1989.
4. A movie based on the novel by Ayn Rand (New York: Bobbs-Merrill, 1943).
5. A. Rand, *Atlas Shrugged;* Idem., "The Objectivist Ethics," in A. Rand (Ed.), *The Virtue of Selfishness* (New York: New American Library, 1964); Idem., *Capitalism: The Unknown Ideal* (New York: New American Library, 1967).
6. *Principles of Industrial Psychology* (New York: Ronald, 1954).
7. "The Contradiction of Epiphenomenalism" (1966).
8. "The Myths of Behavior Mod in Organizations" (1977).
9. See Rand, *Atlas Shrugged* (see also note 27).
10. L. Peikoff, *Objectivism: The Philosophy of Ayn Rand* (New York: Dutton, 1991).
11. See H. Binswanger, "Volition as Cognitive Self-Regulation," *Organizational Behavior and Human Decision Processes, 50* (1991), 154-178.
12. "The Contradiction of Epiphenomenalism" (1966); "Purpose Without Consciousness: A Contradiction" (1969); "Critical Analysis of the Concept of Causality in Behavioristic Psychology" (1972); "The Myths of Behavior Mod in Organizations" (1977).
13. "Is 'Behavior Therapy' Behavioristic? (An Analysis of Wolpe's Psychotherapeutic Methods)" (1971).
14. I am grateful to Anne for her critical comments on two drafts of this essay. She assures the reader that this version represents the "real" me.
15. *A Theory of Goal Setting and Task Performance* (1990).
16. Ibid.

17. Ibid.

18. "Relationship of Goal Level to Valence and Instrumentality" (1992).

19. See Chapter 11 in *A Theory of Goal Setting and Task Performance* (1990) and "Work Motivation and Satisfaction: Light at the End of the Tunnel" (1990).

20. "The Myths of Behavior Mod in Organizations" (1977).

21. See M. Erez, "Feedback: A Necessary Condition for the Goal Setting-Performance Relationship," *Journal of Applied Psychology, 62*(1977), 624-627.

22. A. Bandura, *Social Foundations of Thought and Action* (Englewood Cliffs, NJ: Prentice-Hall, 1986).

23. "Goal Setting, Planning and Organizational Performance: An Experimental Simulation" (1990).

24. "Goal Theory vs. Control Theory: Contrasting Approaches to Understanding Work Motivation" (1991).

25. See Rand, "The Objectivist Ethics" (1964).

26. "The Nature and Causes of Job Satisfaction" (1976).

27. See A. Rand, *Introduction to Objectivist Epistemology* (Expanded 2nd edition, edited by H. Binswanger and L. Peikoff. New York: NAL/Penguin 1990), p. 307.

Dalton E. McFarland

Field of Dreams: Perspectives on the Teaching of Management

DALTON E. McFARLAND

"The field cannot be seen from within the field," declared Ralph Waldo Emerson. But in one of his letters, Carl G. Jung wrote that "It is quite possible that we look at the world from the wrong side and that we might find the right answer by changing our point of view and looking at it from the other side, i.e., not from the outside but from the inside."

For the field of management four observations spring from these contradictory statements. First, it may be more accurate to say that everyone's career in the field traverses different parts of it at different times, entailing the consequences of altered perceptions. Second, we work as though we do see the field from within the field, knowing it in our own way. Third, outsiders can see the field but they do not necessarily see it better than we do. Fourth, in our field it is not easy to tell outsiders from insiders. It is a field of great breadth but less depth than it should have; nevertheless it attracts a growing number and variety of talented teachers and scholars.

Looking back is not as easy as looking forward, for the former is subject to correction by those who know the facts, and we have become inured to the latter by the pseudo-scientific distractions of futurology. Nevertheless the invitation to write an autobiographical essay is a challenge and a delight I could not resist.

Teaching, for me, has been the ideal profession. I see why Gilbert Highet called it "the immortal profession": it's importance for the well-governed society cannot be questioned. Humans are and always will be a teaching species.

In high school I knew it was the occupation I would follow, but only later did I realize that teaching is also a vocation, a calling, and a profession. Later still I was to discover that a career in higher education involved not only very demanding teaching but also hard work in ancillary fields that for others are full-time careers in their own right—consulting, public service, research, writing, editing, and administration.

In high school I was unaware of the vast reaches of higher education; the career that first beckoned was to teach commercial subjects in high school. My teachers doubtless would have encouraged me had they known of my ambitions, but the idea had taken shape gradually and a college education was by no means certain. None of my teachers were a role model, though I liked them for what they exemplified as well as what they taught, and because they liked their work, their students, and each other. The community respected them too, but I could see that its moral prohibitions made them hide sins that today would seem like peccadilloes.

Education and work were the twin pillars of hope for the young in my high school town. A strong work ethic and the importance ascribed to schooling could not be ignored. Though jobs were scarce I found part-time work in several different retail establishments. I learned how to work for tough and demanding bosses, some of whom who were unwitting role models; I found that assertiveness and humor enabled me to cope with difficult people, and saw how work generates friendships, jealousies, animosities, competitiveness, and fun, and how kind yet critical and unrelenting people can be to each other.

My first encounter with higher education occurred when, as a senior, the high school's superintendent included me in a carload of students he took on a two-day visit to the University of Michigan. This episode profoundly stirred my interest in university life. Two vivid scenes remain in my mind: plunging into the huge indoor swimming pool, and the first honors convocation I ever attended. The convocation with its pageantry and ceremony enthralled me, the faculty resplendent in the regalia of ancient times. I listened to speeches that seemed important but which I could not comprehend (a circumstance that has happened many times since). I never recovered from the mental and spiritual impact of this encounter with a first-rate intellectual and scholarly environment.

During my high school years the Great Depression had not yet lost its grip on Sparta, my small West Michigan town. Hard times forged many contrasts in the social and economic climate and taught lessons I later came to classify as "management." I learned about human relations not only from work but from observing the town's delinquents, ne'er-do-wells, alcoholics, and shysters, as well as the prosperous elites, the struggling middle class, and the abysmally poor. Families, churches, schools, and businesses were troubled but worked together for a better future. Most people shared what they could with the less fortunate. Adults cared what became of the young. Rectitude was the standard of judgment for all.

Insights about human relations at work came from hearing my father relive his day's or night's work in stark detail around the dinner table. He was first a machine operator in a foundry and later president of the union local, and still later, a first-line supervisor. The problems he related were very similar at all three stages. He recounted the traumatic and the comic aspects of factory life: political intrigue, insensitive bosses, the tyranny of machines, the failures and successes of the labor union, the postures of petty, stuffed-shirt executives, and more. I realized that his blow-by-blow stories were symptoms of work stress, fear of job loss, and worry about the depression and what the future might hold for his family. After the war, when he found out that I was teaching management in a college, he said "That's not possible. You can't do any such thing." In a way he was right.

By working full time for a year as a bank teller and living at home, I saved enough money to enroll at Western State Teachers College (later to become Western Michigan College of Education and then Western Michigan University). I worked with a group on a dishwashing machine in the union cafeteria, clerked in the college bookstore, and served as a proctor in the new men's dormitory. These jobs too furnished unforgettable lessons about human interaction—perspectives from the bottom rung of the ladder.

At Western I majored in commercial education and minored in economics, but I liked sociology and psychology best. I did not like the work in educational psychology and pedagogy required for practice teaching in Western's high school and for a state teacher's certificate (which I never applied for because World War II and other events intervened).

My teachers at Western were colorful characters of profound learning and good at their trade. Some motivated students through fear and anxiety; whenever they applied this approach to me they seemed to respect my challenges and counter-attacks. Most were tolerant, sympathetic, and helpful beyond the narrow confines of duty, teaching with dedication to their fields and to the social and intellectual needs of students.

Following the attack on Pearl Harbor and before finishing my degree, I enlisted as a Yeoman Second Class in the U.S. Naval Reserve, and was assigned to the Office of Naval Intelligence in Detroit, Michigan. Our domain was the security of Detroit's wartime industrial plants. Two years later, after training for sea duty at the Great Lakes Naval Training Station and officer's training at the University of Notre Dame, I was assigned to ships of the amphibious fleet in the South Pacific.

Four years of naval service didn't teach me much about work, but it surely enhanced my understanding of human relations in organizations. I saw how the Navy rapidly developed an effective fighting force of equipment and trained personnel in an astounding miracle of organization and management. Tough and experienced members of the regular Navy were salted among reluctant amateurs in a ratio of about 1 to 50 in the amphibious fleet, providing a quickly expanding naval force. Reservists necessarily came from all walks of life: rich and poor, educated and unschooled, successes and failures, eager and reluctant, and the strong and the weak. There were alcoholics and lechers, gamblers and dissemblers, realists and dreamers; saints and the selfish, but most were practical and trying to help their country achieve its goals.

Not until I entered graduate school after the war did my managerial observations in business, college, and the Navy shape themselves into a coherent academic focus to help form my personal philosophy of work and shape my career. As my commitment to teaching and research grew, it was clear that graduate school would be the next step. At this point, the wisdom of Ecclesiastes' statement that "Much study is weariness to the flesh" became apparent.

It was a privilege, with financial help from the so-called GI Bill, to attend two of America's finest centers of higher learning: the University of Chicago for an MBA, and Cornell University for a Ph.D. Both had campuses of impressive beauty, Chicago fighting the surrounding poverty and urban decay and Cornell nestled in quiet, pastoral Ithaca, New York. Each had excellent libraries, outstanding faculties, and the unmistakable atmosphere of intellectual quality and integrity.

In the Navy I had managed to finish two correspondence courses for the remaining credits of my B.S. degree and after my return to civilian life in the Spring of 1946, I enrolled in Chicago's School of Business. It was a difficult time for the School with its aging but outstanding senior faculty members and Robert Maynard Hutchins's antipathy toward schools in the University that he accused of offering training rather than education. Nevertheless, Chicago's MBA program was intellectually vigorous and very strong, as it is today, in economics and finance. It was here that I first discovered the endless fascination of the study of management, organizations, and human behavior.

Flexibility in Chicago's program made it possible for me to evade accounting by substituting advanced courses in economics. I also studied theories of education with outstanding faculty researchers in the School of Education without further exposure to the trivia of pedagogical tactics. My main focus, however, was on management and organization, with strong courses on marketing and the social problems of industrial enterprise. The courses on organization and on social problems were among the very earliest of such efforts in universities; textual materials were primitive and scarce, but the lectures and personalities of Lewis Sorrell and William Spencer cemented my conviction that their fields of study should be mine too. Two textbooks nurtured these beliefs: Peterson and Plowman's pioneering *Principles of Organization and Management* (Irwin, 1945), and Chester Barnard's *Functions of the Executive*. Sorrell provided an object lesson on academic freedom in his course on organization by several times filling an entire class hour denouncing in colorful invective what he thought to be the tragic failings of President Hutchins.

A teaching job at the Michigan College of Mining and Technology (later called Michigan Technological University) shifted my focus from high school to college. In the Spring of 1947 I was appointed Assistant Professor of Engineering Administration. The departmental chairman, who was also a Chicago MBA, was in his fifties and still studying there for a Ph.D. that he never completed. He was my first academic role model and mentor, communicating confidence in my teaching and the finer points of the meaning of life. He is the only administrator who ever monitored my teaching by attending my classes. I found it difficult to teach engineering students, most of whom were older than I and who constantly waved their slide rules and spoke mostly in calculus.

The chairman enriched my life with good humor and his practical philosophy of life. He staunchly supported me when the President, spurred by nervous citizens and board members, complained about the leftward slant of the textbook from which I taught economics. It was an ultra-liberal text (John Ise, *Economics*) selected by the department, and my Chairman told the President that he himself was far more liberal in his teaching and beliefs than I. The President let me go. It was a great lesson in academic freedom and responsibility.

In addition to the first course in economics, I taught human relations and personnel management, and basic courses in psychology and sociology. In the summer of 1948 my mentor, seeing the need for seasoning, arranged a consultancy for me with the Director of Industrial Relations of the Allis-Chalmers Company in West Allis, Wisconsin. I observed factory problems, witnessed anti-union strategies and tactics, experienced the contempt of line managers for staff busybodies, and observed that bored fellow office workers were puzzled about what to do until quitting time. One of my assignments was to brief the Director on what to read in the incoming stream of research studies and other reports; another was to give him ideas for program improvement; so far as I know, he never paid any attention to my recommendations.

In 1949 the Graduate School at Cornell University accepted my application for doctoral studies in the newly established New York State School of Industrial and Labor Relations. I first attended a summer school to get the feel of the program and become acquainted with its library and its faculty. Offered an assistantship, I enrolled full-time in 1950 to major in human relations with a group led by William Foote Whyte, finishing my doctoral studies in the spring of 1952.

The NYSSILR was a new state-supported unit in Cornell's unique land-grant system that combined state and privately supported schools on a single campus. The School of Business and Public Administration was new also, but in the private sector. Because my primary interests were personnel management and human relations, and because the NYSSILR faculty members in that and related subjects were so strong, the NYSSILR seemed best for me. It was breaking exciting new ground not only in human relations but also in labor relations subjects.

The broad mission of the NYSSILR called for a balanced approach to labor-management relations, though I thought it an ideal that could only be approached rather than reached. Not until the early seventies, when courses and research in organizational behavior extended existing work in personnel management and human relations, did management theory and teaching in the School achieve a better balance with labor relations subjects.

Faculty research was a major component of all the course work. The School was so well-funded that there was one secretary for every two faculty members and ample funds for supporting faculty research and graduate students. Therefore, it was ideally suited to my objective, which was to obtain an academic post rather than a practitioner position.

For me, management has been an umbrella concept that subsumes and even rationalizes the phenomena of the personnel and labor relations movements, and beyond these, the unexplored frontiers of its relevance for social issues. The School's faculty attracted many successful researchers and practitioners in all these areas for lectures and guest appearances, resulting in a superb mix of the theoretical and the practical.

Human relations was my major field. I chose labor history and personnel administration as my two minors, and also took several courses in cultural anthropology. There was a strong temptation to take all the outstanding courses of able faculty members throughout the university; this collided with Cornell's policy of requiring no fixed number of courses or credits for completing doctoral work. Candidates had to select courses strategically to pass stiff written and oral examinations and finish in a timely manner, but most were tempted to become perpetual students.

In addition to Whyte, the outstanding faculty members whose courses I took included Maurice Neufeld, Vernon Jensen, Arnold Tolles, John Brophy, Temple Burling, Kenneth Beach, Milton Konvitz, and Earl Brooks. Whyte and Brooks were special mentors ready with insights and practical advice to help me avoid pitfalls and traverse the rocky shoals of doctoral work.

Being part of William Foote Whyte's team of researchers and doctoral students in human relations was a magnificent experience and a privilege that profoundly influenced the rest of my life and career. Chris Argyris was a fellow doctoral student; Leonard Sayles, George Strauss, and several other post-doctoral researchers were in the group. Whyte's students, departmental faculty members, and research associates in human relations gathered informally each Monday night at his home in Trumansburg, and most afternoons at tea in the office, to exchange ideas about research, theory, or writing. We advanced our trial balloons on dissertation subjects and reported our individual progress. Members of the group prepared position papers for group discussion of theories, research methods, and new developments in the field; guests were often asked to conduct some of the sessions. These gatherings were casually social but more importantly they provided the inspiration to reach out for new insights and ideas, and to test one's own thinking and research.

Whyte guided my dissertation project—a field study of leadership in a labor union local. I tried hard to master his unique field methods (he was said to be the most directive of nondirective interviewers). I acquired enough practice and insight into nondirective interviewing and the analysis of qualitative data to utilize these methods for the rest of my career. Whyte did not dislike questionnaires and other quantitative techniques; he simply didn't use them much. He didn't preclude students from using them, but I felt more at home without them. I have nurtured a career-long habit of avoiding them on the grounds (sound, I'm sure) that I was better at qualitative methodologies. I knew from the beginning that manipulating statistical data was not my forte and that I preferred clinical approaches to studying organizations and their executives.

Whyte was one of the most successful of the School's faculty members in raising research funds and locating sites suitable for his students' research as well as his own. He received a request from the president of the UEW local at the General Electric Company's plant in Elmira, New York asking for a study of its leaders. Whyte invited me and another student to conduct the studies. We were not allowed to interview or observe behavior in the plant or to talk to managers, so we became skilled in what wags around the School called "pub research," that is, following subjects to taverns and going into their homes for interviews.

The union leader's obvious hope was that the study would clear the local's reputation for left-wing domination. But the president kept his promise that there would be no interference or restrictions of any kind, and that the researchers would have complete freedom of inquiry, including inspection of all documents and files, no limits on who could be interviewed, and freedom to attend all meetings whether scheduled or unscheduled, at any time of the day or night.

From these experiences came another lesson: that unanticipated consequences can pose problems. After I left Cornell, the union leader I had studied issued a news release which appeared in the *Cornell Daily Sun* and other papers, saying that a researcher at Cornell had completely absolved him and the local of any taint of leftist leanings. This I had not done. What I had concluded was that rank-and-file members accepted left-wing leadership because they believed that the local was following good union fundamentals in its relationships with the company. Whyte and the university remained confident in the integrity of my research.

Until going to Cornell my outlook had been essentially midwestern. The School asked me to remain on its faculty to join the group conducting extension programs for managers, but my midwestern orientation won out; I liked the East and its ivy league schools, but did not want to make my home there. John Riegle, then the Director of the University of Michigan's Bureau of Industrial Relations in the School of Business accorded me an interview but declined to make an offer because he thought my business experience was too limited. I was already a published author and somewhat experienced teacher, but I could not dispute his judgment.

My appointment as Assistant Professor of Management in Michigan State University's School of Business and Public Service began in the Fall Quarter of 1952. This left me three summer months to move to East Lansing and to accept a temporary job at the Redmond Company in nearby Owosso, Michigan. Redmond's owner had asked the NYSSILR for someone to assist their new Director of Industrial Relations, but like Riegel he was skeptical about my qualifications. But to get near East Lansing I persuaded him to hire me for clerical work in the employment department. I was now a yeoman with a Ph.D.

A week later, the Director found out about my degree and saw that I was over-qualified for the job. Suddenly I became a consultant to him on upcoming negotiations for a new contract with the U.A.W. local. The Director proved to be an excellent mentor, eager to explain his goals, strategies and tactics. "Forget research," he said. "You can't come to the bargaining sessions as a mere observer, you have to be a company man and do your share of the arguing at the bargaining table." It was a time of high adventure, as when the woman who was president of the local knocked the Director down with a swing of her pocketbook and got fired. She stayed fired, but from then on we had to deal instead with a much tougher international representative.

Two years later, John Riegel asked me to join his Bureau, but by then I was too well situated to make a change. Soon afterward he retired and was succeeded by George Odiorne, for whom I taught occasional courses in his "Management of Managers" executive programs at the University of Michigan.

In my twenty years at Michigan State I benefitted enormously from its dynamic growth, outstanding faculty colleagues, and effective administration. Some years were lean financially, and others not, but over the years resources and moral support engendered first-rate teaching and research. Under President John A. Hannah, Michigan State earned a well-deserved national and international reputation. Hannah had launched a three-fold strategy to achieve its goals: football, facilities, and faculty, almost in that order. The first was well along when I arrived; success in the second was visible and expanding, so much so that Hannah was said to have an edifice complex; and the third grew along with the rest but more slowly.

In my fourth year at Michigan State, I was shocked to read in the newspaper that a new Labor and Industrial Relations Center had been established by the School jointly with the Continuing Education Service. I had not been consulted about this important project in my field, so I delivered a resignation letter to my Chairperson. Surprised at first, he offered to recommend me for a position in the new Center, and I became the Director of its Personnel Management Program Service, alongside the Labor Program Service and a research group. I was also promoted to the rank of Associate Professor of Management, retaining a joint appointment in the College of Business. Three years of administrative responsibilities ensued, but I continued my research and writing along with occasional teaching in the Center and in the Department of Management.

While at Michigan State, I was elected a Fellow of the Academy of Management and a Fellow of the International Academy of Management. These honors lived up to their name in that they provided enduring fellowships with outstanding denizens of the management field.

Reflecting on this period in my career, I see the wisdom in Wayne C. Booth's *Vocation of a Teacher*. In it he describes rhetorical strategies by which teachers can engage radically diverse audiences. He argues that rhetorical skills are required for the teacher to influence a diversity of fellow teachers, students, practitioners, consultants, researchers, and theorists. We occupy a rhetorical maze that we travel mostly by trial and error though occasionally by rational analysis. We do it by instinct, by the ripening of experience, and by pursuing intellectual adventure. I think too much dull teaching results from pedestrian approaches betraying a lack of rhetorical analysis. To Booth's idea I would add, for the same reasons, dramaturgy. In a society sated with the media's professional communicators, with the instant excitement of attending riots and wars all over the world, students have been immersed most of their lives in presentation techniques far superior to those encountered in most classrooms. Obviously rhetoric is only one aspect of the route to success in academic professions. There is also the eclectic, sometimes opportunistic willingness to consider alternative career paths, institutional connections, research interests, and centers of geographical focus. And there are matters of physical health, energy levels, and ambition. Long ago it was plain to me that some persons in university posts hang around a long time without doing much of anything, while others are aggressively self-centered or single-minded in their ambitious strivings. In the middle are those who find their way to balanced progress through reasonable attention to work and other relationships. I think I have been among the moderates, toward the ambitious end of the scale.

The discovery of ancillary careers increased my zest for teaching because working in them enriched it. Teaching, learning, and education were crucial guideposts in my interactions with these adjunct fields; their combination kept university life fascinating in its variety and color. My problem was to avoid dilettantism, so I tried to balance and coordinate my work with the sectors of my professional life as each vied for shares of my time.

Another problem of balance has been that between professional and family life. I tried to stay as flexible as possible in my professional commitments, and to help family members understand what I was doing and why. Though I have probably done less well on this front than I should have, I'm fortunate to have had the love and support of family throughout my career and in retirement.

In allocating my working time, I have been rather eclectic. I have also viewed the several domains of academic activity that interest me as interrelated, and I sought to understand their interconnectedness so as to integrate them into a reasonably productive balance without going overboard on only one or two. Achieving that balance through the natural flow of academic schedules and daily living seemed a natural and easy thing to do. I believe that this did not dilute my energies, deprive my work of sharp focus, produce a dilettante of unsettled mind, or merit the charge of workaholism. I thrived on variety and change, doing what I liked and could do well, and what seemed best and useful to others.

I have enjoyed working close to the problems and people of the business and nonprofit worlds, developing tailor-made educational and training programs for them, and travelling widely around Michigan, the United States, and abroad on research projects and service enterprises. Participating in the exciting duties of this new frontier called "management" enabled me to get acquainted with many of Michigan's best companies and executives, and it enriched my teaching and research and my understanding of university-wide administrative problems. In the early days, I believe, we scarcely thought about the "frontierness" of our subject matter. We were too occupied with our daily tasks to think much about the horizons of the years ahead. It is easy now to look back and see this more clearly, and also to understand that management has lots of frontiers remaining.

During my work for the Center I learned how units that cut across traditional departments complicate the university's organization and administration. Top administrators everywhere were uncertain then (and still are) about how to incorporate institutes, centers and other interdisciplinary functions into the University without conflicts over evaluations, promotions, faculty recruitment, pay, and subject matter when two units must make the decisions.

At first Michigan State's extension programs in business were planned and conducted by its Continuing Education Service, which hired its own faculty of subject-matter specialists. Faculty members in traditional departments successfully protested this duplication, asserting their right to control the offered programs and their contents; the university administration adopted a policy that centers and institutes could no longer design and conduct programs independent of the several colleges, which were instructed to assign their own faculty members to these tasks. I and the other Center administrators held joint appointments in academic departments and so could do some of the program work, but we had to persuade faculty members and departmental chairpersons to staff most of the teaching and research. They were paid for the extra work, but on a more modest scale than they could obtain from outside consulting, lectures, or private seminars and workshops.

At first the Labor and Industrial Relations Center gave no degrees, had no academic courses, and no faculty of its own; in the mid-sixties this was changed and the Center became a degree-granting department of the School of Social and Behavioral Science, with faculty members appointed to tenure-track positions.

On the national scene, while I was still in the Center, the Gordon and Howell and the Carnegie reports appeared, causing upheavals of change in schools of business. At about the same time, a new Dean, Alfred L. Seelye, came to Michigan State's College of Business. In 1958, seeing that he was launching new programs and building a spirited and ambitious new faculty around the impetus of the two reports, I resigned from the Center and returned to full-time service in the Department of Management. Under the new regime David G. Moore had become Chairman of the Department of Management. Several outstanding new faculty members were recruited for the department, including W. Lloyd Warner and his staff of well-funded researchers whom President Seelye and President Hannah lured away from the University of Chicago. With these changes, management teaching and research at Michigan State entered a new era.

While in the Center I had completed the first of five editions of my management textbook, *Management Principles and Practices* (1958). I was promoted to a full professorship in 1959. Three things happened shortly thereafter that significantly influenced my career. I was named editor of the three-year-old *Journal of the Academy of Management* in 1961 after serving as Associate Editor for its first three years of editorship by Paul Dauten at the University of Illinois. In the fall of 1961 I was appointed Chairman of the Department of Management, but in January 1962 I also was named Visiting Professor of Management at IPSOA (Istituto Post Universitaro per lo Studio del Organizatione Aziendale), a post-graduate management school for executives sponsored by the FIAT and Olivetti companies in Turino, Italy.

The nearly simultaneous demands of these three posts meant that I needed the help of colleagues at Michigan State and other universities. Paul J. Gordon at Indiana University helped to edit three issues of the *Journal* while I was in Italy. The position at I.P.S.O.A. combined a three-month sabbatical and an additional three-month leave of absence from my department at MSU, and Dr. Richard Gonzalez substituted for me as Acting Chairman for those six months. Since 1960 I had been serving as Secretary-Treasurer of the Academy of Management, which according to past practice would have resulted in election to the presidency of the Academy after three years. I interrupted this process to go abroad, but was elected president in 1965.

In those days the president of the Academy planned its annual meetings. The 1965 meeting was in the Blackstone Hotel in Chicago. The Academy then had about 600 members; attendance at the meeting, including nonmembers, was around 150. It was the first time the Academy had funds left over after meeting expenses were paid, and it was the first definitive break from meeting on college campuses, and the first to be held at an urban hotel.

My editorship of the *Journal* was interesting not only because I was out of the country for my most of first year as editor, but also because it needed new formats, better contents, and advertiser income to supplement Michigan State's funding, which was generous but insufficient to produce major improvements. A problem that surprised me but shouldn't have was the ire of prominent figures in the management field who didn't like their manuscripts to be rejected. Some of the rejectees were original organizers of the Academy, and some of them had been opposed to the founding of a journal. They reacted emotionally to the swift pace of change. But the day of arm-chair subjectivity was over, and for the Academy a refereed journal had been born. It was also difficult at times to deal with authors dissatisfied with the editor's turnaround time for manuscripts, and subscribers made irate by mistakes in our newborn record system.

To improve the appearance of the *Journal* I had the cover redesigned, reduced the size to its current dimensions, chose new type faces, added new departments, and had an artist design the new logo which eventually became that of the entire Academy, including its journals. To improve the contents I solicited papers from contributors who until then had been unaware of the *Journal*. I carefully edited solicited and unsolicited papers, did all the proofreading, and in addition, with the help of a half-time secretary managed the mailing lists, subscription records, and business procedures. I know that successive editors did these things too, but on a larger scale and with many improvements, a major one being the separation of the editorial and business functions. What I liked best in editorial work were the interactions with management colleagues all over the United States and abroad, and the pleasure of wordsmithing other people's manuscripts.

Much has been written about the role of departmental chairpersons, and in my experience all of it is true and all of it is false, or at least misleading. It is hard to analyze the experience. In my case I was able to continue my academic and scholarly work while also fulfilling administrative duties. Dean Seelye wisely required department chairpersons to teach one course a quarter. In the early 1960s Michigan State had launched a new doctoral program which grew rapidly, and the momentum of foundation support and other encouragements brought about vast changes in MBA and undergraduate curricula. I taught mostly in the MBA and doctoral programs, but also enjoyed teaching occasional undergraduate courses.

Given the desire to combine teaching, research, writing and administration, it was necessary to keep consulting at a minimum and to find a balance among them by combining them in various ways and changing the balance from as new developments took place. As with my colleagues at Michigan State, it was my policy to give first priority to my teaching, then to writing and research and university service, and lastly to consulting and public service. When doing consulting or research in Chicago, for example, we would fly to the campus and back to the city so as not to cancel classes or use substitutes.

Another precept I have followed has been to get more than one result from a single effort: in every consultancy I sought an agreement with the client permitting me to use information (usually disguised) for case and other teaching materials. Consulting work also helped bring reality into my classroom teaching. Consulting often led to research opportunities and research funding, and vice versa. All these activities provided grist for my writing. However successful the balance, combining these activities, each of which could be a profession in its own right, required the flexibility of the traditional academic calendar and the cooperation of university administrators who wisely saw the benefits of such a system for students and the fortunes of the university.

In my consulting I usually worked with one major client at a time; I did not aggressively seek clients or try to produce and sell ready-made programs. My basic approach was to tailor consulting projects to specific needs, help companies and executives quickly get back on their own, and to work at the highest level of the organization necessary for lasting solutions to genuine problems. Early on, much of my consulting involved government and other nonprofit organizations at reduced rates but high in the psychic income of public service.

An interesting adventure while at Michigan State was to help establish the Foundation for Administrative Research. This project originated in a chance encounter between Harold Koontz and Jackson Martindell, a businessman who was publisher of the Marquis Who's Who books in Chicago and president of a research firm in New York City that evaluated the management of leading corporations. Martindell offered the Academy his large office building on Madison Avenue and Koontz, the Academy's president, formed a committee consisting of himself, William Newman, me, and two or three others, to pursue the matter.

Our meeting with Martindell was disappointing because he claimed that he never intended to give us the building, worth millions, but rather his supply of unsold reports on the quality of management in leading companies. We declined his offer but instead decided to set up the new foundation that the Academy would have needed to acquire the building.

The Foundation was established in 1965 as a nonprofit corporation in New York with a 501c(3) status permitting tax deductions for donors. Its fund-raising over the next few years was modest, probably because Board members did not have the time, money, or special know-how for a systematic, large-scale fund-raising effort. Nevertheless it received small grants from corporate donors for a few pilot research projects. It also funded Academy awards and other development programs, and administered projects funded by gifts to other branches of the Academy. In 1989 the law governing federal tax-exempt status for donors was changed and the Academy acquired its own 501(c)3 status. Therefore in 1989 the Foundation became more fully integrated into the Academy's operations, though legally it remains an independent adjunct.

The turbulent times of student activism in the late 1960s assaulted many of the precepts of teaching and administration at Michigan State and other universities, though they have recovered the ethos and philosophy that has assured their integrity and endurance over the centuries. Some beneficial, perhaps lasting changes doubtless came out of the upheavals of that time, but the hysterical if not fanatical demands were out of proportion to the constructive results. Students tried to improve society by revolutionizing the university, oblivious to the futility of insisting that universities cause and therefore must cure all of society's ills. There is much to criticize in today's universities, and indeed in schools of business or management, but books in the muckraking genre of that time as well as now contain nothing new and nothing to guide anyone trying to improve them.

Ill-founded student and public diatribes against business and industry made the teaching of management and business almost an anomaly. Even students with good potential could see little value in careers devoted material gain; they sought a utopian rainbow at the cost of abandoning regular courses or warping them into distorted parodies of learning. It was disturbing to see many so faculty members accept and even encourage students in their rejection of institutional integrity and in their disdain for discipline, their detachment from learning, and their disruption and violence under a mass hysteria founded on misguided or illusory sentiments about the good society. The "if you can't beat'em, join'em" approach alienated those faculty members from colleagues and administrators, whose struggle for fairness and consistency of action turned to weakness and vacillation. The discourse necessary for stability and progress toward mutual goals lost out to chaos and false ideals.

I was glad to see the era of student rebellion give way to orderly change and the renewal of the intellectual and institutional purposes of the university. When the communitarian ethos of the university is disrupted, it is in grave danger, so the emergence of calmer, more deliberate relationships among faculty, students and administrators restored my confidence in them all.

Here I should comment that no one in our profession, including me, succeeds on his or her merits alone. A faculty member is part of an organizational system of goals, resources, and consequences. Progress and success depend on the ability of the people and the organization to pursue mutual goals and interests. I am grateful to Michigan State for its academic opportunities and effective administrators, for able students and colleagues, and for the university's steady commitment to the freedom of intellectual inquiry.

Students, for me, have been a vital influence. I have enjoyed seeing Michigan State's doctoral graduates in management serving in fine universities and earning enviable reputations in their academic careers. Two of them, William Glueck and Kay Bartol, have been president of the Academy of Management; I was fortunate to have chaired their dissertation committees. Students and colleagues in and out of the university provided abundant ideas, criticisms (much too gentle), and stimulating discourse (not so gentle); they knowingly or unknowingly enriched my perceptions, my knowledge, and my writing.

Despite temptations to become a business tycoon, academia maintained its hold on my working life. Opportunities at other institutions were attractive, but Michigan State was the right place for me for twenty years. Perhaps my search skills lacked finesse. On the way to interviews at the University of Wisconsin, I became very ill near midnight on the bus trip to Madison; a doctor who spoke little English thought I was inebriated and sent me to my hotel with two aspirins. With virtually no sleep, I managed to get to the School on time, but exhausted from touring the School's facilities I dozed off in my interview with Dean Dean Gaumnitz. He worked for an hour while I slept, and graciously continued the interview. A most understanding person, he offered me a job which I ultimately declined.

The decision to leave Michigan State was exceedingly difficult. I left for personal reasons rather than dissatisfaction. The idea grew more insistent following the death of my wife in 1970, and the following year I abandoned my departmental chairmanship to return to full-time teaching. It was time for a new beginning; in 1972 I remarried and accepted the post of University Professor of Management and Business Administration at the University of Alabama at Birmingham.

UAB was created in the 1940s by spinning off the state's medical school from the campus at Tuscaloosa and moving it to Birmingham because the medical faculties wanted it to be in the urban center of the state. They also wanted to be in a full-fledged major university complex, so in 1970 University College grew from the nucleus of extension courses conducted in Birmingham by the Tuscaloosa faculties, to provide a structure for schools and departments in the nonmedical sectors of a full-scale university.

These exciting developments included a new School of Business. The campuses at Tuscaloosa, Birmingham, and Huntsville were later combined into the University of Alabama System, each unit with its president and a Chancellor to coordinate them. On paper this system looked good and it pleased the public. People thought it would eliminate duplicate courses and programs, end the competition of the independent units for state funding, and establish controls that assure efficiency. Very little of this happened. The presidents and their branches of the system continued to act independently and competitively, though the branch at Tuscaloosa, its alumni, and the media loftily called it the "capstone" of the system; indeed it maintained its aura of dominance despite the progress of the other two branches.

The dynamic situation at UAB attracted me because the fledgling School of Business was an important part of the plan for the rapidly growing institution. My mission as University Professor, a position which I helped to design, was to build bridges of collaboration and cooperation between units of the top-flight Medical Center and schools of the new University College. The position carried a great deal of freedom for teaching and research across disciplinary and departmental lines. It was clear from the outset that the two divisions were unequal in prestige, resources, and history, and that unless bridging mechanisms could be created, separateness would defeat the purposes for which both were established. I was not the only one working on this problem, though for a few years I was the only University Professor. University College built an excellent faculty and established first-rate academic programs, though the powerful medical center remained dominant in university affairs, heavily financed by federal research grants and income from its medical services while University College had to depend almost entirely on the vagaries of state appropriations. However, each year unity and solidarity grew, and collaborations on academic and scholarly projects greatly increased.

Another attraction to UAB was its urban location in the deep south—a region I had always wanted to learn about first-hand. Alabama's natural beauty, good highways, and excellent parks made the state an interesting place to live, though state and city politics were provincial, uninspired, and often outrageous. I liked Birmingham's mountainous terrain and its excellent cultural environment, but inexcusable slums reminded me of its degrading history of racial disharmony. The city was achieving a measure of racial cooperation and improved opportunities for minorities to find positions in business and government. But its past was never forgotten, and progress has remained a constant goal.

The business community in Birmingham welcomed the university's growth and the new School of Business, contributing to the financial and moral support of the medical center and University College. The University's community spirit, its budget, its reputation as a center of first-rate medical and health training and research and the quality of education provided at moderate cost by University college were vital to the city's progress.

UAB's downtown location and its purchase in 1973 of a large tract of land adjacent to the Medical Center enabled it to expand its physical facilities and to develop a unified and beautiful urban campus. The newer parts of the campus now exhibit an uncity-like quality; the contiguous medical and health facilities are massive and expanding and are more urban in character.

At first I taught undergraduate courses in personnel and human relations, and organizational behavior in the MBA program in the School of Business (my base as a University Professor), and in the Medical Center's master's degree program in nursing administration. By 1978 my teaching and research interests had shifted to social and ethical issues in business-government relations. Vast changes in our country's economic and social milieu encouraged the belief that management knowledge could contribute to the solution of social problems. So I taught graduate courses in social issues, business ethics, and public policy, and wrote a textbook in that field, *Management and Society* (1982). *The Managerial Imperative: The Coming Age of Macromanagement* (1986) was in substance a research sequel to this text.

At UAB I also worked with Medical Center faculty members to develop joint research proposals in health care management and devoted my research time to studies of hospital and health care management, and business-society relationships. I completed a three-year field study of a large multi-hospital system in Birmingham, reported in a *Managerial Innovation and Change in the Metropolitan Hospital* (1979). I also finished *Action Strategies for Managerial Achievement* (1979)—my only "how-to" book—and published the fifth and last edition of *Management Principles and Practices* (1979).

I met with skepticism when I urged the establishment of a doctoral program in management centered in the School of Business. It would have been the first doctoral program in University College. I proposed it as a unique collaboration with the Schools of Engineering, Education, Humanities, and the Behavioral Sciences, but unfortunately this plan did not work out. In due time a different and highly successful collaboration did emerge, however, as a joint program of the Graduate School of Business and the School of Community and Allied Health.

A heart attack in 1981, from which I made a good recovery, stirred reluctant thoughts about early retirement, and in 1983 I was appointed University Professor of Management and Professor of Business Administration Emeritus at UAB. I remained there three more years, grateful to be able to retain my office and secretarial assistant while completing *The Managerial Imperative*, and guiding a doctoral student's dissertation project. During my tenure at UAB my colleagues were always helpful and encouraging; Dean M. Gene Newport and W. Jack Duncan were generous with their time, insights, practical help, and scholarly wisdom, particularly at critical turning points in my work.

Though written largely for scholars, *The Management Imperative* was not a textbook; it sold better to executives in business and public service than in academia. In it I helped pioneer the new concept of macromanagement (which still needs further work). At about the same time, Dr. Philip R. Harris, a management consultant, prolific writer and philosopher of much practical and theoretical wisdom, had discussed the concept in a chapter of his book, *Management in Transition* (Jossey-Bass, 1985). Our books came out so close together that I hadn't seen his and did not cite it in mine. There were slight differences in our definition of the concept which we never fully resolved, but the exchange of our ideas on the subject has been extremely valuable. I have never thought it productive for scholars to quarrel over who first discovered or advanced an idea or a concept, and I'm glad to share the credit with Phil.

Events in the global economy, changes in the political alignments of Eastern Europe and the Soviet Union, and their impact on the social, political and economic systems in the United States are bearing out my assertions in *The Management Imperative* that management theories and practices founded on the concept of the single, domestic, independent though complex organization are anachronisms. No longer can our country or its economic institutions ignore the new opportunities for world markets and accompanying problems of international production and finance. Nor can managers and administrators shun the burdens of greater social responsibility and better ethics in business and government.

Retirement has been a gradual process; it required adjustments whose impact I did not fully comprehend until I experienced them. To relinquish position and status in an organization is also to give up a discipline and an ideology of work to which one has been committed for a very long time. I have continued most of my professional work except regular teaching, but have enjoyed the greater flexibility and variety of activities that comes from the absence of organizational constraints.

Some, seeing me still working, did not realize I had retired, and those who did wondered why work retained its hold on me. The answer is that I like to work and work has become more fascinating when fortified by ample indulgence in leisure-time pursuits. I am largely a creature of habit in my work, but I now give more time to the art of procrastination. I am not now and never have been a workaholic. I like to keep my work and my personal life well organized, but the god of efficiency rules no longer in either.

In 1987, our fifteenth year in Alabama, my wife and I decided to return to Michigan, our home state. For most of my career I worked mostly at my office, appearing daily if in town. Now I work at home in a study I designed for my present needs. Apart from teaching and family responsibilities, reading and writing have been at the center of my life. They were of course necessities of my profession, but they were also an enduring source of personal fulfillment and intellectual growth. My reading in other disciplines has vitalized my perspectives on management. Now writing and related reading are my primary professional and private interests, along with civic duties and community activities.

Giving up regular teaching has been the most difficult aspect of retirement, for students have always stimulated my thinking. I found them always challenging, in and out of class. I like teaching especially when I have discovered something in my own research or that of others worth imparting to students or colleagues. The joy of discovery leads to the joy of teaching, and both lead to the scholar's desire to write.

Traditional policies of "publish or perish" are, I think, the proper standards for promotions and other rewards for faculty efforts, despite their implications of selfishness and aggressive competition. Too often, the processes of discovery and publishing dominate the energy and time of professors, leading to shortcuts in teaching. Yet a teacher's shortcomings waste good educational opportunities. The answer to this dilemma is not to create separate faculties of researchers and teachers, but rather to help each faculty member pursue a balanced career pattern covering the relevant academic functions, while allowing for an emphasis expressive of each person's unique talents and capabilities. To those anticipating or newly embarked on an academic career, I say select your mentors carefully; find a good role model; learn to write.

I am primarily a person of visual rather than aural skills. I learned to listen to research subjects in open-ended, long interviews, but what I see tends to impress me more than what I hear. This is why reading and writing have been important features in my personal and professional life. I'm an inveterate reader of everything except science fiction. It all started early. In high school I read at least half the books in the local Carnegie Library, including nearly every book in a large collection of Greek and Latin classics (in translations). The scheming lives of mythical and historical villains and heroes and the antics of the ancient Greeks and Romans gripped my imagination and sustained me through two years of high school Latin.

I've been an omnivorous but eclectic reader, roaming through fictional and nonfictional works somewhat at random but also concentrating on favorite authors and subjects. I like essays, novels, biographies, plays, and poetry in about that order; I still read avidly in the humanities, especially criticism, history, philosophy, and religion; I keep up with research themes in management, organization, and the behavioral sciences. I collect books not only to read them but to live among them; I annotate and underline almost every book I own. My stack of "books to be read" stays high, reminding me of Sir Kenneth Clark's statement that "After I have owned a book for a while, the impression grows on me that I have read it."

I read selectively when working on an article or a book, but otherwise read almost everything cover-to-cover; I usually remember where I've read something I need, but to make sure I have unstintingly supported the note card and copying industries. Books are a continuing presence in my life, both as to their appearance and in my mind and heart. I can hardly bear to give books away, though I am beginning to sacrifice a few professional ones on subjects I am no longer planning to work on. Still, I am mindful that Heraclitis said "Men who love wisdom must be inquirers into many things indeed."

Reading and writing have always contended with each other for my time. It is every scholar's problem. Erskine Caldwell, obviously thinking of the literary scene, said that "You can be a writer or a reader. I decided to be a writer." I decided to be both, but a perplexing conflict had to be faced: while reading I wish to be writing, and vice versa. And when doing either my neglect of ordinary chores, family and friends haunted my mind. Having an extensive personal library at home and at the office I have often been in the wrong place for what I needed. Probably these conflicts were resolved by losing myself in the tasks at hand, but one of the pluses of retirement is to have all my books, papers and files in one place. Yet the dream of getting really organized persists.

Reading discursively outside the field helps me understand, apply and develop written contributions to the field of management. The works of Erik H. Erikson, Charles Frankel, Ernest Becker, and a host of contemporary philosophers and behavioral scientists are among those that have stimulated my efforts to push management thought beyond the borders that have hemmed it in for the past three decades.

But what of this field called *management*?

Cliches abound, but one I reject is the assertion that management is both a science and an art. I have come to the conclusion that it is neither. It is a congeries of interdisciplinary studies sometimes yielding useful predictions but often only the trite or the bland, or that which springs more readily from common sense than research. As a discipline or a field of study, there has been substantial progress but more is needed. Management is not yet a science, either behavioral or otherwise. Some say it cannot be; others that it should not be. The range between the mundane and the exalted in management thought is enormous, best depicted as a tall, thin pyramid with a large base at the bottom and a wisp of smoke at the top. Qualitative and quantitative studies have added important concepts and practical knowledge to our field, but theories are still a jumble and management remains an elusive and uncertain domain.

One of the mysteries I still find in management as an academic discipline is its amorphous, undefined quality, a lack of assertiveness and direction. I ponder the failures of management scholars to assert the focal mission of their field. Research is abundant but rigorous scholarship is meager; there are too few at work divining the central intellectual and philosophical structure of the field. Theories come and go with little accumulation of explanatory power and hence they are relevant only to small pieces of the pie. We are at the stage where we still justify what we do in management by metaphors that are getting rusty and unreliable.

The idea of management itself lacks sharpness of detail because of its multidisciplinary nature. Management has acquired a trade deficit with other disciplines: it has borrowed more from them than it has contributed to them. Many who regard themselves as teaching or researching in management are, understandably, making their primary careers in other fields. This adds excitement, broadens their outlooks, furthers the aims of their primary discipline, fortunately also illuminating the field of management. It is understandable that many of us yearn to escape from our playpens to triumph in other fields as well as in our own.

Problems of clarity and focus in delineating the field of management are complicated by the mixture of other disciplines that have helped to enlarge and enrich the field as they sought to accomplish purposes of their own. This is not due to cupidity or selfishness, but to the way ancillary disciplines have expanded their primary fields. I do not deplore this, but it reflects the fact that management's identity as a field is in the eye of the beholder. Some believe that management has been dominated by these external interests; I prefer to believe, with Erik H. Erikson, that "the transfer of concepts from one field to another has in other fields led to revolutionary clarifications and yet eventually also to a necessary transcendence of the borrowed concepts by newer and more adequate ones."

Many behavioral scientists writing as organization or management specialists are so much the captive of their mother disciplines that their work ignores or discounts what management researchers in schools of business have already achieved. The fields of ethics, values, and social responsibility are particularly susceptible. One can of course argue that all this makes very little difference in the practical affairs of managers, but I think that more precision and clarity about the nature of the field of management would more closely identify those entitled to speak for it. The root of the problem is that management as a field has an enormous appeal both as a common-sense system of effective endeavors and as a whipping-boy for all that is wrong in society. It has its heroes and its detractors, but their identities are not always clear.

The abundance of concepts, theories, assumptions, methods and empirical studies bestows an ultimate yearning for unity and coherence, grand theory if you will. We need theorists who may some day enjoy pulling it all together. It seems strange that there has been so little progress in this direction. Management remains a discipline without boundaries, fragmented and searching for greater unity and sharper focus.

One reason for this is the confusion surrounding the pattern of subsidiary disciplines within schools of business (or of management). Departments of Management almost never have a dominant role in business schools, while faculties in marketing, finance, accounting, production, communications, operations research, and information processing have in effect adopted "management" as their preferred "umbrella." This trend is reflected in the way prominent schools of business now call themselves schools of management or administration. (For insight on this matter see *Selections*, the Magazine of the Graduate Management Admission Council, Spring 1990, a report of the Commission on Admission to Graduate Management Education).

In *The Managerial Imperative* I espoused the lofty but reasonable idea that management is an integrative discipline embracing all the purposive things that people do or hope to do through their organizational arrangements. Further reflection invites me to temper this view by acknowledging that teaching, education, and research are too often and too generally touted as the best way to solve social problems, and too often used as an excuse for not doing anything else. Education is a slow and uncertain though necessary approach; yet educators themselves are being hauled over the coals for the failures of schools to produce citizens prepared to grapple with their own and society's problems. So education is only one of several things necessary for the preventing or curing such problems as drug abuse, violence, child abuse, fraud, thievery and murder. The world is moving too fast for education alone to keep up, but it can play a meliorative role over the long run.

I still harbor the conviction that better management practice will go along way to ameliorate threats to societal stability and the erosion of human fulfillment. No doubt the rhetorician, the scientist, the physician and many others can also treat their profession as the center of all that is good, and make a case for its value as a central point of view from which to organize some of the chaos in the world. Certainly the fields of business, government, and many others can become stronger if greater attention is paid to the processes and philosophies of management—a task at which educators ought to excel. We ought to teach our students the art of critical understanding, in which case, as Booth suggests, those who learn best may repudiate what we have to teach, and as Booth says, "we can't know whether teaching critical understanding will preserve or destroy our present institutions . . ."

But what do I mean by better management practice and how can we improve it? I can give only a few suggestions that would make a good beginning. First, we need to develop a deeper management philosophy grounded in selected methods and insights of general philosophy. Second, we need to identify the causes of mismanagement, to study its characteristics, and discover the reasons why decision makers so often go astray in both macro and microcosms. Third, we need to overcome the imprisonment of our intellects in fads, cliches, jargon, and the merely fashionable rhetoric which we use to identify ourselves with the cognoscenti. Fourth, we need to examine more fully the interactions key social institutions: business, government, the school, and the church. Fifth, we need to evaluate our work and our works more carefully and to be more critical with each other than we have been.

Teaching and research in management need more and better critical analyses from inside the field, as well as more and better external appraisal. Yes, criticism abounds, but it is sporadic, confined to methodological error, based on casual or poorly constructed opinion surveys and whims of the moment. Our paradigms, philosophy, extant theories, basic assumptions and generalizations, symbolism, and concepts are still virtually unexplored and therefore untouched by our best critical minds.

Signs of progress can be seen in the studies of management education by the American Assembly of Collegiate Schools of Business, particularly that of Lyman Porter and Lawrence McKibbin, in publications of the Graduate Management Admissions Council, and in the works of James Q. Wilson,

Amitai Etzioni, William Frederick, David Vogel, and a few others. Works of this genre spring more from strivings in economics and business administration than management per se; I don't equate them with management, but it is clear that they illuminate much that is missing from mainstream management education and research.

A good source of implied if not explicit criticism comes from students streaming into the social matrix. Fitted with university educations in diverse fields, they bring youth and inexperience into profit and nonprofit enterprises, discounting outworn ways of doing things and creating new ones. In his autobiography Carl Sandburg called them "the young strangers." The young strangers entering the field of management are our students; they are busy transcending and correcting what we thought we taught them with all the authenticity in the world.

It is encouraging that more attention is being paid in management education and research to matters of ethics, social responsibility, and values. Our publics are demanding it, and this is a good place for the melding of management thought with that of general philosophy. It is sad that so many critics of government, business, universities and public schools do not find a focus for their attacks that offers insight into causes and restorative action. The hunt for villains seems appropriate for combating the crime and corruption that pervades organizations and harms decent and innocent people. Still, we often go after the wrong villains and let the worst go unpunished.

I too am troubled by glitches in our criminal justice system, but at the same time I think it is important to focus on the mismanagement that causes and abets many such depredations. Society has no other way of managing its affairs other than at the macro level, that is, with plans and programs on such a large scale as to saddle governments with inevitable forces of mismanagement that are hard to overcome even in private organizations.

I agree with those who say that schools of business and of public administration can do much better in educating individuals for ethical and socially responsible management, but I have reservations about how this is currently being approached. For one thing, most of the work in this sector of management consists of long case studies for use in teaching. Most of them are simply descriptive reports; they center on specific events, times, places, and issues in a single company. Thus they are narrowly drawn; moreover they invite a self-righteous search for villains defined by the emotions of case-writer and teacher, and ignore facts and events occurring after the cases are written. The reason courses rely so much on cases is that basic research on the management aspects of social issues is scant and the philosophy of social responsibility has not been thoroughly analyzed in the context of the social institutions by which society gets its work done. The burdens of comparative analysis, developing critical understanding, nurturing insights, and elucidating enormous complexity falls heavily on the student. Fortunately, there are a growing number of explanatory and systematic textbooks useful in supplementing case work.

In writing this essay I have become aware of the difference between truth and accuracy. It was Samuel Butler who said "I don't mind lying but I hate inaccuracy." I have tried to attain both, but recognize the subjectivity of all that has been said.

Apart from the sciences, analytical philosophy is the only branch of learning putting accuracy and logic of expression foremost. In other disciplines, truth is elusive and writer's writers of the utmost integrity disagree. Historical truth in particular is a quest, not a discrete attainment. But one must keep trying; the search for truth, rather than its attainment, is the heart of the university's purpose.

In his introduction to *Inventing the Truth: The Art and Craft of Memoir*, William Zinsser defines the memoir as distinct from autobiography, as "a window into a life, not a history of the self." By narrowing the frame, he said, "the writer of a memoir takes us back a corner of his or her life that was unusually vivid or intense—childhood, for instance—or that was framed by unique events...and thus achieves a focus that isn't possible in an autobiography." So this essay is not a memoir, though it bears some of its characteristics.

St. Augustine provided an early model for autobiography in his *Confessions*. However, the word "biography" came much later; the *Oxford English Dictionary* gives a quotation from Southey in 1809 as the first example of the word's use. Over the years, autobiography changed from being a narrative of the soul's relations with God to something more akin to psychoanalysis, except that the autobiographer becomes a writer instead of a talker (or hires a ghost), to discover his life's meaning.

In his novel *Deception*, Philip Roth has a character named Philip complain that "I write fiction . . . and am told it's biography. I write autobiography and I'm told it's fiction . . . " There is always the risk of being misunderstood, rejected, or misjudged by one's peers or others in any piece of autobiographical writing; thus the authors of novels are often embarrassed by what is imputed to their lives from their fiction. I recall that Laurence Sterne got around this problem in *Tristram Shandy* by devoting the entire book to the first three years of Shandy's life. Shandy speaks with the utmost adult sagacity to produce startling and penetrating commentaries on Sterne's life and times.

I have never kept a systematic journal or detailed records of events and activities in my career, organizations I have helped, or professional work completed. I should have done so, for it would surely have facilitated a more precise writing of this essay. Booth notes that like Thucydides, Herodotus, Gibbon, and *Time* magazine, he has reported from memory conversations and events that must in fact have been somewhat different. As Thucidides said, "My habit has been to make the speakers say what was in my opinion demanded of them by the various occasions, of course adhering as closely as possible to the general sense of what they really said." In sum, memories are tricky and points of view change over time.

In retirement, I agree with a remark of Primo Levi's in *Other People's Trades*, that the bond between a man and his profession is similar to that which ties him to his country, and that "…it is just as complex, often ambivalent, and in general it is understood completely only when it is broken…"

Retirement has created a sense of detachment which encourages me to reflect philosophically about the past and the present of the field of management. Having castigated the futurists so much, I hesitate to predict management's future, but I know it will be significant for humanity's best interests. We can see the field from within the field but we must be wary of misperceptions and the distractions from objectivity. We can credit outsiders of independent and incisive judgment for seeing our field in ways that increase our objectivity and our fund of knowledge.

I assure the reader that I am not the chap who, asked when he would write his memoirs, said "Why should I? I have nothing to hide."

Dalton E. McFarland
passed away on February 6, 1991

PUBLICATIONS

1947

Community responsiblities of the business teacher in the public high schools of Michigan. *National Business Education Quarterly* (Fall).

1949

Public relations aspects of labor relations. *Public Relations Journal* (November).

1950

[Editor] *Techniques of managerial development*. Fourth Annual Conference of Training Directors, Cornell University.

Construction and analysis of achievement tests. *Journal of Engineering Education* (June).

[Review of *Introduction to labor economics*]. *Personnel Journal, 29*(6).

1951

[Editor] *Organizing and administering the training function.*
Fifth Annual Conference on Training Directors, Cornell University.
[Review of *Problems in labor relations*]. *Personnel Psychology* (January).

1953

Basic aims of a course in personnel administration. *Personnel, 30*(1).

1954

How industry can improve its listening techniques. *Business Topics, 1*(4).
Dilemma of the industrial relations director. *Harvard Business Review, 32*(4).
[Review of *The cse method of teaching human relationships*]. *Journal of Personnel Administration and Industrial Relations, 1*(4).

1955

Management and public relations. *Business Topics, 2*(4).
Bottlenecks in human relations training. *Advanced Management, XX*(2).
Leadership in a labor union local. *LIR Research* (June).
[Review of *Centralizatin and decentralization in industrial relations*]. *Industrial and Labor Relations Review* (July).
[Review of *Effective leadership in human relations*]. *Industrial and Labor Relations Review* (July).
[Review of *Personnel administration*]. *Public Personnel Review* (July).
[Review of *Personnel management*]. *Personnel Journal* (May).

1956

The forward look for the industrial relations director. *The Personnel Administrator, 1*(1), 6-9, 24-29.
Organization health and company efficiency. *Business Topics* (Summer).
(Translated and reprinted in *Alta Direccioin* [March-April, 1967])

1957

Industrial relations directors: An annotated bibliography. *Personnel Journal* (Installments in February, March, April, & May).
[Review of *Human relations for management*]. *Industrial and Labor Relations Review* (April).
[Review of *The foreman on the assembly line*]. *Journal of Personnel Administration and Industrial Relations, 3*(1).

1958

Management: Principles and practices. New York: Macmillan.
The role of the consultant in contract negiotations. *Personnel, 34*(6).

1959

(Editor) *Annual proceedings.* Academy of Management.
Scope of the industrial relations function. *Personnel, 36*(1).
Education for managagement: New directions and new challenges. *Journal of the Academy of Management, 2*(1).
Employee development. *Combined Proceedings of the Thirty-Fifth National Shade Tree Conference,* pp. 98-110.
[Review of *Landmarks of tomorrow*]. *Business Topics* (Spring).

1960

The emerging revolution in management education. *Journal of the Academy of Management, 3*(1).
[Review of *Individual behavior and group achievement*]. *Industrial and Labor Relations Review, 13*(2).
[Review of *Industrial organization*]. *The Accounting Review* (April).
[Review of *Management in the industrial world*]. *Administrative Science Quarterly* (September).
[Review of *Classics in management*]. *Business Topics* (Fall).

1961

[Review of *Management's mission in society*]. *Business Topics* (Spring).

1962

[Editor] *Annual proceedings.* Academy of Management.
Cooperation and conflict in personel administration (Monograph). New York: American Foundation for Management Research, Inc.

1964

Management principles and practices. New York: Macmillan.

1965

Theory as an angle of vision in management education. In *Annual Proceedings* (pp. 3-11). Academy of Management.

1966

[Editor]*Current issues and emerging concepts in management,* Vol. II. Boston, MA: Houghton-Mifflin.

Company officers assess the personnel function(AMA Research Study 79). New York: American Management Association.

Theory as an angle of vision in management education. *Management of Personnel Quarterly, 5*(1), 11-15.

[Review of *Managing the managers*]. *Industrial and Labor Relations Review, 19*(2).

1967

[Edited] With F.C. Wickert. *Measuring executive effectiveness. New York: Appleton-Century-Crofts.*

Management curricula in the 1970's. In A "blue-skies" look at schools of business in the 1970's,

Personnel management in transition. *Arizona Review, 16*(10), 1-3.

Accomodating personal aspirations to organizational goals. In D. Pfannstiel & B. Mathews (Eds.), *Cooperative extension organization and administratin, selected papers.* Madsion, WI: University of Wisconsin, Extension Service.

1968

Personnel management: Theory and practice. New York: Macmillan.

[Review of *Occupational careers: A sociological perspective*]. *Industrial and Labor Relations Review, 21*(2).

[Review of *Occupational sociology*]. *Monthly Labor Review, 91*(9).

1969

The learning and practice of management: One world or two? First Franklin F. Moore Lecture in Higher Education for Management, Rider College.

1970

Management: Principles and practices (3rd ed.). New York: Macmillan.

[Review of *An occupation in conflict: Study of the personnel manager*]. *Monthly Labor Review* (April), pp. 76-77.

1971

Personnel management: Readings (Modern Management Series). Penguin Books.
[Review of *Managing the new generation in business*]. *Monthly Labor Review* (October).

1972

Why confidence is lower in social, political, and economic areas [Guest editorial]. *Birmingham News* (December 27).

1973

Administration de personal. Mexico: Fondo de Cultura Economica. [Spanish edition of Personnel management: Theory and practice).
Some comments on social responsibility of business: A question of ethics. In *Proceedings.*

1974

Management: Principles and practices (4th ed.). New York: Macmillan.
Edited with R.M. Powell. *Management problems in social policy research and action programs.* New York: Institute for Administrative Research, Inc./ Columbus, OH: Division of Research, Ohio State University.
Administrative implications of social policy research and action programs. In R.M. Powell & D.E. McFarland (Eds.), *Management problems in social policy research and action programs* (pp. 110-132). New York: Insititute for Administrative Research.
Administrative ability and leadership are not the same thing at all. *Administrative Management* (July), p. 6.
Management and its critics: A look at social pluralism. *Journal of Business Research, 2*(4).
[Review of *A guide to personnel management*]. *Monthly Labor Review* (June).
[Review of *Personnel administratin and the law*]. *Monthly Labor Review* (June).

1975

From the corporate state to managed pluralism. *The Record, XII*(7), 14-20.

1976

Planning and control. In M.G. Newport (Ed.), *Supervisory management: Tools and techniques.* St. Paul, MN: West Publishing.
Whatever happened to the efficiency movement? *The Record, XIII*(6), 50-55.

1977

Action strategies for managerial achievement. New York: AMACOM.
Management, humanism, and society: The case for macromanagement theory. *Academy of Management Review, 2*(4), 613-623.
[Review of *Corporate lives: A journey into the corporate world*]. *Academy of Management Review, 2*(3).

1978

With N. Shiflett. Power and the nursing administrator. *Journal of Nursing Administration* (March), pp. 19-23.

1979

Management: Foundations and practices (5th ed.). New York: Macmillan.
Managerial achievement: Action strategies. Englewood Cliffs, NJ: Prentice-Hall. (Spectrum paperback.)
Managerial innovation and change in the metropolitan hospital. New York: Praeger.
Research methods in the behavioral sciences: A selected bibliography (Rev. ed.). Monticello, IL: Council of Planning Librarians.
Co-edited with N. Shiflett. Power in nursing [Special issue]. *Nursing Dimensions* (June).
With N. Shiflett. The role of power in the nursing profession. *Nursing Dimensions* (June).
Let's kill bureaucractic overkill. *Birmingham News* (March 4), p. F-2.

1980

Your domain and others. *Supervisory Management, 25*(2), 14-20.
[Review of *Management and consulting: An introduction to James O. McKinsey*]. *Industrial and Labor Relations Review, 33*(2), 282-283.

1982

Management and society. Englewood Cliffs, NJ: Prentice-Hall.
Power as a change strategy. In J. Lancasrer & W. Lancaster (Eds.), *The nurse as a change agent: Concepts for advanced nursing practice.* St. Louis, MO: C.V. Mosby.

1984

[Review of *Reasoned argument in social science: Linking research to policy*]. *Alabama Journal of Medical Sciences* (January 21), p. 109.

1985

Analysis of whistleblowing case. In J.C. Champion & J.M. James (Eds.), *Critical incidents in management*(5th ed.). Homewood, IL: Irwin.
Definition of management. In L.R. Bittell & J.E. Ramsey (Eds.), *Handbook for professional managers.* New York: McGraw-Hill.
Boards of directors. In L.R. Bittell & J.E. Ramsey (Eds.), *Handbook for professional managers.* New York: McGraw-Hill.
Committees. In L.R. Bittell & J.E. Ramsey (Eds.), *Handbook for professional managers.* New York: McGraw-Hill.
Definition of manager. In L.R. Bittell & J.E. Ramsey (Eds.), *Handbook for professional managers.* New York: McGraw-Hill.
Corporate officers. In L.R. Bittel & J.E. Ramsey (Eds.), *Handbook for professional managers.* New York: McGraw-Hill.
Progress in good: It's the measure of the advances toward many ideals [Guest editorial]. *The Birmingham News* (September 8).
[Review of *Managing for excellence*]. *The Alabama Journal of Medical Sciences, 22,* 456-457.

1986

The managerial imperative: The age of macromanagement. Cambridge, MA: Ballinger.
Mismanagement and what to do about it. *Nonprofit World, 4*(2), 26-28.
Lapses in good management got president and his staff in trouble [Guest editorial]. *The Birmingham News* (November 30).
[Review of *The price of power: A biography of Charles Eugene Bedaux*]. *Academy of Management Review, 11*(3), 674-676.

1987

Proper management could have helped the president. *Muskegon Chronicle* (November 22).

1988

[Review of *Managing cultural differences* (2nd ed.)]. *Academy of Management Review, 13*(1).

1989

[Review of *Higher education in partnership with industry*]. *National Forum* (Spring).

[Review of *Bhopal: Anatomy of a crisis*]. *Business in the Contemporary World* (Spring).

1990

[Review of *The generous corporation: A political analysis of economic power*]. *Business in the Contemporary World* (Winter).

Pursuing Diversity in an Increasingly Specialized Organizational Science

JOHN B. MINER

My age at the time (January 1991) of writing this autobiography is 64 years. Thus the view behind me extends over a much more extensive panorama than the view in front. In surveying those 64 years my goal is to highlight the turning points, the major accomplishments, and the failures that have dotted my career. This excursion through the past may be of interest, and perhaps even of value, to others for at least two reasons. To me personally this career has been extraordinarily satisfying; perhaps there is something to be learned here about developing a truly gratifying career. Second, my career has spanned the period of emergence and institutionalization of a field that we now call organizational science. I was first employed in a business school in 1956 and took up residence on a more permanent basis in 1960 buoyed on the waves of the Pierson[1] and Gordon and Howell[2] reports' recommendations that business schools open their arms to "behavioral scientists." Thus there is the possibility of contributing something to the chronicling of events that occurred then, and in doing so to writing history.

But perhaps even more significant is the fact that over the period of this revolution, and then institutionalization, my career has somehow taken a series of new tacks and undergone changes to a point that seems now, looking back, to justify describing it as inherently diverse. Yet this has occurred in an arena that Bedeian,[3] among others, describes, and decries, as permeated with an inexorable march to specialization. Perhaps there is something to be learned from looking briefly into the dynamics and experiences of a person who has gone against the tide in this sense. Surely learning of this kind will do little to enhance the career success of those entering our field, and it could indeed be inherently harmful to their political health. On the other hand if Bedeian is right that the field badly needs individuals who will cross the "harsh terrain" between subfields—following Leavitt's terminology[4]—then looking closely at instances where this has been done could prove useful.

It is important to recognize that autobiographies such as this are not written as lifelong diaries. We do not have the complete, valid reinforcement histories that Skinnerian theory would envisage; not even something close to these histories. In large part we must rely on the vagaries of human memory. Accordingly the reader needs some insight into the type of prism through which the writer views the past. In my particular case it is a prism that has been strongly influenced by my training as a psychologist. My degree is in personality theory and clinical psychology. During the period of my training I underwent a lengthy psychoanalysis. These factors combine to make me focus on the causes of subsequent behavior, and thus attempt to organize and interpret events in adult life around some coherent picture of early experiences. This orientation manifests itself repeatedly in this autobiography. As a result more attention is given to my early years than might otherwise be the case. My goal is to provide insight into why my career has unfolded as it has.

THE YEARS OF PERSONAL DEVELOPMENT: 1926-1946

John Lynn Miner, my father, is probably best described as a pragmatic intellectual. After graduating from Allegheny College, where he was something of a football star, he taught at Roberts College in Istanbul, Turkey for several years and later did graduate work in Germany. Returning to the United States, he began studying for a doctorate at Columbia University, while teaching history at a private school to support himself. Although he got well into his dissertation he did not obtain his doctorate. He was increasingly drawn to private school education and in particular to administration. He helped found and headed the Harvey School in Hawthorne, New York, and subsequently, about the time I was born, repeated the process with the Greenwich Country Day School in Greenwich, Connecticut.[5] He also founded a boys camp in Newport, Vermont, on a bluff overlooking Lake Memphremagog. Basically, his career was spent in founding and heading private educational institutions for young boys from wealthy families, preparing them to attend Eastern prep schools and later on college. He was good at what he did. He was at one and the same time a professional educator, an administrator, and an entrepreneur.

Bess Burnham Miner, my mother, graduated from Goucher College and then went to library school in Pittsburgh. She worked for a time as a children's librarian in Philadelphia. My parents were married in 1916 at roughly the same time my father started at the Harvey School. My mother worked with my father at the school, as she did at Camp Neperan in Vermont. She was not formally involved with the Greenwich Country Day School. Throughout her life my mother maintained an intense interest in books. She worked as a professional librarian at a time when employment of any kind was far from fashionable for young women. Our home was always full of books, many of them with a book review cut from the *New York Times* tucked under the front cover.

At the time of my birth my parents were very actively involved in their professional and other interests—my mother was 43 and my father 41. I was their first child, born 10 years after they were married, and as it turned out their only child. It is my impression that the entry of one child into a family typically introduces few changes in the parents' lives, while two or more children can bring about dramatic changes. In any event much of my time outside of school (Greenwich Country Day School) and camp (Camp Neperan) was spent with adults—either my parents or people who worked for my parents. This created an ideal climate for the nurturance of my intellectual development and for the transmission of my parents' values. It may have been somewhat less ideal in fostering my emotional development. There was very little informal play or undirected activity with groups of children—and practically none with groups including girls. A school for boys and a camp for boys makes for a boy's world growing up.

At the age of 9, when on a camping trip up into the Canadian end of Lake Memphremagog, my life changed dramatically. What had been a close to idyllic existence became a nightmare. As I arrived back at the Camp Neperan dock, word was passed that my father was deathly ill. Ultimately with more understanding this translated into the fact that he had suffered a severe stroke. Nurses, and physicians too, seemed to be constantly running through our homes. He did survive, but with partial paralysis on one side and severely impaired speech. He never returned to the Greenwich Country Day School and he never operated Camp Neperan again. Five years later in 1940, coming off a fall football practice at Deerfield Academy, I received word that he had had a second stroke, and died. The years between had been difficult for me as I struggled to cope with the transition from a strong father figure to a severely impaired one; they were even more difficult for my mother. Yet the finality of death was even more difficult. My father was only 56 when he died. A very successful career and a good life had been cut short. He had been very much in charge. My mother and I were in a real sense cast adrift.

The coping that followed was hesitant and uncertain. My father died during my freshman year at Deerfield and World War II broke out during my sophomore year. My mother struggled to keep me in school as opportunities to take defense-related jobs and later enter the armed forces came my way. To me the beckonings of the larger world of action were much stronger than the feeble calls to class sessions and school meetings. Rules and regulations seemed terribly limiting, and there were sufficient times when my desire to break-out and go my own way surfaced that my tenure as a student was severely jeopardized. Somehow my mother and Mr. Boyden, the legendary headmaster of Deerfield Academy, prevailed over all this. My grades remained good and I graduated on time in 1944 with a scholarship to go to Princeton. We had continued to live in Greenwich during the winter and in Vermont in summer, although in the years before my graduation my mother moved to Amherst, Massachusetts so that we could be closer.

Throughout the first 18 years of my life there was the constant transition from Greenwich during the school year to Newport in the summer. This was more than a geographical change. In Greenwich, and later at Deerfield too, my peers came from affluent families and my lifestyle was influenced by that fact, yet my own family was not wealthy at all. My father worked at the school in Greenwich, while my peers' fathers commuted to Wall Street. In Vermont it was the flip side of the coin. My father ran the camp and hired local people. As I became a teenager my friends in Vermont were high school students, but I went to prep school and lived most of the year in another world. Most important I left before the severe Vermont winters descended.

What resulted from this cycle was a strong sense of being different—not better or worse, although at times both thoughts crossed my mind, but for the most part it was simply a matter of feeling different. Without doubt this feeling was reinforced by the experience of living in a family where my father was partially paralyzed and could not talk very well. Those around him became his communicators and translators. Then after five years there simply was no father. Everyone else among my peers had a father.

In my early years this sense of being different, of not really belonging anywhere, was unpleasant. I fought it and tried to gain group acceptance. For the most part that did not work within the Greenwich-Newport nexus; the feeling of being different remained. Gradually my strategy shifted to one of breaking-out of the cycle. A construction company that had hired me to work during the summer in Vermont wanted to hire me full-time. To me the idea of leaving Deerfield and travelling with the construction company was very attractive. My mother did not think it was a very good idea. The Navy wanted young men to enlist at the age of 17. That seemed attractive, too. My mother did not think that was a good idea either.

Finally, we reached a compromise. The Army had a program where you could enlist at age 17, but would not be called to active duty until after your eighteenth birthday; in my case this meant until after graduation from Deerfield. My mother won one there. However, it would not be necessary to wait to be drafted, a process that might well have taken as long as six months. My mother thought it would be best for me to go ahead and get admitted to college, even though actual matriculation might be several years away. That did not seem too much to ask. My mother won another one there. Admission to college was in fact rather painless. My only application was to Princeton.

Acceptance included a substantial scholarship. My four years at Deerfield had been as a scholarship student also.

As anticipated the Army did beckon rather soon—two weeks after my eighteenth birthday to be exact. From then on things happened quickly. After seventeen weeks of basic training in the swampland and palmetto bush of North Florida, and a brief leave home at Christmastime, we shipped out from New York for England. From there we went across the channel to LeHavre and shortly began shuttling around France in boxcars. The Battle of the Bulge had largely burned out by that time, but many U.S. divisions had been decimated and were badly in need of replacements. We were those replacements.

Our final destination proved to be the town of Dieuze in the Alsace. There my status shifted from an unassigned replacement to a member of Headquarters Company, Second Battalion, 242nd Infantry, 42nd (Rainbow) Division. Pfc. Miner was assigned to an antitank gun crew. This was in early February 1945 and the division was in reserve having suffered heavy losses. My time in combat totalled something over two months. It was a strange experience. From the day we jumped off in the mountains on the attack into Germany we were constantly on the move—lots of little towns and an occasional city—Worms, Wurzburg, Schweinfurt, Nurnberg, Munich, and as the war ended, Salzburg. The assignment to an antitank unit proved to be a blessing. For one thing we could ride not walk. But from a health viewpoint the real blessing was the 57-mm antitank gun. It and our truck repeatedly became stuck in the mud, and the front would move on ahead of us. Then we would hurry to catch-up. Often we became lost; sometimes we ended up behind enemy lines. We never did fire the gun at a tank. It was a bizarre trip through southern Germany. You never knew what would happen next. You learned to live with fear.

The history of our battalion and of the 42nd Division in this period has been chronicled elsewhere.[6] As a young, unmarried new replacement it became my fate to stay on in Austria for well over a year after the war in Europe ended. In many respects it was a pleasant experience. Shortly after the end of fighting my duties shifted to the company supply room, first as a clerk and then as supply sergeant. Although those who know me will find this humorous, the decision to assign me to supply was made because of my skill in using a typewriter. We were constantly shifting the supply room from one location to another, packing up and unpacking. After Salzburg there was a string of small towns in the Alps; beautiful, but isolated. The move to Vienna in January 1946 was a welcome change.

In June 1946 orders came through for my return to the United States for discharge. At that time the division had essentially been disbanded, and my supply room was empty. Everyone else from the combat days was gone. It was time to go back and start on a career. The 23 months in the Army, and especially the 18 months in Europe, had been a very maturing experience. I was a lot more dedicated to getting on with my life's work, whatever it was to be, when it came time to start classes at Princeton than would have been the case had there not been this intervening experience.

THE CONSEQUENCES OF PERSONAL DEVELOPMENT

To understand what my career has become it is important to know what kind of a person undertook and carried on that career. This is the heritage of my education in personality theory. Questions of etiology and development are always central.

The best way for me to answer questions of this kind is to present some test results for myself. This is the medium in which I deal professionally. The tests are the Miner Sentence Completion Scales—Form H (1961), Form P (1977) and Form T (1984). They were completed in December 1985 at a point when the scoring system for the last of the three measures had just been put in final form. Now, there is a great deal wrong with interpolating from these three tests completed at age 59 to a career spanning almost 45 years. To do this is probably not good science, and the reader deserves to know why. One problem is that we have no idea how much of what emerged in the tests so many years later was present during my twenties, or even thirties and forties. Furthermore I wrote the test items, did the item-selection research, and developed the scoring system. Accordingly we have three projective techniques which have been stripped of their projective clothing. Worse still, I scored the tests. The net result could very well be that the scores are substantially inflated in a positive direction.

Yet, there are some counterarguments also. The period up through the 'teens does seem to be the time of greatest flux in personality; after that people stabilize more, and test results obtained longitudinally often reflect this. There is a chance that the results at age 59 are retroactive. We find only very little by way of age correlations with these measures among adults (see my 1993 book *Role Motivation Theories*). In addition, the tests were completed in 1985 for my information and to deal with my curiosity. There was no idea then of publishing the results, or providing the scores to others. Thus the incentive to honesty was substantial. Why lie to myself if there was no reason to do so? Yet the most compelling argument is the test results themselves. They make a great deal of sense against the backdrop of the preceding discussion.

The range of possible Total Scores for the hierarchic (or managerial; Form H) scale is from −35 to +35 and for the professional (Form P) and task (or entrepreneurial; Form T) scales it is from −40 to +40. Using the percentiles to make comparisons, it appears that all three Total Scores are rather high, but professional motivation is dominant. Given my father's education and his career as an educator, plus my mother's training and work as a professional librarian, this is not surprising. Being an only child and having considerable adult interaction provided me with many opportunities to learn about and appreciate professional work. The other two Total Scores are high enough to have meaning. They fit well with my father's experiences, although not my mother's. My father was an administrator (a headmaster) throughout most of his career. He also founded or helped found three organizations—two schools and a camp. He was in fact both a manager and an entrepreneur. One way of interpreting the Total Scores in the table below is that they reflect the influence of my father, but that the professional scale score is higher because in that instance my mother, too, exerted an influence.

Miner Sentence Completion Scale Results - December 1985*

The Hierarchic (or Managerial) Scale		
Total Score	+ 9	(81st)
Authority Figures	+ 3	(89th)
Competitive Games	+ 1	(43rd)
Competitive Situations	+ 2	(93rd)
Assertive Role	0	(45th)
Imposing Wishes	+ 2	(81st)
Standing Out from Group	+ 1	(54th)
Routine Administrative Functions	0	(36th)
The Professional Scale		
Total Score	+16	(91st)
Acquiring Knowledge	+ 1	(64th)
Independent Action	+ 6	(96th)
Accepting Status	+ 6	(98th)
Providing Help	+ 1	(35th)
Professional Commitment	+ 2	(77th)
The Task (or Entrepreneurial) Scale		
Total Score	+ 13	(76th)
Self Achievement	+ 5	(86th)
Avoiding Risks	+ 5	(93rd)
Feedback of Results	− 1	(36th)
Personal Innovation	+ 4	(64th)
Planning for the Future	0	(32nd)

Note: * Figures in parentheses are percentile equivalents for corporate managers, professionals, and entrepreneurs, respectively.

The theories of hierarchic, professional, and task motivation underlying the data in the table are in fact joined by a fourth theory dealing with group motivation (see *Role Motivation Theories*, 1993). This is the type of motivation hypothesized to be needed to function effectively in autonomous or sociotechnical work groups, voluntary groups, and the like. No measure of group motivation has been developed. If one were, my expectation is that my scores would be low. Peer group interaction is not my strong suit. This is consistent with my difficulties in the area of group acceptance while growing up. It appears that I came to reject what I did not feel I could have. It may be symptomatic of this that there are Forms H, P, and T of the Miner Sentence Completion Scale, but no Form G (Group). It has been hard for me to get motivated to carry out the very substantial amount of work required to create a Form G.

The subscales of the three measures have score ranges from -5 to +5 in the case of the hierarchic scale and -8 to +8 in the other instances. Due to the lower reliability of the subscales, interpreting scores not at the extremes is not recommended. Given that the lowest subscale score is at the 32nd percentile, one cannot conclude that any motivational pattern is rejected outright. On the other hand there are a number that appear to be supported. The 90th percentile appears to be the best cutting-point for this purpose, but dipping down to the 85th percentile may be warranted. Using these criteria there are two subscales on the hierarchic scale, two subscales on the professional scale, and two subscales on the task scale that require discussion.

The hierarchic data indicate a generally positive attitude toward authority figures and a strong competitive drive. In the former instance there appears to be some reflection of my frequent exposure to adults during my formative years. Perhaps even more important is what happened during psychoanalysis. My impression is that a certain initial negative transference gave way later to a strong positive transference during therapy; these effects may well still linger. I have on occasion gone against authority figures who seemed to be abusing their authority during my career, but this is extremely difficult for me. It may well elicit psychosomatic symptoms. The manifestation of a strong competitive drive will come as no surprise to those who know me, and perhaps have played tennis with me. Part of this is straight-out value teaching by my parents. I was the only child they had; they were winners and their child was supposed to be, also. However, I have also observed that people with not-fully-resolved oedipal strivings tend to score high on Competitive Situations. Given that my father was incapacitated during my early years and then died, leaving me with my mother, there is every reason to believe that the not-fully-resolved oedipal interpretation may apply to myself as well.

The professional results clearly go back to my childhood. The sense of being different appears to have translated into a strong need for independence at an early age. Certainly this need was clearly in evidence during my Deerfield years. Mr. Boyden used to comment often on my excessive desire for freedom during our discussions when rules were broken. My reasoning appears to have been that if I was going to feel different from others anyway, then why not go ahead and enjoy being different and do things my own way. The desire for status on the professional scale, too, seems to go back to an early time. Greenwich, Deerfield, Princeton—this was my upbringing and it has rubbed off. My mother in particular was a very status-conscious person. This is part of my legacy; no doubt it has some relation to my competitiveness, also.

On the task scale the Self Achievement index is elevated, although perhaps not to a really pronounced degree. This measure reflects a tendency to obtain satisfaction from putting substantial effort into something where the end product can be clearly identified as one's own. Such people really enjoy being able to sit back and look at the results of their efforts, such as a company they founded, and being able to say "I did it myself." Needs of this kind can be born out of early insecurities such as those that characterized my childhood. The products that one creates represent a constant statement of one's self-worth and lack of vulnerability. Finally there is the high Avoiding Risks score. Gambling has not been part of my life except in the Army. My parents taught me not to gamble, to hold on to what you had in life and not risk losing it. Much of this no doubt was part of what has been called "the depression mentality," and my formative years occurred during the Great Depression. However, it is also true that on this measure older people, who have more, often score higher than younger people who have nothing to lose. Probably my score in this instance has risen over the years.

THE YEARS OF PROFESSIONAL DEVELOPMENT: 1946-1955

At the time of entering Princeton, my intention was to major in geology. However, my first clash with chemistry convinced me that my career prospects in any field that required that type of knowledge were dim. At the same time it became increasingly apparent that the social sciences, which were not part of my Deerfield education, were a strong spot. The decision to seek a doctorate in clinical psychology came early—sometime toward the end of my freshman year—and my course work from that point on was formatted toward that end. Actually my exposure to the field outside of the classroom was quite limited. There were no clinical psychologist role models around me, and an attempt to learn by doing (as an aid at a private mental hospital during the summer) actually turned out to be quite unpleasant.

Yet the course work in psychology was fascinating. Princeton did an excellent job at that time of exposing undergraduates to its major professors. Those who influenced me the most then were Silvan Tomkins, Hadley Cantril, Leo Crespi, Irving Alexander, Charles Bray, and Sheldon Korchin. We were required to do an undergraduate thesis, and mine was a study of the personality characteristics of institutionalized alcoholics using the Thematic Apperception Test. Unfortunately there was no control group and so the research never was published. However, the impact on me personally was tremendous. I was hooked on doing research forever. My major advisor for the thesis was Silvan Tomkins, who also gave me my first real exposure to personality theory via a year-long graduate course he taught. All the other students in the class were at the graduate level.

At the end of my sophomore year I was married to Sally Tollerton of Newport, Vermont. This was not accomplished easily. Sally was a Catholic, while I was not much of anything. Sally's mother wanted us married in the church; the Catholic Monsignor did not. Finally it was agreed that we could be married in a small room on the edge of the church. Then there was a problem at Princeton because in those days undergraduates were not supposed to marry. Finally permission was obtained from the Dean of the College on the grounds that my graduation actually would have occurred by that time were it not for my military service. Lastly there was my mother. My mother simply did not care for my marrying a girl from Newport who never had gone to college at all. Moreover, she did not like Sally. This problem never was resolved over the ensuing 18 years of marriage. In any event we persevered and the marriage occurred.

My grades in college actually improved with marriage in spite of working half-time at the Educational Testing Service as an assistant in the research department. My overall grade-point average at graduation was just over B+, but the psychology grades were considerably higher. All of this was good enough to get me elected to Phi Beta Kappa in my senior year; that in turn helped in applying to graduate school and trying to obtain support. My scores on the Graduate Record Examination were at about the 85th percentile in the verbal area and almost 20 percentile points lower in the quantitative area, but my performance on the advanced test in psychology put me at the 98th percentile. That is the pattern of an overachiever. Eight years later on the Admission Test for Graduate Study in Business the differential in favor of verbal over quantitative ability was much the same, with an overall score of 670 (95th percentile). All those books in our home growing up apparently had their effect.

Looking back it seems safe to say that my initial decision on graduate school was thoroughly botched. The first offer from the University of Texas came in early and was turned down, but then Clark University offered a Veterans Administration traineeship with added scholarship incentives. Having read some of Heinz Werner's work, and pressured somewhat to make an early decision, I mailed my acceptance to Clark. Shortly afterward, a much more attractive fellowship offer from Harvard arrived in the mail. After agonizing for some time, my conclusion was that it would be unethical not to honor my original agreement with Clark. Based on my experience since, this decision has to be viewed as questionable. In any event, we moved to Worcester, Massachusetts during the summer of 1950 after a stint as a camp counselor on Martha's Vineyard. It was not a good move.

The thing that remains strongly positive in my mind about Clark is that my clinical training was excellent. Thelma Alper was my major advisor and

Heinz Werner, Fred Wyatt, and Robert Schafer taught me as much as anyone could hope for. In that sense it was a good experience. But clinical work in the Veterans Administration and other aspects of the experience were disenchanting. It simply was not up to expectations based on my Princeton background. The environment of a psychiatric hospital was unpleasant, and the idea of constantly fighting psychiatrists for recognition and status was unattractive. By the end of the first year it was quite clear that this was not for me.

My M.A. thesis at Clark had involved work with a tachistoscopic index of illusory motion, the Rorschach, the Thematic Apperception Test, and the Tomkins-Horn Picture Arrangement Test (PAT). This background was particularly attractive to Silvan Tomkins at Princeton who was in the process of negotiating a grant for research to standardize the PAT. Accordingly, we moved back to Princeton after two years in Worcester. My major area of study changed from clinical psychology to personality theory, although my comprehensive exam actually covered both the clinical work at Clark and my new major. Most of my graduate course work in psychology was taken at Clark, not Princeton. After one year the grant to standardize the PAT came through, and we spent two years working with the Gallup Poll people and various mental institutions across the country collecting test protocols. It was a fascinating experience. Ultimately it resulted in three books, and a couple of articles as well, during the mid- and late-1950s. It was this work that really initiated my career.

Right after we moved back to Princeton in 1952 my daughter Barbara was born. My son John was born just as my doctorate was awarded in 1955. The children brought new responsibilities and financial demands. The latter were particularly acute because of my entry into psychoanalysis shortly after returning to Princeton. During the preceding year or so I had experienced rather frequent anxiety attacks. An attempt to deal with these through short-term therapy in Boston had been unsuccessful, and it was apparent to me that something more drastic was needed. My solution was to enter psychoanalysis with Russell Carrier who was just starting a practice and a hospital in Belle Meade, New Jersey. This involved four sessions a week, with time out during the summer, for almost five years. In a very real sense this was personal development, but it was professional development also. The experience helped me to handle many of the problems of an emerging professional career more effectively. It did not cure the anxiety attacks, but it did control them and make it possible for me to cope with them. Gradually over the years they have disappeared.

Toward the end of my years at Princeton my career began to take on a new dimension. Although many aspects of clinical psychology had not proven very attractive, one aspect that was appealing was its applied nature. That aspect was missing from a career devoted entirely to scholarship in the field of personality theory, and the gap bothered me. My solution was to attempt to research and write my way into some degree of legitimacy as an industrial psychologist. The process started slowly simply because there was no industrial psychology at Princeton. There was some industrial sociology, however, and that provided a start. Wilbert Moore taught a doctoral seminar on the subject and auditing that seminar proved of considerable help. My doctoral dissertation research utilized intelligence test data that we had collected during the PAT standardization project, and involved analyzing them from a national manpower utilization perspective. There was no one on the psychology faculty who was really conversant with the type of analyses this required. Wilbert Moore, although not formally a member of my committee, was extremely helpful.

My committee consisted of Silvan Tomkins, Hadley Cantril, and Ledyard Tucker. Doing a dissertation outside the areas of expertise of my committee members presented many problems. Coming at intelligence test data on a national sample from a manpower utilization perspective led me to certain theoretical formulations and analyses that Ledyard Tucker in particular found unacceptable. The first version of the dissertation contained eight chapters and was in fact book length. After lengthy discussions we agreed to disagree, and the final product accepted for the degree was devoid of both the theoretical chapters and the manpower utilization analyses; it was less than half the length of the original. Frankly, there was not a great deal left. Two years later, however, my friend Bernhard Springer brought out what was essentially the initial unabridged version in book form (Springer Publishing, 1957).

With the work in industrial sociology, considerable reading on the side, the dissertation research, and an article in the *Journal of Applied Psychology*, it was time to declare myself an industrial psychologist. My original intention was to obtain a job in the business world that would confirm my legitimacy in the field and also improve my financial position. That did not work out, but the old maxim that "if you cannot do it, teach it" came into play. A job offer came through to teach industrial psychology in the summer school at Georgia Tech. Shortly thereafter a similar opportunity for a full-time appointment at Brooklyn College became available. The psychology faculty there really did not care much for industrial psychology, but had to meet a substantial student demand; the idea of hiring someone who in their minds was really a personality theorist for this purpose had great appeal.

PREPARING FOR A BUSINESS SCHOOL CAREER: 1955-1960

To label these five years as preparation for a business school career is not to say that my intention was to prepare for such a career. Only with hindsight is this an apt description for the period. In fact, initially my knowledge of business schools was practically nil; neither Princeton nor Clark had had one. My first, really peripheral, exposure came after one semester at Brooklyn College. As might have been guessed, the Brooklyn College experience did not work out well. The teaching load was 15 hours, the commute from Princeton took five hours a day, and it became increasingly evident to me that teaching industrial psychology without having practiced it was not going to permit me to live up to my own expectations.

Luckily, Douglas Bray and Eli Ginzberg bailed me out of that situation. Doug was working for Eli on a manpower utilization project at Columbia University and had just been asked to come to AT&T to initiate the introduction of assessment centers into the Bell System. He needed someone to replace him at Columbia. He had been familiar with my manpower research at Princeton and was favorably impressed with it. Consequently, in early 1956 my academic base shifted from Brooklyn College to Columbia, and my commute was cut almost in half. The Conservation of Human Resources project was associated with the Graduate School of Business at Columbia for at least part of my stay there. However, it was in large part a self-contained entity, and my appointment was entirely as a researcher. As a result, there was only limited exposure to the business school and its faculty. In actual fact my contacts with the people at Teachers College such as Irving Lorge and Donald Super were at least as frequent.

My stay at Columbia turned out to be rather brief also. The work was extremely interesting, taking me into many areas of human resource management that previously had been completely unknown to me. There was also a continued opportunity to publish—a co-authored book, my masters thesis, and several articles based on our research into the causes and consequences of ineffective performance among World War II soldiers. On the other hand, my family's financial status did not improve much with the move to Columbia, and the projects we worked on were all ones that Eli Ginzberg brought in. I began to chafe a bit; the need to be my own person professionally began to take hold. With the winding down of my psychoanalysis it seemed time to move on, to make some money, and to get the business experience that was still lacking. Doug Bray's success in moving from my position at Columbia to AT&T was a clear incentive.

The result of a brief search was a move to Philadelphia to join the Personnel Research staff at The Atlantic Refining Company and, after a short orientation, to take charge of the company's psychological services. The irony of this was that my efforts to find a business position two years earlier had also led to Atlantic, but not with any success at all. Now, with the Columbia experience behind me, things were different.

Strangely this large corporation with its entrenched bureaucracy did allow me the professional freedom that Columbia had not. We were a staff service, and if you could find a problem and sell an approach to solution, you were off and running. Often the solutions which came out of extensive research did not get implemented in the long run, but that did not become evident to me for some time. In any event Atlantic did provide the opportunity to learn industrial psychology firsthand and in fact to learn many aspects of human resource management as well. We conducted projects of one kind or another in the areas of selection, placement, management development, compensation, safety, labor relations, internal communications, organization planning, and performance appraisal; there was also considerable employee counseling. Ultimately three books or monographs and part of a fourth, as well as some ten articles, were an outgrowth of this experience. It was a demanding yet exciting time. It became evident to me that practicing industrial psychology can be fun. The field is one of very few in the social sciences where one can practice and do research at the same time.

Living became a little more financially comfortable during the Atlantic years, although two more children—Cynthia born in 1957 and Frances born in 1960—absorbed their share of the gain. Nevertheless my proclivity for exploring new horizons went on unabated. It was not long before my path led to the Wharton School at the University of Pennsylvania, where my initial objective was to obtain an MBA in marketing. That proved infeasible given my Atlantic commitments, but there was a possibility that something could be worked out in the industrial relations area where the courses were scheduled at better times for me. In any event it was quite evident that a knowledge of labor relations would be an asset at Atlantic. Thus started my brief joust with an MBA curriculum which actually lasted only one year and was restricted entirely to course work in labor relations and labor law.

George Taylor had taught my labor relations class and he was at that time Chairman of the Industry Department at Wharton. He was responsible for the briefness of my MBA experience. He offered me an opportunity to teach a course in what would now be considered organizational behavior. It would have been impossible to teach the course and continue in the MBA program, and the teaching won out. Toward the end of that academic year (1959-60), George approached me again about a permanent appointment at Wharton. He was very much aware of the ferment over introducing behavioral scientists into business schools because of his close association with Frank Pierson at Swarthmore who had just completed the Carnegie Foundation report on business schools. The idea was that my appointment would be at the Associate Professor level. It passed all the necessary faculties and committees at Wharton, but ran into trouble from an unexpected source. Morris Viteles in the Psychology Department was unalterably opposed. He did not want a competing industrial psychology program to arise across the street.

In the end Viteles prevailed and any prospects of an appointment at Wharton ended. George offered to help in any way possible to get me a job at some other business school. Viteles contacted me about the possibility of taking an Assistant Professor opening he had. Given what had happened, that did not seem very attractive. Victor Vroom later took that position. In the meantime I had become a candidate for a major promotion at Atlantic. Nels Mann had been shifted from Marketing Personnel Manager to Director of Purchasing. Nels recommended me as his replacement. However, seniority and strong ties preexisting my entry on the scene clearly controlled the decision. Again things did not work out well for me. I lost round two also. With George on my side and the market for psychologists in business schools burgeoning, it seemed best to avoid a round three in Philadelphia and to seek employment elsewhere. This whole scenario was as much a product of my own ambition as anything else, but the chance to move in on the opportunity created by the Carnegie and Ford Foundation reports was unmistakable. At last the fact that I had somehow unintentionally been preparing for a business school career came home to me; but at the same time the possibility of such a career emerged out of nowhere. It was not planned.

Another search in the marketplace yielded offers from the Universities of Wisconsin, Washington, and Oregon. We decided upon the latter, largely because we had heard much about the university and Eugene from the daughter of a former president who was a close friend during the Princeton years. We headed west in 1960, just after Frances was born, into a world of uncertainty occasioned not only by geography, but by the changing nature of business schools themselves. It was hard to establish what was happening there. What looked like opportunity might turn out to be a pipe dream.

STRUGGLING IN AND OUT OF BUSINESS SCHOOLS: OREGON, BERKELEY, AND McKINSEY

The next decade certainly was something different. My initial reaction to the University of Oregon was that it was much like moving back and forth from Greenwich to Newport; acceptance was hard to come by, and one was always an outsider who had not lived through the winter (or summer). In this early period the business schools were having a very hard time digesting the behavioral scientists that the Ford and Carnegie Foundations had served up to them.

One outgrowth of all this was the formation of a group made up of psychologists in business schools which met regularly at American Psychological Association meetings to share information and hopefully reduce stress. If my memory serves me correctly, the major figures in the group who either chaired it or served on the steering committee were Bernard Bass, Raymond Katzell, Donald Marquis, Fred Massarik, and myself. We even did what psychologists in groups of this kind usually do: we surveyed ourselves (see my articles "Psychology and the School of Business Curriculum," 1963; "The Psychologist's Impact Upon Collegiate Management Education," 1964; and "Psychologists in Marketing Education," 1966). That the group gradually faded out of existence in the mid-1960s probably reflects the fact that it was no longer needed; psychologists had come to the business schools to stay.

Another outgrowth that was not so pleasant was the conflict that developed between a colleague and myself at Oregon. This colleague came to the university at the same time I did to occupy an endowed chair. My initial appointment was at the Associate Professor level, with a promotion to Professor two years later, and tenure a year after that. Sometime around that time the colleague was made head of the newly formed Personnel and Industrial Management Department. I supported that appointment because he was clearly the senior member of the department, and out of my respect for the research he was then conducting. He seemed to view the department as the bottom link of a hierarchic chain of command; he was in charge. My view was more like a community of scholars with a senior scholar representing the group. Obviously the two views clashed. Furthermore, this colleague did not appear to be comfortable with psychologists such as Abraham Korman and myself on the faculty. At that time he may well have not understood what we were doing. In any event things got so bad at one point that my courses, and myself with them, were all transferred to the Accounting and Business Statistics Department. When that move was countermanded by a dean returning from sabbatical, it became evident that something had to change.

As it developed, a large number of things did change. Some time before, West Churchman had asked me to spend a visiting year in the business school at Berkeley. At the time the invitation was extended my promotion to full professor had just come through, and Dean Richard Lindholm asked me as a quid pro quo to delay the visit a year. By the time that year was up there had been some drastic changes in the behavioral science group at Berkeley and the invitation was not re-extended. Now, however, Lyman Porter asked me to replace him in the Psychology Department while he was visiting at Yale. That would have been my sabbatical year, but Oregon would not approve a sabbatical to teach elsewhere. Accordingly the sabbatical was delayed a year, and I went to Berkeley for the 1966-67 year.

As it turned out, the move was not only to Berkeley, but also to the San Francisco office of McKinsey and Company. Robert House, who at that time was employed by McKinsey in New York, had been trying to work out something between the firm and myself for some time. He was very much interested in management development then and had been favorably impressed by my *Studies in Management Education* (1965). What we ultimately came to was that the San Francisco office would use my services two days a week as a consultant on behavioral science applications to McKinsey's client services, and also as advisor on the recruiting and selection of new Associates with the firm. For several years the possibility of going back into the business world had been nagging at me. Now things seemed to be moving in that direction. There was one more change to come, however. During the summer of 1966, just before the move to Berkeley, problems that had long existed in my marriage became acute. During the Princeton days Sally and I had discussed divorce, but the agreement one makes prior to entering psychoanalysis, not to take any drastic action of this kind, precluded my pursuing the matter. During the ensuing years the children were simply too young to have their home disrupted. But, by the time of the Berkeley move, the distance between us was so pronounced that almost anybody could recognize it. For myself I can only say that the love and respect that I felt in the early years had completely evaporated. My mother's early forebodings were fully vindicated. Sally did not move to Berkeley. We were divorced before the end of the year.

The year at Berkeley was productive, but reinforced my belief that my values and those of a psychology department did not mesh. Edwin Ghiselli was a great help in dealing with issues surrounding the graduate student strike and protests against the war in Vietnam, but the very fact of seeing certain of my fellow faculty members support that strike was terribly disturbing. The demonstrations were beyond belief for someone like myself who had considerable faith in established authority, and certain psychology professors were part of the problem. The thought that it might be desirable to return to a psychology department was vanquished from my mind during the Berkeley year, but returning to a business such as consulting was not. On a completely different note, Mary Green Thompson and I were married in 1967.

My original intention was to spend the sabbatical year in the San Francisco area working with McKinsey. However, as things developed, the firm transferred me to New York. Since my mother was getting rather frail and my children were in the East also, the return to the New York area was welcome. We lived in Greenwich, and commuting once again became a major part of my life. During that year we carried out a number of studies related to the selection and career progress of consultants at McKinsey; it was a great opportunity.

However, as the year wore on there was an increasing need to decide what to do next. Returning to Oregon was out of the question. The pay scale there was rather low relative to other parts of the country, and because of this it would have been impossible to meet my child support commitments. The difficulty with colleagues would remain. Also, before leaving Oregon, for several years, I had diversified into educational administration, working with doctoral students in the School of Education and holding a half-time research appointment in the Center for Advanced Study of Educational Administration (CASEA). Due to some changes in U.S. Office of Education policy, the CASEA appointment would not be available any longer. That was a disappointment, especially in view of the fact that my research in educational administration had begun to appear in print (see my 1967 monograph *The School Administrator and Organizational Character* and the article "The Managerial Motivation of School Administrators," 1968).

There was some possibility of staying in consulting, either with McKinsey or with another firm, but the prospect of continually being at the beck and call of clients while travelling almost non-stop became less and less attractive as the nature of consulting work became clearer to me. It is a highly risk-laden occupation: no clients, no job. Tenure is much better. In any event, after discussions with several universities, we moved to the business school at the University of Maryland with a considerable raise in pay over what would have been possible at the University of Oregon. Meeting the child support commitment was no longer a problem. The work with McKinsey continued for about another year with frequent commutes from Maryland to New York City; then it was finished. I had returned to business schools for good.

PURSUING DIVERSITY WITHIN THE BUSINESS SCHOOLS: MARYLAND, GEORGIA STATE, AND BUFFALO

By 1968 my career path had led through clinical psychology, personality theory, industrial psychology, personnel management, organizational behavior, and educational administration. My publications spanned all of these areas. In the ensuing years clinical psychology, personality theory, and educational administration largely disappeared from my list of competencies, although all three fields continue to influence my thinking and research. Industrial (/organizational) psychology, personnel (human resource) management, and organizational behavior have remained major areas of activity until the present.

Throughout my five years at the University of Maryland these three areas represented the primary focus of my activities. During this period, a substantial proportion of my time was devoted to administration—as Chairman of the Behavioral Science Division, a unit in many ways comparable to a department. Also my wife, Mary Green Miner, began to become increasingly interested in a career. She started working part-time for the Bureau of National Affairs (BNA) in Washington, D.C., where she had been employed a number of years before, and she began to collaborate with me on some of my writing. As time went on we collaborated more and more with the explicit objective of advancing her career; she did not have an advanced degree. Toward the end of my time at Maryland the opportunity to edit the *Academy of Management Journal* was extended, and Mary worked with me as we got that effort under way.

Several factors eventually contributed to my leaving Maryland. For one thing it was impossible to obtain any support or assistance from the university in carrying out my editorial duties. Probably this was related to the fact that the business administration area was undergoing a major reorganization at this time, but it was true nevertheless. Second, my administrative duties provided a number of advantages in terms of reduced teaching load and extra compensation. As my initial term came to a close, there was a vote within the division which indicated substantial disenchantment with my performance as an administrator. Although this disenchantment was by no means universal, there were several individuals who clearly did not like me. The net result was that my first term as chairman of the division was my last. With the disappearance of the perks that went with administration, Maryland was no longer a particularly attractive place to work. Although it was never entirely clear to me what the whole problem was at Maryland, part of it apparently was my tendency to do "my thing" without being adequately responsive to group members. An example cited was the visiting appointment I decided to take at the University of South Florida for a quarter during 1972.

In any event, just as things came to a head at Maryland, Georgia State offered an appointment as Research Professor which contained all the elements missing at Maryland—a secretary to work on the *Journal*, a one-course teaching load, a 12-month contract, and so forth. Thus we moved on to Atlanta. As we did my mother, who had been in a nursing home for some time, died.

Just prior to the move to Atlanta, Frank Khedouri, my editor at Macmillan, had gotten in touch with me about the possibility of teaming up with George Steiner on a policy/strategy book. After lengthy deliberations, a contract was signed with the idea that George would handle the material in areas like social responsibility, planning, and strategy formulation, while my role would be to write on decision making, consulting, aspects of implementation, and entrepreneurship. Our objective was to bring together the research in the field to produce a substantial amount of text in addition to cases and readings. No such research summary existed at that time, and both of us had a great deal of literature to review. Partly to help in accomplishing that review I introduced a doctoral course in strategy at Georgia State shortly after arriving there. Thus began my diversification into policy/strategy, a field in which my prior experience was very limited. It resulted in several dissertations in that area as well as a number of publications.

In many respects the 1970s were the Academy of Management years. My movement within the Academy was rather typical. We founded the Organizational Behavior Division in 1970, and I progressed from executive committee member to chairman. Then there was the editorship of the *Journal* and, subsequently, election into the sequence which ultimately resulted in my becoming President in 1977-78. A highlight was the creation of the *Academy of Management Review*. Almost from the beginning of my work with the *Journal*, it had seemed to me that we needed another publication. Eventually my protestations resulted in the formation of a committee to deal with the issue. We met in Irvine, Calif., and that is where the *Review* began. It should be said that the series of elections that brought me to the presidency of the

Academy were really a surprise. Viewing oneself as different, one does not expect to be elected; I am not a politician, much more an individualist. The whole thing took me back to when Princeton awarded me the Phi Beta Kappa key. Both elections were equally unexpected. Yet with my desire for status, both were very satisfying. I was truly honored to be made President of the Academy.

The early years at Georgia State saw not just the movement into policy/strategy but also an increasing commitment to organization theory at the macro level. One manifestation of this was the expansion of my managerial role-motivation theory, which previously had dealt only with bureaucratic forms, into a full-scale organizational typology. These ideas were presented first at various conferences and then published in the edited volumes that resulted (see "The Uncertain Future of the Leadership Concept: An Overview," 1975 and "Limited Domain Theories of Organizational Energy," 1980). Another move into organization theory was the publication of *Theories of Organizational Structure and Process* (1982) as a companion volume to *Theories of Organizational Behavior* (1980). It is my belief that the successes experienced in the Academy of Management gave me the courage to branch out into these new fields at that particular point in time.

As my career became more interesting and exciting, my marriage was moving in the opposite direction. Mary was increasingly involved with her work for BNA and spent a considerable amount of time in Washington. In the early years our marriage served to assist her career; now she seemed to view it as a limitation. As so frequently happens with dual-career couples,[7] signs of competition between us began to emerge. For my part, the prospect of continuing the marriage in a form where we both went off in completely different directions was unattractive. We were separated and later divorced during 1978. Mary did not continue to write with me after the divorce; in fact, she did not continue to write at all. She moved back to the D.C. area to take a management position at BNA.

My marriage to Barbara Williams occurred in 1979. Barbara had been my assistant going back to the work on the *Academy of Management Journal*. During 1978 she assumed the position as Production Editor of the *Journal* that Mary had vacated just prior to our separation. Later, in 1982, she became Production Editor of the *Academy of Management Review* as well, and still later added the responsibility for Academy of Management advertising. With the birth of our children, Jennifer in 1981 and Heather in 1983, it became increasingly obvious that what had been a part-time job with the Academy was now more than a full-time job, and more than Barbara could handle without cheating the girls. By 1985 she decided to call it quits with the Academy and concentrate on the family.

In 1978 my duties at Georgia State were extended to include working for a three-year term as Doctoral Program Coordinator for the School of Business

Administration. That position gave me more of an overall view of the various disciplines and combined with my experiences in the Academy at about the same time to ignite an interest in serving as a business school dean. That did not actually happen, but it almost did. There were serious discussions at Santa Clara, Washington State, and Georgia Tech among others; there were several opportunities. Ultimately, my conclusion was that to serve as dean in the type of research-oriented university that was attractive to me it would be necessary to work as an associate dean first. The prospect of doing that was exceedingly unattractive. Whatever my competencies as a dean might have been, it is absolutely certain that I would have been neither happy nor successful in the associate dean role. Unless the dean involved was a very unusual person, my proclivity for independent action and desire for a sense of personal achievement inevitably would have led to actions viewed as far removed from what should be expected from a good team player.

There is one more aspect of the Atlanta years that needs discussion. During this period my consulting and outside activities developed in some very interesting directions. One such activity was serving as an expert witness in equal employment opportunity cases. My introduction to this type of work came at Maryland when the Equal Employment Opportunity Commission contacted me about helping with the AT&T case (see my article "Psychological Testing and Fair Employment Practices: A Testing Program that Does Not Discriminate," 1974). In Atlanta there was much more opportunity to explore the area, working primarily with law firms representing corporate clients. In many of these instances the case required conducting research. Also, toward the end of my stay in Atlanta, an opportunity arose to help develop an honesty or integrity test. The result of our efforts was an instrument called True Test published by Intergram, Inc. Work on this test continues to the present (see "True Test Scores of Prison Inmates," 1990). Finally in 1976, I started a small publishing organization primarily to publish my own tests, scoring guides, and some books. This is my only true entrepreneurial start-up. It remains a very small-scale effort, but Barbara and I continue to operate it today under the title of Organizational Measurement Systems Press.

Overall my years at Georgia State were a very positive experience, although they ended on something of a sour note. It was possible for me to be very productive there, although the lack of a research culture and the widespread failure to value my scholarship were a source of annoyance. However, recognition from the cosmopolitan world more than compensated for the lack of it on the local scene. My basic strategy was to go my own way working with the doctoral students and a few faculty colleagues, notably Donald Crane and Max Holland. Many might have found this difficult to do. It was difficult for me on occasion, but it gave me the free time to accomplish a great deal.

With my sixtieth birthday in July 1986 the opportunity to take early retirement from Georgia State became available. Given that a comparable position could be found elsewhere, this had a great deal of appeal. It would add to our income substantially. Also there was considerable evidence that the culture at Georgia State was, probably unwittingly, producing a certain amount of age discrimination. At least a number of us believed that was the case. The University simply did not appear to be an attractive place to spend one's later years. These two factors combined to push me into seeking a position elsewhere, although leaving Atlanta would be difficult.

The result of that search was a very attractive offer from the State University of New York (SUNY) at Buffalo. The contrast between Georgia State as we knew it and what we found at Buffalo could not have been more extreme. SUNY/Buffalo is a first-class research university, and it has the culture to go with it. It is a pleasure for a person like myself to be part of that culture. One consequence of being aligned with one's culture, however, is that one gets called upon to do many things within it. My initial appointment was to an endowed chair, the Donald S. Carmichael Professorship in Human Resources. That assumes my continuing to be a productive researcher and scholar. Two years after arriving in Buffalo, Dean Joseph Alutto asked me to take over as Chairman of the Department of Organization and Human Resources from Raymond Hunt, who wanted to step down. That assumes a substantial amount of time devoted to administrative activities. Also, the School of Management was developing a new outside program for established entrepreneurs at the time of my arrival and Joe asked me to become Faculty Director of the Center for Entrepreneurial Leadership which was the umbrella for that program. That assumes frequent interaction with entrepreneurs to help them develop their businesses. Clearly, the free time and isolation created by the cultural mismatch at Georgia State has not been characteristic at SUNY/Buffalo.

Yet, there has been continuing diversification, fostered in large part by my Center for Entrepreneurial Leadership activities. From the mid-1970s, entrepreneurship had been an area of considerable interest to me, although my knowledge in the field was rather limited prior to coming to Buffalo. There were a few publications on the subject, primarily with Norman Smith, a marketing professor who came to Oregon at about the same time as my move there, but this was not a major focus for me until the scoring guide for Form T was published in 1986. On coming to Buffalo, I found a real vacuum in the area at the University and a real need in the business community to help develop small home-grown firms that would substitute for the absentee-owned plants that had moved out. We introduced courses in entrepreneurship into the curriculum, interested doctoral students in research in the area, and worked with established entrepreneurs through the Center for Entrepreneurial Leadership; my research in the area accelerated. More than half of my teaching is now in the entrepreneurship field. This latest plunge into diversity has been a real pleasure. Entrepreneurship is a fascinating field to study, especially for one with my motives.

ON PURSUING DIVERSITY AS A CAREER STRATEGY

Industrial/organizational psychology, organizational behavior, and human resource management have now been extended to policy/strategy, organization theory, and entrepreneurship, and to a great deal of ground between these fields of organizational science. Whatever it may be, this is not narrow specialization. Furthermore, this treatment has not dealt in detail with the development of my various role-motivation theories, all of which are meso theories extending across the micro organizational behavior-macro organization theory interface. These theories and the research on them, much of it done with doctoral students at Oregon, Maryland, Georgia State, and SUNY/Buffalo, are described in detail elsewhere (see *Role Motivation Theories*, 1993).

My belief is that many who feel secure in their own well-defined specialization will say that Miner is not really a legitimate figure in the policy/strategy, or organization theory, or industrial/organizational psychology, or whatever field. Over time certain individuals in all of these fields have said just that to me; I am different from them and don't really belong. In the early years this did bother me. Growing up feeling different did not necessarily mean that different was pleasant. Yet across the years it has become part of my identity. I really like exploring new areas and proving myself, at least to me and perhaps to a handful of others. It is a challenge, and it is pleasing to win over some of those who were initial doubters. Maybe this is what Maslow really meant by his concept of self-actualization (not to be confused with others' interpretations of his concept). To me at least always being the "new kid on the block" has come to be a pleasure. It is for me a means "to become more and more what one is, to become everything that one is capable of becoming."[8]

Was all this planned in advance? Far from it. My planning tends to be short-term at best—perhaps a few years out front, with the vagaries becoming more pronounced as time extends outward. Many would view me as an opportunist, waiting to grasp the gold ring as it passes by. There is some truth in that. Many, but not all, of my ventures into new fields have occurred because some new stimulus got me started in a new direction, and with that the new challenges and opportunities became more clearly visible.

Is there some message in all this? Probably a rather bland one—people differ. Yet, at another level, my experience leads me to believe that pursuing specialization in a burgeoning field like organizational science is the natural route for most. It is comfortable and most people probably reach their greatest potential in that manner. Yet for others, who are different, pursuing diversity produces the greatest rewards, at least those of an intrinsic nature. We are different, in one sense a minority, but we are not necessarily better or worse than others for being different. Whether we contribute more or less is essentially an empirical question to be determined one case at a time. It does seem to me, however, that if one's personal development is such as to foster the pursuit of diversity, one should not fight it. Some people, like myself, can find a great deal of gratification in a diversified career. Hopefully the majority will not snuff out this type of flame in the years to come, wherever it may spring up.

PUBLICATIONS

1955

With S.S. Tomkins. Contributions to the standardization of the Tomkins-Horn Picture Arrangement Test: Plate norms. *Journal of Psychology, 39*, 199-214.
With J.E. Culver. Some aspects of the executive personality. *Journal of Applied Psychology, 39*, 348-353.

1956

Motion perception, time perspective, and creativity. *Journal of Projective Techniques, 20*, 405-413.

1957

With S.S. Tomkins. *The Tomkins-Horn Picture Arrangement Test*. New York: Springer.
Intelligence in the United States. New York: Springer.
With S.S. Tomkins. *Tomkins-Horn Picture Arrangement Test Profile Chart*. New York: Springer.
With S.S. Tomkins. *Scoring cards for the Tomkins-Horn Picture Arrangement Test*. New York: Springer.

1958

With J.K. Anderson. Intelligence and emotional disturbance: Evidence from Army and Veterans Administration records. *Journal of Abnormal and Social Psychology, 56*, 75-81.
With J.K. Anderson. The postwar occupational adjustment of emotionally disturbed soldiers. *Journal of Applied Psychology, 42*, 317-322.

1959

With E. Ginzberg, J.K. Anderson, S.W. Ginsburg, & J.L. Herma. *The ineffective soldier: Volume II–Breakdown and recovery*. New York: Columbia University Press.

With S.S. Tomkins. *Picture Arrangement Test interpretation: Scope and technique.* New York: Springer.
With E.E. Heaton. Company orientation as a factor in the readership of employee publications. *Personnel Psychology, 12,* 607-618.

1960

The effect of a course in psychology on the attitudes of research and development supervisors. *Journal of Applied Psychology, 44,* 224-232.
The Kuder Preference Record in management appraisal. *Personnel Psychology, 13,* 187-196.
The concurrent validity of the Picture Arrangement Test in the selection of tabulating machine operators. *Journal of Projective Techniques, 24,* 409-418.

1961

Management development and attitude change. *Personnel Administration, 24*(3), 21-26.
On the use of a short vocabulary test to measure general intelligence. *Journal of Educational Psychology, 52,* 157-160.
The validity of the Picture Arrangement Test in the selection of tabulating machine operators: An analysis of predictive power. *Journal of Projective Techniques, 25,* 330-333.
Selection or development: Management's perennial dilemma. In *Business Developments 1961* (pp. 29-34). Eugene, OR: University of Oregon School of Business Administration.
Miner Sentence Completion Scale: Form H. New York/Buffalo, NY: Springer Publishing and Organizational Measurement Systems Press.

1962

Personality and ability factors in sales performance. *Journal of Applied Psychology, 46,* 6-13.
Conformity among university professors and business executives. *Administrative Science Quarterly, 7,* 96-109.
Performance failure in a competitive economic system. *Oregon Business Review, 21*(5), 1-7.

1963

The management of ineffective performance. New York: McGraw-Hill.

Evidence regarding the value of a management course based on behavioral science subject matter. *Journal of Business, 35,* 325-335.

Occupational differences in the desire to exercise power. *Psychological Reports, 13,* 18.

Psychology and the school of business curriculum. *Journal of the Academy of Management, 6,* 284-289.

1964

Scoring guide for the Miner Sentence Completion Scale. New York: Springer.

The psychologist's impact upon collegiate management education. *Academy of Management Proceedings, 23,* 62-68.

1965

Studies in management education. New York: Springer.

A statistical model for the study of conformity. In F. Massarik and P. Ratoosh, (Eds.), *Mathematical explorations in behavioral science* (pp. 95-111). Homewood, IL: Irwin.

The prediction of managerial and research success. *Personnel Administration, 28*(5), 12-16.

The management of ineffective performance. In L.E. Davis (Ed.), *Proceedings–Seventeenth Industrial Engineering Institute* (pp. 38-40). Berkeley and Los Angeles, CA: University of California.

1966

Introduction to industrial clinical psychology. New York: McGraw-Hill.

Psychologists in marketing education. *Journal of Marketing, 30*(1), 7-9.

With V. Glaudin, J.L. Wallen, R.D. Boyd, W.G. Klopfer. What models for the professions of psychology? *American Psychologist, 21,* 820-823.

1967

The school administrator and organizational character. Eugene, OR: University of Oregon Press.

1968

The managerial motivation of school administrators. *Educational Administration Quarterly, 4,* 55-71.

Early identification of managerial talent. *Personnel and Guidance Journal, 46*(6), 586-591.

Bridging the gulf in organizational performance. *Harvard Business Review*, *46*(4), 102-110.
Management appraisal: A capsule review and current references. *Business Horizons*, *11*(5), 83-96.

1969

Personnel and industrial relations: A managerial approach. New York: Macmillan.
Personnel psychology. New York: Macmillan.
With N.R. Smith. Managerial talent among undergraduate and graduate business students. *Personnel and Guidance Journal*, *47*, 995-1000.
Management development and its ethical limitations. *The Federal Accountant*, *18*(3), 54-62.
With R.J. House. Merging management and behavioral theory: The interaction between span of control and group size. *Administrative Science Quarterly*, *14*, 451-464.
An input-output model for personnel strategies. *Business Horizons*, *12*(3), 71-78.
Simplified scoring procedure for the Tomkins-Horn Picture Arrangement Test. Philadelphia, PA: Wittreich Associates.

1970

With F.E. Dalton. The role of accounting training in top management decision making. *Accounting Review*, *45*, 134-139.
Psychological evaluations as predictors of consulting success. *Personnel Psychology*, *23*, 383-405.
Executive and personnel interviews as predictors of consulting success. *Personnel Psychology*, *23*, 521-538.

1971

Management theory. New York: Macmillan.
With W. Wittreich. People: The most mismanaged asset-Rational selection and promotion. *Business Horizons*, *14*(2), 68-77.
Personality tests as predictors of consulting success. *Personnel Psychology*, *24*, 191-204.
Success in management consulting and the concept of eliteness motivation. *Academy of Management Journal*, *14*, 367-378.
Changes in student attitudes toward bureaucratic role prescriptions during the 1960s. *Administrative Science Quarterly*, *16*, 351-364.

1972

Management appraisal: A review of procedures and practices. In H.L. Tosi, R.J. House, & M.D. Dunnette, (Eds.), *Managerial motivation and compensation* (pp. 412-428). East Lansing, MI: Michigan State University.

1973

The management process: Theory, research, and practice. New York: Macmillan.
With S.J. Carroll, & F.T. Paine. *The management process: Cases and readings.* New York: Macmillan.
With M.G. Miner. *Personnel and industrial relations: A managerial approach* (2nd ed.). New York: Macmillan.
With A.N. Nash. *Personnel and labor relations: An evolutionary approach.* New York: Macmillan.
With M.G. Miner. *A guide to personnel management.* Washington, DC: Bureau of National Affairs (BNA) Books.
Intelligence in the United States (reissue). Westport, CT: Greenwood Press.
With H.P. Dachler. Personnel attitudes and motivation. *Annual Review of Psychology, 24*, 379-402.
The management consulting firm as a source of high-level managerial talent. *Academy of Management Journal, 16*, 253-264.
The real crunch in managerial manpower. *Harvard Business Review, 51*(6), 146-158.
Personnel strategies in the small business organization. *Journal of Small Business Management, 11*(3), 13-16.
The OD-management development conflict. *Business Horizons, 16*(6), 31-36.

1974

The human constraint: The coming shortage of managerial talent. Washington, DC: Bureau of National Affairs (BNA) Books.
Motivation to manage among women: Studies of business managers and educational administrators. *Journal of Vocational Behavior, 5*, 197-208.
Motivation to manage among women: Studies of college students. *Journal of Vocational Behavior, 5*, 241-250.
The selection interview. In W.C. Hamner & F.L. Schmidt (Eds.), *Contemporary problems in personnel* (pp. 86-92). Chicago, IL: St. Clair Press.
The cross-cultural perspective to work motivation. In S.K. Roy & A.S. Menon (Eds.), *Organizational effectiveness, motivation, and productivity* (pp. 29-42). New Delhi, India: Shri Ram Centre for Industrial Relations.

With J.R. Rizzo, D.M. Harlow, & J.W. Hill. Role motivation theory of managerial effectiveness in simulated organizations of varying degrees of structure. *Journal of Applied Psychology, 59*, 31-37.

The organization for motivation. In J.W. McGuire (Ed.), *Contemporary management: Issues and viewpoints* (pp. 575-578). Englewood Cliffs, NJ: Prentice-Hall.

Psychological testing and fair employment practices: A testing program that does not discriminate. *Personnel Psychology, 27*, 49-62.

Student attitudes toward bureaucratic role prescriptions and the prospects for managerial talent shortages. *Personnel Psychology, 27*, 605-613.

1975

The challenge of managing. Philadelphia, PA: W. B. Saunders.

Case analyses and description of managerial role-motivation training. Philadelphia, PA: W.B. Saunders.

The uncertain future of the leadership concept: An overview. In J.G. Hunt & L.L. Larson (Eds.), *Leadership frontiers* (pp. 197-208). Kent, OH: Kent State University Press.

1976

With J.F. Brewer. The management of ineffective performance. In M.D. Dunnette (Ed.), *Handbook of industrial and organizational psychology* (pp. 995-1029). Chicago: Rand-McNally.

Levels of motivation to manage among personnel and industrial relations managers. *Journal of Applied Psychology, 61*, 419-427.

With M.G. Miner. Managerial characteristics of personnel managers. *Industrial Relations, 15*, 225-243.

Relationships among measures of managerial personality traits. *Journal of Personality Assessment, 40*, 383-397.

With N.R. Smith, & K.G. McCain. The managerial motivation of successful entrepreneurs. *Oregon Business Review, 34*, 3.

1977

With G.A. Steiner. *Management policy and strategy.* New York: Macmillan.

With G.A. Steiner. *Management policy and strategy: Text, readings, and cases.* New York: Macmillan.

Motivation to manage: A ten year update on the "Studies in Management Education" Research. Buffalo, NY: Organizational Measurement Systems Press.

With M.G. Miner. *Personnel and industrial relations: A managerial approach* (3rd ed.). New York: Macmillan.

With M.G. Miner. *Policy issues in personnel and industrial relations.* New York: Macmillan.

With S.J. Carroll, & F.T. Paine. *The management process: Cases and readings* (2nd ed.). New York: Macmillan.

Implications of managerial talent projections for management education. *Academy of Management Review, 2*, 412-420.

Motivational potential for upgrading among minority and female managers. *Journal of Applied Psychology, 62*, 691-697.

Miner Sentence Completion Scale: Form H (Multiple Choice Version). Buffalo, NY: Organizational Measurement Systems Press.

1977 supplement–Scoring guide for the Miner Sentence Completion Scale. Buffalo, NY: Organizational Measurement Systems Press.

Miner Sentence Completion Scale: Form P. Buffalo, NY: Organizational Measurement Systems Press.

1978

The management process: Theory, research, and practice (2nd ed.). New York: Macmillan.

With M.G. Miner. *Employee selection within the law.* Washington, DC: Bureau of National Affairs (BNA) Books.

With M.G. Miner. Organizational communications. In L.R. Bittel (Ed.), *Encyclopedia of professional management* (pp. 140-147). New York: McGraw-Hill.

The Miner Sentence Completion Scale: A reappraisal. *Academy of Management Journal, 21*, 283-294.

Twenty years of research on role motivation theory of managerial effectiveness. *Personnel Psychology, 31*, 739-760.

1979

Leadership: Our nation's most critical shortage. In F.E. Kuzmits (Ed.), *Leadership in a dynamic society* (pp. 1-13). Indianapolis: Bobbs-Merrill.

The role of organizational structure and process in strategy implementation: Commentary. In D.E. Schendel & C.W. Hofer (Eds.), *Strategic management: A new view of business policy and planning* (pp. 289-302). Boston: Little, Brown.

With P. Hesseling, & W.H. Money. Technological versus cultural imperatives: A critical evaluation. In G.W. England, A.R. Negandhi, and B. Wilpert (Eds.), *Organizational functioning in a cross-cultural perspective* (pp. 211-222). Kent, OH: Kent State University Press.

Managerial talent in personnel. *Business Horizons, 22* (6),10-20.

1980

Theories of organizational behavior. Hinsdale, IL: Dryden Press.
With M.G. Miner. *Uniform guidelines on employee selection procedures.* Washington, DC: Bureau of National Affairs (BNA).
Limited domain theories of organizational energy *and* A rationale for the limited domain approach to the study of motivation. In C.C. Pinder & L.F. Moore (Eds.), *Middle range theory and the study of organizations* (pp. 273-286, 334-336). Boston, MA: Martinus Nijhoff.
With A. Holland. Leadership potentials. In R.H. Woody (Ed.), *Encyclopedia of clinical assessment* (pp. 984-995). San Francisco, CA: Jossey-Bass.
The role of managerial and professional motivation in the career success of management professors. *Academy of Management Journal, 23*, 487-508.

1981

Scoring guide for the Miner Sentence Completion Scale: Form P. Buffalo, NY: Organizational Measurement Systems Press.
Theories of organizational motivation. In G.W. England, A.R. Negandhi, and B. Wilpert (Eds.), *The functioning of complex organizations* (pp. 75-110). Cambridge, MA: Oelgeschlager, Gunn and Hain.
With N.R. Smith. Can organizational design make up for organizational decline? *The Wharton Magazine, 5*(4), 29-35.
With D.P. Crane. Motivation to manage and the manifestation of a managerial orientation in career planning. *Academy of Management Journal, 24*, 626-633.

1982

Theories of organizational structure and process. Hinsdale, IL: Dryden Press.
With G.A. Steiner. *Management policy and strategy* (2nd ed.). New York: Macmillan.
With G.A. Steiner & E.R. Gray. *Management policy and strategy: Text, readings, and cases* (2nd ed.). New York: Macmillan.
With N.R. Smith. Decline and stabilization of managerial motivation over a twenty-year period. *Journal of Applied Psychology, 67*, 297-305.
The uncertain future of the leadership concept: Revisions and clarifications. *Journal of Applied Behavioral Science, 18*, 293-307.
A note on theory and research for developing a science of leadership. *Journal of Applied Behavioral Science, 18*, 536-538.

1983

With R.P. Butler & C.L. Lardent. A motivational basis for turnover in military officer education and training. *Journal of Applied Psychology, 68,* 496-506.

With J.N. Pearson. An evaluation of business and economics doctoral student selection. *Collegiate News and Views, 37*(1), 15-19.

The unpaved road from theory, over the mountains to application. In R.H. Kilmann, K.W. Thomas, D.P. Slevin, R. Nath, and S.L. Jerrell (Eds.), *Producing useful knowledge for organizations* (pp. 37-68). New York: Praeger.

With N.R. Smith. Type of entrepreneur, type of firm, and managerial motivation: Implications for organizational life cycle theory. *Strategic Management Journal, 4,* 325-340.

1984

The unpaved road over the mountains—From theory to application. *The Industrial Psychologist, 21*(2), 9-20.

The validity and usefulness of theories in an emerging organizational science. *Academy of Management Review, 9,* 297-306.

Participation and management. In B. Wilpert & A. Sorge (Eds.), *International Yearbook of Organizational Democracy* (Vol. 2, pp. 183-196). New York: Wiley.

With N.R. Smith. Motivational considerations in the success of technologically innovative entrepreneurs. In J.A. Hornaday, F.A. Tarpley, J.A. Timmons, and K.H. Vesper (Eds.), *Frontiers of entrepreneurship research* (pp. 488-495). Wellesley, MA: Babson College.

Miner Sentence Completion Scale: Form T. Buffalo, NY: Organizational Measurement Systems Press.

1985

The practice of management. Columbus, OH: Charles E. Merrill.

Introduction to management. Columbus, OH: Charles E. Merrill.

With M.G. Miner. *Personnel and industrial relations: A managerial approach* (4th ed.). New York: Macmillan.

People problems: The executive answer book. New York: Random House.

Sentence completion measures in personnel research: The development and validation of the Miner Sentence Completion Scales. In H.J. Bernardin & D.A. Bownas (Eds.), *Personality assessment in organizations* (pp. 145-176). New York: Praeger.

With N.R. Smith, & B. Ebrahimi. Further considerations in the decline and stabilization of managerial motivation: A rejoinder to Bartol, Anderson, and Schneier (1980). *Journal of Vocational Behavior, 26*, 290-298.

With F.E. Berman. Motivation to manage at the top executive level: A test of the hierarchic role-motivation theory. *Personnel Psychology, 38*, 377-391.

With N.R. Smith. Motivational considerations in the success of technologically innovative entrepreneurs: Extended sample findings. In J.A. Hornaday, E.B. Shils, J.A. Timmons, & K.H. Vesper (Eds.), *Frontiers of entrepreneurship research* (pp. 482-488). Wellesley, MA: Babson College.

1986

With G.A. Steiner. *Management policy and strategy* (3rd ed.). New York: Macmillan.

With G.A. Steiner & E.R. Gray. *Management policy and strategy: Text, readings, and cases* (3rd ed.). New York: Macmillan.

Scoring guide for the Miner Sentence Completion Scale: Form T. Buffalo, NY: Organizational Measurement Systems Press.

Managerial role motivation training. *Journal of Managerial Psychology, 1*(1), 25-30.

1987

With N.R. Smith, & J.S. Bracker. Correlates of firm and entrepreneur success in technologically innovative companies. In N.C. Churchill, J.A. Hornaday, B.A. Kirchhoff, O.J. Krasner, & K. H. Vesper (Eds.), *Frontiers of entrepreneurship research* (pp. 337-353). Wellesley, MA: Babson College.

With M.G. Holland, & C.H. Black. Using managerial role motivation theory to predict career success. *Healthcare Management Review, 12*(4), 57-64.

1988

Organizational behavior: Performance and productivity. New York: Random House.

With D.P. Crane. Labor arbitrators' performance: Views from union and management perspectives. *Journal of Labor Research, 9*, 43-54.

[Review of Tannenbaum, Margulies, and Massarik's *Human Systems Development.*] *Contemporary Psychology, 33*, 423-425.

Development and application of the rated ranking technique in performance appraisal. *Journal of Occupational Psychology, 61*, 291-305.

1989

With N.R. Smith, & J.S. Bracker. Role of entrepreneurial task motivation in the growth of technologically innovative firms. *Journal of Applied Psychology, 74*, 554-560.

With J.M. Wachtel, & B. Ebrahimi. The managerial motivation of potential managers in the United States and other countries of the world: Implications for national competitiveness and the productivity problem. *Advances in International Comparative Management, 4*, 147-170.

1989 supplement-Scoring guide for the Miner Sentence Completion Scale-Form H. Buffalo, NY: Organizational Measurement Systems Press.

1990

With M.H. Capps. True Test scores of prison inmates. *Polygraph, 19*, 68-71.

The role of values in defining the "goodness" of theories in organizational science. *Organization Studies, 11*, 161-178.

Entrepreneurs, high-growth entrepreneurs, and managers: Contrasting and overlapping motivational patterns. *Journal of Business Venturing, 5*, 221-234.

1991

With C.P.M. Wilderom. Defining voluntary groups and agencies within organization science. *Organization Science, 2*, 366-378.

With C.C. Chen, & K.C. Yu. Theory testing under adverse conditions: Motivation to manage in the People's Republic of China. *Journal of Applied Psychology, 76*, 343-349.

Psychological assessment in a developmental context. In C.P. Hansen & K.A. Conrad (Eds.), *Handbook of psychological assessment in business* (pp. 225-236). Westport, CT: Quorum.

Individuals, groups, and networking: Experience with an entrepreneurship development program. *International Council for Small Business Proceedings, 2*, 82-90.

With B. Ebrahimi. The cultural dynamics of managerial motivation among students from Pan-Pacific Basin countries. *Journal of Global Business, 2*, 87-98.

1992

Industrial-organizational psychology. New York: McGraw-Hill.

With N.R. Smith, & J.S. Bracker. Defining the inventor-entrepreneur in the context of established typologies. *Journal of Business Venturing, 7*, 103-113.

With N.R. Smith, & J.S. Bracker. Predicting firm survival from a knowledge of entrepreneur task motivation. *Entrepreneurship and Regional Development, 4,* 145-153.

1993

Role motivation theories. London/New York: Routledge.

In Press

With D.P. Crane. *Human resource management: The strategic perspective.* New York: Harper Collins.

With D.P. Crane. *Advances in the practice, theory, and research of strategic human resource management.* New York: Harper Collins.

With D.P. Crane, & R.J. Vandenberg. Congruence and fit in professional role motivation theory. *Organization Science.*

With S. Stites-Doe. Applying an entrepreneurship development program to economic problems in the Buffalo area. In A.K. Korman (Ed.), *Contemporary human resource dilemmas/problems.* New York: Guilford.

NOTES

1. See F.C. Pierson, *The Education of American Businessmen: A Study of University-College Programs in Business Administration.* New York: McGraw-Hill, 1959.

2. See R.A. Gordon, and J.E. Howell, *Higher Education for Business.* New York: Columbia University Press, 1959.

3. See A.G. Bedeian, "Totems and Taboos: Undercurrents in the Management Discipline." *Academy of Management News, 19*(4, 1989), 1-6.

4. See H.J. Leavitt, *Corporate Pathfinders: Building Vision and Values into Organizations.* Homewood, IL: Dow Jones—Irwin, 1986.

5. See S.D. Elia, R.F. Seblatnig, and V.P. Storms, *Greenwich Country Day-A History: 1926-1986.* Canaan, NH: Phoenix Publishing, 1988.

6. See H.C. Daly, *42nd "Rainbow" Infantry Division: A Combat History of World War II.* Baton Rouge, LA: Army and Navy Publishing Co., 1946; J.L. Reith, and W.A. Vaughn, *Mission Accomplished-History of the 2d Battalion, 242d Infantry Regiment, 42d Infantry Division, The Rainbow Division.* Salzburg, Austria: Salzburger Druckerei and Verlag, 1945.

7. See P.A. Wallace, *MBAs on the Fast Track: The Career Mobility of Young Managers.* New York: Harper and Row, 1989.

8. See A.H. Maslow, "A Theory of Human Motivation." *Psychological Review, 50*(1943), 370-396.

Twenty-five Years Later... The Illusive Strategy

HENRY MINTZBERG

ADMONITIONS

I was going to close this piece with advice to the young scholar that you should always take your work seriously but never yourself. I put it here instead to express my apprehensions in doing this. I think it is useful to have on record comments on how careers that were lucky enough to emerge successfully unfolded, but there is the danger that the person in question will be taken, and will take him or herself, too seriously. To have succeeded in studying something or other has never made anyone intrinsically interesting; indeed I find some of my successful colleagues terrible bores.

In line with this, I try here to avoid discussing my private life. That is my own business; the issue in question is my working life. But because the two are obviously intertwined, I would like to make a single comment here about them. When I wrote on the back cover of *Mintzberg on Management: Inside Our Strange World of Organizations* (1989) that it "is written for those of us who spend our public lives dealing with organizations and our private lives escaping from them," I was not joking. That, if anything, has characterized much of my behavior. I am intrigued by organizations; all my work has set out to understand them. But when I play, I distance myself from them as far as possible. For example, I love to cycle on back roads in Europe, but I would never dream of taking an organized tour. Sure, I need an airline to get me there, but once I get off the plane, typically with a friend or two, we just get on our bikes and go. I hate to be organized by organizations. So my fascination with them works best at a distance, in commitment at least—not space, because I love to get inside them, as an observer or temporary advisor, and sense their behavior.

To tell my career story, I shall begin with how I fell into this business—
academia as a vocation—and about business itself, or at least organizations
in general. Then I shall outline my career in three phases. But in order to do
this, I shall present some hard data—tracks of some patterns in my behavior
over time. I can explain this in terms of the title of this essay.

I spent a semester (Fall 1990) at the London Business School. A member
of the strategy group there called me in Montreal in the summer to arrange
a faculty seminar and I was to get back to him on the title. When I didn't,
he left a message that it would be called "The Illusive Strategy." Perfect, I
thought, I'll speak to that. It was an inspired suggestion (of Charles Hampden-
Turner).

Strategy formation has been my most sustained subject (as will be seen in
the data): it is the subject of my first article, my greatest number of articles,
and my steadiest stream of articles. Much of this work has revolved around
the definitions of strategy as realized (pattern in action) in addition to intended,
and emergent (realized despite intentions) in addition to deliberate (intentions
realized).[1] Nonetheless, my own realized strategies have, if anything, tended
to be rather deliberate. At least until recently. In the talk in London, I wished
to review my work at that time, which involved a rather wide-ranging collection
of papers and projects. Because the patterns among them may not have been
clear, I thought it would be fun to use the talk to search them out—to infer
my own strategies. Hence the appropriateness of the suggested title there, and
my use of it here.

In 1978, I wrote a working paper titled "Ten Years Later: Some Personal
Reflections on Management and Methodology," to review the first ten years
of my career (parts of which appeared in "An Emerging Strategy of Direct
Research" [1979b]). So here we have "twenty-five years later," more or less.[2]

One final warning. This is my career story as told by me. It is not reality
but my own reconstruction of reality through my own perceptions. I did some
research for this paper—went back into old files and documents, reviewed all
the c.v.s I did over the years, reread some of my earliest papers, did a systematic
analysis of my publications and course teaching, and so forth. That helped
me to pin some things down, but it also revealed the fallacy of my memory
if not my outright biases. While such a reconstruction may be of interest in
and of itself, it should be read only for what it is.

ORIGINS OF MY CAREER

I was hiking on the moors of Somerset with a friend a few weeks before writing
this when he suddenly asked, "How did you come to study organizations
anyway?" "I don't know," I answered, "it just happened. . . . One thing led
to another. I never really thought about it. But it's worked out quite well."

I guess I should try to answer his question here, which will require a bit of personal background.

I was born to a pretty comfortable family; my father owned a successful small firm that manufactured women's dresses. It may be true, as I claimed in the preface to my first book, that as a young boy I wondered what my father, as manager, did at the office. But this was certainly no more than a passing curiosity. Overall, I think I grew up as a pretty ordinary kid, not a bad student but never one in danger of being selected "most likely to succeed."

After reasonable grades in high school, I entered engineering studies at McGill, in mechanical because I used to love to tear engines apart (although I could never quite put all of them back together again). I really wanted to do industrial engineering, but McGill had no such program. My grades were average or a bit better, but in any event, engineering grew into an excuse to do extracurricular activities. Summers were spent mostly working in factories, from die making to time studies.

When graduation came, I do not recall having very clear intentions, other than that I was determined not to work for my father. I had to know if I could make it on my own. So I halfheartedly registered for the cycle of company interviews, and after discussing the future prospects of the McGill Redmen (football team) with several personnel types who read on my c.v. that I had been sports editor of the *McGill Daily*, I walked into an interview with Canadian National Railways. Imagine, this guy had a beard! (The year was 1961; only Fidel Castro had a beard then.) Not only that, but he was a biologist, working for the railroad, and talking about these strange studies he and a mixed group of colleagues were doing under what he called "operational research." When he looked at my c.v. and asked "What did you *accomplish* as sports editor of the *McGill Daily*?," I knew this was the place for me.

So there I found myself, doing OR when it was still common sense analysis rather than a lot of greedy technique. The CN was an exciting place to be in those days, one of the most progressive railroads in the world.

It was a good way to begin. For example, at one point I found myself fishing in a hump yard. A hump yard sorts incoming trains by passing them over a hill, off which they roll one car at a time, switched into the appropriate outgoing track and braked automatically according to various parameters fed into an analog computer—the distance to the last car on the track, coefficients for the friction effects of the track and the car, and so forth—to ensure an impact speed great enough to couple and gentle enough to spare the car and its contents (about 2-4 mph. as I recall). It was wonderful, new technology. Even if the yard was littered with the debris of broken coupling gears. So a Rube Goldberg type in the CN lab made a fishing rod, with a magnet for a hook and a speedometer on the reel, and I went a-fishing—to catch a histogram of impact speeds. Amid great blasts of mating from cars labelled "chinawear—do not hump," I drew my chart of coupling speeds: a fair proportion at zero that never made it, some in the desired range, and many others on up (well into the double figures, I recall—anyone who wants to learn about organizations should just once stand next to two boxcars meeting at 12 m.p.h.). The upshot was a meeting of the executive committee in which a presentation by a regional vice president about the glories of his Montreal hump yard was followed by the flinging of my histogram on the table by our vice president of research and development. A political battle ensued, and I was learning about organizations—at the top and the bottom, as well as all that empty space in between!

I always intended to go to graduate school, certainly not one of those soft business schools with all those obnoxious (later-to-be called) "fast trackers," but for a master's degree in industrial engineering or operational research, to become a consultant to small businesses. An uncle of mine, Jack Mintzberg, with whom I was rather close, had encouraged me in this direction, in fact hired me the previous summer to develop a costing system for his tag and label company after sending me to learn about it on a course in the United States. (My c.v. still lists my very first speech—in 1963, four years before my second— to the Society of Paper Box Manufacturers of Quebec, arranged that summer by Jack. I should add that despite his directing me toward business, it was Jack, I later came to realize, who first planted the seed of an academic career in my mind. As a young man, he had worked as a research assistant for Hans Salye, the eminent physiologist, and always regretted having given in to family pressures to go into business. But if the image was set back then, it was deeply buried in my subconscious, because I recall having no pretensions whatever of a career in academia. It was not that I dismissed my academic record an insufficient; I no more aspired to be a professor than to try out for quarterback of the Green Bay Packers.)

At the suggestion of an acquaintance, I applied to the industrial engineering master's program at New York University, well ahead of time. Finding myself one day in New York, after having been accepted, I called to meet someone in the department. After getting the runaround on the telephone, I decided this would never do, and so went over to Columbia to apply to their department. Still I would not consider a business school. But, of course, MIT was not a real business school; it was then called the School of Industrial Management and it gave a Master of Science degree. There was no way I would get in with my grades, but on a lark I applied anyway. For some reason (perhaps my extracurricular activities) they accepted me, so I had a decision to make. I went to see Sebastian B. Littauer, the grand old man of industrial engineering at Columbia, and he said "Go there; we could never do for you what they will do." One of those critical moments of one's life.

And so this aspiring industrial engineer went to MIT, and within weeks was writing articles in the student newspaper condemning the excessiveness of quantitative materials in the curriculum. I even published an editorial in November dismissing any claims that they couldn't change the program by

January. (I still had a bit to learn about professional bureaucracies!) The old journalist in me had come out once again (I would likely have ended up in journalism had I not become an academic . . . maybe I did!), not only literally in my extracurricular activities but also in my attraction to the softer interpretations of reality in place of the hard core analyses that surrounded me in the classroom.

I am not sure why I applied to the doctoral program at MIT. Perhaps it was the easy thing to do (easier than getting a job), perhaps I was getting increasingly interested in some of the softer questions of management—probably a bit of both. My grades in the master's program had been good but certainly not top; my GMAT of 602 was not bad for those days (though, based on figures I have seen recently, I would probably not even be considered for the current MIT master's program).

I applied to do the degree in policy. At the time, MIT had no area of policy, no professor of policy, no doctoral concentration in policy. All that obviously suited fine someone who wanted to escape the control of organizations. That it also suited the doctoral committee is, I believe, a tribute to its members' open-mindedness. A professor of operations management named Edward (Ned) Bowman, who had just returned from a year out as assistant to the president of Honeywell Computers, and was teaching one first policy course, had just taken over the chairmanship of the committee, and on informing me of my acceptance also said he had decided to supervise me himself, to find out what this field of policy was all about.

It was an unusual course of study to say the least—in terms of American doctoral program conventions, if not European. I went into Ned's office one day to ask what I should read for my comprehensive examinations, and he replied, more or less: "I don't know. Why don't you just draw up a reading list and read it." He did add a few books to the list I drew up from my own reading, helped by a visit across the river to Roland Christensen at Harvard which had lots of policy doctoral students. I also recall vividly—though the now chaired professor of policy at Wharton does not—that after walking away from a brief meeting with Ned in the hall, he called out that "I've decided there is no future in policy." "You'll change your mind," I called back.

I had a clear mission in my studies. Theory was challenging cases in those days, inspired by the Carnegie Graduate School of Industrial Administration innovations of Bach, Simon, Cyert et al., and MIT was one of the faithful adherents. But policy, and management in general, were stepchildren in these schools, often barely taught at all.[3] Why could policy not be taught conceptually as marketing and finance were then so commonly done? So I set out on a search for conceptual materials—mostly in related fields, as there was little research base in policy itself—and began to outline a theoretical approach to the field. In December 1965, just a few months into the doctoral program, I submitted a course paper titled "The Future of Business Policy," which I wrote was "in response to a request by my program supervisor, Ned Bowman, to try to define the field. The explicit objective of this paper is to argue for the recognition of Business Policy as a management discipline at MIT." I viewed the field in terms of two processes, "guiding the firm: strategy making and planning" and "leadership: purpose, relationship to society, leadership style, and power." A section on "The Research Base" categorized the "underlying research" in terms of power, game theory, the Carnegie School, military strategists, and organizational goals, and the "applied research" in terms of leadership, firm in society, business policy texts, systems analysis (PPBS), and long-range planning, all supported by numerous references. (An appendix listed forty-two books that I had read.) I concluded that while "the literature is growing rapidly," the field appears to be less developed "largely due to the fact that there has been almost no attempt to classify and identify the literature that has been printed."

Ned Bowman left MIT before I started thesis work (to take on the controllership of Yale, later the business deanship at Ohio State, before going to Wharton, with periods back at MIT in between), but he was still there for my comprehensive examinations, which must have happened in late 1965. My major was in policy (but Ned did not present me with an examination that read "Write a comprehensive examination in Policy and answer it"), with minors in "Organizational Studies" and "Information and Control Systems." My underlying discipline was Political Science, which included some weird course material on all kinds of ways to fight a nuclear war.

With the exams behind me, there was merely the question of the thesis. Strategy making was my main interest, but in truth I had no sense of what I wanted to do, and I wasted six months finding out.

Igor Ansoff's book, *Corporate Strategy* (1965), had just appeared, and I was as taken with it as everyone else. So I decided I would try to extend the application of the Ansoff model from mergers and expansions to strategic planning in general. (Another course paper I wrote in December 1965 had considered "the arguments for and against planning" and outlined a model based on the conclusion "that bureaucracies can and must plan." I also came across a thick file of thesis proposals from March to September 1966, about a "Programmed" or "An Analytical Procedure for Strategic Planning.") But, once again, I was saved from myself: I could not find an organization in which to apply the model (or, nearer to the truth, my feeble attempt to convince the new dean at MIT to let me do so in the management school failed).

Some time earlier, James Webb, who headed up NASA in the Apollo era, approached that same individual (Bill Pounds) to be studied personally, as a manager. He believed NASA would ultimately be evaluated by its technological spin-offs on this planet, and he counted among these its own management advances (including, evidently, his own managerial style). As the only doctoral student at this school of management interested in management, I was approached to do this as a thesis. I dismissed the idea quickly—studying one chief executive was no way to make your way through the bastion of science that was MIT. I did, though, get a wonderful tour of NASA installations with several faculty members.

That was in late April 1966, and immediately upon my return to MIT, a conference took place to discuss "The Impact of Computers on Management."[4] There I saw a number of impressive individuals bog down on the question for lack of a conceptual framework within which to consider managerial work. Gulick's POSDCORB (*p*lanning, *o*rganizing, *s*taffing, *d*irecting, *co*ordinating, *r*eporting, and *bu*dgeting[5]) was not of help, and in their discussions, they could scarcely get beyond attempts to equate computers with programmed activities and managerial work with the unprogrammed.[5] It occurred to me, having listened to people who certainly "knew" what managers did—all were involved with management in one way or another, including a number as successful managers themselves—that they did not "know" conceptually. And without that second kind of knowing, many of the most critical issues in management simply could not even be addressed. Clearly we needed to take a closer look at what managers really do.[6]

And so, bastion of science and all that notwithstanding, I came to study managerial work for my doctoral thesis. No one had bothered to tell me that doctoral dissertations are supposed to probe narrow, researchable issues; I don't bother to tell my own doctoral students either. (One professor did once tell me that an MIT dissertation should be "elegant"; he was referring to the method, not the results, and I have always prided myself on the inelegance, or at least the simplicity, of the methodology I used to study managerial work.)

Webb was no longer available, and I decided that I would observe the activities of five chief executives. That number had no special significance, other than being several and manageable, nor did my choice of organizations, except to ensure that all were in different domains. (Years later, having done a categorization of organizations,[7] I realized there was somewhat of a bias toward professional bureaucracies and adhocracies. But I doubt this much influenced the dimensions I was studying.)

I started to write letters to possible subjects. I hit it lucky quite early. James Gaven, who headed up the Arthur D. Little consulting firm, accepted immediately by return mail. He was well known in the United States at the time as the first retired army general to have publicly criticized the Viet Nam war effort. Thus, when I received a telephone call from the secretary of John Knowles, head of the Massachusetts General Hospital, saying he wouldn't do it but that he would like to talk to me, and after he offered various reasons, I chipped in with "That's too bad because General Gaven has accepted," and without loosing a breath, Knowles added "and that's why I can't do it for at least several weeks!" (Knowles was a wonderfully extroverted subject; years later he told me someone gave him an article I did on the research with the comment, "John, this sounds exactly like you!") I do not recall having to ask more than about ten chief executives altogether; the others who accepted were Bernard O'Keefe of E.G. & G., Inc., Harry B. (for Bulova) Henshel of the Bulova Watch Company, and, of course, Charlie Brown, this one head of the Newton Massachusetts school system. They were a wonderfully cooperative group.

Jim Hekimian, an MIT professor of control with an interest in policy, took over the chairmanship of my committee, which included Charlie Myers in industrial relations, and Don Carroll in operations management. (As Jim left MIT to become dean at Northeastern, Don ended up officially signing the thesis as chairman, before he too went off deaning, at Wharton.) For the most part, they knew as much—or, I should say, as little—about the subject as I did, except for Charlie Myers who had touched on it in his book with Harbison, *Management in the Industrial World* (McGraw-Hill, 1959). But they formed a wonderfully enthusiastic support group that encouraged me to put in everything (hence the host of asides in my thesis).

When the time came to defend the thesis (an event of obvious consequence at MIT—one doctoral student showed up aside from my committee), after I presented the results, having been assured earlier by Charlie Myers that there was nothing to worry about, the committee deliberated for about twenty minutes. An anxious me was finally informed that, oh, they were just discussing the publishing possibilities.

Having been assured by someone like Charlie Myers that the thesis was publishable, I kind of dropped it in the mail to a publisher (McGraw-Hill as I recall), not quite with a note as to where to send the checks. The reply was in kind, more or less to "occupant," saying "No, thank you." Not to worry, it must have been a mistake, so I sent the thesis off to a second publisher. Perhaps a dozen publishers later, I had no contract. So Charlie Myers stepped in and proposed it to the MIT Press. It seemed headed for publication when someone on their board questioned it and out it went for another review. I met that reviewer years later, who apologized to me. Carnegie-Mellon methodology jock meets sample of five, and I was back at the beginning.

It was at that time that I surprised my wife one evening by blurting out that I knew this was an important piece of work—that I just knew it would be prominent one day—and so, in the face of all those rejection letters, I would rewrite it and proceed. I was not prone to such claims, and I was not expressing a wish or some manifestation of arrogance so much as what felt like a certainty.

And so I rewrote the thesis and resubmitted it to the whole cluster of publishers. Again they all rejected it, luckily except for Harper & Row and Random House. And so the former published *The Nature of Managerial Work* in 1973. To quote the last line of Philip Roth's *Portnoy's Complaint*: "So (said the doctor). Now vee may perhaps to begin. Yes?" (Random House, 1967, p. 274).

SOME REAL HARD DATA

My occasional diatribes notwithstanding, hard data is not a bad thing; indeed some of my own articles are full of it. It helps to pin down some of the vagueness (and in turn to create some of its own). So I thought it might be useful to present some tangible traces of my own work, before I begin to describe the phases of my career, as I see them. I took all my publications of any consequence (i.e., excluding letters, short newspaper articles, and so forth), whether good or bad, academic or not, and categorized them in three ways: first as to whether they were empirical (deriving directly from my own research, interpreting this rather narrowly as articles rooted in the research rather than drawing off it), substantially conceptual, or practitioner (intended to populize findings); second as to subject matter, comprising strategy making, managerial work, organization (including structural and power issues), management in general (including a few publications on research and on the field of policy), analysis and/or intuition, and decision making; and third, as to coauthorship. The histograms for all of this are shown in Figure 1. Books are shown shaded in; obviously each was the equivalent work of many articles.

I published my first article, called "The Science of Strategy Making," as a doctoral student in 1967, and with the exception of 1969, my second year as a professor, I have published every year ever since, from a single article in five of the twenty-five years in question to as many as six articles and two books in 1983. (Figures for 1991 include material already accepted for publication; I write this in February 1991.) Probably the most consistent substream is the empirical, almost regularly one per year, interspersed by some empty years and a few with two publications. But the conceptual stream is far fuller, with more than double the number of publications and sometimes quite frequent in a single year (e.g., 1983 with the two books and five articles). Partly this reflects my propensity to conceptualize, but it also reflects the fact that conceptual articles, especially when spun off books in which I had already worked out the issue, were easier to do than empirical ones. But I should add that I always took great care and time with almost all of my writing, books as well as articles, conceptual and practitioner-oriented as well as empirical, with five drafts or more being the norm. Practitioner publications represent a thinner stream, more sporadic, but indicating my commitment from early on to trying to reach both audiences. Indeed, in mid-1976 I took great pride in having published at the same time one article in *Administrative Science Quarterly* and another in the *Harvard Business Review*.[8]

In terms of content, it could be concluded from the data that I passed from one focus to another, initially on managerial work in the early 1970s, then over to analysis and its relationship with intuition from the mid-1970s, then to a heavy concentration on organizational issues (especially structure, power, and forms of organizations) from 1979 to 1984, and then to a heavier and more

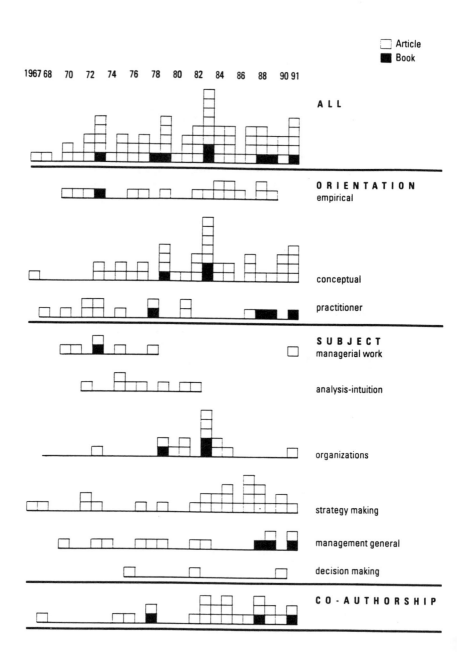

Figure 1.   Publications

sustained focus on strategy making through the rest of the 1980s, with a rise at the end in the management-general category, representing especially two editions of a textbook[9] and one summary book for practitioners.[10] Three articles on decision making are shown, well spread out, the heaviest concentration of work being for the first one. That was published in 1976,[11] although the work was done in 1973 (indicating the need to take into account what can be long lead times in these figures). Management-general shows a thin trickle from early on to 1983, representing some of my practitioner articles as well as ones on research and on the field of policy. Finally, while strategy making clearly peaks as by far my heaviest concentration of articles, through most of the 1980s, that is a theme I have returned to throughout my career. Indeed, that first article as a doctoral student, in 1967, opened with a comparison of two approaches to strategy making that anticipated my much later comparison[12] of deliberate and emergent strategy:

> Man's beginnings were described in the Bible in terms of conscious planning and grand strategy. The opposing theory, developed by Darwin, suggested that no such grand design existed but that environmental forces gradually shaped man's evolution.
> The disagreement between the biblical and Darwinian theorists is paralleled on a more mundane level in the study of strategy-making. There are those who envision grand calculated designs for the corporate entity, and there are those who cite current practice to argue that organizational strategy evolves, shaped less by man than by his environment.[13]

I have included a histogram on coauthorship for what it may reflect. In general, I was a solo writer for most of my early years (although I did coauthor my second article with Jim Hekimian, in 1968). There was some joint work in the mid-1970s, based on a contracted monograph,[14] as well as my first article on decision making with two of my students,[15] but coauthorship became a serious and sustained activity only after Jim Waters joined the McGill faculty in 1976. Jim left McGill several years ago, and we suffered his tragic loss a short while ago. In the last few years, I have had an equally delightful collaboration with my colleague, Frances Westley, again around issues of strategy, although in recent years my variety of coauthorships has increased significantly (as can be seen, alongside everything else here, in the attached list of these publications). Finally, I should mention my collaboration with Danny Miller. Danny was my first doctoral student, and we have shared ideas closely and energetically for many years, although our formal collaboration has been restricted to that 1975 contracted monograph and one published paper called "The Case for Configuration" (1983).[16]

In Figure 2, I plot all my teaching activity. (My accessible records here are not complete, so there may be some inaccuracies, but this should not affect the overall patterns. The year recorded refers to the first of the whole academic year. For example, the Carnegie course shown in 1972 was actually taught in the Spring of 1973.)

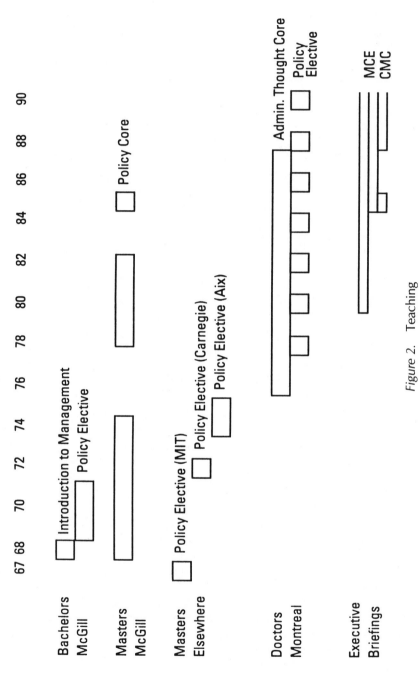

Figure 2. Teaching

334

As can be seen, I have not taught a great variety of courses, given the number of years. The mainstay of my teaching was mostly the MBA policy course; I was hired at McGill in 1968 to take over the full year core course that had fallen into disarray. In general, I taught one or two sections of it in almost all my years at McGill until recently, aside from periods of sabbatical or leave (to France in 1974-76 and Switzerland in the winter of 1983) and a three and a half year spell running the doctoral program in the late 1970s. I taught a similar master's elective course as a doctoral student at MIT, again as a visiting professor at Carnegie-Mellon in the Spring of 1973, and again on a sabbatical followed by a year's leave of absence in Aix-en-Provence, France in 1974-76 (technically in a "third cycle doctoral" program, but coded, as I see it, as master's level). I also taught some undergraduate courses in my early years at McGill—an introduction to management in my very first year and an elective "Seminar on Organizational Strategy" in the next three. In 1986 I negotiated myself out of McGill MBA teaching altogether to concentrate my efforts on research, writing, and doctoral training, at a reduced salary. (Figure 3 tabulates my appointments, sabbaticals and visits, etc.)

Our doctoral activity started up (as a joint program among the four Montreal universities) in 1976; I played a major role in its design and championing, and when I returned from Aix-en-Provence in 1976, near its inception, I was asked to run it, which I did for three and a half years. For many years, I cotaught the introductory required course for all doctoral students, called "Fundamentals of Administrative Thought," and I have also offered a policy elective every second year, more or less, beginning in 1976 and occurring again right now, which remains my only teaching commitment at McGill.

Finally, the chart shows a stream of "executive briefings" beginning in 1980. This is a two-day public program that I do myself, which draws much of my work together for managers, who register from a wide variety of contexts. Originally offered by the Management Centre Europe (a Brussels-based training group associated with the American Management Association), it has become a regular activity, expanding in Europe from one program a year to two in 1985, and then to Canada on a regular basis by their sister organization in 1988.

These data suggest (to me at least) that there has always been a clear pedagogical focus in my work. In fact, one central course has always served to integrate much of my thinking and activity, including the stimulation and direction of much of my writing. In the earliest years of my career, it was the McGill MBA core policy course. After my return from France, that focus shifted to my doctoral teaching, particularly the administrative thought course. And in recent years, the two-day briefings have emerged as the focal course, directing me to particular issues and helping me to address them. As I shall specify later, the *push* of theory has gradually been replaced by the *pull* of issues in my approach to the world of organizations.

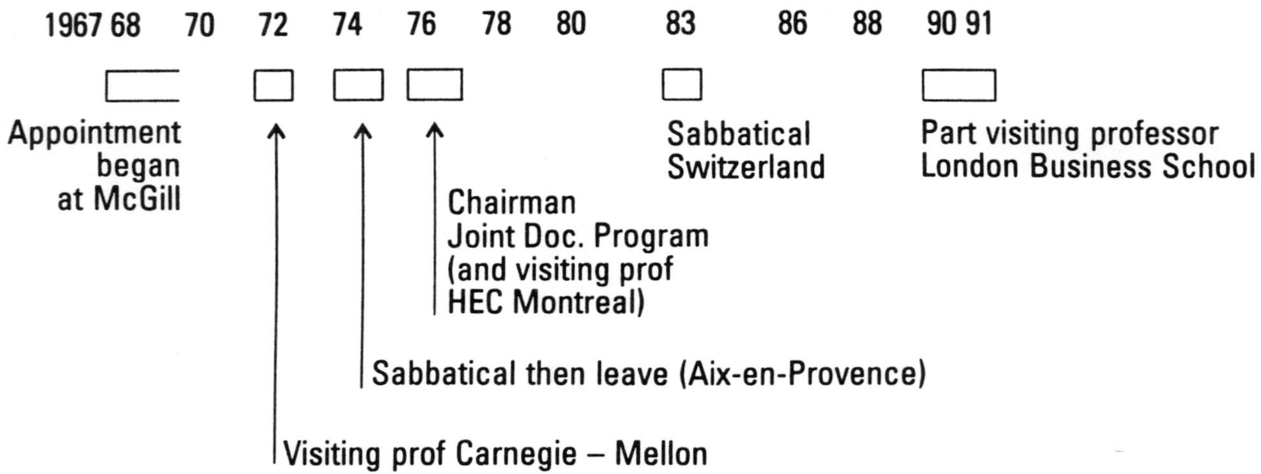

Figure 3. Appointments

336

Those hard data that tell the story best I shall save for later. These are the diagrams that I have used in my publications over the years. When, as part of this exercise, I begin to consider all of them chronologically, the results were most startling: they clustered into three clearly distinct groups.

All of these findings, reinforced (or produced in the first place) by my prior beliefs, cause me to see my career as having unfolded in three fairly distinct phases. I can, in fact, identify the commencement of all three with rather tangible events, although the second and third took some time to manifest themselves fully. It is not so much that one phase ended when another began. Rather the second and then the third added to the first, as my mindset shifted over time. As we travel through life, we don't so much replace baggage as add to what we already have. To be discussed in the following sections, the three phases can be labelled as follows:

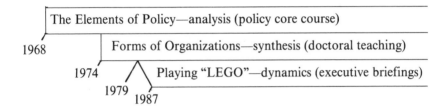

RECTANGLE PHASE (ANALYSIS): THE ELEMENT OF POLICY (FROM 1968)

I returned to Montreal in 1968 with not only a thesis but also an outline for a book to be called "The Theory of Management Policy." I then set out to write it, chapter-by-chapter, week-by-week, the first time I taught the McGill MBA Policy course. I am still writing it!

The MIT management school back in those days was also a bastion of theory (as was McGill's, it should be added, Canada's representative in that small club of the late 1960s), what we saw then as one of the Carnegie-inspired lights of conceptual clarity glowing in the darkness of all that Harvard case study chatter. Harvard's policy textbooks (*the* textbooks of the time) were (and remain) either devoid of conceptual material or else soft peddled bits of it lightly. Policy or general management was, as a result, almost absent from these theory-based schools. But my doctoral studies had convinced me that it need not have been: lacking was not teachable theory so much as someone to pull together all the relevant theory that did exist, much of it in related disciplines. I intended to be that someone. I simply misjudged the task, or at least my obsessive way of going about it.

The outline I had developed by 1968 was not, I suspect, much different from the earliest one I could now find, dated 1973, shown in Figure 4, which itself

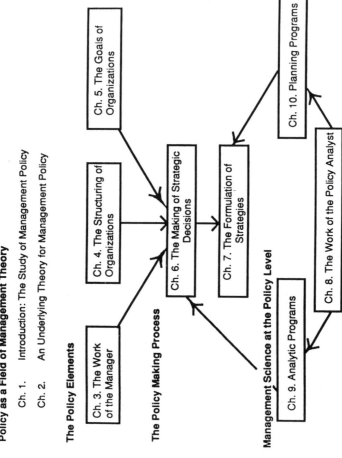

Policy as a Field of Management Theory

Ch. 1. Introduction: The Study of Management Policy

Ch. 2. An Underlying Theory for Management Policy

The Policy Elements

Ch. 3. The Work of the Manager

Ch. 4. The Structuring of Organizations

Ch. 5. The Goals of Organizations

The Policy Making Process

Ch. 6. The Making of Strategic Decisions

Ch. 7. The Formulation of Strategies

Management Science at the Policy Level

Ch. 8. The Work of the Policy Analyst

Ch. 9. Analytic Programs

Ch. 10. Planning Programs

Management Policy Tomorrow

Ch. 11. The Future of Management Policy

Figure 4. Outline of "Theory of Management Policy" circa 1973

did not much change subsequently.[17] I opened files on each chapter, to collect notes and relevant articles. Pendaflex folders soon became boxes, and the boxes soon began to overflow and multiply. I code named each chapter TT1, TT2, and so forth (for *The Theory of Management Policy*) for purposes of filing notes, and so forth. And so I had my writing plan all set out for me—my intended strategy was well formulated, merely to be implemented.

As I wrote the chapters, I began to bind them together to hand out as a kind of text in my MBA policy course. The oldest version I have of this (and probably the first, bound at least) is dated July 1972, although I did find the 1970-71 course outline which showed me handing out Chapters 1, 2, and 3 (the latter on goals), 4 (on structure), and 7. The 1972 text opened with a fifteen-page bibliography, followed by a working paper titled "Policy as a Field of Management Theory," which argued:

> The student of Business or Management requires a useful conceptual framework with which to view the world of Policy that he shall face during his career. He requires answers to the following questions:
>
> - What is the job of the manager?
> - How do organizations determine goals?
> - How do different organizations develop their structures and which are appropriate for each?
> - By what processes are significant decisions made?
> - What are the organizational strategies, and how are they made?
> - What is the role of management science at the Policy level?
>
> The Management Policy Course should provide answers to these questions on the following bases:
>
> 1. *The answers to questions of Policy must be based on empirical research.* We must observe and study the management process in a systematic way. Then, what we teach our students should be researched or at least researchable.
>
> 2. *The answers should blend into an integrated theory of Management Policy.* We must bring together the theories that we now have, integrate them based on some underlying theory, and use research to fill in the gaps that remain. We have much to do, but we have the basis for a beginning. Many theories are available that provide partial answers to our questions, although they are often not recognized as Policy theories. But so long as they shed light on the questions asked in the Policy course, they must be used there.
>
> 3. *Description must precede prescription.* There has been too great a tendency to prescribe in the literature of Policy, to tell managers how to manage without first understanding why they do what they do.... We must avoid the temptation to arm our students with simplistic prescriptions (e.g., planning is good per se); rather we and they must come to understand the complex processes of management. Prescription is meaningful only when it is grounded in valid description.
>
> 4. *The Policy course should integrate the lessons of management science.* The Policy course is the integrative one of the MBA curriculum, linking the applied fields of marketing, finance, and production. The modern curriculum places increasing emphasis on the scientific tools of these fields (e.g., marketing research, capital budgeting, mathematical programming). The Policy course can maintain its integrative

role by serving to interpret the lessons of management science for the policy maker. The Policy student should learn to assess the relevance and weaknesses of each management science technique (especially strategic planning) in the light of his or her knowledge of the actual management process. The Policy course must walk a line between behavioral science and management science, drawing on one for descriptive theory, on the other for prescriptive theory.

5. *The Policy course must link theory with practice.* Theory alone is no better than practice alone. The reality of Policy is sufficiently complex to require that the student have the opportunity to assess the relevance of theory in practice. Ideally, the students armed with theory will observe reality firsthand, via a field study or live case. Alternately, he can assess his theory in the context of a written case or business game.[18]

That working paper became Chapter 1, which was rewritten in 1974 and 1978. Chapter 2, titled "An Underlying Theory for Management Policy," sought to build some roots for the material to follow by combining the administrative theory of Herbert Simon with the general systems theory of Ludwig von Bertalanffy.[19] Although over twenty years old (and also rewritten in 1974 and 1978) and never published, I still intend eventually to turn it into some kind of article!

Chapters 3, 4, and 5 dealt with the "policy elements." There was no chapter on managerial work in that first edition, and never has been. I was just publishing my thesis as a book and knew I could easily summarize it in chapter form when necessary. I did write an early chapter on structure titled "Organizational Structure and the Coupling of Programs" (undated) which took up 67 pages in that 1973 edition, and an early chapter (dated 1970) titled "Influences and the Organizational Goal System," which took up 60 pages, the framework of which appeared in print only in one article for French speaking practitioners.[20]

Chapters 6 and 7 considered the "policy-making process," first in terms of strategic decision making (single important choices) and then strategy making (streams of choices over time). A very long version of the latter was written in the early 1970s (125 pages, undated), under the title "The Strategy Concept," although I included only parts of it in the 1973 edition. These comprised material I published as "Strategy Making in Three Modes" (1973) and three pages of propositions under the label "A General Theory of Strategy Making," each backed up by considerable text in the full version (and never published).

For Chapter 6, the 1973 edition contained one page with the words "Chapter 6 to come." It came the next year. In January 1973, I took off to Carnegie-Mellon for a semester, to soak up the energies of that famous school of administrative thought (Simon, Cyert, March, etc.), and, appropriately, I thought, to write up some data I had been collecting on the making of strategic decisions, which together with a literature review, was to become Chapter 6. Carnegie did not distract me from that task: it turned out that there was nothing left of those energies. Simon had gone off to the psychology department, Cyert was doing administration instead of writing about it, and March had long since left. For the doctoral students from Europe roaming the corridors, like me, in search of that glorious past, I became the closest thing to a resident expert on administrative theory! (I was, after all, writing a paper on decision making!) And so I did the chapter, quite large, about 80 pages, single spaced. It also remains unpublished, although its essence was captured in "The Structure of 'Unstructured' Decision Processes," (1976), with Duru Raisinghani and André Théorêt, McGill students in the MBA and doctoral programs respectively, who had helped with the earlier analysis of the data. Figure 5 reproduces a representative decision process from that article.

The third, prescriptive section of the book, on "Management Science at the Policy Level," consisted of chapters on the work of the policy analysts and their analytic programs for decision making and planning programs for strategy making. It was represented in that 1973 edition only by a six-page piece titled "A Program for Strategic Planning" (dated January 1969), my rendition of the classic strategy model (which I now prefer to call the "design school").[21] A Chapter 8 on "The Role of the Analyst at Policy Level" did appear in 1978 (52 pages), which I shall discuss later.

And so I devoted much of what I am calling the first phase of my career (up to 1974) to writing the chapters of that book as well as to pursuing research that fitted in with those chapters—notably on strategic decision making and strategy formation. An initial proceedings publication (the only one in my reference list) outlined a major project that I was undertaking on strategy making through the analysis of patterns in behavior.[22]

Likewise, most of my publications of this period related to these chapters, two on strategy making[23] and several on managerial work, including my first book,[24] based on my thesis, and various articles spun off of it,[25] including one that delved into the information systems consequence of the findings.[26] Figure 6 shows the book's depiction of the manager's working roles. Miscellaneous publications of the period included two for Canadian practitioners[27] and one for a Canadian government publication,[28] spun off a consulting assignment, that sought to describe government activities in terms of Maslow's needs-hierarchy theory.[29]

I should also mention a project carried out for the U.S. National Association of Accountants and the Canadian Society of Industrial Accountants. They wondered why managers didn't use accounting information the way (accountants at least) thought they should, and were prepared to fund research to find out. One project came to us, to do a kind of compendium of *Normative Models in Managerial Decision Making*, the title of the monograph published in 1975 (b), coauthored with Danny Miller, who came to McGill in 1972, and Larry Gordon, a professor of accounting. But I felt they were wasting a lot of money funding original research when many of the answers were already in the published literature. So for a tiny fraction of their budget, I surveyed

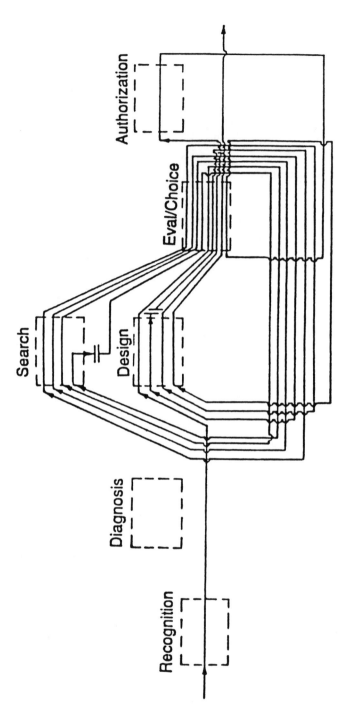

Source: "The Structure of 'Unstructured' Decision Processes" (1976, p. 273)

Figure 5. Illustration of Strategic Decision Process

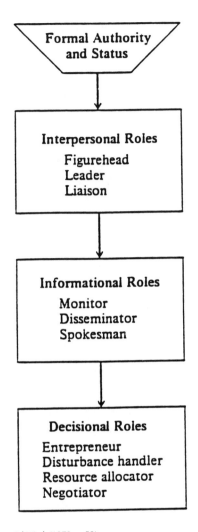

Source: *The Nature of Managerial Work (1973, p. 59).*

Figure 6.   The Manager's Working Roles

the literature and produced another monograph, called *Impediments to the Use of Management Information* (1975). It laid the blame on hard information itself (too limited, too aggregated, too late, unreliable), as well as on the nature of organizations (rigid objectives, politics, verbal nature of managerial work) and the nature of our own brains (cognitive limitations, biases, psychological reactions to failures).

Looking back on that phase of my career, I see myself as a rather conventional academic, except for my obsession with that textbook. I had my world neatly compartmentalized—organizations conveniently chopped up into various elements and processes—for myself probably more than for my MBA students. But they did serve as the focus of my pedagogical activity, the market force if you like, which in turn served to focus my writing and research. To bring some reality to the classroom, not to mention to myself, beginning with my first course in 1968 I sent those students out in groups to study Montreal organizations of their own choosing.[30] In fact, in the early years they were given a sequence of assignments that corresponded to the main chapters: to study one manager, to describe an organization's structure and its goals, influencers, and coalitions, to trace one of its strategic decision processes (some of the reports of which became the data base for the 1976 article on decision making), and to describe its strategy making process. Over the years, these studies provided me with a wonderful variety of examples, as well as the opportunity to test the applicability of my theoretical materials in practice, and to enrich them.

Research and especially conceptual development is what drove me in the first phase of my career, with a decidedly academic orientation, although I did do several practitioner articles. Despite some rumblings about my upcoming attention to emergent strategies and managerial intuition, in retrospect I see my work then as most decidedly deliberate and analytical. One need only look at all those nicely sequenced sets of rectangles in the figures (4, 5, and 6) that I was drawing in those days!

BLOB PHASE (SYNTHESIS): FORMS OF ORGANIZATIONS (FROM 1974)

Leaving for sabbatical to Aix-en-Provence in the fall of 1974 proved to be a turning point in my life, or at least coincided with one. Personally I opened up to the splendor of southern France, finding my escape from organizations in that rugged nature, and professionally an important shift began to occur in my mind.

I began serious work on a rework of the structuring chapter before I left, having read all the literature collected in my boxes and setting out to develop a detailed outline to take with me. My memory is generally awful about many details, but one event I do recall vividly in the spring of 1974 is sitting in my basement office at home when a friend dropped in, and expressing to him my intense frustration in trying to draw the huge, disparate, and awfully narrow literature on organizational structuring into some kind of comprehensive framework. Bivariate relationships concerning "administrative ratios," "amount of control," "environmental hetrogeneity," and the like just didn't help. As Danny Miller and I explained in a later article,[31] that was why the museums of organizational structuring were empty of people even if its archives were full.

Pradip Khandwalla joined the McGill Faculty of Management in 1971 after completing his doctorate at Carnegie-Mellon. We soon became close colleagues and good friends. In his thesis, Pradip found that organizational effectiveness depended less on doing any particular thing (such as planning formally or decentralizing power over decision making) than on the interrelationship among several such things done (such as centralizing power *and* staying small *and* remaining informal). Early on, as I recall, I thought of this finding as configurational. There the seed was probably planted for the resolution of my frustration in the basement.

I have often tried, without success, to recall exactly how the idea of synthesizing the literature of organizational structuring around distinct configurations, or "ideal types" of organizations, came to me. All I do remember is the critical role played by the occasional insight, most notably in the work of Joan Woodward[32] on forms of technology. On at least two occasions, my struggles with anomalies in my notes were suddenly resolved as I looked through her rich description.

By the time I left for Aix in September 1974, I carried a 200-page outline of the "chapter," so specific that I wrote the first draft of what was to become a 512-page book, *The Structuring of Organizations* (1979), by December. (I keep that outline handy today, perhaps to remind myself of what I am capable of doing though never did before or since.) The full book, of course, loaded with references and quotes as befits a determined young academic, took much longer. (But later, I took much of that out for a textbook/practitioner version called *Structure in Fives* [1983].)

The first parts of the book laid out various elements of structure and the findings I had extracted from the research literature, more or less in their own terms. But this was a prelude to the last part of the book, which described five basic forms of organizations, labelled simple structure, machine bureaucracy, professional bureaucracy, diversified form, and adhocracy. Everything seemed to fall naturally into place in these five forms, so that the book achieved an integration that delighted me, down even to the link between the opening and closing stories. It remains my favorite publication, in form if not also substance. Part of the fun in doing the book was in my use of a funny little diagram which has become my logo of sorts, overlaid and distorted in various ways to integrate graphically across the text, as reproduced in Figure 7. I gave my rough sketch of it to a young American woman artist in Aix to render it clean, and she took one look and declared it obscene—"everyone will see the same thing." Well, I certainly hadn't, and over the years this pseudo-Rorschach has been described as a mushroom (in China!), my nose (by London Business School students), a telephone (at AT&T), the cross section of a rail, a woman's uterus, a kidney bean, and who knows what else. To me, it's just an organization!

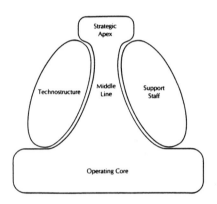

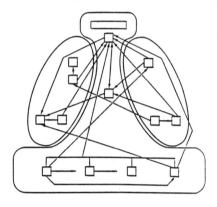

The Flow of Informal Communication

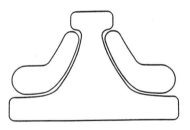

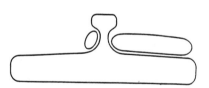

Machine Bureaucracy   Professional Bureacracy

Source: *The Structure of Organizations: A Synthesis of the Research* (1979).

Figure 7.   Structuring Book Use of Logo

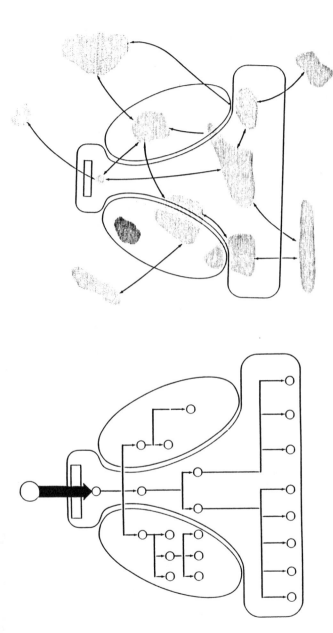

The Instrument

The Complete Political Arena

Figure 8. Power Book Use of Logo

Source: *Power In and Around Organizations* (1983).

347

The sabbatical was so enjoyable that I decided I needed another. Happily, the Aix business school (the Institute d'administration des enterprises of the Université d'Aix-Marseilles) invited me to stay another year at their expense, and McGill granted me a leave. So I set out to write the next chapter on goals and power. That went less quickly: I failed to do a detailed outline, and paid the price for it in rewrite after rewrite over the next six years or so (although it should be added that this literature was far more diffuse and nuanced, and so far harder to integrate, than that of structure, even if I did have the notion of configuration from the outset). *Power In and Around Organizations*, exactly 700-pages long, was finally published in 1983. It laid out the elements of the power game, within and around organizations, to draw them together into configurations described in terms of power relationships. The Logo renditions of these are shown in Figure 8. (I should add that I dragged along to Aix my file on another "chapter"— two full boxes, as I recall, on strategy making—and dragged them back to Montreal two years later, unopened!)

The thought had dawned on me by the time I left Aix, perhaps as a result of having to carry around those 512 and 700 page "chapters," that my textbook was becoming something else. So, back in Montreal, I convinced Prentice-Hall, the eventual publisher of both, to label them "The Theory of Management Policy Series," so that the original conception of the textbook could at least be maintained in a series of books. One day they might even be able to issue all the "chapters" in one jacket! (With this in mind, Prentice-Hall kindly negotiated permission to reprint *The Nature of Managerial Work* in the series, which it did in 1983, and I still have contracts, dated 1977 and 1982, for one volume on decision making and another on strategy making. Maybe I should frame them!)

The significance of these two books to my work was that, whereas before them I was cutting up the world of organizations in my terms—the conceptual categories of the academic—as a result of them I began to cut that world up in its own terms—forms of whole organizations. If before I saw the world like this

managerial work
—————————————————————————————————————
   structure
—————————————————————————————————————
     power
—————————————————————————————————————
       strategy making, etc.
—————————————————————————————————————

with the horizontal lines slicing through organizations, now I was perceiving it this way,

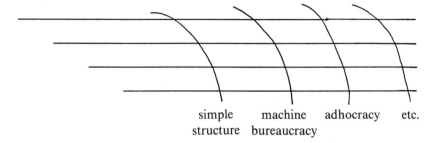

| simple | machine | adhocracy | etc. |
| structure | bureaucracy | | |

seeking to combine the elements in identifiable contexts, however idealized. I began to realize—perhaps best articulated in my article with Danny Miller on "The Case for Configuration" (1983)—that the field of organization theory needs to distinguish its species no less than did that of biology. Otherwise we would continue to distort our description and prescription, extrapolating research findings out of context and following the long and costly tradition of promoting that ever changing "one best way."

Thus, not long after I returned to McGill in 1976, I began to open a new set of files, with names such as machine bureaucracy, adhocracy, missionary, and typologies, although I maintained the old ones too, especially the unfinished one on strategy making, whose literature was soon to mushroom. In effect, my mental set had been turned from the pat categories of organizational dimensions to the (no less pat) categories of organizations themselves. But that represented an important gestalt shift for me.

There was another shift, too. Before I left for France, I had drawn up a proposal for a McGill doctoral program in management. When the other Montreal schools got word of it, given the need for approval at the level of the provincial government and the fear that our program might preempt others, they produced proposals of their own. The government committee reviewed our horse and countered with what looked like a camel—that we all get together and produce a joint doctoral program. So we sat down and did just that, and I believe (if some others don't) that the results have been excellent. Institutions are notoriously reluctant to cooperate, especially in academia. But somehow the 2 × 2 arrangement, two English, two French language schools, in each case one older and more established, the other newer and more applied, fell into a natural balance. The program was quite innovative—blending European self-study with American coursework, and involving serious cooperation in all aspects, including courses and individual student committees. Today it registers 175 students, a plurality in the policy area.

My return was greeted with a request that I run the new program, which I accepted to do. So the management of adhocracy came to life, as I entered the world of mutual adjustment—no subordinates, just peers with whom to negotiate and cajole. I learned that I could do it, also that I could think strategically, but I also learned that the "calculated chaos"[33] of practising management was not very compatible with the concentrated life of scholarship, and so I was glad to return to where I felt I belonged after three and a half years of managing.

There has been a long and solid Jesuit tradition in the schooling of French Quebec, such that philosophy runs deep in its best students. I, on the other hand, was educated in Quebec's pragmatic English schools, and became an engineer who never had a philosophy course in his life. So when a kind of philosophy course was proposed for the joint program, to be required by students from all areas and all schools, I was not terribly enthusiastic. Little did I suspect that upon my return from France, I was designated as McGill's representative to teach the course (alongside a colleague from each of the other schools). "Fundamentals of Administrative Thought" turned out to be one of the great pedagogical joys of my life; I remained with it for about ten years, using it to help socialize the incoming class into a coherent unit and to play intellectually with a wide range of ideas, as one can only do in a course that doesn't have to convey some established body of theory. A number of my ideas developed in that course, particularly concerning Herbert Simon and the role of intuition in management. I consider my (1977) review of his *New Science of Management Decision*, which grew out of work I prepared for that course, to have been an important step for me, as I shall discuss below.

I also began to teach a doctoral seminar on policy every second year, which I continue to do today. Thus, while I picked up my MBA policy course again, after completing my chairmanship of the joint doctoral program, my pedagogical focus was shifting from 23-year-old aspiring managers to thirty-plus-year-old aspiring scholars.

Configurations had entered my mind, but the elements of the original textbooks's outline hardly left my behavior. In fact, by far my most concerted effort after returning from France was my research on strategy making. It had been conceived in the early 1970s[34] around the notion of (realized) strategy as pattern in actions (originally decisions).[35] With a sizable research grant, we began to track the behaviors of organizations over time, isolating streams of activities, inferring patterns in them as strategies, combining these strategies to infer distinct periods in their histories, and finally brainstorming around the results to develop theory about the formation (not just formulation) of strategy. (So now the logic of this paper should be evident, which means, of course, that it would have to be tabulated on Figure 1 as empirical!)

I found a new colleague at McGill when I returned from France, named Jim Waters. We hit it off immediately, and after he convinced me to rename "emergent" what I had originally called "retroactive" strategy, a most productive collaboration emerged on this research, some of this also including student co-authors.[36] Of course, the configuration notion was not lost; gradually we began to see the influence of organizational form on the strategy-making process (e.g., entrepreneurial[37] adhocracy[38]; also professional bureaucracy, in a conceptual article with Cynthia Hardy, Ann Langley, and Janet Rose[39]; a first attempt by Jim and myself to draw these together;[40] and my latest book in which I added descriptions of the strategy making process to the chapters on each of the configurations[41]).

I published a variety of other articles in what I am calling this second phase of my career. A number were spun off of my two books,[42] including a few from a last section of the power book (titled "Who Should Control the Corporation?") that took me into the new realm of broader social issues.[43] A major piece titled "Beyond Implementation: An Analysis of the Resistance to Policy Analysis" (1979), based on a Chapter 8 that I finally wrote in 1978 (52 pages), was produced for an operations research conference.

I also published two articles on research methodology. One, titled "If You're Not Serving Bill and Barbara, Then You're Not Serving Leadership" (1982), was a diatribe of sorts, done in my role as commentator for a conference on leadership research. Realizing how dismal was most of that research, I argued for the getting rid of definitions, measurements, instruments, variables, and so forth, not for shock effect but because I really believed that they didn't serve a phenomenon as fuzzy as leadership style. Bill is a close personal friend (who edited both my thesis and my latest book), and Barbara was his colleague in marketing at the National Film Board of Canada, both the kind of intelligent practitioners who, I argued, should be used as gatekeepers to decide who gets funded and published in the field of leadership research. Their comments on the papers at the conference, which I included in my own paper, merit reading in and of themselves.

The other article, "An Emerging Strategy of 'Direct Research'" (1979), outlined the approach that has characterized my own research—its descriptive and inductive nature, its use of simple ("inelegant") methodologies, the presence of a systematic focus (always addressing a clear issue if never testing a hypothesis), concern with synthesis (particularly around the notion of configuration), the need to measure, where appropriate, in real organizational terms (e.g., the pattern of store openings as opposed to "amount of control" on some perceptual 7-point scale), and always supporting systematic data by others of a richer, anecdotal nature in order to explain and not just describe what has been found (and so to theorize). Were I to add one more prescription today, it would be to cherish anomalies. Time and again, as I worked with dozens or hundreds of little notes all over the place, it was my inclination to hang onto those I could not explain, and to return to them periodically, that made all the difference. I suspect that weak theorists tend to dismiss the anomalies, while others succeed because they don't let go of them until they are explained.[44]

Finally, I published two articles in the *Harvard Business Review* during this phase of my work, each of which made a big difference in its own way. The first, "The Manager's Job: Folklore and Fact" (1975), published while I was in Aix, summarized the conclusions of my thesis for a wide practitioner audience. That it reached, with a bit of vengeance, although one additional year in Aix shielded me from its full influence.

The other, "Planning on the Left Side and Managing on the Right" (1976), had quite a different effect, on me personally. I am not particularly prone to "knocking off" an article—getting an idea, writing it up quickly, and sending it off. But on a quiet farm in the summer of 1975 in the Perigord region of France, where we were subsequently to spend many months of August, I read Robert Ornstein's, *The Psychology of Consciousness* (Freeman, 1975), about the consequences of Roger Sperry's research on the two hemispheres of the brain. I had a sense of revelation—it seemed to explain so much of what I had found in my own research, including those two kinds of knowing things, managerial work as "calculated chaos," the realization in studying strategic decision making that everything that seemed to matter (such as diagnosis and design) remained a great mystery while whatever didn't (such as the evaluation of alternatives) was crystal clear. Whether or not the physiology was correct—and that debate continues vigorously, but to my mind less a question of scientific validity than of scientists' propensities to draw inferences—to me there was clearly a critical message here.

The title came first—"Planning on the Left Side and Managing on the Right"—and then I wrote the article, rather quickly. I sent it to the *Harvard Business Review*, which accepted it, and in March 1976 I sent a copy to Herbert Simon. He replied soon after, commenting in his letter that "I believe the left-right distinction is important, but not (a) that Ornstein has described it correctly, or (b) that it has anything to do with the distinction between planning and managing or conscious-unconscious." He referred to it as "the latest of a long series of fads."[45] A day or two later, as I recall, the *Harvard Business Review* wired me to France that they needed the final draft immediately.

Herbert Simon was to me not just the most eminent management theorist of our time but one with no close equal. He had been devoting the later part of his career to intensive research on issues of human cognition, in the psychology laboratory. And here I was about to go into print in direct contradiction to his conclusions, based on the casual reading of a popular book he referred to as a "fad"! Did Simon know something I didn't, or was there some kind of block in his thinking? My heart battled with my head (or was it my right hemisphere with my left?), over whether hearts sometimes know more than heads, and after an agonizing day or two, the "right side" won.[46]

I had a comment in the original paper that both I and the *Review* editors deleted independently in the final version as too controversial: "I am tempted to raise the issue of extra-sensory perception here. There is clearly too much evidence to dismiss this as a medium of communication, at least for some people, and as Ornstein suggests, it is presumably a right hemisphere activity." Simon had picked up on this in his letter. "The temptations are so great to romanticize about human performance (and even to credit it with ESP for which there is no evidence)!" My decision turned on rereading that sentence. I am certainly no mystic, not even a numerologist (William McKelvey's worries in *Organizational Systematics: Taxonomy, Evolution, Classification* [University of California Press, 1982] about my playing with the number five notwithstanding), and I have as much trouble entertaining the notion of precognition as anyone else. But for Simon to dismiss the possibility that we pick up information in as yet unspecified ways— for example, when we "read" someone's eyes or "feel" tension in a room—struck me as a blockage. And so I decided to go with my inner "sense" instead of Herbert Simon's learned knowledge.[47]

I believe our lives are determined in large part by the occasional choice that later proves to have been a turning point. In other words, we don't get to choose critically very often, and we can, in fact, hedge and stall and do all kinds of dumb things day in and day out, but every once in a while we had better get it right. And getting it right at those times usually seems to mean listening to that inner voice, which goes by the name of "intuition," not to the babble of the social world or the logic of formal analysis.

My intuitive decision to opt for intuition subsequently opened up my work to that concept and myself to that process. It was as if I had been climbing up to a knife edge of analysis-intuition ever since I joined the operational research group at the Canadian National. The Simon letter put me right on that edge, and the decision I took began my journey down the other side.

Subsequently, my attention turned increasingly to the softer notions in management, and I broke increasingly with the long dominant rationalist view, perhaps the one real paradigm in the field, represented especially in the work of Simon himself (who, in recent years, has come to define intuition as "analyses frozen into habit"[48]). Today I am inclined to compare a "cerebral" with an "insightful" approach to management, one based on words and numbers (in academia, Harvard's words or Stanford's numbers, both equally cerebral), the other on images and "feel" (as in strategic "vision" or being "in touch"). In a recent paper on decision making (discussed in the next phase), I wrote a section that characterizes Simon's "bounded rationality" as really a "cerebral rationality" because it slights people's ability to perform great feats of synthesis (such as Simon's own writing of *Administrative Behavior* [Macmillan, 1957]).

My debate with Simon continued with some sporadic correspondence as well as a critical review in 1977 of his revised *New Science of Management Decision*. This associated excessive rationality with the excesses of the Vietnam War, especially as reflected in the "professional management" of Robert McNamara. It concluded by juxtaposing Simon's claim that "We now know a good deal about what goes on in the human head when a person is exercising judgement or having an intuition, to the point where many of these processes can be simulated on a computer"[49] with Roger Sperry's conclusion that "The right [hemisphere], by contrast [with the left] is spacial, and performs with a synthetic space-perceptual and mechanical kind of information processing not yet simulateable in computers."[50] Simon was awarded the Nobel Prize in economics in 1978; Sperry won his in physiology in 1981!

So what am I to make of this second phase of my career. This was certainly a time of loosening up and of opening up, a time of shift from the rather analytic to (what I like to think of as) more balance between the analytic and the intuitive, certainly a time in which synthesis more vigorously entered my work and thinking. I would not label my realized strategy of this period as emergent, but surely it had become less formally deliberate. One might describe it, using our own labels,[51] as umbrella in nature, guided by the notion of configuration, with, of course, that old textbook outline, now compromised by the size of its "chapters," still providing one sense of direction. I also started to become more playful in this period, both literally in my private life and figuratively in my work. One need only look back at those blob forms in Figures 7 and 8!

CIRCLE PHASE (DYNAMICS): PLAYING "LEGO" (FROM 1979/1987)

Alain Noël joined our doctoral program in September 1978, and about five months later, after having read my work on structure and power, asked me a question that was to change my thinking a second time: "Do you mean to play jigsaw puzzle or LEGO with the elements of organizations?"[52]

I had to reply that I guess it was jigsaw puzzle, at least for my readers: I was asking them to select known images of their organizations, to put the elements of structure together in one of five predetermined ways. But Alain's question so intrigued me that I soon opened a file called "LEGO," to collect examples of all those weird and wonderful organizations that refused to fit into one or other of my pat categories. It was not that I couldn't find examples of ones that did—I knew from my own experiences, and those of others, that many effective organizations conformed remarkably well. (I later began to ask the McGill MBA students to record their perception of fit with their field organizations: in just over half the cases recorded—66 out of 123—the students felt a single form fitted best.[53]) But some of the most effective organizations, and certainly many of the most interesting, did not. For example, there were seemingly bureaucratic machines that managed to innovate when they had to (McDonald's? IBM?), and what seemed like adhocracies that had rather tight control systems (Hewlett-Packard? 3M?). These became of increasing interest to me.

I show the third phase of my work as beginning on a diagonal line from 1979, when Alain first posed that question, to 1987, when I began work on a serious answer (published in *Mintzberg on Management* [1989] as "Forces and Forms in Effective Organizations"; see preferably my *Sloan Management*

Review version of 1991). Here I did not so much dismiss the five forms as covert than to a set of five forces, arranged around the nodes of a pentagon, each drawing the organization in a different direction. In the middle, I added from my power book the two forces of ideology and politics (the former of "cooperation," pulling together, and the latter, "competition," pulling apart) which I described as catalytic (centripetal and centrifugal). Altogether, shown in Figure 9, this constituted what I have found to be a most useful framework by which to diagnose the problems of organizational design.

In 1980, I was invited to do a "top management briefing" for the Management Centre Europe (MCE)—two days, me alone, with senior European executives. I guess I always subscribed to Jim Water's guide of tying a rope to a rock, the other end to your ankle, and then throwing the rock over some attractive cliff. It's called commitment. But when the time came, I was petrified, more worried than I had been for any other working engagement. I slept not a wink the night before, and making it through the first day was somewhat of a miracle. I recall in the afternoon sitting up near the ceiling of the room listening to me talking down below (a phenomenon I have heard described by others), and praying that guy wouldn't make any mistakes. Fortunately he didn't, and after a good night's sleep, and a successful second day, with all of me together on the ground, I have been doing MCE briefings ever since. By 1985, I was doing two per year, and in 1988 I began to do one regularly in Canada as well. These programs are exhausting and I limit the number, but they have come to represent the core of my thinking, focusing my writing, research, and general mental set much as did the MBA policy course when I began teaching at McGill. They force me to ask questions of relevance: how do all the concepts I teach help practicing managers to deal with serious problems.

These briefings have thus become part of a shift in my mind from the *push* of concepts to the *pull* of issues. Push promotes some idea, technique, or angle, whether transaction cost in the university or strategic planning in the corporation. It reflects the rule of the tool, that given a hammer everything begins to look like a nail. Pull begins with a problem or issue, and then draws on whatever it takes to deal with it, sometimes including concepts and techniques. Business schools, especially in America, have become prisoners of push, to their great discredit. So has much of American business practice, given its obsession with technique driven by that almighty "bottom line." I believe it is time for pull.[54]

My shift from push to pull should not be interpreted as a change to a prescriptive, applied orientation; indeed, sometimes the result has been exactly the opposite. Having to address the concerns of thoughtful managers (as Europeans in general and MCE attendees in particular tend to be) can be a helpful experience for even the most theoretical academic. To take a not incidental case in point, my description of managerial roles in *The Nature of*

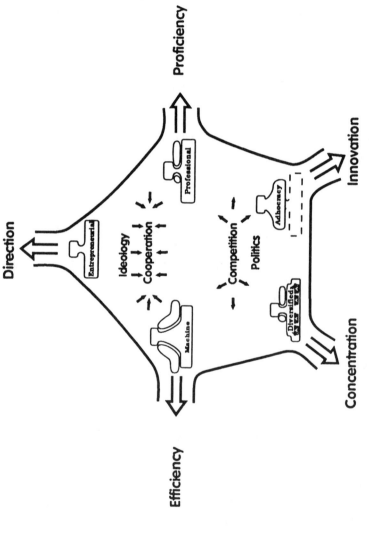

Figure 9.   Framework to Play "Organizational LEGO"

Source: *Mintzberg on Management: Inside Our Strange World of Organizations* (1989, p. 256, with modification).

Managerial Work (1973) has never worked in the MCE briefings. In an effort to provide a framework by which my materials on strategy and structure (which do work) can be assessed in the attendees' own jobs, I have, therefore, had to rethink the roles.

In 1985, I served as the faculty representative on a McGill university-wide committee on budgeting problems. I proposed—seriously as an idea but with no expectation of implementation—that the university could eliminate its deficit if it paid professors for what they really did. McGill remains a very collegial and responsible institution, a place with a real sense of its own excellence despite a battering by a sometimes hostile milieu. But like any other, it has its share of faculty who have retired from research but not from drawing full salary. Since I consider research part of professors' duties—in other words, we are paid full time to work more or less full time—people who have stopped doing research should be receiving something like sixty percent of their salaries.

It soon occurred to me that I should really do just that myself, with a slightly different twist. I was becoming increasingly disillusioned with conventional management education.[55] It just did not make sense to me anymore, socially or economically, to continue the pretense of training barely experienced hotshots to be managers. The MCE experience had convinced me that management education should be reserved for people who know how organizations work, whose experience is deep as well as tacit, and whose place in the classroom is determined by their accomplishments rather than their aspirations.

So I decided to stop teaching the MBA policy course, proposing to the McGill administration that I go on reduced load and salary and concentrate my university work on writing, research, and doctoral supervision and the biannual course. In other words, I would divide my labor between scholarship in the university and application (including pedagogy) in the field. Long ago (in 1969), *Fortune* magazine published an article by S. Zalaznick titled "The MBA—the Man, the Myth, and the Method" that concluded that the real contribution of the American business schools lay not in its graduates from teaching so much as its insights from research. I always thought that to be true—now I was putting it into practice myself.

The arrangement has worked out marvellously well. All at once, I relieved myself of significant pressure (from doing what felt wrong more than from trying to do too much), clarified my efforts, and ironically, significantly increased the time I had for what I like to do best, namely scholarship. McGill has a rule of a maximum of four days of consulting per month for full-time faculty; even now, on reduced load, I do not yet reach it. Much of the time that went into MBA teaching now goes into my writing and research.

Outside the university, I do those few two-day programs, a number of one-day public conferences in Europe that I am directing more toward what I like to call "discovery conferences" (where a panel of us from theory and practice addresses some pull issue in a mostly unrehearsed way, for example, the management of strategic change), an occasional in-house workshop in the form of executive retreats, and so forth, as well as a certain amount of consulting, which tends to take on a wide variety of interesting forms. Recently, for example, I helped a couple of McKinsey consultants rethink the structure of a large South American firm and decided with people at the Brookhaven Laboratories in New York whether or not nuclear power plants are best thought of as machine bureaucracies (concluding yes and no, depending on whether one chose to play jig-saw puzzle or LEGO).[56]

These latter experiences offer me wonderful opportunities to discover issues and to root my theoretical concerns in the realities of messy practice. I do not pretend that they constitute research. (I have always considered so-called "action research" to be an attempt by some academics to have their research cake and eat the consulting fees too.) But I do find them invaluable for drawing me toward issues that seem to be significant, for exposure that frames reality in my head, and even for enhancing the scholarship in my work. Direct exposure has always been my best stimulus; lately I have been able to request tours of a fascinating variety of physical facilities, through which I also meet operating people. That has made an enormous difference—not only for the consulting work itself but also for my own development of conceptual material. At Brookhaven, for example, I asked to tour a nuclear power plant, and what I saw in just one morning made all the difference to my conclusions. Similarly, a friend in London took me out to a hospital recently, and after listening to the National Health Service regional manager talk about negotiating a new facility through the politics of the bureaucracy, followed by a tour by the head nurse who revealed her wonderful intimacy of the operations, I came home talking about "managing up" and "managing down." Where those meet—in fact, whether they meet—strikes me as a critical issue in the practice of management today. I feel privileged to have this kind of varied access to organizations at this stage in my career.

I explain all this before discussing my publications of this third phase because the order of presentation reflects the phase itself. These are the things that have increasingly begun to drive my work in the past several years. As befits more pull and closer connection to practice, my writings have also become more disparate; hence the "illusive strategy." But I should add here that when we drew conclusions about "Strategy Formation in an Adhocracy" (1985) in our own research, which we found to have oscillated between periods of convergence and divergence (typically about six years of concentration on particular product/market themes, followed by about equal periods of less focused experimentation, of "riding off in all directions"), it turned out that the organization was sometimes most effective during the periods of divergence. In other words, focused strategy is not necessarily a prerequisite to success, at least not perpetually in some kinds of organizations (which also means, I guess, that my own behavior has shifted from that of professional bureaucracy toward adhocracy!).

To make the link between my practice and my writing, I should perhaps begin with my most applied recent efforts, two books in particular. As noted earlier, I have always sought to produce a stream of work aimed at practitioners. Some of this has been easily accessible to them—articles in the *Harvard Business Review*, for example—while other material was not. And so I accepted an invitation from Bob Wallace at the Free Press to do a kind of practitioner compendium of my work. It was initially meant to be a packaging job of existing materials, but (surprise!) I ended up writing and rewriting a good part of it. The book contains some new materials (including some of the Simon exchange and the forces and forms paper discussed above, as well as other two pieces to be discussed below), and it presents the configurations renamed (as in the pentagon in Figure 9) and rewritten to encompass the dimensions of managerial work and strategy formation. The publisher calls it *Mintzberg on Management*; I prefer the subtitle *Inside Our Strange World of Organizations* (1989). The book draws together almost all of the themes in my work over the years, such that it is probably the closest thing in print to my original textbook, although not so organized, and with a particular slant (that I shall discuss below). It is aimed at the practising manager, but also, I had hoped, a far broader audience. As I noted in the introduction, in today's world of organizations, "pop organization theory" should be as important to the general public as pop psychology.

As the for second book, James Brian Quinn of the Tuck School at Dartmouth approached me a few years ago to collaborate on a textbook. He had developed a series of excellent cases on strategic management, and proposed that I do the text. I agreed, but not in the usual way. Rather than writing it, I suggested we *design* it by pulling together the best work of other authors in the field, carefully edited for conciseness, interspersed with our own published writings. I just could not face the thought of doing a conventional "gather-around-children-while-we-tell-you-about-strategic-management" textbook. Why should intelligent students not be exposed to what intelligent writers had to say in their own words. *The Strategy Process* was published in 1988, also co-authored with Bob James, and the second edition appeared in 1991.

There is, of course, a lovely irony here. Finally given the chance to do a real policy textbook after so many years of struggling with one, indeed with most of the chapters already written and awaiting publication, I casually turned my back on it!

Turning to my work of a more scholarly nature, many of my publications up to the late 1980s were in fact manifestations of the previous phase, especially the coming to fruition of our studies of strategy formation (already listed), followed by an article called "Crafting Strategy" (1987) to draw out the broad conclusions. More recently, my pace of writing on this subject has not slowed down so much as shifted (not fully reflected in the Figure 1 histogram, due to the size and publication lag of some of this work), meaning that I continue to pursue work of the first stage too.

I took another sabbatical, this time to a tiny village in an obscure valley in the Swiss Jura mountains, during the first six months of 1984. I dragged along what amounted to many boxes of the old Chapter 7 on strategy making, and spent all that time reading and organizing it. (The analyst in me still likes to keep score, so I recorded somewhere that I read 1,495 items—I calculated it would have stood fourteen feet high.) It was all intended to write the chapter that this time I knew would be a book. Well, I was wrong again. It may be recalled that my first book, on managerial work, was 298 pages long, my second, on structuring, was 512 pages, and my third, on power, exactly 700. One need not even be the statistical jock I am to conclude that the next book in the "Theory of Management Policy Series" has to be about 900 pages long. In fact, the outline I brought home from Switzerland divided that book into two volumes, the first called *Strategy Formation: Schools of Thought*, intended to review the literature, and the second, *Strategy Formation: Towards a General Theory*, to extend the configuration notion to strategic stages across the evolution of organizations.

A number of other subsequent commitments, as well as an increasing propensity to go with ideas that come up (to be detailed below), have slowed this work down somewhat, or at least its publication, because I have in fact already produced a sizable quantity of material for the first volume. Chapter 1 on the concept of strategy has been written, and published as two articles.[57] The rest of the volume is devoted to the schools, ten in number. A lengthy chapter exists on the first, design school, much of it published in a recent article,[58] and I finished in 1985 a 358-page "chapter" on the planning school, which I am now revising for book publication. I also began work several years ago on the "positioning school" chapter, which exists as a long, untyped manuscript, one part of which has appeared as "Generic Strategies: Toward a Comprehensive Framework" (1988, also in shortened form in 1991). I might add that in doing this chapter, I was having a wonderful time playing Michael Porter: my own work may hardly be loaded with nuance and affect, but as a consummate categorizer, I was revelling in developing the rather purely logical typologies of strategy content. The chapters on the other schools— entrepreneurial, cognitive, learning, political, cultural, environmental, and configurational—remain unwritten, although I did publish a very long paper titled "Strategy Formation: Schools of Thought" (1990) that summarized them all.

Since this is my final comment on "The Theory of Management Policy," I thought it might be helpful to include an accounting of where that book now stands, which I do in Exhibit 1.[59] So near and yet so far.

Exhibit 1.   Current Status of "The Theory of Management Policy

Chapter	Title	State
1	The Field of Management Policy	Chapter (1974, 1978) and two articles
2	An Underlying Theory for Management Policy	Chapter (1974, 1978)
3	The Structuring of Organizations	Book, several articles, and chapter (1980)
4	The Nature of Managerial Work	Book and several articles
5	Power In and Around Organizations	Book and several articles (early chapter [1970] superceded)
6	The Making of Strategic Decisions	Chapter (1973) and article
7	The Formation of Strategy	Two volume outline, of which several articles and chapters, one as book manuscript (early chapter [1970] superceded)
8	The Role of the Policy Analyst	Chapter (1978) and article, also book manuscript on planning
9 or 16	Toward Effectiveness in Organizations	Article (forces and forms)
9-15	Possible chapters on seven configurations:L Entrpreneurial, Machine, Diversified, Professional, Adhocracy, Ideology and the Missionary Organization, Politics and the Political Organization	Chapters in other books

Alongside the volumes on strategy formation has been my research work in that area with Frances Westley, who joined the McGill faculty in 1983. Frances is one of those rare people who came out of the push of a strong discipline and slipped ever so naturally into the pull of the management field. As a result we have developed a wonderful collaboration, of her sociological affect with my engineering effect, by which we have worked out some tricky conceptual issues with great glee. (Having made a habit of doing so just before conference presentations, we have decided that our real talent lies in "just-in-time theorizing"!) We published two articles on strategic vision,[60] and after many go-arounds are now preparing to publish another on a general model of strategic change. As shown in Figure 10, it is conceived in terms of circles and cycles, one representing the concentric levels of change, a second the means of change, a third the episodes of change, and a fourth, the evolving cycles of change.

A. Concentric Cycles
    • contents and levels of change

B. Circumferential Cycles
    • means and processes of change

C. Spiraling Cycles
    • sequences and patterns of change

D. Spiraling Cycles
    • sequences and patterns of of change

Figure 10.   Overall Cycles of Organizational Change

Source: "Cycles of Organizational Change" (1993, p. 41).

One characteristic of this third phase of my work, as already noted, is my greater willingness to go with ideas as they come up, much as did our adhocracy, the National Film Board of Canada, in its periods of divergence. This has resulted in a number of "one-off" papers and articles, mostly co-authored, one with Joe Lampel (ex of our doctoral program) on customizing strategies (in draft), another with Maria Gonzalez (ex of our MBA program) on strategies for financial services,[61] based on a consulting assignment, a third with Angela Dumas of the London Business School on managing design.[62]

Two major activities of late have included revisiting work I did initially in the first phase of my career. I have already mentioned my return to the managerial roles because of the difficulties of using them in my MCE program. Moreover, it occurred to me, based on my own notion of emergent strategy and Karl Weick's concept of "sensemaking,"[63] that the order in which I had presented the roles (interpersonal providing information enabling decision making, as shown in Figure 6) could just as easily have been reversed; in other words, I had a list, not a theory. An invitation to speak at a celebration of the eightieth birthday of Sune Carlson, author of the classic study of managerial work titled *Executive Behavior: A Study of the Work Load and the Working Methods of Managing Directors* (1951), sent me back to this literature (specifically to my two unopened boxes of Chapter 4). There I realized that, at best, all the other descriptions were no more than lists themselves.[64] So I set out to develop something better, and last fall in London, out of a series of seminars (rocks going over cliffs, each preceded by some JITT), it all came together, quite literally so in a framework of concentric circles. [Figure 11 shows the framework as finalized in 1993.]

I think there is something to the fact that this figure (developed in considerably more detail) preceeded the outline. What matters in developing theory about mangerial work, in my opinion, is not so much the fully articulated text as the comprehensive representation of the model. People need to *see* the various dimensions that appear to constitute managerial work all in one place. That way, they can begin to discuss the job of managing comprehensively and interactively. I have found this to be true as I started to use the model to develop the theory, and when I drew the diagram for Bill at dinner one evening, he immediately began using it to diagnose the problems of managing in his own firm.

For different reasons, I have for some years now wished to revisit the subject of strategic decision making. The tendency to show it as the linear unfolding of sequences of steps, in our own work[65] no less than that of others, somehow seemed to miss something important. This subject (in effect, the old Chapter 6) was not, however, on my agenda, especially given my heavy commitment to strategy formation. But with the new spirit of one-off papers, combined with a pedagogical idea I had been considering for awhile, I made room for it.

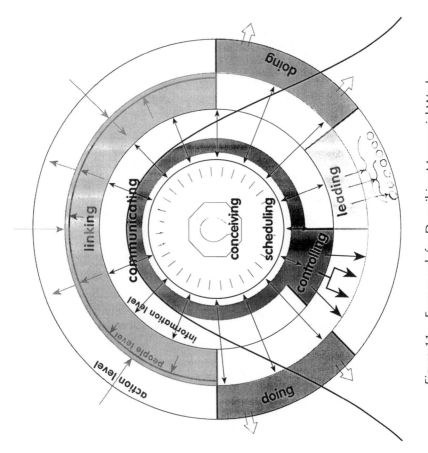

Figure 11. Framework for Describing Managerial Work

Doctoral study is really an apprenticeship. Courses are fine, as far as they go, and research assistantships can be useful, but they often subordinate the students' interests to those of the professor. So I developed the idea of a "research cell," somewhere between the two, in which a small team of selected faculty members and doctoral students could address an issue together. Five of us, including one other colleague and three doctoral students (from all four Montreal universities, as it happens), took on the issue of "opening up decision making," seeking to reconceive what we perceived to be this narrow line of research. A most exciting paper has resulted (submitted for publication), which opens up the concept of decision itself to the ambiguities that surround the moment of choice, opens up the decision maker to history and experience, affect, insight, and inspiration, and opens up decision making to a host of dynamic linkages such that isolated processes of decisions come to be seen as networks of issues.

Finally, there is the side of my current work I call the polemics, which address some broader social issues. Two papers were published as chapters in my last book, *Mintzberg on Management* (1989). One, called "Training Managers, Not MBAs," explains my dissatisfaction with conventional management education. And the other, "Society Has Become Unmanageable as a Result of Management," expresses my concerns about the prevailing practices of management. These chapters give the book a somewhat caustic flavor, but not, to my mind, one unwarranted in today's world of bottom-line banality. Still, I felt the need to back off after these, and so the work I continue to do on broader social issues is perhaps more provocative than polemic. Last fall, for example, invited to give a speech to a large management congress in Prague on "East Meets West," I used the occasion to do some reading and thinking on the issues facing eastern Europe. The resulting paper (just submitted for publication) emphasizes the need for grass roots strategic learning rather than formal planning in times of difficult change, and suggests that it was not capitalism that "triumphed" in the west so much as balance in our economic system, a balance that, ironically, risks being upset by these very changes.

I like what I have been doing recently. I like the style of life I have established for myself and I like the variety of work I can do, so long as it remains under the umbrella of the themes that have always rooted my work—to understand management and organizations, especially with regard to strategy (setting direction) and structure (establishing state and process). Everything seems to fit together very nicely. So I have no intentions of making any changes now; I foresee no fourth stage in the near future (but neither did I earlier foresee a second or a third). I hope to consider the issue of intuition more carefully, especially to develop the idea of an "insightful" face of management in contrast to its long dominant "cerebral" face. I wish to consider via direct exposure, certain of the trickier organizational contexts, notably the delivery of public professional services (especially health care), the management of the softer sides of government, the organization of corporations across businesses and boundaries, and the long standing problem of rendering adaptive our bureaucratic machines. I intend to redo *Structure in Fives* as "Structure in Sevens," so that I can play more elaborate LEGO; to do another research cell, on organizational effectiveness; and, of course, to keep plugging away at "Chapter 7" on strategy formation.

So where is that illusive strategy? Not so illusive, I conclude, unless one insists on the kind of deliberate plan that drove my earliest work. As my activities have grown more varied, I believe that the overall thrust has become more integrated. It all comes together around the themes that have been struggling to get out these past twenty-five years: thinking, designing, acting, and learning to achieve more effective and humane organizations. Organizations do this, biased perhaps toward that order, while I do it perhaps with a growing bias toward the opposite order. Gradually I have come closer to organizations while always maintaining my distance, being able to consider their impact more broadly while probing more narrowly into their details. Overall, I have been searching for their deceptive effectiveness, first through study of their elements, subsequently combined to describe their forms, and then exposed to reveal their dynamics, all the while attuned to their dark recesses of intuition hidden amidst the brilliance of their formal analysis. Cycling has characterized my own behavior as well as the actual theory I have been developing recently, as I have come to see organizations in increasingly dynamic terms. One need only look back at the circling and cycling diagrams I have been doing in recent years, illustrated in Figures 9, 10, and 11! Thus this third stage of my work can be depicted as follows:

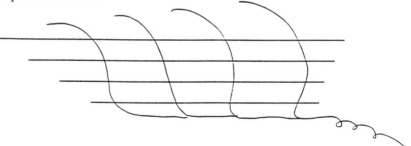

"We shall not cease from exploration," wrote T.S. Eliot in one of my favorite quotes, "and the end of all our exploring will be to arrive where we started and know the place for the first time."

This ends my story. When Art Bedeian informed me, rather casually, of the page limit, I thought to myself, who in the world would ever write that much about himself. Now look what I've done. And me who started with the admonition about not taking yourself too seriously. Could we, perhaps, just attribute this to me taking my work very seriously?

PUBLICATIONS

1967

The science of strategy-making. *Industrial Management Review* (Spring).

1968

With J. Hekimian. The planning dilemma. *The Management Review* (May).

1970

Structured observation as a method of study managerial work. *The Journal of Management Studies* (February).
Making a science of management. *Canadian Business* (March).

1971

Managerial work: Analysis from observation. *Management Science* (October).

1972

Research on strategy-making. In *Proceedings of the Academy of Management Conference.*
A framework for strategic planning. *Canadian Forum* (January-February).
The myths of MIS. *California Management Review* (Fall).

1973

The nature of managerial work. New York: Harper & Row. (Reissued by Prentice Hall, 1983)
Policy as a field of management theory. *Journal of Business Policy* (Summer).
A new look at the senior manager's job. *Organizational Dynamics* (Winter).
Strategy-making in three modes. *California Management Review* (Winter).
Jeu des influences et buts organisationnels. *Commerce* (juin).

1974

A national goals hierarchy. *Optimum.*

1975

Impediments to the use of management information. Monograph of the National Association of Accountants (U.S.) and Society of Industrial Accountants (Canada).

With L. Gordon & D. Miller. *Normative models in managerial decision-making.* Monograph of the National Association of Accountants (U.S.) and Society of Industrial Accountants (Canada).

The manager's job: Folklore and fact. *Harvard Business Review* (July-August).

1976

With D. Raisinghani & A. Théoret. The structure of "unstructured" decision processes. *Administrative Science Quarterly* (June).

Planning on the left side and managing on the right. *Harvard Business Review* (July-August).

1977

Policy as a field of management theory. *Academy of Management Review* (January).

[Review of] New science of management decision. *Administrative Science Quarterly* (June).

Strategy formulation as an historical process. *International Studies of Management and Organization* (Summer).

1978

With W. Balke & J. Waters. Team teaching general management: Theoretically, experimentally, practically. *Exchange: The OB Teaching Journal* (June).

With J. Lorsch, J. Baughman, & J. Reece. *Understanding management.* New York: Harper & Row.

1979

The structuring of organizations: A synthesis of the research. Englewood Cliffs, NJ: Prentice-Hall.

An emerging strategy of "direct" research. *Administrative Science Quarterly* (December).

Beyond implementation: An analysis of the resistance to policy analysis [Proceedings of the 1978 IFORS Conference]. In Haley (Ed.), *Operational research '78* (pp. 106-162). Amsterdam: North-Holland.

Organizational power and goals. In Schendel and Hofer (Eds.), *Strategic management.* Boston, MA: Little, Brown.

Patterns in strategy formation. *Management Science* (May).

1980

Structure in 5's. *Management Science* (March).

1981

Configurations of organizational structure. In Meltzer and Nord (Eds.), *Making organizations humane and productive: A handbook for practitioners.* New York: Wiley.

Organization design: Fashion or fit. *Harvard Business Review* (January-February).

What is planning anyway? *Strategic Management Journal.*

1982

With J. Waters. Tracking strategy in an entrepreneurial firm. *Academy of Management Journal.*

A note on that dirty word efficiency. *Interfaces* (October).

If you're not serving Bill and Barbara, then you're not serving leadership. In Hunt, Sekaran, & Schriesheim (Eds.), *Leadership: Beyond establishment views.* Carbondale, IL: Southern Illinois University Press.

Commentary. In Ungson & Braunstein (Eds.), *Decision making: An interdisciplinary inquiry.* Kent Publishing.

1983

With D. Miller. The case for configuration. In G. Morgan (Ed.), *Beyond method.* Beverly Hills, CA: Sage.

Structure in 5's: Designing effective organizations. Englewood Cliffs, NJ: Prentice-Hall.

Power in and around organizations. Englewood Cliffs, NJ: Prentice-Hall.

With J. Waters. The mind of the strategist(s). In S. Srivasta (Ed.), *Executive mind.* San Francisco, CA: Jossey-Bass.

With C. Hardy, A. Langley, & J. Rose. Strategy formation in the university setting. *The Review of Higher Education* (Summer).

A note on the unionization of professionals from the perspective of organization theory. *Industrial Relations Law Journal.*

Why America needs, but cannot have, corporate democracy. *Organizational Dynamics* (Spring).

The case for corporate social responsibility. *Journal of Business Policy* (Fall).

1984

With J. Waters. Researching the formation of strategies: The history of Canadian Lady, 1939-1976. In R.B. Lamb (Ed.), *Competitive strategic management.* Englewood Cliffs, NJ: Prentice-Hall.

With W. Taylor & J. Waters. Tracking strategies in the birthplace of Canadian tycoons: The Sherbrooke Record 1946-1976. *Canadian Journal of Administrative Sciences* (June).

Power and organization life cycles. *Academy of Management Review.*
Who should control the corporation? *California Management Review* (Fall).

1985

With J. Waters. Of strategies, deliberate and emergent. *Strategic Management Journal.*
With A. McHugh. Strategy formation in an adhocracy. *Administrative Science Quarterly.*
The organization as political arena. *Journal of Management Studies.*
With F. Westley. Imagining strategy. *Journal of Management.*

1986

With P. Brunet & J. Waters. Does planning impede strategic thinking? Tracking the strategies of Air Canada from 1937 to 1976. In R.B. Lamb & P. Shivastava (Eds.), *Advances in strategic management.* Greenwich, CT: JAI Press.
Crafting strategy. *Harvard Business Review* (September-October).
Five Ps for strategy. *California Management Review* (June).
Another look at why organizations need strategies. *California Management Review.*

1987

With J. Jorgensen. Emergent strategy for public policy. *Canadian Public Administration* (Summer).

1988

With J.B. Quinn & R.M. James. *The strategy process: Concepts, contexts, and cases.* Englewood Cliffs, NJ: Prentice-Hall.
With F. Westley. Profiles of strategic vision: Levesque and Iacocca. In J. Conger & R. Kanungo (Eds.), *Charismatic leadership: The elusive factor in organizational effectiveness.* San Francisco, CA: Jossey-Bass.
Generic strategies: Toward a comprehensive framework. In R.B. Lamb & P. Shivastava (Eds.), *Advances in strategic management.* Greenwich, CT: JAI Press.
With J. Shamsie, S. Otis, & J. Waters. Strategy of design: A study of "Architects in co-partnership." In J. Grant (Ed.), *Significant developments in strategic management.* Greenwich, CT: JAI Press.

1989

Mintzberg on management: Inside our strange world of organizations. New York: Free Press.

With F. Westley. Visionary leadership and strategic management. *Strategic Management Journal.*

With A. Dumas. Managing design, designing management. *Design Management Journal* (Fall).

1990

With J. Waters. Does decision get in the way? *Organizational Studies.*

Strategy formation: Schools of thought. In J. Frederickson (Ed.), *Perspectives on strategic management.* Ballinger.

The design school: Reconsideration of the basic premises of strategic management. *Strategic Management Journal.*

1991

With J.B. Quinn. *The strategy process: Concepts, context, cases* (2nd ed.). Englewood Cliffs, NJ: Prentice-Hall.

The effective organization: Forces and forms. *Sloan Management Review.*

Managerial work: Forty years later. In the S. Carlson, *Executive behavior* (Republished edition).

With M. Gonzalez. Strategies in the financial services industry. *McKinsey Quarterly.*

Commentary. In D. Wong-Reiger & F. Reiger (Eds.), *Globalization: Separating the fad from the fact.*

SUBSEQUENT PUBLICATIONS

1991

Strategic thinking as "seeing." In J. Nasi (Ed.), *Arenas of strategic thinking.* Helsinki: Foundation for Economic Education.

Learning 1, planning 0 (Reply to Igor Ansoff). *Strategic Management Journal.*

With A. Dumas. Managing the form, function, and fit of design. *Design Management Journal* (Summer).

1992

Learning in (and from) Eastern Europe. *Scandanavian Journal of Management.*

1993

With F. Westley. Cycles of organizational change. *Strategic Management Journal.*

The rise and fall of strategic planning. New York: Free Press.

NOTES

1. For example, "Research on Strategy-making" (1972); "Patterns in Strategy Formation" (1979); "Of Strategies, Deliberate and Emergent" (1985); "Strategy Formation in an Adhocracy" (1985); "Emergent Strategy for Public Policy" (1987).

2. Pardon the slight ambiguity; "Ten Years Later" was meant to date from the start of my teaching career; the data I present on my publications cover exactly twenty-five distinct years, back into one year as a doctoral student.

3. See L.R. Sayles (1970, April). Whatever happened to management—Or why the dull stepchild? *Business Horizons, 13*(2), 25-34.

4. This was the title of the subsequent book of proceedings; see C.A. Myers. (Ed.) (1967). *The Impact of Computers on Management*. Cambridge, MA: M.I.T. Press.

5. See L.H. Gulick (1937). "Notes on the Theory of Organization." In L.H. Gulick & L.F. Urwick (Eds.), *Papers on the science of administration*. New York: Columbia University Press.

6. When this occurred to me I am not exactly sure. The conference was in April and I began work on the dissertation by November at the latest. I have on file a dissertation proposal called "Programmed Strategic Decision-Making" dated September. So there must have been some kind of delayed reaction. On the other hand, I did a course paper in May 1965 called "On-Line Real-Time Presidents? A Study of Computer Applications at the Presidential Level" that included interviews with two Boston chief executives and descriptions of their work. So the topic had been on my mind even before the Webb approach.

7. *The Structuring of Organizations* (1979).

8. "The Structure of 'Unstructured' Decision Processes" (1976) and "Planning on the Left Side and Managing on the Right" (1976).

9. *The Strategy Process* (1988, 1991).

10. *Mintzberg on Management* (1989).

11. "The Structure of 'Unstructured' Decision Processes (1976).

12. *Patterns in Strategy Formation* (1979).

13. "The Science of Strategy-Making" (1967), p. 71.

14. *Normative Models in Managerial Decision-Making* (1975).

15. "The Structure of 'Unstructured' Decision Processes" (1976).

16. As Danny used to be somewhat reluctant to travel and get personal exposure, we had this line about Danny Miller being the pseudonym I use for my quantitative articles.

17. See, for example, the comparable published diagrams in *The Structuring of Organizations* (1979, p. iv) and *Power In and Around Organizations* (1983, p. viii).

18. For published versions of this paper, see "Policy as a Field of Management Theory" (1973, 1977).

19. See H.A. Simon (1957). *Administrative Behavior* (2nd ed.). New York: Macmillan; and L. von Bertalanffy (1968). *General Systems Theory*. New York: Braziller.

20. "Jeu des influences et buts organisationnels" (1973).

21. See "The Design School" (1990).

22. "Research on Strategy-Making" (1972).

23. Ibid.; "Strategy-Making in Three Models" (1973).

24. *The Nature of Managerial Work* (1973).

25. "Structured Observation" (1970); "Managerial Work" (1971); "A New Look" (1973).

26. "The Myths of MIS" (1972).

27. "Making a Science of Management" (1970); "Jeu des influences et buts organisationnels" (1973).

28. "A Framework for Strategic Planning" (1972).

29. A. Maslow (1954). *Motivation and Personality*. New York: Harper and Brothers.

30. See "Team Teaching General Management" (1978).

31. "The Case for Configuration" (1983).

32. J. Woodward (1965). *Industrial Organization: Theory and Practice*. London: Oxford University Press.

33. See F. Andrews (1976, October 29). "Management: How a Boss Works in Calculated Chaos." *New York Times*, in reference to my own study of managerial work.

34. See "Research on Strategy-Making" (1972).

35. See "Does Decision Get in the Way?" (1990).

36. "Tracking Strategy in an Entrepreneural Firm" (1982); "the Mind of the Strategist(s)" (1983); "Research the Formation of Strategies" (1984); "Tracking Strategies in the Birthplace of Canadian Tycoons" (1984); "Of Strategies, Deliberate and Emergent" (1985); "Does Planning Impede Strategic Thinking?" (1986); "Does Decision Get in the Way?" (1990).

37. "Tracking Strategy" (1982).

38. "Strategy Formation in an Adhocracy" (1985).

39. "Strategy Formation in the University Setting" (1983).

40. "The Mind of the Strategist(s)" (1983).

41. *Mintzberg on Management* (1989).

42. "Organizational Power and Goals" (1979); "Structure in 5's" (1980); "Configurations of Organizational Structure" (1981); "Organization Design" (1981); "A Note on that Dirty Word Efficiency" (1982); "A Note on the Unionization of Professionals" (1983); "Power and Organization Life Cycles" (1984); "The Organization as Political Arena" (1985).

43. "Why Ameirca Needs" (1983); "The Case for Corporate Social Responsibility" (1983); "Who Should Control the Corporation?" (1984).

44. Besides, anomalies can be fun. Some people collect stamps; I collect typographical errors. I write badly, and so my secretaries over the years have obliged with wonderful ones: "statistics quo," "Karl Propper," "consultants tend to come in times of charge," and, best of all, "diversifiction" (what a difference an "a" makes). I use these almost subliminally in my executive programs.

45. This and subsequently referenced correspondence with Simon has been reprinted with his permission in *Mintzberg on Management* (1989), pp. 58-61.

46. I must admit to something a bit sneaky here. As Ornstein points out, there is a good deal of symbolism associated with right and left, the former correct, strong, straight (in French), masculine, and so forth, the latter "gauche" (which means left in French), "sinister" (left in Italian and Latin), mysterious, feminine, and so forth. Of course, these refer to the right and left sides of the body, which are controlled by the opposite hemispheres of the human brain. By titling the article "Planning on the Left Side and Managing on the Right," with references to hemispheres instead of arms, I was turning the effect of that symbolism to my advantage.

47. In a letter of reply to Simon, I quoted Turing ("Computing Machinery and Intelligence, *Mind*, October 1950), the great British mathematician, who wrote in his famous article (before computers) on why it should not be assumed that machines cannot think:
I assume that the reader is familiar with the idea of extrasensory perception, and the meaning of the four items of it: telepathy, clairvoyance, precognition, and psychokinesis. These disturbing phenomena seem to deny all our usual scientific ideas. How we should like to discredit them! Unfortunately the statistical evidence, at least for telepathy, is overwhelming. It is very difficult to rearrange one's ideas so as to fit these new facts in... This argument is to my mind quite a strong one. One can say in reply that many scientific theories seem to remain workable in practice, in spite of clashing with ESP; that in fact one can get along very nicely if one forgets about it. This is rather cold comfort, and one fears that thinking is just the kind of phenomenon where ESP may be especially relevant.

48. H.A. Simon (1987, February). "Making Management Decisions: The Role of Intuition and Emotion." *The Academy of Management Executive*, pp. 58-59.

49. H.A. Simon (1977). *New Science of Management Decision*. Englewood Cliffs, NJ: Prentice-Hall, p. 81.

50. R. Sperry (1974, January). "Messages from the Laboratory." *Engineering and Science*, p. 30.

51. "Of Strategies, Deliberate and Emergent" (1985).

52. A passage written earlier for the Preface to *The Structuring of Organizations* (1979) reads:

> In retrospect, I felt I had been working on a giant jigsaw puzzle, with many missing pieces. Some of the pieces I had seemed to fit in obvious places, and once enough of them were placed, an image began to appear in my mind. Thereafter, each new piece in place clarified that image. By the time I finished, I felt I had found a logical place for all the pieces available to me. (p. xii)

53. See *Mintzberg on Management* (1989), pp. 259-260, 266.

54. This year I even redesigned my doctoral seminar in policy around pull. Whereas I used to hand out a set of readings each week on some aspect of organizations (not unexpectedly, strategy, structure, managerial work, etc.), to be discussed in class, this time the students and I identified a series of issues—organizing across borders and boundaries, managing professional institutions, effecting strategic change, and so forth—which they introduce and we all discuss each week, backed up by some related readings to stimulate understanding.

55. See *Mintzberg on Management* (1989), Chapter 5.

56. Ibid, pp. 267-268.

57. "Five Ps for Strategy" (1987); "Another Look at Why Organizations Need Strategies" (1987).

58. "The Design School" (1990).

59. The latest materials I could find in the files still reflecting a real textbook, are the bound chapters dated 1980-81 and an outline dated November 1981. The former shows Chapters 1,2,3 (now on structure), 5,6, and 8 as written, while 4 (now on managerial work) and 7 list published materials. The later outline shows efforts to incorporate the notion of configuration, with one new chapter on "Elements of Situation," another on "Configurations" themselves, and seven at the end on each configuration as well as a final one on "Transitions." I also found a document dated May 21, 1980, called "Management: Another View," that outlined a trade version of the book which was more integrated around the configurations and listed a "LEGO" chapter. Another scribbled note read "TT writing in 1976-77: concentrate on integrating the chapters." Sometime later I had crossed out the two decade 7s and replaced them with 8s, and sometime after that (in this case at least whimsically) I had crossed out the 8s and put in 9s!

60. "Profiles of Strategic Vision" (1988); "Visionary Leadership and Strategic Management" (1989).

61. "Strategies in the Financial Services Industry" (1991).

62. "Managing Design, Designing Management" (1989); I have long been fascinated with the subject of design, not just the concept in my professional work but the aesthetics in my personal reading—or preferably, looking at the pictures. In engineering school, in fact, I harbored the idea for a time of becoming a packaging consultant.

63. K.E. Weick (1979). *The Social Psychology of Organizing* (2nd ed.). Reading, MA: Addison-Wesley.

64. See "Managerial Work" (1991).

65. "The Structure of 'Unstructured' Decision Processes" (1976).

The Takeoff

WILLIAM H. NEWMAN

The study of managing as a distinct social process, separable from the immediate purpose of the activity being managed, is a recent affair. In a period of fifty years this delimiting of a field of study—and area of professional expertise—has grown from the speculation of a handful of individuals to a worldwide recognized source of economic and social progress. It has been a surprising, fascinating, and important development.

So, when Arthur Bedeian invited me to contribute a retrospective essay to the present volume I recalled anew the exponential growth in the attention focused on managing per se. Having had more opportunity than many contributors to take part in the early days of the development, I shall write mostly about the "takeoff."

These essay are, by design, expected to deal with personal experiences rather than a broad review of a subject. Personal perceptions and biases are to be aired instead of avoided (camouflaged). In keeping with these instructions, after a few background notes, my comments will center on three early developments in which I took an active part: (1) The McKinsey approach to strategy; (2) managing—a basic social process; and (3) Executive education.

PERSONAL BACKGROUND

Although born in Philadelphia in 1909, I soon became a typical midwesterner—growing up in a Chicago suburb and going to college in Iowa and Kansas. My older brother, Eddie, was a precocious kid whose active mind I never even aspired to match (in professional life he long served as a professor of psychology at Harvard). Instead, I compensated by concentrating on outdoor sports, camping, and the like. The woodshop in high school—directed by a super teacher—and diverse nonacademic activities in college—notably intercollegiate debating—probably taught me more than I absorbed in the classroom.

Looking for "a better way" was as normal in my boyhood home as getting out of bed in the morning. My father, a modestly paid social worker, felt that social practices should be improved; the *New Republic* rather than the *Saturday Evening Post* regularly appeared on the parlor table. And my mother—a teacher in Philadelphia for sixteen years prior to marriage—had no doubt that there were better ways for my brother and me to behave. As for myself, I concluded at an early age that there were more rewarding ways to earn a living than being a social worker—probably "in business."

None of us was particularly unhappy or felt persecuted. Rather, the norm was that our respective spheres could be better, and with patient effort each of us could and should improve our lot and the world around us. It was just a typical Yankee restlessness—seasoned with book learnin' (both parents had two college degrees).

Actually, the attraction of business stuck with me. Following an A.B. degree from Friends University in Wichita, Kansas, I could no longer postpone a decision about getting a job. And a decision to leave Kansas for a Master's degree in business at the University of Chicago simply reflected a recognition that in 1930 I was so naive and young that no progressive company would hire me. But then the Great Depression intervened. The very few jobs available called for people with a recognizable differential advantage. Fortunately, my good fellowship at Chicago enabled me to go straight through to a Ph.D. while still twenty-four years old. The atmosphere was grim; anyone privileged to do full-time study was obligated to put forth maximum effort. And study I did— for the first time. The self-discipline and work focus developed during those years continues to haunt me.

If a person unsullied by business experiences was needed for the "takeoff" innovations described in the following pages, I was a qualified candidate.

THE McKINSEY APPROACH TO STRATEGY

McKinsey the Consultant

Depressions provided opportunities for a scattered few. One such person was James O. McKinsey, founder of the now renowned worldwide management consulting firm and part-time professor at the Business School of the University of Chicago. By the 1930s McKinsey's attention had moved from the first published book on business budgeting to organizing a company to utilize budgetary control, and then on to "business policy"—or the content of overall company budgets.

When the depression struck McKinsey had in hand a method for assessing a company's total strengths and for projecting a company's plan for confronting its turbulent competitive environment. Battered companies, often prodded by their commercial bankers, could benefit greatly from such an integrating approach. So, it is not surprising that McKinsey's consulting firm grew steadily while most of the economy was in disarray.

My exposure to this early version of strategic planning was unusual. By 1934 McKinsey had his academic teaching narrowed down to an 8:00 a.m. class four days a week on the Midway campus; his chauffeur picked him up promptly at 8:50 a.m. and he was in his office by 9:15 a.m. The catch, however, were frequent trips out of the city. Any consulting staff member careless enough to be in the office in a late afternoon was exposed to the risk of a pinch-hitting assignment at the University early the next morning. This was not a popular arrangement among the staff (most lived miles from the campus had neither chauffeur nor a thirst for early morning teaching), nor did it help the continuity in the business policy class.

Using me to provide stability in McKinsey's class probably had more influence on my getting a job in his consulting firm than my newly minted Ph.D. The arrangement was that I went to the class every day; if McKinsey was absent for any reason I could pick up the discussion where it ended the previous day. The beauty of the plan for me, however, were the frequent rides into the city with McKinsey—sans telephone or other interruptions. Sometimes he would elaborate on the case he had just been discussing—always a camouflaged client. More often it was an unsolved problem that the consulting firm faced. And I was cocky enough to raise embarrassing issues. The relationship was informal, candid, and relaxed—and for the very junior member highly informative.

While innovative and personally ambitious, McKinsey evaluated ideas in terms of their usefulness to business managers. Models and theories took on value when they had normative connotations. "So what?" was always a pertinent question. The answer might not be pleasant to a client, but it had to be sound, long-run advice. For McKinsey, professional integrity eschewed glitzy and pompous language that complicated basic issues; also he disdained unnecessarily elaborated studies that might look impressive but add little significant insight—and he believed similar criteria should apply to academic research.

The General Survey Outline

The McKinsey consulting firm had a distinctive focus. In contrast to the major management consultants of the 1930s which dealt with functional problems of production, engineering, selling, personnel, or the like—perhaps centered on particular industries—each McKinsey engagement was expected to at least scan (a) the overall company—all the departments and their *interdependencies*, and (b) changes in the external competitive setting. Within the firm, terms such as a top management view, a general survey, or a way of thinking were used to identify the focus, but the most concrete guide was an emerging "general survey outline." This outline covered many of the key elements in what is now (1990) embraced in "business-unit strategy." The main headings were: Outlook for the industry; Position of the company in the industry; Sales policies; Production policies; Purchasing policies; Personnel policies; Organization structure; Executive personnel; Facilities; Methods and procedures; and Financial situation and possibilities.

In the 1930s such an approach was new in both business and academic circles. Especially for outside consultants to intervene in these top management issues was usually considered presumptuous and threatening by company executives.

In practice, no report to a client ever followed the general survey outline exactly, nor were all topics studied in each client company. A preliminary diagnosis of problems and opportunities facing the particular client set the agenda for what would be investigated. The dominant purpose of the outline, in McKinsey's words, was "a way of thinking about company problems."

The industry outlook and company capabilities (the first two headings in the outline) set the stage; then key modifications of company policies which would significantly improve the company prospects were recommended; next modifications essential to carry out the revised policies in company organization, key personnel, facilities, methods and procedures would be noted; finally (in keeping with McKinsey's 1921 concept of budgetary control) the impact of the outlook and the revised operations would be summarized in projected profit-and-loss and balance sheet statements. Just change the word "policy" in this framework to "strategy" and the approach is close to the concept of business-unit strategy so popular fifty years later.

McKinsey himself was reluctant to put the general survey outline into writing because he feared that his staff people would follow it slavishly instead of being selective in what to emphasize. (Position in the outline did not prejudge importance of a variable.) In discussions with prospective clients he rarely mentioned the framework: instead he asked penetrating questions that were prompted by his "way of thinking." Reports likewise were tailor-made. Nevertheless, the outline was very useful within the consulting firm (1) as a ready-made sorting device for the many scrambled bits and pieces of information that analysts learn about a company, (2) as an aid in quickly identifying interdependencies among parts of a company, and (3) as a device for converting descriptive material into an action mode.

For scholars interested in strategy formulation, we might note that the approach was intended to be normative rather than descriptive. Attention to interdependencies was vital, but there was no doctrine about dependent and independent variables; which variable was manipulated to achieve a viable "fit" depended upon local situation. New and timely synthesis was at least as important as refined empirical verification.

Birth of a Book on "Business Policies"

The refinement and application of McKinsey's approach to company-wide strategy received a jolt when McKinsey accepted the position of Chairman and CEO of Marshall Field & Company—then one of the most prestigious businesses in Chicago. Less than a year later, I left the consulting firm to become McKinsey's Assistant in his new position. Among my assignments was helping Chairman McKinsey give a management development course to the top managers of Fields's main retail store. (Again 8:00 a.m. was the starting hour.) For this occasion, McKinsey decided to have the "general survey outline" written out to assign as advance reading. My main role was to produce a chapter per week as the text.

This task was eased by previous experience in the consulting firm where I often found myself in the unenviable role of drafting reports to clients. While in the firm, McKinsey personally read all major reports, and his fertile mind invariably turned up ways to improve such documents. Often he told me in a general way what was lacking, and I had to serve as mediator between the proud author of a major study and the boss. It was a hot spot for learning what wording and ideas would please the maestro.

One fallout of preparing readings for the retail store training program was that McKinsey had arranged with his editor at South-Western Publishing Co. to use the material in a textbook for undergraduate business courses. At this stage McKinsey suddenly died (at the age of 46). South-Western's editor then came to me with a proposal that the text be substantially enlarged with examples and cases which would make the concepts meaningful to inexperienced students. Thus, the plan for *Business Policies and Management* (1940), was laid.

This was the first textbook on business policy ever published (Richard D. Irwin, Inc. did not start publishing collections of Harvard cases until after World War II). What small market existed at that time was defined primarily as an "integrating course for business majors," and the War snuffed out most of these. Nevertheless, the book prospered. In its various revisions and expansions covering half a century it has gone through ten editions, and is now titled simply as Strategy.[1] Although I doubt that a single sentence has survived in this evolutionary process, McKinsey's approach to business strategy continues to serve as the basic framework for the book. Also, in the business world his "way of thinking" about top management issues is now widely accepted.

The "validity" of the framework does not rest on deductions from abstract generalizations or on statistical analyses of opinion polls. Rather, it has been tested by application in hundreds of companies and found to be useful. It is valid in the sense that it is known to work well as a diagnostic and planning instrument.

Aside from consulting, the McKinsey approach to strategy has served me well especially in executive education—to be discussed later in this paper. Of course, over the intervening years concepts have been substantially elaborated as is shown in *Strategy in Action* (1982).[2] Nevertheless, for me and for many others the "takeoff" push goes back to McKinsey's way of plotting the trajectory for a total business.

MANAGING: A BASIC SOCIAL PROCESS

A second major thrust in my career sprang from experiences during World War II. I was initiated into the swirling activities in Washington, D.C., first, in establishing gasoline rationing. Within five months a small band of us devised a rationing system that sharply altered the personal travel patterns of a majority of people in the United States. Then, for about two years I worked in the Organization Planning Office within the War Production Board—the regulating agency for most of the nation's industries. From there I transferred to the Petroleum Administration for War, ending up as Executive Officer with responsibilities for annual appropriations from Congress, Civil Service appointments of personnel, and related activities. Overall, this was a very intensive, though untypical, course in government administration.

Widely Applicable Skills of Managing

A major characteristic of both the War Production Board and the Petroleum Administration for War was the use of high-level, experienced business executives in most of the substantive (operating) positions. These were people who had successful careers in their respective companies.

A striking fact was that the effectiveness of these executives in their new jobs varied widely. Many were able to adapt quickly to their new mission with its unusual resources and a minimum of socialization. Others simply did not fit; they undoubtedly had knowledge and skills that were valuable in the particular setting of their previous employer but those strengths were not transferable.

For an erstwhile professor concerned with managing, the tantalizing question was "What did the effective group have that the second group lacked?" During the War we were much too pressed with current performance to attempt any systematic study of the phenomenon. But it was clear that a transferable knack of managing was possessed by some, though not all, of these successful executives. The issue haunted me—partly because I had participated, just prior to the War, in a project for identifying ways to develop officers in the twelve Federal Reserve Banks.

Viewing Management as a Coherent Social Process

A useful lead to partial answer to that quandary turned up in an unexpected source. Billy Goetz had sent me a draft of a paper by L.C. Marshall (former dean of the business school at the University of Chicago) on the development of advanced civilizations. The paper centered on *social processes* such as transfer of authority to administration and managers, the division of labor and recognition of specialists, recognition of the long-run value of capital goods, and the like. Cultures that refine these socializing processes advance.

The implication of Marshall's view was that managing, too, could be considered as a social process. The transfer of authority by individual hunters, farmers, and other craftsmen to managers suggests that certain functions can be more effectively performed by a different sort of specialist—a manager. *And* in this elementary sense, quite similar functions of managing are probably applicable to many kinds of group activities.

The effective managers in the War, then, had a mastery of the basic elements of managing which they could apply to a situation that differed sharply from their previous jobs. The ineffective mangers could not separate managing from the particular settings with which they were already familiar. Or, stated another way, there are common elements of managing production, marketing, construction, universities, and circuses; recognition and skill in dealing with these common elements can add substantially to the effectiveness of a manager even in diverse settings.

The body of concepts addressed to these common elements we call "general management." Moreover, it is useful to think of managing as a social process— a way for people to work together toward common goals. This implies that the managers and the managed share many cultural norms, and that these norms are evolving over time, becoming more intricate and "sophisticated."

Today, over forty-five years after I read Marshall's paper the idea of viewing managing as a basic social process seems obvious. But back then it was not a common concept. For me, at least, it was a liberating construct. It provided a rationalization for seeking widely applicable instruments of managing. And the prevailing ideas about how to manage readily fell into an interrelated framework (a "model" in the same sense that McKinsey's general survey outline was a model).

Setting Forth an Integrated Conception

In 1946-1947, back into a civilian role, I started to put the pieces into place. First in a seminar at the Wharton School and the following year in a graduate course at Columbia University, I tried out the ideas on the restless war veterans who were swamping our classes during that period. By 1948 mimeographed chapters were available for assignments, and Prentice-Hall had the book, *Administrative Action* in print in 1951.[3] The parts of the book depict the now familiar framework: Planning; Organizing; Mobilizing Resources; Directing; and Controlling.

As an aside—the title was troublesome. I had used "Principles of Management" on the manuscript, but the editor at Prentice-Hall noted that "management" (at that time) tended to be associated just with production. So we shifted to "administration" as a more comprehensive term—as had the Business School at Harvard. The text, however, uses the two terms interchangeably. The U.S. Bureau of the Budget at that time had a division called "administrative management"!

The book is normative. As the preface states: "This book seeks to (1) bring together existing knowledge regarding the basic processes of administration, (2) state these ideas in a practical and useful form, and (3) add new ideas and interpretations that will assist executives in administering dynamic enterprises." Note also that the prime target audience was practicing business executives. We hoped to also reach academics, and this straddle was fairly successful. Nevertheless, the writing style clearly reflects my continuing interest in influencing professional behavior rather than indulging in more scholarly debates that make good footnotes.

The book was pioneering in the sense that it fit into no established niche. Although seminars dealing with general management undoubtedly existed at scattered universities, management per se was an unknown subject in business schools and elsewhere in university curricula during the late 1940s. The Academy of Management at that time had a small scattered membership of about fifty people. The American Management Association did have a "General Management" division, but papers presented there dealt mostly with boards of directors, company policy, and miscellaneous issues which did not fit into the other AMA (functional) divisions. The absence of an integrating, cohesive framework made both academics and reflective business executives doubt that focusing on general management would be rewarding.

Administrative Action was the first book that clearly laid out an action-oriented model for thinking about general management. It led the parade.

A Confluence of Thoughts

Fortunately, the central theme of *Administrative Action* was "an idea whose time had come." For example, General Electric Company—at the urging of its future president Ralph Cordiner and the supervision of vice president Harold Smiddy—conducted a major study of the practices of its outstanding managers. The conclusions were stated in a framework (and in an internal textbook used to train GE future managers) that closely matches the framework of *Administrative Action*. The main GE headings are planning, organizing, integrating, and measuring.

Soon, the National Industrial Conference Board made a comparable study, and sent its researcher—L.A. Allen—on a nationwide tour expounding a similar gospel. On the academic side, Harold D. Koontz and Cyril O'Donnell came out with their popular *Principles of Management* (McGraw-Hill, 1955) four years after *Administrative Action*, using the same framework. Meanwhile, John Mee mustered resources for a Ph.D. program at Indiana University that was an important early source of professors trained in general management. And the activities just mentioned are only examples of the epidemic-like interest in a process approach to general management that arose in the early 1950s. There is no way of knowing how much influence *Administrative Action* had in this ferment, even though its leading publication date is clear.

Forerunners

Of course, many lines of thought contributed to the planning-organizing-directing-controlling framework. Important among these were: Discussions in the Taylor Society applying F.W. Taylor's concepts to an ever-wider range of operations; published works on military organization and planning; discussions of government administration, notably Luther Gulick's PODSCORB article in *Papers on the Science of Administration* (Institute for Public Administration, 1937); Ralph C. Davis' introduction to his *Industrial Organization and Management* (Harper & Brothers, 1940), a forerunner of his analysis of *Top Management* (1951); Chester I. Barnard's seminal book on *The Functions of the Executive* (Harvard University Press, 1938); Paul E. Holden, L.S. Fish, and H.L. Smith's study of *Top Management Organization and Control* (Stanford University Press, 1941); J.D. Mooney and A.C. Reiley's historical study of large organizations titled *Onward Industry!* (Harper & Brothers, 1931). However, a sign of our provincialism at that time is virtually no use of Max Weber's *Theory of Social and Economic Organization* (The Free Press, 1920), or Henri Fayol's *Industrial and General Administration* (Issac Pitman & Sons, 1916). I, at least, was unacquainted in the 1940s with these major works.

A broader perspective on the unfolding of general management as a field of study is sketched in the diagram on the next page.

The diversity of these contributing lines of thought suggests that managing was becoming a more critical activity during the second quarter of the twentieth century. People in quite different settings were thinking about it. Then for many people, including myself, World War II thrust managers into strange situations; pressures to accomplish results in new ways with scarce resources were great; changes came rapidly. Those elements of managing which are transferable

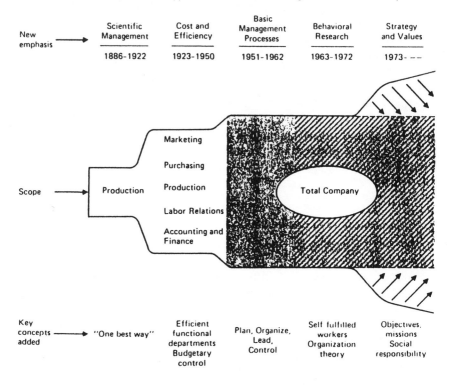

Expansion of Management Concepts. Dates shown suggest when a concept was making its greatest impact on the development of management thought. For each approach there were earlier roots, and each approach continues to have significant influence today.

Source: William H. Newman, E. Kirby Warren, and Andrew R. McGill, *The Process of Management*, 6th ed. (Englewood Cliffs, NJ: Prentice-Hall, Inc., 1987), page 25. Reproduced by permission.

became especially valuable. This stirring the pot set the stage for a very rapid growth in the concepts of general management that we rely upon today.

Revisions of the Faith

At this point let me deviate a bit from the central "takeoff" theme of this paper. Skeptics did appear.

In light of rapid changes in technology and social norms that took place after World War II, some people predicted that the process of managing would also change sharply. The forecast was that the planning-organizing-directing-controlling model discussed in the preceding pages, would become obsolete.

Two approaches, in particular, were cited as likely replacements: operations research or organization behavior. And, indeed, we at the Columbia Business School moved promptly into each of these developments in the 1950s.

Contribution of Operations Research

Up through the early 1950s Columbia Business School relied on the Industrial Engineering Department in the School of Engineering to give instruction in production management. The rise in Business School enrollment coupled with a big stir about the role of operations research, which was linked with (but not limited to) production management, led to the establishment of a "production and operations management" division within the Business School. This new arrangement would facilitate, we hoped, the melding of operations research and general management.

In practice, not much melding has taken place at Columbia or elsewhere. Both operations research—which grew into "management science"—and general management have flourished, but as separate disciplines. Management science does provide a distinctive approach to designing the operating structure of an organization. And in some circumstance this can be quite helpful. However, the resulting designs, while changing the status quo, usually fit easily in the management process framework. So, the use of management science does not undercut the concepts embraced by the planning-organizing-directing-controlling model.

Operations research, then, has not yet provided—much less required—a reformulation of the management process model, as was predicted in the 1950s. My guess is that the current computer craze will have a similar supplementing influence. Instead of a currently predicted sharp change in the way organizations (and individuals) make decisions and the way individuals interact—which would revolutionize the way companies are managed—I foresee computers and related communication devices improving and speeding up information flows and processing. But the social process of managing will continue essentially as it has been.

Contributions of Studies in Organization Behavior

A second potential source for revising the management process model are those branches of behavioral science which deal with "organization behavior." Here again, I jumped on the bandwagon early. The Samuel Bronfman Chair at Columbia in 1951 also provided for an assistant professor. I elected to fill that new position with a behavioral scientist. This was the beginning of a flow of impressive faculty members at the Columbia Business School with such a background. The rationale was that if managing was to be treated as a social process individuals trained in the behavioral disciplines would help shape the basic concepts.

Also, in an early effort at melding the general management and organization behavior concepts, Charles E. Summer and I wrote a text on *The Process of Management* (1961).[4] A major purpose of this book was to integrate insights from the behavioral scientists with the framework laid out ten years earlier in *Administrative Action*. Being directed to college students rather than experienced managers, the book added cases, discussion questions, and other features to facilitate classroom use. The behavioral scientist were unimpressed, or more likely did not bother to examine the book at all. For management professors, however, the additional perspectives on management processes were welcome. The book sold well, won a prize, and is now in its sixth edition. And it anticipated the large migration of behavioral scientists into business schools.

Especially during the 1960s and 1970s the increase of U.S. business school faculty members trained as behavioral scientists was dramatic. Most of these people came from social psychology; sociology and anthropology were also well represented. This influx did not represent converts to a new discipline of the process of managing. Rather, most of them were missionaries dedicated to their mother discipline nourished in "arts and sciences."

Several factors contributed to this influx of missionaries. First, enrollments in business schools were increasing rapidly and previous sources of business school professors were inadequate to fill the need for enlarged faculty. Consequently, jobs were available and faculty salaries were generally higher than those available in arts and science departments.

Second, the influential studies of business schools sponsored by The Ford Foundation and The Carnegie Foundation in the late 1950s both strongly recommended adding faculty trained in the social science disciplines. Business schools were to become respected members of the university community. And, indeed, a marked change in the status of business schools occurred. It became almost respectable among academic scholars to take one of those higher paying business school jobs.

Third, for some reason unknown to me the American Psychological Association and other behavioral science associations did not provide an attractive "home" and forum for the growing number of faculty people focusing on organization behavior. The Academy of Management did provide a place where people interested in studying organization behavior in *business* firms could meet and exchange ideas. (This separate professional development contrasts with the field of economics where the American Economic Association has continued to be a major professional home for economists who strayed into business schools.)

Considering the size and backgrounds of this new faculty in organization behavior, one might expect substantial revision of concepts in management processes. I recall at a ceremony in the mid-1960s at which *The Process of Management* received the McKinsey award a well-known behavioral scientist congratulated me on a fine book and added, "I predict that this book will be best known as the last of an era. Within the next few years the new concepts of management will make the style of management that you describe obsolete."

This has not happened. Since that time scores of new books oriented around the process framework have been widely studied throughout the world. In my biased view, we have seen a wide variety of refinements but no major paradigm which outmodes the "classical" process approach. For example, the Tavistock Group developed new ways to organize work groups on the factory floor, OD (organization development) has modified the role of a supervisor in many companies, participation in planning is much more common and may extend into some degree of self-regulation, and other ways to improve the quality of working life are being tried. We are more sophisticated in the selection and training of employees. The process for changing management practices has been explored at length. The list could go on and on. Valuable as these techniques are when applied in the right place and right way, the organization behaviorists have not made planning-organizing-directing-controlling obsolete.

Looking back, it is now clear at least to me that expecting behavioral scientists to redesign the basic processes of managing was unwarranted. The basic processes of managing have persisted for centuries—from the building of the pyramids and Jethro's advice to Moses to select able men...and make them rulers of tens, rulers of hundreds...[in a management hierarchy]. Behavioral scientists have helped us adapt those processes to current cultural norms—an important, continuing role. But to expect them to devise, say, a non-hierarchical airline is presumptuous.

My guess is that the basic process view of managing will not be replaced due to being obsolete. Instead, additional ways of thinking about the phenomenon of managing will become popular because they are useful—that is, they help managers to do a better job of managing. They will supplement the basic framework. Furthermore, to stretch the point, my guess is that behavioral scientists will not be the creators and proponents of such new approaches which become widely accepted. The reason for prophesying a constrained role for behavioral scientists is that their "discipline" will continue to restrict their range. What receives attention, the way such elements are researched, and often the values attached to outcomes all narrow the concepts that are endorsed. In contrast, new widely useful approaches to managing will probably spring from people who focus on the total role of managers and employ eclectic ideas and methods to form innovations.

EXECUTIVE EDUCATION

Returning to the early "takeoff" theme, a third cluster of my activities strongly reinforced my interests in business strategy and general management, which have been the focus of the first two sections in this paper. The third leg on the stool was executive education. Continuing education of practicing executives, while challenging in itself, also provided an excellent forum for testing and enlarging concepts incubated in sheltered university halls. And for me, validating managerial concepts with experienced people who will soon apply the concepts is worth more than tons of questionnaires to eager undergraduate students.

Let me first describe our particular "laboratory" and then comment on the impressive benefits of using such testing grounds.

Columbia Executive Programs

In 1951 Averell Harriman gave to Columbia University his family home, Arden House, a ninety-six room mansion located on the top of a small mountain in Bear Mountain Park about fifty miles north of New York City. The home was to be used as a conference center, firstly for The American Assembly. However, the university officials who obtained the gift—Dwight Eisenhower and Philip Young, then president and dean of the business school respectively—recognized that meetings of The American Assembly would utilize Arden House only a small percentage of time. The second and larger group of guests at the home were to be high-level executives honing their skills for managing businesses.

Thus Columbia Executive Programs were conceived. We had a unique facility; next we had to design a program and find the participants who would match this auspicious start.

In the absence of precedents, we did establish several parameters that served us well:

- *Participants*: person concerned with overall management of a self-contained business; company sponsored.
- *Duration and location*: six weeks, full-time residence at Arden House; complete relief from company duties during this period.
- *Instruction:* succession of topics—not concurrent "courses" as at Harvard AMP; small group role assignments (to utilize participants' experience) combined with group reports and full class discussions; faculty leaders the best in the country, not restricted to Columbia.
- *Main themes:* industry and company outlook; company policy (strategy); organization and control to execute strategy.

Harvard Business School already had its Advances Management Program in operation—a 13-week, on campus set of courses patterned after its regular MBA courses. However, the Columbia program was the first of its length and format. In response to inquiries we explained that "by omitting functional courses and restricting reliance on cases we covered in six weeks what Harvard did in thirteen and we did it better"!

The idea of high-level mangers taking time off to go back to school was very new in the early 1950s. So, a lot of missionary work was necessary to recruit participants of the required status. Nevertheless, as indicated in the earlier discussion of interest in general management, the timing was right for innovations in management education.

The participants starting with the first session of Columbia's "Executive Program in Business Administration" have been an able lot. Most of them were already in or soon were promoted to senior posts in their companies. The group even in the early pioneering years included future CEOs of IBM, Johnson & Johnson, Prudential and Metropolitan life insurance companies, Texaco and Continental oil companies, Coca-Cola, and duPont—to name only some of the larger firms. This was, indeed, an opportunity for the teacher to learn more from the students than vice versa.

My role in these early programs was "faculty coordinator." With one or two colleagues, we planned the programs, recruited faculty, and hovered over the daily educational activities at Arden House. The informal give-and-take among participants, often running well into the night, was as important as classroom sessions.

The subjects discussed in Executive Programs, as already noted, drew heavily on the McKinsey approach to strategy and on the basic process concepts of general management. And these Arden House assemblies were an excellent forum in which to test and refine top management issues. Compared with faculty approved courses in a university degree program, there was greater flexibility in content as well as sharper and faster feedback. The development of ideas moved at a much faster pace than on the campus.

Foreign Executive Programs

A related sort of executive education was also enriching. Foreign countries, literally around the world, were keenly interested in U.S. management in the decades following World War II. And our federal government, especially in its A.I.D. programs, supported the training of local business managers. Consequently, there were many opportunities for those of us already involved in executive education to spread the word. In many countries we helped pioneer the idea that management should be regarded as a profession with a body of knowledge that could be learned. And, we tried to explain Yankee concepts in a manner that could be applied to the local culture and conditions.

My first dunking was in Chile in 1956 where a newly formed management association made headlines by sending many of the country's business leaders back to school. Later, our business school entered into a five-year cooperative plan—which I helped negotiate—with the University of Buenos Aires in Argentina. And we made a similar arrangement with a business association in Belo Horizonte, Brazil; this was part of an extensive regional development plan for a second industrial center that would relieve the crowding in Sao Paulo.

The interest in management education grew in both developed and developing countries. I personally have participated in intense programs ranging from several weeks to several months in England, France, Spain, Yugoslavia, Turkey, Lebanon, Nigeria, South Africa, Iran, Australia, and China—in addition to the South American ventures in Argentina, Brazil, and Chile—and shared in related projects in Japan and India. American colleagues have, of course, been in many other locations.

The fact that the study of managing as a distinct, widely applicable social process could spread in a single lifetime from a few score of professors and executives (in the 1930s) to a worldwide recognized ingredient of economic growth is fascinating. We are experiencing a very rapid diffusion of management technology as well as physical technology. And by now refined concepts have sprung up in many places. Even in these diverse locations, however, the process view of managing (planning, organizing, directing, controlling) is one of the most useful paradigms that we have. Because the process approach is both basic and action-oriented, managers in any country can use it.

Benefits of Executive Education

Executive education, both locally and abroad, is doubly rewarding. Faculty leaders as well as the students (executives) gain. However, the nature of these benefits—on both sides—differs from the usual teacher/pupil input and outcome.

In the normal teacher/pupil relationship the teacher spends a lot of time conveying descriptive knowledge, and in this respect the teacher is in a superior and authoritative role. In contrast, experienced managers already know the facts of life; indeed they usually know more about specific problems in their industry and company than does a faculty leader. Participants in an executive program typically increases their breadth of knowledge—largely by talking with other participants. And the main contribution of the faculty leader typically is a mental framework for bringing meaning out of this conglomeration of data. The framework(s) provided by the faculty leader helps to sort, select, relate and synthesize; the aim is to simplify and interpret into action-oriented conclusions. In this respect, a faculty leader is more like a coach than a source of information. And it is the participant, not the faculty leader, who is in a power position to decide what is correct for a specific situation.

This relationship, of course, puts the faculty leader on the spot. Perhaps a proposed framework is eagerly accepted; it helps participants master their environment. At other times the proposal falls flat; the impatient participants see little value in it. Then the faculty leader must seek a better way to explain the concept, and/or try to find out why the concept does not fit the participants' needs. And this reexamination leads to revisions and qualifications. With smart experienced participants, such feedback is indeed stimulating—and fun.

A related aspect of executive education is the perspective it provides on academic research. Jargon has to be translated into managerial English, and this has a therapeutic effect on the use of vague and obscure language. Also tests of validity are much closer to application of a concept than come from refined statistical manipulation of indirect data. The participants' response to an idea is not always correct, but I find that their batting average is better than the conclusions I read in the *Administrative Science Quarterly* or the *Academy of Management Journal*. (Part of this difference reflects the higher weight that participants give to relevance.)

Moreover, personal relationships developed with executives, especially in residential programs, open opportunities for in-depth research. Frank discussion about internal pressures and competitive moves may be possible to a degree rarely extended to outsiders. Although much of this sort of data is confidential, it provides insights and has an authenticity that supplements published material.

Executive education, then, is an advantageous activity for schools of business. It can provide a distinct input to the professional development of individuals who are already in positions where they can promptly use concepts presented. And, it can contribute significantly to the personal development and research of the faculty leaders.

Certainly I benefitted greatly from my work in executive education. My early starts with both business strategy and general management were amplified and refined in the Arden House dialogues. At the same time the McKinsey strategy model and the social process model of general management served as useful frameworks for the Arden House programs. There was an invigorating synergy between the three thrusts—strategy, general management, and executive education.

PUBLICATIONS

1940

Business policies and central management. Cincinnati, OH: South-Western.

1948

Government-industry cooperation that works. *Public Administration Review.*

1951

Administration action. Englewood Cliffs, NJ: Prentice-Hall.
Cases for administrative action. Englewood Cliffs, NJ: Prentice-Hall.

1953

Basic objectives which shape the character of a company. *Journal of Business* (October).

1955

With J.P. Logan. *Management of expanding enterprises.* New York: Columbia University Press.

1956

Overcoming obstacles to effective delegation. *Management Review* (January).

1961

With C.E. Summer. *The process of management.* Englewood Cliffs, NJ: Prentice-Hall.

1963

Contemporary adjustments in managerial decision-making and planning. Bureau of Business Research, University of Texas-Austin.
Managing external relations. *California Management Review* (Spring).

1967

Shaping the master strategy of your firm. *California Management Review* (Spring).

1969

Industrial management. *Encyclopedia Americana.*

1970

Is management exportable? *Columbia Journal of World Business* (January).

1971

Strategy and management structure. *Academy of Management Proceedings.*
Selecting company strategy. *Journal of Business Policy* (Winter).

1972

Cultural assumptions underlying U.S. management concepts. In J.L. Massie & J. Lytjes (Eds.), *Management in an international context*. New York: Harper & Row.

1975

Constructive control. Englewood Cliffs, NJ: Prentice-Hall.

1978

[Editor] *Managers for the year 2000*. Englewood Cliffs, NJ: Prentice-Hall.
Control: Past of future. In L. Benton (Ed.), *Management for the future*. New York: McGraw-Hill.
With H.W. Wallender, III. Managing not-for-profit enterprises. *Academy of Management Review* (January).

1979

External integration of the firm. In M. Zimet & R.G. Greenwood (Eds.), *The evolving science of management: The collected papers of Harold Smiddy by others in his honor*. New York: AMACOM.
Company politics: Unexplored dimension of management. *Journal of General Management*. (Autumn).

1980

With H.E. Klein. How to integrate new environmental forces into strategic planning. *Management Review* (July).
With H.E. Klein. How to use SPIRE: A systematic procedure for indentifying relevant environments for strategic planning. *Journal of Business Strategy* (Summer).
Research methodology for the design of integrated systems. Research Working Paper 295A, Graduate School of Business, Columbia University.

1982

With B. Yavitz. *Strategy in action*. New York: The Free Press.
With B. Yavitz. What the corporation should provide its business units. *Journal of Business Strategy* (Summer).

1984

Managerial control. Chicago: Science Research Associates.

1985

With J.P. Logan & W.H. Hegarty. *Strategy, policy, and central management* (9th ed.). Cincinnaati, OH: South-Western.
The chief executive as synthesizer. In *Proceedings of meeting of the fellows*. International Academy of Management, Irish Management, Irish Management Institute.

1986

The role of company culture and internal politics. In J.R. Gardner, R. Rachlin, & H.W.A. Sweeny (Eds.), *Handbook of strategic planning*. New York: Wiley.

1987

With E.K. Warren & A.R. McGill. *The process of management* (6th ed.). Englewood Cliffs, NJ: Prentice-Hall.
With M.L. Tushman & E. Romanelli. Convergence and upheaval: Managing the unsteady pace of organizational evolution. *California Management Review* (Fall).
With J.P. Logan & W.H. Hegarty. *Multi-level strategy: Fusing departmental with strategic moves*. Working Paper 57, Graduate School of Business, Columbia University.
Faculty for the future: An industrial hurdle. In *The evolution of education in collegiate schools of business: Past, present, and future*. Conference Proceedings, School of Business, Hofstra University.

1989

With J.P. Logan & H. Hegarty. *Strategy: A multi-level, integrative approach*. Cincinnati, OH: South-Western.
With J.A.F. Stoner. Teaching executives and MBA students. Working Paper 88-103a-2, Graduate School of Business Administration, Fordham University.
With J.A.F. Stoner. Better vision for old dogs: Teaching experienced managers. *Academy of Management Proceedings*.

1992

Birth of a successful joint venture. Lanham, MD: University of Press of America.
Focused joint ventures in transforming economies. *The Executive* (February).
Launching a successful joint venture. *California Management Review* (Fall).

NOTES

1. *Business Policies and Central Management* (First edition: 1940, Second edition: 1947. Third edition: 1953. Fourth edition: 1959; Indian translation: 1959. Japanese translation: 1962. Fifth edition: 1965). *Strategy, Policy, and Central Management* (Sixth edition: 1971. Seventh edition: 1976. Eighth edition: 1981. Ninth edition (with J.P. Logan & W.H. Harvey): 1985). *Strategy: A Multi-Level, Integrated Approach* (with J.P. Logan and W.H. Harvey), 1989.

2. *Strategy in Action* (with B. Yavitz) (Paperback: 1984. Finnish translation: 1984. Spanish translation: 1985).

3. *Administrative Action* (First edition: 1951. Dutch translation: 1959. Spanish translation: 1962. Second edition: 1963; Asian translation: 1963; English edition: 1963; Italian translation: 1963. Portuguese translation: 1969; French translation: 1969. Japanese translation: 1972.

4. *The Process of Management* (with C.E. Summer) (First edition: 1961; Recipient of the 1961 McKinsey Award for One of Five Best Books in Management. Japanese translation: 1962. Indian translation: 1964. Second edition: 1967. German translation: 1968. Indian translation: 1970. Third edition: 1972; Spanish translation: 1972. Chinese translation: 1974. Hebrew translation: 1974. Fourth edition: 1977. Portuguese translation: 1980. Fifth edition: 1982. Spanish translation: 1985. Sixth edition (with E.K. Warren & A.R. McGill): 1987.

An Almost Random Career

CHARLES PERROW

PRELUDE

I find it amusing that a field so characterized by rationality and functionalism, as organization theory surely is, should have been chosen by me in such a non-deliberate, casual and even accidental manner. But that is what my retrospect now lays before me. In a word, I wandered out of previous career possibilities for want of sufficient talent and application and, for no apparent reason, wandered into organization theory. Once in the sociology of organizations at the best time and in the best places, randomness evaporated and I surprisingly found myself capable of immense application. I found a reasonable talent to be sufficient.

A modest talent was all that was needed, because, to use the parlance of today, an enormous niche opened before those of us who ventured forth at the end of the nineteen fifties. Organization theory, like both the sociology and business administration of which it was a part, and like academia in general, flowered from abundant resources; all were given over to addressing the problems the consumption of abundant resources had left us with. After World War II the United States sailed forth as number one in the world, business expanded, universities sought to catch up with it, and all this expansion and prosperity trickled down to doctoral students in sociology. Even with little talent survival was guaranteed, and moderate talent carried a lot of us a long ways, allowing us unwittingly to set directions and define standards that would be responsive to our limits and strengths.

The first time a thought of a teaching career crossed my mind was when it was placed there by an English professor at the University of Washington in 1945. At the end of a conference he asked me if I had ever considered going into teaching. I had not, but the glow of twenty minutes of discussion in his hushed and book filled study on campus made the novel idea, at least momentarily, very pleasurable. I had written an essay on Milton in his freshman English course. Quite innocent of all that had gone on before in scholarly discussions of *Paradise Lost*, I argued that Milton couldn't have been much of a Christian, for all his professions to that effect, if the only interesting character to be illuminated by his dense language was Satan.

I had one other earlier communication from this professor, whose name I cannot even recall. We were all required to write a brief essay in order to either be placed in the fairly remedial freshman English course or one of the more advanced ones. Upon reading my essay he was strongly inclined to allow me to do an advanced course. This was based upon the character and insight of my essay, he said. But its grammar, punctuation, and spelling was, he noted, so execrable as to put to shame any high school in Seattle. He could not have known that I came from an even more shameful high school system, that of neighboring Tacoma, where I managed only a C average. Three years of tedious military service had extended my reading range but not my grammar.

The assignment in question was to write a "how to do something" essay, such as catch a fish or learn to ski. Being fairly incompetent at most things I had tried, I decided to bend the rules of the essay and write upon something that I could not possibly as yet have successfully executed—"how to commit suicide." One might say that I had the imagination for it; indeed I was much preoccupied with it, but lacked the grammar and spelling to carry it out.

I did not want to be a professor at that time. For lack of discipline and diligence I had failed to become a jazz trumpeter, though the music stayed with me to the present, and one of the many virtues of the woman I am devoted to is that she is a violinist. One knows fairly soon that one will not make it as a trumpet player, but not so with my other dream—novelist. Writing the great American novel was clearly dear to my heart. I had not read many at all, but I figured it would not require the discipline of endless hours of trying to produce sustained, golden tones and even pragmatic scales on the trumpet. Writing the novel would come as I lived a great American life.

I moved on from the University of Washington after one quarter, most notable for having lived in a dank basement room that required going outside, up the walk, and into the back door of the house if one wished to use a toilet which was adjacent to the laundry. (I was fairly poor, but I believe I thought myself poorer than I really was, and might have done better. It was a tenacious condition with me, born of suffering during the Great Depression and only gradually abandoned in the recent decades of middle-class prosperity.) I hitchhiked from Seattle to a curiosity called Black Mountain College in the fair state of North Carolina. An acquaintance in the army had told me about it enthusiastically. As I recall, he was probably what the country would soon label a communist, but the irony was that the article that he passed on to me extolling the virtues of Black Mountain College was from the super orthodox *Readers Digest*. It described an apolitical community of scholars and students. Perhaps he knew of that which the editors of the *Digest* did not, that it was intensely political and very left. He detected in me a concern with social issues and social responsibility I am sure, since he plied me with literature (which I rarely read), such as Dos Passos. But more important he detected in me a want of background and knowledge for these matters, due no doubt to my impoverished childhood and high school, but surely also to my capacity for reverie. Black Mountain, it seems, would provide the rigor and depth I needed, he felt. Little did he know how perfectly that great indulgence, which Black Mountain in many respects was, would suit my nature.

One could not get into Black Mountain in the month that I was mustered out of the infantry, but I was able to catch the spring quarter at the University of Washington, as I have related. I figured I then could go on to Black Mountain if the University of Washington proved lacking. At the end of the spring quarter nothing held me there, certainly not my dank room, and I had made no friends. Hitchhiking was still fairly safe in those years and six days later I showed up with my backpack for an admission interview at Black Mountain College, near Ashville, North Carolina. I was enraptured. It was mutual, the officials later told me. They drew from the urban northeast, which to them was New York City; they had almost no one from the west coast and never dreamed of anyone showing up from a place called Tacoma, Washington. After the interview I went on up the east coast to find a summer job (on a Connecticut dairy farm, pasteurizing the milk) and spent the next two years, except for another summer off to make some money, at one of the strangest college experiences in the nation's history.

It was at Black Mountain that an occasional nickname from my childhood— my mother sometimes called me Chicken Little, out of affection, I am sure, rather than any premonition that decades later I would be prophesying Bhopals, Challengers, and Chernobyls—came to stick. There were four students named Charles; I was the last to arrive and all the other names had been appointed—Charles, Chuck, and Charley. I mentioned that I was sometimes called Chick by my mother and it stuck.

There were about eighty students, almost all of them I thought from New York City, and twenty teachers, half of them, it seemed, refugees from Hitler's Germany. We had a farm and we all worked at it; we washed dishes and helped with cooking. The faculty salaries were very low and based on family size, and we even had two or three black students, who risked more in coming to us in the South before the civil rights movement than we risked in seeking them out. I was perhaps the only country mouse, and while I had indulged myself in the likes of Thomas Wolfe, Ambrose Bierce, and Poe, here I was to read Rimbaud, Dijuna Barnes, and Carl Rodgers.

Carl Rodgers?! Yes indeed. The early stirring of group process, or group dynamics as it was later called, was sending up very tender shoots in this extraordinary college. A psychologist named John Wallen had studied with Nathaniel Cantor, a student of Rodgers, and had brought a new book by Cantor with him, *Dynamics of Leadership*. He also introduced us to the slim works of Mary Parker Follett. A group of us took over the student body and ran what would now be called T-groups to aid and abet the community decision-making practices. The results of this were, in our estimation, fairly disastrous. The split between the social sciences and literature (us) and the painting, music and crafts group (the European immigrants and their closest followers in the student body), long patched and smoothed over by civility and concern for the fate of the fragile community, was revealed by the search light of openness for all to see. Try as we did to dig down to where that common ground was sure to be found, the digging only revealed highly emotional and fairly irrational bases of disagreements, ones that no democratic process could alleviate. At the end of my second year at the college it fell apart and half the students and half the faculty left; we "Democrats" left it to those we righteously considered the "Fascists." They struggled on for a couple of years and then this wonderful experiment and institution, founded in the bleak 1930s, wound down and disappeared in the prosperous late 40s and early 50s.

All the community struggle, infighting, and politics succeeded in distracting me from my task of writing at least some short stories, if not a novel. (I was head of the student body for some time, and if anything could characterize Black Mountain, my institutional success there would be it, for in my three years of military service I succeeded only in making private first-class three times, the last a nearly automatic and symbolic gesture before discharge.)

Failing to write, the community struggles may have stimulated some interest in organizational processes. Black Mountain was a wonderful laboratory. A community of one hundred and twenty-five souls, isolated in a beautiful valley in the wooded hills of North Carolina with a strong social consciousness (easy to have in an isolated valley where we doted on Henry Wallace for President), it was both an organization and a community. It was not so much that organization and community overlapped but that they were inseparable, and I grew to believe that this was the source of many of the fierce firestorms that swept over us. We didn't "study" at Black Mountain; we lived and argued and suffered and tried to be creative as individuals. As a country mouse I had much catching up to do in living and arguing; it was perhaps a sufficient excuse for not having written more than one or two short stories.

But a philosopher there, William Levi, had a profound effect upon me, and I began an education in the social sciences. We read Karen Horney and Karl Jaspers, brand new then, as well as Mill and Plato. Had I gone to a more conventional school or, much the same thing, stayed at the University of Washington, and been required to write stories and especially to read them, it might have all turned out differently. If I had not become a writer as the result of more conventional schooling, I could have ended up as an English teacher or have played some other role in the literary world. But at Black Mountain my studies were unfocussed, the community/organization struggle demanding, and self-exploration the real goal.

After leaving Black Mountain, the next few years were unpleasant and do not bear much accounting since they neither reflect well upon myself, nor are they especially pertinent to my life as a sociologist. I hung out with what would later be called the beats and hippies on the Lower East Side of New York City for a year. But I cannot resist one anecdote from this intensely literary, and political, and self-consuming atmosphere. After a couple of days of wandering about the Lower East Side looking for a cheap apartment I was struck by the fact that the clumps of people sitting on the stoops in the hot weather appeared to spend all their time telling Jewish jokes. Then I realized that the only vehicle for Yiddish accents in my limited experience had been the endless round of Jewish jokes told, with accomplished accents, by so many of the students at Black Mountain. It was a language and an accent that could be used to simply pass the time of day and communicate, I finally realized.

I found a four-room "railroad flat" basement apartment on East Sixth Street and First Avenue, where only the rooms at each end had windows to the outside; the windows of the other two rooms opened on to each other. Since I truly had little money and was not inclined to work more than part time, it served me well. The extra rooms were loaned to an endless stream of visitors, acquaintances, and friends of friends. The novelist Jimmy Baldwin, for example, was there for a month and a half, electrifying me, my girlfriend, and our acquaintances, with his intellectual intensity and fierce living.

But no novel came forth so I hitched across the country again, this time to Reed College in Portland, Oregon, where I stayed for only eight weeks since it seemed such a large and stuffy college, and because I had such a disastrous love affair there. I needed some psychological help so I moved to the Bay Area, finally settling for a year in Oakland, California, working as a dishwasher in a delicatessen and starting some extremely helpful psychotherapy. Then, still in the hands of my therapist, who would know me for three more years, I went to a real college—the University of California at Berkeley.

BERKELEY

Here I filled in the immense space between the Thomas Wolfe of my army days and Rimbaud of Black Mountain, and read James and Conrad and Eliot; the space between Bix Biderbeck of my youthful record collection and John Cage (who taught at Black Mountain) with the late Beethoven quartets; shifted from Wallace to Adlai Stevenson; and tried to convince the university administration that they should give me credit for two years of self-exploration and group dynamics at Black Mountain. (They didn't. I took final exams in physics and other subjects to salvage the better part of a year's credit.) And, most germane to this account, I inadvertently wandered into a sociology course.

I had no major. I still wanted to be a writer, though I must have noticed that I had written almost nothing. Sociology had a solution looking for problems, and I had a problem. We came together, in the parlance of garbage-can theory, in a year-long course called grandly enough, The Idea of Progress, taught by Kenneth Bock. Despite some homeopathic applications of Nietzsche and Karl Jaspers to a soul suffering some anguish, I had never before encountered the skeptical idea that progress was only an idea and not a fact; that it was a social construction of reality, which in reality could not be satisfactorily defended but needed, as we say today, deconstruction. That some held there was nothing but decline rather than progress amazed me, though it was a commonplace lament; that still others, the Manichaenism could see an alteration between good and evil and no forward movement; that Vico could see larger oscillations ever returning in circular form—all this amazed and energized me. With the atomic bomb hanging over us, and poverty everywhere in the world, I felt impelled to think some grand thoughts about how we got here and if we were following any discernable trajectory.

Bock was dry, ironic, witty, and subtle. In his sociology I found immense learning which could be put to some remote good—it provided an aspect, a view, a position, a metering device, a sense of proportion, almost a sense of engagement with detachment. I signed up for his sociology at the shabby department office, at his suggestion.

For me, being at Berkeley in those years (1950-1958), must have been like being on the Left Bank in the 1920s, or Vienna in 1895, or Greenwich Village and the East Village in the 1940s and 1950s, where, indeed I had been for one year. Can one really be sure one is in the beginning of a renaissance? ("Dear diary, today the One Hundred Year War began.") I, and I dare say the other students, certainly didn't. Berkeley Sociology could have been third-rate in the late 1950s and its new offspring would have been none the wiser.

I did not know it was spring time for sociology at Berkeley when I signed on as a sophomore, and there was no reason to expect it. The department was soon in receivership as a result of a split between the historical sociologists (of whom my mentor, Kenneth Bock was the most junior member) and some other branch that I couldn't possibly characterize now, and because of the lingering effects of the McCarthyite university loyalty oath which had found some strong detractors within the department, and alas some supporters. After a year of stewardship by Professor Edward Strong from Philosophy (who was later to resign from the university in high dudgeon over the antics of the students in the free speech movement), Herbert Blumer was brought in from Chicago to remake it. He brought in some stimulating people, including Philip Selznick, and since I had no other plans at graduation, I just kept going.

I don't know whether I take greater delight in finding some general principles or laws operating that can explain the world—the traditional sociological quest—or in finding that the principles and laws we endorse fail to give any explanation and are indeed often contradicted—the skeptical, critical side of sociology. The attentive reader will note that much of my deprecatory tone in this essay is meant to alert one to the contradiction of received principle. Occasionally I shall point them out directly, as now.

Blumer was an extremely staunch proponent of a particular view—symbolic interactionism. One might say he was even fanatical, except that it wouldn't fit with that stolid body and gentle courtliness, itself so unusual in a former professional football player for the old Chicago Cardinals. We students thought he would fill the department with that strange breed that doted on Charles Cooley and George Herbert Mead, and was just beginning to be called symbolic interactionism. George Herbert Mead (the full name was mandatory) was long since dead and indeed had left little in the way of publications. But he left a devoted following of scribes who kept supposedly careful notes of his lectures and then published them. (Since I found the thoughts of Chairman Mead very dull and dense I could only assume that the scribes were more careless than careful, since I was reluctant to assume that Mead's thought was equally dull and dense.) And here was one of Mead's foremost devotees coming to rebuild our department.

I had no hostility I was aware of to the persuasion (and have since realized its importance more and more), but I feared for any candidate who was singularly unpersuaded when it came to hiring. I'm delighted to say that I was very wrong. Herbert Blumer brought in William Kornhauser, Philip Selznick, Seymour Martin Lipset, Kingsley Davis, and others of disparate persuasions. Indeed only Tamatsu Shibutani could be counted as a near relative to Blumer and Mead, and Erving Goffman as a distant one. All of these new hires joined Reinhard Bendix and Robert Nisbet who were already there. In the five years I resided in that graduate department, the department probably jumped from tenth to first place in the country.

The graduate students were, as is often held to be the case, as important as the faculty itself—Arthur Stinchcombe, Bennett Berger, Amitai Etzioni, Guenther Roth, Thomas Scheff, Arlene Daniels, and many others that went on to fine careers and positions. One had simply to be dense, even defective, to not have gotten much smarter very quickly in that atmosphere. Not knowing any better we even started a journal which is still running, now called *The Berkeley Journal of Sociology*. I can't speak for my more prominent colleagues, but I rather expect that they were as naive as I was when we ventured forth to our first positions. I remember getting an offer from Humboldt State College and being thrilled. Another from the University of Michigan at the Flint campus. I took it into Blumer and asked him what he thought of the place. Selznick was appalled that I hadn't made any efforts to apply to the top institutions; how could I, since I wasn't sure which ones they really were? Sociology, as a bona fide enterprise, with big classes, was being born, and we had only vague notions of Chicago, Harvard, and Columbia. Morris Janowitz, at the University of Michigan, needed a director for a project that he and Robert Vinter (of the Michigan School of Social Work) had just gotten money for, so Selznick fixed me up with a job in those, all-so-halcyon days, when a phone call would do it.

At Berkeley it took some time to wean me from my introspective, psychological and literary conceits so that I could thrive on the formal, detached and rationalistic world of organizations. I was still interested in group dynamics, and Charles Cooley and even George Herbert Mead were cousins to my Black Mountain experience. But that experience suggested a larger role for manners than for honesty, for avoidance than for encounter, than I had expected. My master's thesis was on the primary group, but significantly it was chaired by Reinhard Bendix. I must have been moving to a more structuralist position. It was Selznick that was decisive. I could savor his gift of language readily enough and his moral concerns. He was tough, and like all professors in those days, distant. I of all people thought I knew how to write, so it was devastating when my first seminar paper came back with the first page and a half totally covered with cramped and crabby comments and revisions. And then a note that said "Rewrite the whole paper along these lines and I will continue reading it." He did this more than once, until I realized that he was teaching me to think clearly, and when that happened, good writing was comparatively easy. I could write well enough; it was my thinking that was, so to speak, ungrammatical.

I worked as a research assistant on a project that Selznick co-directed, studying the Townsend old age assistance organizations in California, a political movement. I also served as a research assistant one summer for Lipset reviewing the literature on leadership, trying to match it with the propositions of his study of the International Typographical Union. I gradually came to perceive the students clustered around Shibutani and Goffman as a cult, and unfortunately never took any of their courses. Still, the pull from Selznick, Lipset, and Bendix could just as well been towards political sociology, historical sociology, or even stratification rather than organizations, but for the lack of funding in those directions.

The audience that reads these pages knows that funds are important, but how little we seem to reflect upon funds when giving accounts. Money matters affected me but little during my two years at Black Mountain College (except that I had to take often risky summer jobs, as in a New England textile mill where all of my coworkers had lost at least one digit of their fingers). There were many well-off students and even some rich ones at Black Mountain, but a deliberate effort kept that from making a difference there. My undergraduate days and part of my graduate days were hounded by the responsibility of working twenty to twenty-five hours a week as a dishwasher, supermarket cashier, carwash attendant, and counterman in small restaurants. My childhood was a long string of paper routes, magazine routes, peddling my mother's cookies door to door, lawn mowing and pennies counted. Thus, when Blumer mentioned to me that Mount Zion Hospital in San Francisco was looking for somebody to head up a research effort to evaluate a home-care program, and that it would pay considerably more than a teaching assistantship (I was one of his), I jumped at it. I could not get much of a dissertation out of the home care program (my ambitions were beginning to soar) but it was intimately involved with and run out of a very progressive hospital, and perhaps there was something of interest there. If not, it would still be an interesting and well paid job. Reflecting upon this now, I am astounded as to how little thought must have gone into that choice of site and job. I had no plans for a dissertation topic and no plans to turn this job into a dissertation opportunity. I wound up my affairs as soon as I could with exams and such like, and eventually moved over to San Francisco to study Mt. Zion Hospital, now with Edith who, fresh from an MSW degree at Berkeley, took a job in a family agency. We would soon marry.

Quite possibly there is no accurate, honest retrospect but only reconstruction. But if I may be permitted a retrospect, I eased myself into the sociology of organizations in that experience, just as I might have gone into political sociology, stratification, or even social psychology with another funding source. My micro interests in the human group and especially the primary group were indulged by watching the extraordinary administrator of that hospital carry it through some exciting days. My social consciousness was indulged by pointing out how little concern there was for the outpatient department with its rising number of minority patients, while all attention was riveted upon the prestige-gathering heart surgeons and their research. Kenneth Bock's course, The Idea of Progress, followed at Berkeley by some wonderful history courses, led me into the bowels of the institution to find out if there was anything in its past that might account for the present state of affairs (at that time, and for some future decades, this was a rare question for sociologists of anything). Indeed there was. It had once been run by wealthy philanthropists, then by doctors, and now by my administrator. And didn't the goals change at every step of the way, each change surrounded by controversy? And didn't the power reside in those groups that controlled the most important source of resources coming into the institution? Thus were my organizational interests regarding goals and structure prefigured and nourished. In the year and a half or so that I spent in the field, working half-time on the home care project and full-time at trying to understand the hospital, I unwittingly constructed the outline of my approach to organizations. In a way there were yet no competing approaches that I could be even aware of, other than Selznick's writings, which did guide me. But a few years ago when I looked at the introduction of that dissertation for the first time since writing it, I was amazed that I defined the organization explicitly as an arena of conflicting interests, with shifting centers of power over time, and with multiple goals depending upon the uses of each group. I didn't know I knew this then. (Learning appears to be a process of combined re-invention, each invention dearly won but only marginally different from its preceding invention.) I was developing a political side of Selznick (found in his TVA study), and down playing his institutional side (found in his book on leadership and administration). But the point I want to make is that it was chance that placed organizations in my purview, indeed, sociology itself. I had no time for the trumpet now, and had not tried a short story since my anguished, lonely days in Oakland. It certainly was *bonne chance*; I now not only had friends, but a wonderful wife and a profession to which I gave enormous application.

However, for a time it seemed I almost would not have a degree. Two foreign languages were required, and my high school Spanish was not one of them. I had had two years of French and somehow got through that exam. But my two years of German were insufficient and I flunked the German exam. I dropped everything and tried again. I flunked it again. By now I had accepted a job at Michigan and my field work was almost completed. I believe it was Bendix who came to my rescue, giving me a passage to translate from Max Weber's famous essay on bureaucracy that I virtually knew by heart in English. Others were not so kind. The key defense of my dissertation outline was rather savagely attacked by Lipset, presumably settling scores with Selznick thereby. I passed the exam but it was not judged a distinguished performance. Before my wife and I left Berkeley for the terrors of the midwest I showed a rough draft of most of the chapters to the hospital administrator. He liked it and said he did not think it was necessary to disguise the name of the hospital. I was overjoyed. The last obstacle seemed to have fallen and I would have it finished by December. I was off by a year. The final version enraged the Board of Trustees of the hospital, so every page bearing the hospital name had to be retyped, and, for a time, the U of C library declared that the copy filed with them was not accessible to anyone!

I find it hard to hurry over those graduate student days at Berkeley. It was summer, and everything since then has been autumn with touches of winter. I no longer had to work in carwashes and restaurants, yet seemed to be able to live on nothing, or a TA-ship which amounted to the same thing. Our friends were as abundant as the sunshine, even in foggy San Francisco where we loved the young woman across the hall, cherished a young pianist, and knew slews of other graduate students. I had a *new* car, one of the early VWs where we beeped at each other on the roads. I was invited to a conference on health systems in Roanoke, Virginia, leaving the day after our wedding, and I wouldn't have missed it even for a marriage! Famous people were there and one of them invited me to come up to Columbia before going back, and give an informal seminar on my dissertation. I was astounded that anyone would care and that they would pay my expenses. I happened on the weekly sherry party at Columbia, where I introduced myself to Robert Merton, my mentor's mentor, and the leading sociologist in the United States: "I'm a student of Philip Selznick, and I know he would want me to send regards." Merton ignored me and turned away, but I was thrilled to even be snubbed by him. Almost 30 years later, when we met for the first time and discussed those early days, he noted that I was his "grandson." Paul Lazersfeld was kindly and interested. The few people at the seminar also were curious as to what this new department of sociology was turning out, and were surprised at the breadth and scope of my dissertation. The products of the "lab" at Columbia were narrowing.

Edith and I left the Bay area in August 1958, just as the silent generation of the 50s was beginning to stir. The first political party on the Berkeley campus, SLATE, had just won control of the student government. The Committee on Unamerican Activities was in full sway. Loyalty oaths were everywhere. But the students had organized, and the south was stirring with sit-ins. Edith and I filled up the Volkswagen and left the beautiful Bay area for Michigan, tears in our eyes. I didn't know it, but I was heading for one of the best departments that I could have gone to. We left via the Golden Gate Bridge, going up the coast to Tacoma for a short visit with my two older brothers, who had raised me from the age of ten. Then we headed due east, the prairie winds so strong against the boxes on the VW's roof that we were forced to tack across the wide expanse. After Berkeley and then San Francisco, Ann Arbor as a hometown was a shock. We could not believe that people could prosper in such weather and provincialism.

ANN ARBOR

The years from the fall of 1958, when we arrived in Ann Arbor, to the fall of 1963 when we left for the University of Pittsburgh, seemed to me a period when organizational analysis first took hold, and incredibly enough I was at the university where much of it was happening. Thus, for me, it was a period of professional training and personal exploration of my now chosen field. It was also a time when I learned some important rules of the game, which I will communicate shortly insofar as I understand them, and was also, at the end of the period, sufficiently secure to discard them and to leave that intellectual oasis for a far more risky venue. More prosaically, I spent the first year full-time on a research project codirected by Robert Vinter and Morris Janowitz; the next two years part-time on that project and part-time teaching in the Sociology Department; and the two years after that full-time in the

Sociology Department. I eased my way in but the union was never really consummated. I left because the tenure prospects pictured to me by the Department Chairman were sufficiently compromised with ill-suiting stipulations that I decided to risk leaving the main stream for a few years. Pittsburgh offered what the University of Michigan could not (a multitude of large organizations and large city), and would not (a chance to teach courses in organizations, research funds, and only a reasonable amount of committee work).

I think there is a mode of cognitive reasoning that reconstructs choice situations such that we read into them preordained, and even favorable outcomes. People are adept at justifying what they did do and discounting the other options at the time. I will have more to say about this when I come to my departure from Michigan, but want to raise immediately the difficult issue now as to whether my choice to depart was wise, whether I even had a choice, and whether it made any difference at all in the long run. Sorting through those years at Michigan will turn up a lot of valuable learning experiences, some musings of moral concerns, and, I suspect but cannot be sure of, the solidification of my dominant prospective. Let's watch for all of these as I narrate those years.

It's hard to recall how primitive organizational analysis was in 1958. Simon had written *Administrative Behavior*, most noted for its attack upon the proverbs of classical administrative theory, but I found it dull, obvious, and irrelevant to an emerging notion that organizations were a key force for shaping society. The March and Simon volume, *Organizations*, was somewhat more promising in its second part, but mechanically psychologistic in its first part. The first part deals with choices, and from economic atoms add up the pluses or minuses of joining or leaving an organization or cooperating and working in it or not, and the resulting sums tell us what each atom will do. Somehow or other they will form together to make an organization. The counterpart today is agency theory and my reaction to it today is the same as in 1958— organizations are profoundly social, and like all social life, require enormous amounts of disinterested or other-regarding cooperation, and self-interest maximization can only be a small part of the picture.

But the second part of the book abandoned the psychologistic orientation and the stricture that "organizations are made up of human beings" and thus that organizational analysis is a problem of psychology, and looked at the context of behavior—the control of premises, what I later came to call "unobtrusive controls," and it invented new terms such as uncertainty absorption and organizational slack and other structural concepts. To paraphrase an economist, the first part was about atoms making choices, and the second part about how they had precious few choices to make. But, remarkably enough, I learned almost nothing from reading this book the first time in 1958, and since the chairman did not allow me to teach courses in organizations at Michigan, I never had occasion to seriously go over it again until that opportunity was presented to me when I moved to Pittsburgh. Some of it must have reached me in 1958, but by and large it had a delayed impact.

The project that I walked into at Michigan, as field director, was, I believe, the first thoroughly comparative organizational study, designed to gather identical data from several organizations. It was certainly the first to gather systematic questionnaire data from the lowest members, in this case the inmates of juvenile correctional institutions, all the way up to the director. We were to find three organizations that were fairly treatment-oriented in handling the kids, and compare them with three that were fairly custodial in their orientation. Then we would see what were the impacts of the two settings upon the clients, and to some extent upon the staff. No plans were made to judge the success of custody versus treatment in terms of later recidivism rates, since these would be difficult to obtain, and more important, extremely difficult to interpret given the quite different context to which the boys returned. Next, the study was quite unique for its time in that it involved two measurements of the same population; what was to become referred to as a panel study. In between those measurements we conducted seminars for the executives, feeding back the information from the first wave of observations, interviews, and questionnaires. We also had access to a state-of-the-art IBM 650 in a huge air-conditioned room at Michigan, and not only would we cross-tab everything with lightening speed, doing many runs in an hour if the machine was up, but we would be doing factor analyses no less. This was 1959-1961.

I threw myself into the project with unbelievable enthusiasm and worked harder than I had ever dreamed I could work. A good part of the enthusiasm came from the sustained contact with Robert Vinter, who, along with Morris Janowitz, was coprincipal investigator. (Janowitz was spending the year at the new think tank in Palo Alto, the Center for Advanced Study in the Behavioral Sciences.) I was in awe of Vinter. I had never met anyone with that much savvy about the world of social welfare. He was immensely critical of it and committed to making the social welfare establishment a positive force for the poor, rather than for the Scouts, middle-class Ys, and those in individual therapy. What was so fascinating was that my inchoate liberal or even radical instincts were subject to devastating scrutiny and cynicism by Bob, yet his own strategies and those for the project were realistic, tough-minded, and actually idealistic. My fascination with him was in direct proportion to my naivete, and as I learned from him, I began to pull away from his concept of organizations.

Vinter and Janowitz had a "leadership" and "one best way" view for the project. What happened in these institutions depended upon the quality of the director, and most particularly his ability to accept and develop a therapeutic intervention model. It was consistent with the leadership model that Selznick had developed, where the leader has the vision and summons the energy of the organization. I came to a somewhat different perspective. It struck me that there was nothing that much wrong with the directors' leadership of the custodial institutions; they simply believed that the raw material they were dealing with was in bad shape because it had never been disciplined and taught to respect authority. The institution could remedy that, sometimes with shaved heads and bread and water in a tiny dungeon without light for days. I certainly didn't agree with their diagnosis and was so appalled by the treatment that, at one institution in West Virginia, every time that I returned to my dingy motel room after a day's field work, the first thing I had to do was take a long shower, as if to cleanse myself of participation in the horror. (I learned that the job of the field worker was to *understand*, get inside the perspective of not only the boys, but the staff too. This required empathetic interviewing. The distasteful task continued as I interviewed top executives in corporations, where bigoted stereotypes were often in evidence.)

But there was no vouchsafing the sincerity of the directors' view of the nature of the problem and the solution they had chosen. They had a different raw material, or thought they did, than the keepers of the treatment institutions, and thus applied a different technology than the keepers of the treatment institutions. Everybody had agreed that helping and remaking delinquents was their goal, not punishment, and certainly not custody. To the insight that I was trying to formulate in my dissertation, that organizations had multiple and contradictory goals, and the goals changed over time as different groups got control, I was beginning to add the insight that "operative" goals, what the organization did rather than what it said, were limited by the techniques that it used to transform its raw materials, and these in turn depended upon management's definition of those raw materials.

Though in the long run I think the differences in our approaches were probably quite small, at the time they loomed so large that I almost withdrew from putting my name upon the final volume. I wrote a good deal of the first draft, but much of that got cut or changed, and put back into a leadership perspective. But meanwhile I thought I was on to something, and I was looking for a way to explore it further. I engaged in a bit of entrepreneurship on my own part that the project did not really provide. I had come across an article by James March in a political science journal about the political process of goal setting, and it seemed to me to be a formulation that went beyond my dissertation and initial published articles, but I felt that we were traveling in the same direction. I immediately wrote an appreciative note to March and "thoughtfully" enclosed copies of *ASR* and *AJS* articles from my dissertation. About nine months later I got a letter from him asking if I would write a chapter on hospitals for the *Handbook of Organizations*. I wrote it in my last year at Michigan and it allowed me to conceptualize the delinquency study in the way that I wished, and to apply that conceptualization to general and mental hospitals. March, upon receiving the draft, wrote that on first reading he thought it had far too little to do with hospitals for a handbook of organizations, but that upon second reading, that it said far more about hospitals, as well as other organizations, than the kind of review article he was expecting. The chapter in the *Handbook* became an important part of my intellectual development and of my career.

As I suggested, I really grew up at Michigan. Part of this was due to the charisma of Bob Vinter with respect to how organizations really worked—he could be spellbinding on that subject. But a good part of it was due to three people who were nominally my subordinates, since I was project director, and they were there to write their dissertations on the data set: Mayer Zald, David Street, and Rosemary Sarri, nee Conzemius. We four had a seminar that was immensely productive. My authority was very nominal, since we were all really in the same position of being graduate students, on the first large scale project on organizations that at least we had ever heard of, and with guidance from a star of sociology, Janowitz, and a fierce fighter from social work, Vinter. Just as happened at Berkeley, with all those graduate students, the four of us had to get smarter at Michigan.

I, at least, also got wiser to the ways of organizations and departments. There was a good deal of friction between the Institute for Social Research (ISR), populated largely by psychologists and survey researchers, and the sociology department where the interest in organizations was more broadly political and dynamic. I taught from 1959 on, with Janowitz and then with Albert J. Reiss, social organization seminars that explored political, institutional, and structural views of organizations, while Rensis Likert, Floyd Mann, Basil Georgeopolus, Stanley Seashore, and others explored the ways in which workers could be made more productive. The conflict was more general than views of organizations; when the brilliant Harold Wilensky was being wooed by Berkeley, Angus Campbell, one of the brilliant leaders in ISR, was reported to have gone around the department's back to the Dean arguing that Wilensky should be let go. I don't know whether it is a measure of my past naivete and my present cynicism, or an actual change in the way these institutions function, that I could be shocked by this then and so used to it now.

I was not particularly interested in the Institute's work in organizations, though arguably it was the most productive center for organizational studies for a decade or more. I thought it served management far more than workers, relied too heavily upon attitude research, thought that organizations were really quite benign things and if only run well could do immense good. It ignored the larger structure or setting in which they operated (e.g., capitalism and racism), and the force of historical traditions. And so on. It came as a shock to me, then, when my chairman told me that to get tenure at Michigan I would have to go over to ISR, join with someone like Floyd Mann, and do a sound, empirical "hard-cover" questionnaire study (not a book that would be sold as a paperback). This was to be in addition to the sound, empirical hard-cover study that Janowitz, Vinter, David Street, and I were then producing. I suppose that I didn't have the votes from the ISR voting members of the department, and could not prevent the end runs to the Dean at that time. But if I were a good boy, it was implied, I could gather the votes.

The occasion for this advice from the chairman of sociology was an offer from the lesser-ranked University of Pittsburgh, and a joint offer at that, with half-time in sociology and half-time in an abomination called GSPIA, the initials of which had something to do with public administration. (I obviously didn't know what GSPIA was all about when I joined it.) I had gotten an inquiry from Pittsburgh and asked my chairman for advice. He said: "It is always good to get known and you will learn something by going down there and giving a talk." When I went down I found out that I could raise my salary from $7,000 a year (9 months) to $13,000 (yearly), cut back on my teaching load, teach as many organizations courses as I wanted at either the graduate or undergraduate level, have seed money for research, and I would be near heavy industry which I wanted very much to study. There were bright people in the sociology department, and Pittsburgh was heaven after Ann Arbor— it was a real city with ethnic groups, slums, corruption, power, industry, and everything a sociologist felt was representative of life in the United States.

I went back to the chairman with the offer and he said, "It sounds great; we could never match it." "What would I need to get tenure at Michigan?" I asked. The chances were marginal at present (a book was in the works on the correctional institutions, but that was coauthored; there were four and five articles and the *Handbook* piece, but that was not enough). With the ISR book in a couple of years things would look good, he said. So I left. I left a department where the chairman told me to shave my beard off when I returned from summer vacation before I'd be allowed to teach (the year was 1960), where I was saddled with loads of committee work (especially since I was an elected junior representative of the executive committee, where my feeble voice matched the tremulous tones of assistant professors at that time), where it took a revolt by myself and others to avoid having to use the textbook written by the key department members when teaching the large sections of the American Society course, or Introductory Sociology, and where the chairman could hoard courses for himself or his favorite graduate student. The place was stacked to the rafters with bright and productive people, and in my five years in Ann Arbor, and especially the last two years as full-time in the department, I profited immensely from them. But I was getting a reputation of my own and knew that organizations were not to be defined by morale questions nor made socially responsive by Likert's System Four.

Edith and I also longed to get into a real city with real problems and restaurants. We had a baby on our hands, our son, and the prospects of some decent income for a change—Edith had worked in the local state hospital and in a family agency as a psychiatric social worker, neither of which paid very well. (Part of my education there was absorbing the frightening, penetrating tales of life in the back wards of the huge psychiatric hospital she brought home so many nights.) The thing we would miss most, collectively, was the art and music scene in Ann Arbor, which was extraordinary. This was a time of great experimentation and we were in awe of it.

PITTSBURGH

Pittsburgh can be briefly covered. One or more of the key members of the sociology department had a long-term relationship with a nearby CIA-front research organization, and there seemed to be less of the 60s protest in that department than in most. There was a great president, Edwin Litchfield, the only university president I ever voluntarily went to hear address the faculty—and he bawled us out for our unwitting support for racism—but he died in a plane crash in my second year there. My other appointment, in GSPIA, was in an institution even more tightly linked to the powers-that-be that were fighting the Vietnam War. It was a client of the Agency for International Development and through that, I believe, the CIA. Its members went off to various places of insurgency around the world and did the necessary work. They published articles about developing the Third World, stabilizing primitive economies, and fighting communism. The head of GSPIA organizations was thoroughly untrustworthy in the estimation of some of us. As one colleague put it when I was raising a storm about something, "Chick, you can't practice virtue in a whorehouse." With about three exceptions the graduate students were poor. But it allowed me to spend a lot of time in a few industrial organizations, just hanging out, learning the technology, and trying to absorb the norms. I was able to sit in on board meetings and shop floor meetings, read a fair bit of correspondence and in some cases to serve as an informal shrink to top management.

As much as I learned from Michigan I hadn't learned nearly enough. At the end of the first year at Pittsburgh I drafted a proposal to the National Science Foundation to do a comparative study of several industrial organizations, along the lines that their tasks or technology might determine their structure. It came back with a devastating letter from the resident sociologist, Carl Bachman, I believe, saying that while the notions were good and interesting, they hadn't been thought through seriously enough to do any decent research. "What kind of organizations? How many? What kind of questions? To whom? Is there any way that your theory could be proved wrong given the kind of data you would be gathering? If you wish, you can revise your application and try to meet the deadline in six weeks, but the change would have to be substantial." Furious, stung, but goaded, I completely revised it and in the process thought the whole thing through seriously for the first time since writing the *Handbook* article. I am still immensely grateful to that sociologist for the tough, straightforward, penetrating criticisms of what I had thought had been a splendid proposal. (I think if I'd been at Michigan and run it by somebody in ISR they would have been able to do the same thing for me. But Pittsburgh was not like Michigan.)

Funds in hand I went out into the field in earnest with two good graduate students in tow (Ernest Vargas and Jeffrey Guest), and we did great interviewing and field work, but again Michigan had not had time to fully train me. At Michigan I had demanded of the project staff that every question they submitted for inclusion in the questionnaire be justified theoretically and contain a dummy table showing what they expected to find and what its significance would be. It was a terrific discipline and we had a stunning questionnaire. At Pittsburgh there was nobody to do this to me, and more important, there wasn't the culture of careful questionnaire construction and attention to scaling. Incredibly enough, I ended up with many key questions having three, or even only two, alternatives. Rensis Likert was one of the first people I met when I moved to Michigan—I sat next to him at the first departmental meeting and his name meant nothing to me. But by the time I left I certainly knew who he was and what he had done for questionnaire construction, but here I was making these stupid errors. I think it had something to do with the climate of the place. GSPIA faculty were all consulting; those doing questionnaire studies in sociology could never show us any of their data or the pieces they wrote from it because they were all classified; the rest of the sociology department were philosophers. This was a major reason why I decided that the three years that I had planned on allotting to Pittsburgh was just right.

That questionnaire was lousy and I barely used the data; it became a pretest for a much better questionnaire which was funded by NSF again, and which I conducted after I moved to Wisconsin. But the latitude that I had in terms of the kinds of courses I could teach, teaching load, support for spending time in the field, and a few contacts with Jim March and others at Carnegie still paid off handsomely I believe. I could think about the problems, and it takes a long time to do any serious or productive thinking—years in some cases, for what then appears to be a simple, even obvious idea.

CONTINGENCY THEORY

Midway through my Pittsburgh stay, probably around the time when we were giving out questionnaires, I remember a project meeting when I was trying once again to formulate and get across some still inchoate notions of technology and structure. "It's not a routine-non-routine continuum," I said. "It's got to be more complex. There is another dimension. We can see it in the engineering firms that we are studying in contrast to [a particular firm that was making highly specialized steel for the defense industry.]" I went to the board and drew a four-fold table (sociology's Sesame Street) and rapidly began to fill in the cells with organizations and attributes. I knew I had it, and for the first time.

I dropped everything and wrote a piece called "A Framework for Comparative Organization Analysis" and sent it off to the *American Sociological Review* who published it forthwith (that is, a year or so later). Unfortunately, when the data began to roll in, the world, rolled flat and shiny by my functionalist theory, burst forth again in a riot of weeds and flowers and hillocks and craggy rocks. An organization that should have followed a machine-like bureaucratic model because its production was very routine, looked like what we would today call a garbage can, full of power, prejudice, preferences, and wealth. The president did little, the vice-president ran the place, but to keep the president from knowing how he was running it, he refused to use organization charts or assign true responsibility, or even install a decent recordkeeping system. He was smart and he knew where the problems were popping up and he had those people, from workmen on up to assistant vice-president report to him directly when their area heated up. Otherwise he ignored them. It was an immensely wasteful organization in terms of almost all of its resources, but it was in a market that was taking off and you would have to be totally incompetent not to make money. And we saw the opposite, nonroutine processes overlaid with bureaucracy so that the functional fit between technology and structure alluded us in our questionnaire data.

It was a good theory, one that a variety of us were coming up with at the time, but only a partial one. After my first year at Wisconsin the students put on a skit at the end of the year where they lampooned the professors. I was delighted to be lampooned (the unkindest cut of all is to be ignored), and I took note of the caricature. Throughout the evening, especially when the sets for the skits were being changed, somebody with a beard like mine would come out with a pail and a mop vigorously moping the floor. Finally somebody asked him what the hell he was doing. "My name is Perrow, and I'm using technology to sop up all the variance in the world, don't you see!"

It was certainly one source of variance, but not the only one. I was not alone in arguing that research organizations should be, and in most cases probably would be, structured differently from routine manufacturing, and elite psychiatric hospitals differently from routine people processing state hospitals. Joan Woodward in the late 1950s had conducted a survey of firms in the midlands of England and had first formulated this idea. Sociologist Robert Dubin, then at the University of Oregon, came across her obscure publication and through his reference to it in an article, I got hold of it while I was at Pittsburgh. I was ready for it because of the work on correctional institutions and the formulation, in primitive form, that I had made in the *Handbook* chapter. I made some comments about technology and structure at an

American Sociological Association meeting and Paul Lawrence and his student, Jay Lorsch, of the Harvard Business School, came up afterwards and said, "We should talk; we are thinking along the same lines."

They also knew of some work of Gerald Bell at North Carolina that fitted in, and we all knew of the work of James Thompson, with whom I was in frequent communication. We decided that we had something going, and they had just become aware of Woodward's work, so Paul and Jay organized two conferences. At first the principals, Lawrence, Lorsch, Bell, Thompson, Woodward, myself, and three or four others met to discuss our similarities and differences, and to prepare an agenda for the second—the Coonamasset Conference, named for a resort on Cape Cod which was beautiful in the late fall. There a distinguished gathering of economists, organization theorists, and other social scientists (from Harvard, MIT, etc.) met. We presented our astounding view to them. There is, we said, no best way to run an organization, and that organizations differ systematically in terms of either the technology, as I was putting it, or their environment, as Lawrence and Lorsch were putting it. I can't recall now how overwhelmed the audience was, and I'm not sure I knew at the time, but we principals were all impressed.

The next year, 1967, my publication, "A Comparative Framework for Organizational Analysis" came out, and Thompson's book, *Organizations in Action* came out, and Lawrence and Lorsch's book, *Organization and Environment* came out. Two years before Woodward had beaten us all with *Industrial Organization: Theory and Practice*. (Tom Burns and G. Stalker had also prefigured this work with *The Management of Innovation* in 1961.) But prefigured though it was, 1967 was a great vintage, and the wine aged delightfully over the next ten years until reservations, problems with empirical demonstration, complexities and new interests eroded it.

So far in my career I had had at least three base hits—the article on goals in the *American Sociological Review* in 1961, the *Handbook* article in 1965 (written in 1962-63), and now the 1967 framework article. Many years later when asked to write a commentary on this article for the Social Science Index, *Current Contents*, which apparently picks out frequently cited pieces and asks the author to comment on the subsequent history of the ideas, I argued that it was still fairly sound, but that power, institutional and cross-cultural factors weakened it far more than I had anticipated. And furthermore, the interests of organization theory should not be in the best way to organize, even if that way was contingent upon environment or technology, but on what organizations were doing to transform societies, and on the role of power within organizations, and the power of some organizations over others and the rest of society. But "contingency theory," as Lawrence and Lorsch aptly dubbed it, was a necessary development, I believe. It is hard to realize that this simple idea had not been formulated until Woodward came along and had not gotten into the literature until the 1967 harvest.

Prior to that, organizations differed by their goals—profit making, health care, education, or whatever in the excessively functionalist and normative view of sociology that we inherited from Talcott Parsons and others. Since the turn of the century, theorists have been looking for the one best way to organize. Indeed, the Institute for Social Research at Michigan had finally found it, and System Five was the one best way. Business organizations continued along the same lines, emphasizing leadership and/or "fundamental organizing principles." The notion that organizations might have to change rapidly as the environment and the tasks changed was even slower in getting recognition. The search of most of the social sciences up until the '70s, and still in most quarters, is for the stable, the regularities, the predictabilities, and above all, the rationalities. Contingency theory unsettled that view and made it easier for me, at least, to appreciate the cognitive and social constructionist's revolutions around the corner that preoccupy so many of us today.

MADISON

After two years at Pittsburgh I knew it was time to prepare to move on. The market was still great, departments were still building, the war on poverty had not been completely enfeebled as yet, and President Johnson had not yet turned upon the insurgent movements. The University of Wisconsin beckoned and I was thrilled; it had one of the best sociology departments in the country. When my appointment was virtually certain, it was cancelled when a higher-level committee turned it down. Russell Middleton, the chairman, called with the sad news and I learned that they had balked about my moving as a full professor when I had just become a tenured associate the year before at Pittsburgh (when I moved there I received nontenured associate). I immediately said, "I'll come as an associate." "But your salary will be much less and we think you should be a full professor." "I don't care about the salary, and I don't care what you call me; in fact, I'll come without tenure." It was speedily arranged, and after a few months there, I was promoted to a tenured professor, effective the next year, with a reasonable but moderate salary (oh, those salad days!).

Once at Wisconsin I was imbued with the standards of research that had been maintained at Michigan, and I completely redid my study of industrial organizations. It was a tremendous amount of work, since I did it while I was teaching and in summers; it had a large questionnaire and fourteen different organizations, and a ninety-three percent response rate from all salaried exempt personnel. It was a good questionnaire, asking questions of these people that they always wanted to be asked and allowing them to say what they always wanted to say about controversial matters, such as the war between production and sales, or the failure of top management to innovate, or the failure of R&D

to support the stable product lines, and so forth. But, as I indicated before, only some of the organizations fitted the mold; too many other variables, unmeasured but still known to us, entered in to reduce the requisite correlation levels and significance tests. The results just did not play out in the pattern that we had predicted, and we uncovered measurement problems that made me forever suspicious of organizational surveys.

For example, on a questionnaire the foreman in a routine bottling plant would check that he had "a lot of power or say" over a process that was unpredictable and demanding, whereas we knew that that was not so. In our view he was immensely constrained by the production process and only engaged in fine tuning. On the other hand the foreman in a semiconductor plant, where yields were only sixty percent and could be disturbed when a nearby canning factory vented acids from cooking tomatoes into the air, or a thousand other contingencies, would check that he had "little power or say" over things that affected his job. We knew otherwise, since he could shut the line down, call in engineers and research scientists, tell sales that orders would have to be cancelled, and in effect control large swings in profits. But to his mind all these contingencies and uncertainties meant that he was powerless, and all he could fall back upon were the routines. Scrambling over the line, conferencing, working far into the night, and not really understanding the process, he felt he was in the grip of meaningless and vagrant demands and forces.

I was so surprised that the bottling foreman scored high on power and the semiconductor foreman low that I checked the coding of the original questionnaires. Then I went back and talked to them, anticipating with a sinking feeling what I was to find: for these foremen certainty meant power; uncertainty meant lack of it. It was not what we had intended in the questionnaire, and worse yet, it was not the way many other respondents conceived of it.

We also had data from one large organization on rank, but for the others we had to rely on a question which said, more or less, "think of 6 levels, with the president and vice-presidents as level one, and foreman and salesmen and salaried finance people as level six: where would you put yourself?" We asked this question at the first organization, where we had the independent data, and then compared the responses.

The first problem we encountered was an all-day, very contentious staff meeting where we tried to reconcile the official rank data with what we each thought the hierarchy was. (We had not yet coded the self-rankings.) "You can't give him a 5; he has 40 people under him and it is a key process, while this other guy who gets 5 has only 4 people under him and no one pays any attention to them." ("I'll agree to 4 there, but you have to give this other bunch a 6.") We *bargained* our way to consensus. The second problem was worse: we compared both our view and the official ranking with the self-ranking. As I recall (I really should have published this, but it was very sensitive data at the time); the highest of the three different correlations were about .3! Neither our view nor the official view had better correlations with the self-ranking, and the self-ranking was quite absurd. Yet we go on treating the most key variable in our surveys, hierarchy, as if it can be measured by self-reports or official ranks. I learned, finally, to treat questionnaire responses as data, but not necessarily the data we thought we were getting. One last example: We expected morale to be high in the zinging technologically-advanced firms where management skills were high, people were bright, and the hours long. It was frightfully low there. Morale was high in the sleepy, routine firms where education was low, tenure long, favoritism rampant, effort casual, and innovation and profits minuscule. I carried with me a "social construction" of organizations that bore more resemblance to Michigan's ISR than I realized. It took some time for these findings to sink in and, of course (perhaps unfortunately), I didn't think the *Administrative Science Quarterly* would welcome them.

Wisconsin in those years was a great place for an organization theorist with an uncertain macro-leftist tilt. Michael Aiken and Jerald Hage were there, collaborating furiously; Robert Alford was doing his important work on health-care politics, from the book of the same name; Maurice Zeitlin was just finishing a seminal and even path breaking long piece attacking the Berle and Means thesis and opening the door for subsequent research and debate on that topic; Jay Demerath was working in the cultural area; and Richard Hamilton was finishing his important book on class and politics in the United States. We were all on the same floor, often had lunch together, and shared ideas and disputed ideas. The left politics of Hamilton, Zeitlin, and Alford probably had the greatest influence upon me; they provided the intellectual figured base to the antiwar arias that the students were singing.

The atmosphere was sufficiently open at Wisconsin that a group of students, most of them graduate students, proposed that *they* offer a seminar for faculty members on the new left. About twenty of us signed up and met weekly for a semester, with attendance falling off to about ten at the end. We read Marx, Peter Collier, the Port Huron Statement, Ernest Mandel, Baran and Sweezey, and so on. Much of it was an eye opener for me. The four graduate students that ran the seminar welcomed our arguments and dealt with us patiently. Two of them disappeared as Weathermen a few years later. When the state police and the national guard arrived to quell the "Dow Chemical riots" some of us seminar members were on the streets getting gassed (so was Edith).

When I left in the summer of '68 for a fellowship at Berkeley, my students presented me with a World War I gas mask as a symbol of what had happened to me at Wisconsin and what might well happen at Berkeley. They were right. I got gassed again during the People's Park demonstrations at Berkeley, cornered with a large number of people in a cul-de-sac, and sprayed by a helicopter, with the police beating us as we exited through a narrow passage.

I heard the shot that killed the student a block away from me that day. I remember writing a two-in-one letter to Mayer Zald, the first dealing with academic matters, and the second, interleaved between the lines of the first, dealing with the craziness at Berkeley. I artfully designed the first four or five lines so that they could be read as if it were a single-spaced letter. The effect was the desired one; I was living in a schizophrenic world. I wasn't required to do any teaching, but I planned to teach a graduate seminar in the business school anyway, and then found that, when I cancelled it because of the occupation of the campus by the national guard, I was the only business school faculty member to cancel classes! Sometimes you just luck out.

THE CRITICAL ESSAY

A more revealing intellectual and biographical incident occurred during the tumultuous 1968-69 year at Berkeley. I was working on *Complex Organizations: A Critical Essay*. The first book I had published, *Organizational Analysis: A Sociological View*, had been something of a quicky. Vic Vroom had talked me into writing it for a series, and I had written it quickly and knew that it didn't really hang together all that well. The *Critical Essay* was going to be, I hoped, an important work. By the time most of that year was over I had written the book (I had started it long before), but I was having a great deal of trouble with what was then the last chapter, on the institutional school. It just wouldn't come off, and I turned to other writing and research tasks. (One of which was gathering the material together for a semiedited volume called *The Radical Attack on Business*, where I was to present a sympathetic interpretation of the new left that would, I hoped, be utilized in business schools. It was in some, but coming out in 1971 it missed the rising wave and crest, and got lost in the repression of the 1970s.)

After the fellowship I returned to Wisconsin and, caught up in that world, did not get a chance to do much at all on the book until the following summer. Then I sat down and in a burst of speed and articulateness that I had never experienced before, and perhaps not since, I wrote a draft of the last chapter on the institutional school. I then realized what had happened. While at Berkeley I had occasionally seen my mentor, Philip Selznick, and the last chapter was going to be much about him. But it was to be critical, and while I was in Berkeley, I guess I just couldn't do it. A year later in the sticky summer of overheated Wisconsin, I had the distance I needed.

Early that fall I met Selznick at a conference and mentioned that I had just finished a long chapter that was very critical of him. He said, "Well, send it to me Chick. I'd love to see it." I said, "But, I don't think you're going to like it at all and I am embarrassed by that." He replied with a casual laugh, saying "Students always feel that way when they first criticize their professors, and they don't realize that the professors are well aware of many of these problems themselves. Send it," he said. I did and I got back several single-spaced pages of vigorous rebuttal and argument. Selznick was clearly upset by the chapter. I was upset by his response, but the response was so well-argued, and so measured, that it allowed me to see the theory, the institutional theory that he was trying to develop, and has ever since embraced, much more clearly. I set to work revising the chapter, to not only take into account his objections, but to make the critique even more pointed. I'm writing now as if this is a monumental intellectual effort occupying a couple of summers, and it is not that at all. Perhaps ten printed pages is all that was in contention, but in terms of my intellectual development, they were extremely significant.

The postscript is that after the book came out in 1972, I came across a student of Selznick's who had just had a seminar with him. They had spent two weeks discussing *Complex Organization*, the second week entirely devoted to the last chapter. Selznick disagreed, he said, but thought the issues were important enough that the seminar should go into them in detail. All students should be so lucky as to have a mentor such as this.

REPRESSION

The University of Wisconsin at Madison was all that one could hope for in terms of a strong sociology department and strong social science and history departments. The School of Business Administration was still somewhat sleepy, but the Institute for Poverty Research and the Industrial Relations program more than made up for that in my view. There were so many brilliant scholars on campus that it often wasn't until years later that I learned that the person that I was reading in political science, or history, or psychology had actually been "a colleague" of mine during my Wisconsin days. Why would one ever leave? The most trivial but still important reason was the dreadful winters and the steaming summers. More important was the midwest isolation. We looked back upon Pittsburgh as a vital eastern city that we missed. If you can say that for Pittsburgh, it reflects upon the place you are saying it from. Both Edith and I were in a sense Easterners; I had loved New York City since my first youthful visit there on a furlough, and Edith had been born there. Her parents still lived, and still are living there.

But the most important immediate reason was the poisonous gas of repression that settled over the Wisconsin campus. I didn't think Stony Brook, to which I moved, was going to be all that freer, though it was, but it was the liberal atmosphere of the campus that allowed one to put up with the other deficits of living in Madison. When that was destroyed, there was less to hold one there. We had policemen in our sociology courses dressed as students, except for their tell-tale heavy black oxfords that gave them away. They took notes and reported on us. Maurice Zeitlin organized a referendum on the Vietnam War in the city of Madison (it failed), and for his efforts the Trustees went after him. He had accepted a Rockefeller Fellowship to continue his work on the ruling class of Chile (oh, the ironies of the left!), and once he had signed the papers, the Trustees turned around and deliberately refused to accept the grant from the Rockefeller Foundation, leaving Maurice, as they and we all thought at the time, without funding for a year. It was unheard of to turn down a fellowship that was given to the university for a prominent scholar. Fortunately, the lawyer that we hired discovered that Maurice had inadvertently been given the wrong form to sign, the form that indicated leave with pay rather than leave without pay. The Trustees, embarrassed, admitted they would have to pay his salary and then quietly, after denying that they would do so, reaccepted the Rockefeller Grant so that the university wouldn't loose the money.

But they didn't stop there. The President of the Board of Trustees called the President of the Santa Barbara campus of the University of California, where Maurice was going to do most of his work, and persuaded him to refuse to give an office and a mailbox and a library card to Maurice. More money was raised, this time at Santa Barbara, and another lawyer hired. The sociology department at Santa Barbara quietly gave him an office without a name on the door, a mailbox without a name on the box, and a book runner that would search the stacks for him. Zeitlin wasted most of the year in a series of court battles with the University of California administration until the issue finally became moot because the year was over. So the Regents triumphed after all.

These are just two instances of what I was spending most of my time fighting, it seemed, at Wisconsin. Why not at least be on the East Coast where you could read the *New York Times* in the morning, and get to a museum now and then. I made inquiries; SUNY, Stony Brook was enthusiastic; and I left. About six tenured people left Wisconsin that year, at least four of them for political reasons, including one of the people I was to miss the most, a brilliant demographer and wonderful storyteller, Norman Ryder, who went to Princeton. Within three or four years everybody that I mentioned earlier on in this section had left. Even many of the terrific crop of junior people, such as Donald Treiman and Sy Spilerman departed. (The department came back; they usually do.)

STONY BROOK

In terms of research and theory, I dropped out of the organizations field when I got to Stony Brook; I was shaken by the wave of repression in 1970, and I turned more directly to social issues. I felt that the late 1950s and the 1960s had made some important changes in American society, but the momentum was now stalled and where it continued it was in the hands of a very radical fringe. In fact the day before Edith and I, and now two children, left Madison for Long Island, a bomb in a science building on the Madison campus, set by some hard-core "revolutionary," exploded, killing a student. Students that I had gotten to know on the campus were making secret phone calls from pay booths wanting to hide out for a night or two at our house or to get some money to survive. One called after the Chicago "Days of Rage," and I found it was very hard to harbor her after what struck me as an extremely futile and worse, counterproductive demonstration.

Yet the students had done an enormous amount. They made it somehow harder to keep the war going; they introduced reforms in the universities; they made the American population uneasy about the environment, corporations, foreign policy, and civil rights. The new feminist movement came from there, I believe. They got things on the agenda that were never there in the 1950s, even if they didn't remake America.

What caused it, the activism and protest, and how could it be brought about again? I spent the next few years on a research project on insurgency that was immensely productive for a large group of quite brilliant students (they existed in abundance at Stony Brook), but which resulted in only one small publication of my own, a last minute conference presentation, and a piece with Craig Jenkins. The students published several books directly or indirectly related to the project, however, and I was very pleased with that. The main reason that no master publication came out of the project, and that I published next to nothing, was that our only *general* findings were negative. We found substantial evidence to undermine every major theory about that stormy decade, and were able to only do historically specific accounts of the various strands of the movement, for example, black civil rights, abortion reform, welfare protests, environmental protests, women's liberation, Catholic church reform, such as it was, and of course the antiwar movement. It's bizarre to think that they were unrelated, and we found evidence of interrelatedness, but whatever underlay these diverse movements, we were unable to find it. Some were born of affluence, some of poverty; some were related to the draft and the war, but most were not; some died out quickly; others such as the black civil rights movement persisted for a decade or more (thus casting doubt on the mechanistic "attention-span" theory); some were driven by the young, but those of the middle-age were in great number and spawned, lived, and died with their movements. It was something to keep one busy in the bleak early '70s.

Meanwhile, organization theory continued to diversify and blossom, breaking out of the rationalistic confines of contingency theory, which in turn had been a breaking out of the simple-minded leadership and goals theories of the past. Most notably, the great garbage can was dropped upon an unsuspecting organizational world (with a computer program inexplicably embedded in it). I was enchanted, and later when the first book by Jim March and Johan Olsen came out I gave it a long, very enthusiastic review in the sociology review journal, *Contemporary Sociology*. But my concerns with organizations were broadening. The political implications of the '60s and the repression that started in the last year of the Johnson administration and continued through the Nixon years made me search more widely. Also, I think there is a fairly natural progression from internal processes of organizations or small organizational sets to a concern with organizations' impact on society, more generally the world, and in my case, upon history. The beginnings of a still unwritten book to be called *A Society of Organizations* were beginning to stir.

In retrospect, to which we should always remain suspicious, many roads pointed in that direction. I developed a large undergraduate course on social change and technology, where I tried to make organization theories, along with many others, interesting and palatable to largely indifferent undergraduates. (Stony Brook had an astoundingly good sociology department and graduate students, but the state bureaucracy must have been one of the worst in the country, and the undergraduate students were the most difficult ones I ever tried to teach.) I started reading about the history of technology and found myself reading about the history of organizations, indirectly. Another strand was a brilliant graduate student, Daniel Clawson, a trenchant, burning lefty, who asked me to sit on his dissertation committee, the problem being to show that control was a more important motive in the establishment of bureaucracy in the nineteenth century than efficiency. I had long emphasized the control aspect of bureaucracy, but also acknowledged its efficiency dimensions. I was dubious about downplaying efficiency and quoted my other mentor from graduate school days, Reinhard Bendix, pulling the book off the shelf and reading the quotes to Dan about the origins of bureaucracy and Max Weber. He persisted, and I knew that he was very capable and might even be brilliant. (In a seminar he took with me, he had the habit of handing out ditto copies of his critiques of my views each week! Wrong-headed and perverse as they of course were, I took notice.) Clawson carried off his dissertation research with aplomb and published a brilliant book, *Bureaucracy and the Labor Process: The Transformation of U.S. Industry, 1860-1920*. I had been reading other kinds of history, William A. Williams, Brody on the steel workers, and so forth; I was teaching about organizational and technological developments in my undergraduate class; and now I had Dan Clawson's stunning chapters coming in every couple of months. In the 1978-79 school year I put my thoughts together and formulated the basic ideas for *The Society of Organizations* volume, and announced its imminent appearance. Little did I know what was going to happen over the next twelve years.

NORMAL ACCIDENTS

The accident at Three Mile Island in March 1979 was, of course, of great interest to me, then as a student of technology as well as a student of organizations. But I followed it no more closely than my colleagues, and probably was more concerned about the social movement and collective behavior aspects of it than the accident itself. Perhaps I absorbed more of the details of the accident than I realized, but I was certainly not prepared to comment with any more authority than many of my colleagues who, on the whole, were a brilliant bunch. (I regretted leaving the star-studded department at Wisconsin, not realizing that luck and chance were still with me, and I walked into a department that was already fairly star-studded, especially in its younger people, and was soon to be propelled into the first rank in my view.)

In July 1979 I got a call from David Sills of the Social Science Research Council saying that Cora Marrett, one of the commissioners appointed by the President to study the accident (I was a member of her dissertation committee at Wisconsin), had convinced the commission that they should have some social science input. Compared to the engineering and economics input, it was to be minuscule, but we were glad to have Cora get that much for us. "Could I do a paper on failure rates in industry?" Why, I asked. "Because there is some question as to whether this is such a unique event or something that happens to all plants in due course." I knew nothing about failure rates in industry and had no interest in it, I said, but I'd love to do an organizational analysis of the accident. "Well, Chick, that would be great but the other part of the story is that you would only have a month to do it; we don't have any money for research assistants." (I forget whether we ever even got an honorarium as panel members, but it was not important! This was a national crisis.) The hearings were going on at that very time. "Could you send me the transcripts of the hearings?" "Sure." "I'll do it."

Two days later a huge Federal Express truck got lost in the low-rent foothills of the Berkshires where we had a small vacation home, and after wandering around for an hour finally found our cabin. They rolled up the huge back door and out came this little box of transcripts. I was so naive that I had the image that the truck had driven all the way from the hearing rooms in Washington, D.C., since Federal Express was fairly new to me. I went through the transcripts that afternoon and couldn't get to sleep. When I got to sleep I had the worse nightmares I'd had since my army days. The testimony of the operators made a profound impression upon me. Here was an enormously, catastrophically risky technology, *and they had no idea what was going on for some hours.* Could we have risky systems with catastrophic potential watched over by uncomprehending operators, who testified that alarms were always going off and had to be ignored, that valves were frequently set wrong, that there was no dial among the thousands of dials indicating the core was uncovered, that the plant did not really work properly in the two or three months that it had been on-line, and so on? I suddenly realized that I was in the thick of it, in the very middle of it, because this was an *organizational* problem more than anything else, and that I was an organizational theorist.

The kids were off at camp, and Edith and I were alone. I wanted to go back to Stony Brook to be near a library but we had rented our Stony Brook house so I couldn't. I called a couple of graduate students down there that I had worked with, and told them to rush me everything from the library they could find on nuclear power plants that would tell me how they worked, to burn up the xerox machines and I'd pay them later. They did. Then I read the few hundred pages of testimony over again, and paced about like a caged tiger. Late in the evening, a couple of days after the materials had arrived, I called out to Edith that I had it. "It's a normal accident" I said with triumph in my voice. "How can you have a normal accident; don't be silly, it's a contradiction in terms." "You don't understand. It was normal for this plant to have this accident, and I know it because everything I've read in here I have seen at the university at Stony Brook or at Wisconsin, or in the corporations I've studied. They all have failures all the time. Nothing can be perfect. But they don't come together like this to create an unmanageable, irretrievable system failure." I might have added that they also were not radioactive.

"And I know I've got it because it's what I've been working on in the society of organizations project. When you have a lot of small units in a bunch of clusters spread about, failure in one will not spread rapidly to other parts. But when organizations come along and grow large by absorbing all these smaller units, you end up with big organizations bumping into each other, and they have interactions within them and between them that are incomprehensible. It's as if we had a bunch of wood burning fireplaces all over, any one of them dangerous in itself but not to any of the others, and we replaced it with a nuclear power plant. It's big, it's complex, it's tightly coupled and it can do immense damage. That is the problem with our society. Three Mile Island is an analogy for what we face."

Now I'm not quite sure that that's an exact quote! But it was something like that. I had preformed a "hammer analysis." Give a little boy a hammer at Christmas and he discovers that everything in sight is in want of pounding. I had a primitive theory about complexity and coupling and when they handed me the transcripts I pounded them with it and broke it open. It was one of the most thrilling writing experiences I have ever had. In thirty days I had produced a 45-page paper that applied the theory to Three Mile Island, to tanker collisions, aircraft failures, chemical plant explosions, and suggested why most factories would not have "normal accidents" or, in a more technical term, what I call "system accidents." The students at Stony Brook sent a steady stream of material and critiqued my rough drafts and ideas. My long paper had to be reduced to ten pages because the commissioners had a lot to read, and as we soon learned, the social science set of papers were among the several thousand that they never got around to reading. (They are no different from business executives who rely, as very good data tells us, on visual and auditory information, and rarely read for background purposes.)

It was clear that I had caught something significant by the tail. I tried to go back to the society of organizations, thinking that this would be a small section of one chapter of it, but these ideas had their own momentum and people were very interested. I wrote pieces for this and that and then realized I had a major project on my hands, turned to our major and extremely important resource, the National Science Foundation, and got a grant to keep going.

Meanwhile, independent of this I believe, I had been asked to be a fellow for a year at Center for Advanced Study in Palo Alto. I had already set the 1981-82 year for that glorious experience and it worked out beautifully. I spent much of the next three years writing *Normal Accidents*, and had an immense amount of fun with it. I had labored hard over *Complex Organizations: A Critical Essay*, and was extremely fond of that book, and worked hard at the subsequent revisions. It was much the same with *Normal Accidents*. I mention this because it is not always thus. My first book was not a labor of love, and my most recent one, on AIDS, was fairly agonizing. *Complex Organizations* was great for me because I was in a sense building a hammer or a tool, and trying to get it right. *Normal Accidents* was great because the hammer that developed out of *Complex Organizations* and my growing historical concern seemed to work. The guiding thesis that my coauthor Mauro Guillen and I used for the AIDS book did not seem as fruitful and as powerful to me, the failures that we discovered there were more depressing than those for the accident book, and I was unprepared for the politics of writing about stigmatized groups.

I said goodbye to Stony Brook because in the meantime I had accepted an offer at Yale. I had no intention of leaving Stony Brook, was not looking, and had misgivings about the politically conservative tone of the Yale campus, its faculty and students. For a long time it was not certain that I even had an appointment, even though initially I'd been assured that it would be pro forma. Some felt that a quantitative person was needed and there were some dicey episodes I gather. The thing I was most proud of was that the junior faculty, everyone of them worth their weight in gold and all having gone on to great careers, some even at Yale, got wind of an impending negative vote at the college level, and drafted a wonderful letter supporting my appointment and signed it nearly unanimously, the first time that anything like that had happened in the department, and perhaps in the college.

Though I worried about the conservative cast of the university, I left Stony Brook for three reasons. It was resource starved. If you didn't have a grant, and sometimes I didn't, you couldn't make a long distance telephone call without getting a key from the head secretary to unlock the telephone room, and you can imagine what happened when you would find the line was busy. Next, it was difficult to teach the students. I cut down substantially on lateness to class, and absenteeism, by starting off giving two or three questions that would very likely be on the exam, reading them off slowly, and then giving the answers to them, slowly, and then building my lecture for the day around those questions and answers, saying why they were important. If more than a third of the students still missed the questions on the exam, I repeated the process and asked them on the next exam (there were four in the semester). In this way students would learn why it was important to be able to distinguish Karl Marx from Max Weber, and unfortunately it took this technique to do so. What I didn't anticipate, however, was that it made me prepare my lectures more! Controls are often reactive.

The final and most important reason I left, and the one I felt the most ambivalent about, was intellectual. I had been in a great sociology department at Stony Brook for eleven years, with one year off at the London Graduate School of Business, and I felt I had gotten an immense amount out of John Gagnon, Lewis Coser, Mark Granovetter, Michael Schwartz, Jim Rule, and others. But my interests had changed. I was now more interested in history, and Yale had David Montgomery who was more interested in political science, and Yale had Charles Lindblom in economics, and there was Sidney Winter and Richard Nelson in cognitive psychology, and there was Robert Abelson. Stony Brook could not match these and the depth that lay behind these particular figures in all these departments. That was my main reason for going.

YALE

When I got to Yale I found that my expectations were surpassed. It was more politically conservative than I have even anticipated and more stuffy, ingrown, and cautious. But the undergraduates were even better than I thought they would be, and the intellectual environment was stunning. It was like a vast candy story in which you thrust your hand into huge containers full of faculty seminars and working groups and stuffed yourself. There shouldn't have been time to go to all those seminars—especially when you had to read the material ahead of time—two, sometimes three of them a week. But somehow or other there seemed to be more time to do things at Yale than anyplace else I've been, during the first few years. That has changed, of course, as committee assignments, dissertations, and new facets of interests accumulated.

But Yale was a year off. First Edith, Darragh, and I spent a splendid year at Palo Alto (our son, Nicholas, was already off at the University of Oregon). Officially everyone agrees that the year at the Center is the best year of their intellectual life, and that was true for me. Up until mid-December I did very little work on the accident book, but went to seminars on the Stanford campus (who could resist listening to Amos Tversky) and visited several of the working groups that were going on at the Center. I read fairly widely for the first in a long time, and with the help of John Ferejohn, who was at the Center that year, got into computers and learned enough primitive programing to write a primitive word processing program for the primitive IBM PC which had just come out that fall. (There were no programs that would work on it until Camilo Wilson came along with his extraordinary *Volkswriter* program.) Then I settled down to work, and worked long days and nights, going back to the office three or four nights out of the week. Both Edith and Darragh were thoroughly engaged in their own pursuits and were glad when I stopped bothering them about taking time off for trips around the Bay Area. Most of *Normal Accidents* was written there. I traveled about, poking my way into chemical plants, nuclear plants, and naval training bases, and wrote and wrote voraciously. It took most of another year at Yale to really tidy things up and get it into good shape, but the book was really written between December and August in sunny California.

Since that was my last major effort to date (I am too close to *The Aids Disaster: The Failure of Organizations in the U.S. and the Nation* to judge it). I'm tempted to end there, but two comments might be appropriate. First, when I sent *Normal Accidents* off to the editor I thought I was through with it and would go back to *The Society of Organizations*. But not long after that we had, in quick succession, Bhopal, the Challenger, and Chernobyl. I couldn't not comment on them, but I made no discoveries or major revisions to anything that I'd done before, except that it is very hard to have a catastrophe. We are inundated with near misses because you need just the right combination of six or seven conditions to come together in the right way to produce a Bhopal. Chemical plants are producing near-Bhophals all the time.

Second, I think the most important thing I've done since *Normal Accidents* was an essay which appears also as a chapter in the third edition of *Complex Organizations*, on economic theories of organizations. I'm embarrassed to say how much work I put into reading that literature, and how long it took me to come to and formulate some fairly obvious statements about it. But much of our work seems to be like that. Many parts of *Complex Organizations* involved a struggle with a recalcitrant literature and stubborn ideas. I fear as much for *The Society of Organizations*, which may account for its endless postponement, but the 1990-91 year at the Russell Sage Foundation should help it along. The idea for *Normal Accidents* just came up like a full moon on that August night and that was it; the rest was hard, but it was refinement and detail. I should only be that lucky again.

PUBLICATIONS

1957

Are retirement adjustment programs necessary? *Harvard Business Review,*
    35(4), 109-115.
Gemeinschaft and gesellschaft: A critical analysis of the use of a polar typology.
    Berkeley Publications in Institutions and Society, 2(1), 20-43.

1959

With M. Berke, J.D. Gordon, & R.I. Levy. *Study on the non-segregated*
    hospitalization of alcoholic patients in a general hospital (American
    Hospital Association, Hospital Monograph Series 7).
Research in a home care program. *American Journal of Public Health, 49*(1),
    34-44.
With M. Berke, J.D. Gordon, & R.I. Levy. Nonsegregated hospitalization of
    alcoholic patients in a general hospital. *Hospitals* (Journal of the
    American Hospital Association), *33*, 45-48.

1961

Organizational prestige: Some functions and dysfunctions. *American Journal*
    of Sociology, 66(4), 335-341.

1963

Reality shock: A new organization confronts the custody-treatment dilemma.
    Social Problems, 10(4), 374-382.
Goals and authority structures, a historical case study. In E. Freidson (Ed.),
    The hospital in modern society (pp. 112-146). New York: The Free Press.

1965

Sociological perspective and political pluralism. *Social Research, 31*(4), 411-
    422.
With J. Maniha. The reluctant organization and the aggressive environment.
    Administrative Science Quarterly, 10(2), 238-257.
Hospitals: Technology, goals and structure. In J. March (Ed.), *Handbook of*
    organizations (pp. 910-971). Chicago: Rand-McNally.

1966

With D. Street & R.D. Vinter. *Organization for treatment: A comparative study of juvenile correctional institutions.* New York: The Free Press.
Reality adjustment: A young institution settles for humane care. *Social Problems, 14*(1), 69-79.
Technology and organizational structure. *Proceedings of the Nineteenth Annual Meeting of the Industrial Relations Research Association* (December), 156-163.

1967

A framework for the comparative analysis of organizations. *American Sociological Review* (April), 194-208.

1968

Organizational goals. In *International encyclopedia of the social sciences* (rev. ed., Vol. 11, pp. 305-311). New York: MacMillan.
The professional army in the war on poverty. *Poverty and Human Resources Abstracts* (January-February).
Technology and structural changes in business firms. In B.C. Roberts (Ed.), *Industrial relations: Contemporary issues* (pp. 205-219). New York: MacMillan.

1969

Some reflections on technology and organizations. In A.R. Negandhi et al. (Eds.), *Comparative administration and management* (Comparative Administration Research Series, No. 1). Kent, OH: Kent State University Press.

1970

Organizational analysis: A sociological view. Belmont, CA: Wadsworth Publishing Co.
Members as a resource in voluntary organization. In W. Rosengren & M. Lefton (Eds.), *Organizations and clients* (pp. 93-116). Columbus, OH: Merrill.
Departmental power and perspective in industrial firms. In M. Zald (Ed.), *Power in Organizations* (pp. 59-89). Nashville, TN: Vanderbilt University Press.

1972

Complex organizations: A critical essay. Glenview, IL: Scott, Foresman.
    (Revised edition, 1979. Third edition: Random House, 1986).
The radical attack on business. New York: Harcourt Brace Jovanovich.

1973

The short and glorious history of organizational theory. *Organizational
    Dynamics, 2*(1), 2-15.

1974

Zoo story, or life in the organizational sandpit. In *People and organizations.*
    Milton Keynes, UK: Open University Press.
Is business really changing? *Organizational Dynamics, 3*(1), 30-44.

1977

The bureaucratic paradox: The efficient organization centralizes in order to
    decentralize. *Organizational Dynamics, 4*(4), 2-14.
Three types of organizational effectiveness. In P.S. Goodman & J.M. Pennings
    (Eds.), *New perspectives on organizational effectiveness* (pp. 96-105). San
    Francisco, CA: Jossey-Bass.
With C. Jenkins. Insurgency of the powerless: Farm worker movements, 1946-
    1972. *American Sociological Review, 42*, 249-268.

1978

Demystifying organizations. In R.C. Sarri and Y. Hasenfeld (Eds.), *The
    management of human services* (pp. 105-122). New York: Columbia
    University Press.

1979

The sixties observed. In M.M. Zald and J.D. McCarthy (Eds.), *The dynamics
    of social movements* (pp. 192-211). Cambridge, MA: Winthrop Publishers.

1981

The president's commission and the normal accident. In D. Sills et al. (Eds.),
    The accident at Three Mile Island: The human dimensions. Boulder, CO:
    The Westview Press.

Disintegrating social sciences. *New York University Education Quarterly,*
     12(2), 2-9.
Markets, hierarchies and hegemony: A critique of Chandler and Williamson.
     In A. Van de Ven & W. Joyce, (Eds.), *Perspectives on organization design*
     and behavior (pp. 371-386, 403-404). New York: Wiley-Interscience.
This week's citation classic. *Current Contents, 14,* 14.
Normal accident at Three Mile Island. *Society, 18*(5), 17-26.

1982

Three Mile Island: A normal accident. In D. Dunkerley & G. Salaman (Eds.),
     The international yearbook of organization studies (pp. 1-25). London:
     Routledge & Kegan Paul.
The organizational context of human factors (Tech. Rep. DTIC No. ADA
     123435). Washington, DC: Office of Naval Research, U.S. Navy.

1983

The organizational context of human factors engineering. *Administrative*
     Science Quarterly, 28, 521-541.

1984

Normal accidents: Living with high risk technologies. New York: Basic Books.
     (German ed.: Campus Books, 1987.)

1985

Journaling careers. In L.L. Cummings & P.J. Frost (Eds.), *Publishing in the*
     organizational sciences (pp. 220-230). Homewood, IL: Irwin.
Comment on Langton's "Ecological theory of bureaucracy." *Administrative*
     Science Quarterly, 30, 278-283.

1986

Cognicao e Catastrofe: Os Acidentes de Alto Risco [Cognition and catastrophe:
     High-risk accidents]. *Analise & Conjuntura, 1* (3).
Risky systems: The habit of courting disaster. *The Nation* (October 11), 24-
     37.
Journaling careers. *Sociological Forum, 1*(1), 169-177.
Economic theories of organization. *Theory and Society, 15,* 11-45.

1987

Lernen wir etwas aus den jungsten Katastrophen? [Do we learn anything from the latest catastrophies?] *Soziale Welt:Zeitschrift fur sozialwissenschaftliche Forschung und Praxis, 37*(4), 390-401.

1988

Le Organizzazioni Complesse: Un Saggio Critico [Complex organizations: A critical essay]. Milano: Franco Angeli Libri.

1989

A society of organizations. *Kulter und Gesellschaft, 24.*
Normal accidents. *Technische Rundschau, 13* (January).
On not using libraries. In *Humanists at work* (pp. 29-42). The University Library, University of Illinois at Chicago.

1990

With M. Guillen. *The AIDS disaster: The failure of organizations in New York and the nation.* New Haven, CT: Yale University Press.

1991

A society of organizations. *Theory and Society, 20*, 725-762.

1992

Small firm networks. In S.E. Sjostrand (Ed.), *Institutional change: Theories and empirical findings.* Armonk, NY: M.E. Sharpe.
Accidents in high risk systems. *Technology Studies, 1*(1).
Unfalle und Katastrophen—ihre Systembedingungen. *Journal fur Sozialforschung, 32*(1).

Management Laureates:
A Collection of Autobiographical Essays

Arthur G. Bedeian, *Department of Management, Louisiana State University*

Volume 1, 1992, 416 pp. $86.25
ISBN 1-55938-469-7

CONTENTS: Preface. **A Profile in Intellectual Growth,** *H. Igor Ansoff.* **Looking Backward and Inward In Order to Contribute to the Future,** *Chris Argyris.* **A Transformational Journey,** *Bernard M. Bass.* **The Fruits of Professional Interdependence for Enriching a Career,** *Robert R. Blake.* **Green Lights All the Way,** *Elwood S. Buffa.* **History and Management Practice and Thought,** *Alfred D. Chandler, Jr.* **Calling, Disciplines, and Attempts at Listening,** *Larry L. Cummings.* **A Journey Through Management in Transition,** *Keith Davis.* **Life in a Pretzel-Shaped Universe,** *Fred E. Fiedler.* **From the Ranch to System Dynamics,** *Jay W. Forrester.* **Mid-Career Perspectives in My Work,** *Robert T. Golembiewski.*

Volume 3, In preparation, Fall 1993 $86.25
ISBN 1-55938-471-9

CONTENTS: Preface. **An Almost Random Career,** *Charles Perrow.* **An Unmanaged Pursuit of Management,** *Lyman W. Porter.* **The Academic as Artist: Personal and Professional Roots,** *Edgar H. Schein.* **"Watch Where You Step!" Or Indiana Starbuck Amid the Perils of Academe (Rated PG),** *William H. Starbuck.* **My Roads to Management Theory and Practice,** *George Steiner.* **Spectator at the Beginning: Some Personal Notes on OB's Early Days and Later,** *George Strauss.* **Guilty of Enthusiasm,** *Eric L. Trist with Richard C.S. Trahair.* **Up the Management Mountain,** *Stanley C. Vance.* **Improvising and Muddling Through,** *Victor H. Vroom.* **Turning Context into Text: An Academic Life as Data,** *Karl E. Weick.* **From Participant Observer to Participatory Action Researcher,** *William F. Whyte.* **From Practice to Theory: Odyssey of a Manager,** *James C. Worthy.*

Future volumes will be available annually and may be ordered on a standing order basis.

JAI PRESS INC.
55 Old Post Road - No. 2   P.O. Box 1678
Greenwich, Connecticut 06836-1678
Tel: (203) 661-7602   Fax: (203)661-0792

JAI

PRESS

Advances in Entrepreneurship, Firm Emergence and Growth

Edited by **Jerome A. Katz** and **Robert H. Brockhaus, Sr.**, *Jefferson Smurfit Center for Entrepreneurial Studies, Saint Lewis University*

Volume 1, 1993, 248 pp. $73.25
ISBN 1-55938-514-6

JAI PRESS INC.

55 Old Post Road - No. 2   P.O. Box 1678
Greenwich, Connecticut 06836-1678
Tel: (203) 661-7602   Fax: (203)661-0792

Advances in the Study of Entrepreneurship, Innovation, and Economic Growth

Edited by **Gary Libecap,** *Director, Karl Eller Center, University of Arizona*

Volume 6, New Learning on Entrepreneurship
1993, 192 pp. $73.25
ISBN 1-55938-5200

CONTENTS: Introduction: New Learning on Entrepreneurship, *Gary D. Lipecap.* **American Economic History and the Entrepreneur,** *Jonathan Hughes.* **Change and Innovation in a Post-Schumpeterian World Economy,** *David L. McKee.* **Entrepreneurship and Technological Change in Historical Perspective: A Study of 'Great Inventors' During Early American Industrialization,** *B. Zorina Khan and Kenneth L. Sokoloff.* **Entrepreneurship, Property Rights, and Economic Development,** *Gary D. Libecap.* **Specialization in Entrepreneurship,** *Thomas J. Holmes and James A. Schimtz, Jr.* **Innovation and Technological Change: THe New Learning,** *Zoltan J. Acs and David B. Audretsch.* **Entrepreneurship and Small Business Growth: A Case Study,** *Zoltan J. Acs and David S. Evans.* **Entrepreneurship and External Sources of Technology,** *Albert N. Link.* **About the Authors.**

Also Available:

Volumes 1-5 (1986-1991)
+ Supplement 1 (1989) $73.25 each

JAI PRESS INC.

55 Old Post Road - No. 2   P.O. Box 1678
Greenwich, Connecticut 06836-1678

Tel: (203) 661-7602   Fax: (203)661-0792

Advances in
Strategic Management

Edited by **Paul Shrivastava**, *Department of Management,
Bucknell University*, **Anne Huff**, *College of
Business and Commerce, University of Illinois*
and **Jane Dutton**, *Graduate School of Business
Administration, The University of Michigan*

Volume 8, 1992, 404 pp. $73.25
ISBN 1-55938-519-7

CONTENTS: Introduction. **PART I. Exploring Theoretical
Boundaries. Strategy Theorizing: Expanding the Agenda,**
J.C. Spender, Commentary by C. Marlene Fiol. **Integrating
Organizational Behavior and Strategy Formulation
Research: A Resource-Based Analysis,** *Jay Barney,
Commentary by Mike Lawless.* **Relating Economic and
Behavioral Perspectives in Strategy Research,** *Edward Zajac,
Commentary by James Walsh.* **Strategy, Environment, and
Intelligence,** *Charles I Stubbart and James M. Wilson III,
Commentary by Charles Snow.* **Organizational Economics
Within the Conversation of Strategic Management,** *Joseph
T. Mahoney, Commentary by Kathleen Eisenhardt and Shona L.
Brown.* **The Use of Experimental Economics in Strategy
Research,** *Keith Weigelt, Colin F. Camerer, and Mark Hanna,
Commentary by Erhard Bruderer and Will Mitchell.* **PART II.
Evolving Strategic Management Tasks. Crisis Management
and Strategic Management: Similarities, Differences and
Challenges,** *Ian I. Mitroff, Chris Pearson and Thierry C. Pauchant,
Commentary by Denis Smith.* **Vision Worlds: Strategic Vision
as Social Interaction,** *Frances Westley, Commentary by Karl
E. Weick.* **Gearing Strategic Public Enterprises for Interna-
tionalisation: The Indian Case,** *Pradip N. Khandwalla,
Commentary by Prakash Sethi.* **PART III. New Syntheses of
Strategic Issues. Generic Strategies: Classification,
Combination and Context,** *Danny Miller, Commentary by
Gregory G. Dess and Abdul M. A. Rasheed.* **Business Strategy
and Business History: A Framework for Development,** *John
Hendry, Commentary by John Kimberly.* **Consequences of
Group Composition for the Interpersonal Dynamics of
Strategic Issue Processing,** *Susan E. Jackson, Commentary
by Donald C. Hambrick.*

Also Available:
Volumes 1-7 (1983-1991) $73.25 each

Advances in Applied Business Strategy

Edited by **Lawrence W. Foster,** *College of Commerce and Business Administration, University of Alabama*

Volume 3, 1992, 244 pp. $73.25
ISBN 1-55938-512-X

CONTENTS: Introduction. PART I. US/JAPAN TRADE RELATIONS IN THE 1990s. **Japan vs. the U.S.? Uchi and Soto, Inclusion and Exclusion,** *Lawrence W. Foster.* **The Evolution of Japan's Science and Technology Policy, Strategic Responses of U.S. Firms to the Japaneese Competitive Challenge,** *William R. Boulton and Jung Wha Han.* PART II. US/JAPAN INDUSTRY COMPETITIVENESS. **Global Competitive Strategies of Japaneese Firms: A Cross-Indutry Analysis and Generic Model,** *Richard W. Wright and Gunter A. Pauli.* **United States-Japan Relations in the Post Cold War Era,** *James A. Auer.* **A Strategic P:erspective: The U.S. Auto Industry,** *James Cashman.* **Techno-Global Competition in the Integrated Circut Industry,** *David T. Methe'.* **Toward a National Technology Strategy,** *Warren E. Davis.* **Perspectives and Directions of Management Strategies in the 1990s,** *Tadahiro Sekimoto.* **"Collaboration": The Japaneese and the U.S. View,** *Katsuyuki Horinouchi.* **The Overseas Transfer of Japaneese Corporate Culture,** *Motofusa Murayama and Stacey Allen.* **Spirit of "Co-existence and Coprosperity",** *Akira Ochida.*

Supplement 1, Global Manufacturing: Technological and Economic Opportunities and Research Issues
1993, 291 pp. $73.25
ISBN 1-55938-513-8

Edited by **William A. Wallace,** *Rennsselaer Polytechnic Institute*

CONTENTS: Introduction. **What We Can Learn From the Past: A Comparison of Historical Manufacturing Systems with Computer-Integrated Manufacturing,** Laurie Rattner, Daniel L. Orne, and William A. Wallace. **Competitiveness and Global Manufacturing: The Contribution of Information Technology,** *Tagi Sagafi-nejad and John Burbridge. Impact of Global Change on International Business Strategy, Jack Baranson.* **The Shifting Playing Field in Global Competition,** *Arlyn J. Melcher and Bernard Arogyaswamy.* **Manufacturing Risk and Global Markets,** *George K. Hutchinson.* **Implications of Global Manufacturing for Strategy and Organizational Design,** *William G. Egelhoff.* **International Manufacturing Strategies and Computer-Integrated Manufacturing (CIM): A Review of the Emerging Interactive Effects,** *Daniel L. Orne and Leo E. Hanifin.* **Strategy Research: Methodological Issues and Options,** *Daniel L. Orne and Suresh Kotha.*

Also Available:
Volumes 1-2 (1984-1990) $73.25 each

Advances in International Comparative Management

Edited by **S. Benjamin Prasad,** *Department of Management, Central Michigan University* and **Richard B. Peterson,** *Department of Management, University of Washington*

Volume 8, 1993, 240 pp. $73.25
ISBN 1-55938-618-5

Also Available:
Volumes 1-7 (1984-1992)
+ Supplements 1-2 (1984-1987) $73.25 each

JAI PRESS INC.
55 Old Post Road - No. 2   P.O. Box 1678
Greenwich, Connecticut 06836-1678
Tel: (203) 661-7602   Fax: (203)661-0792